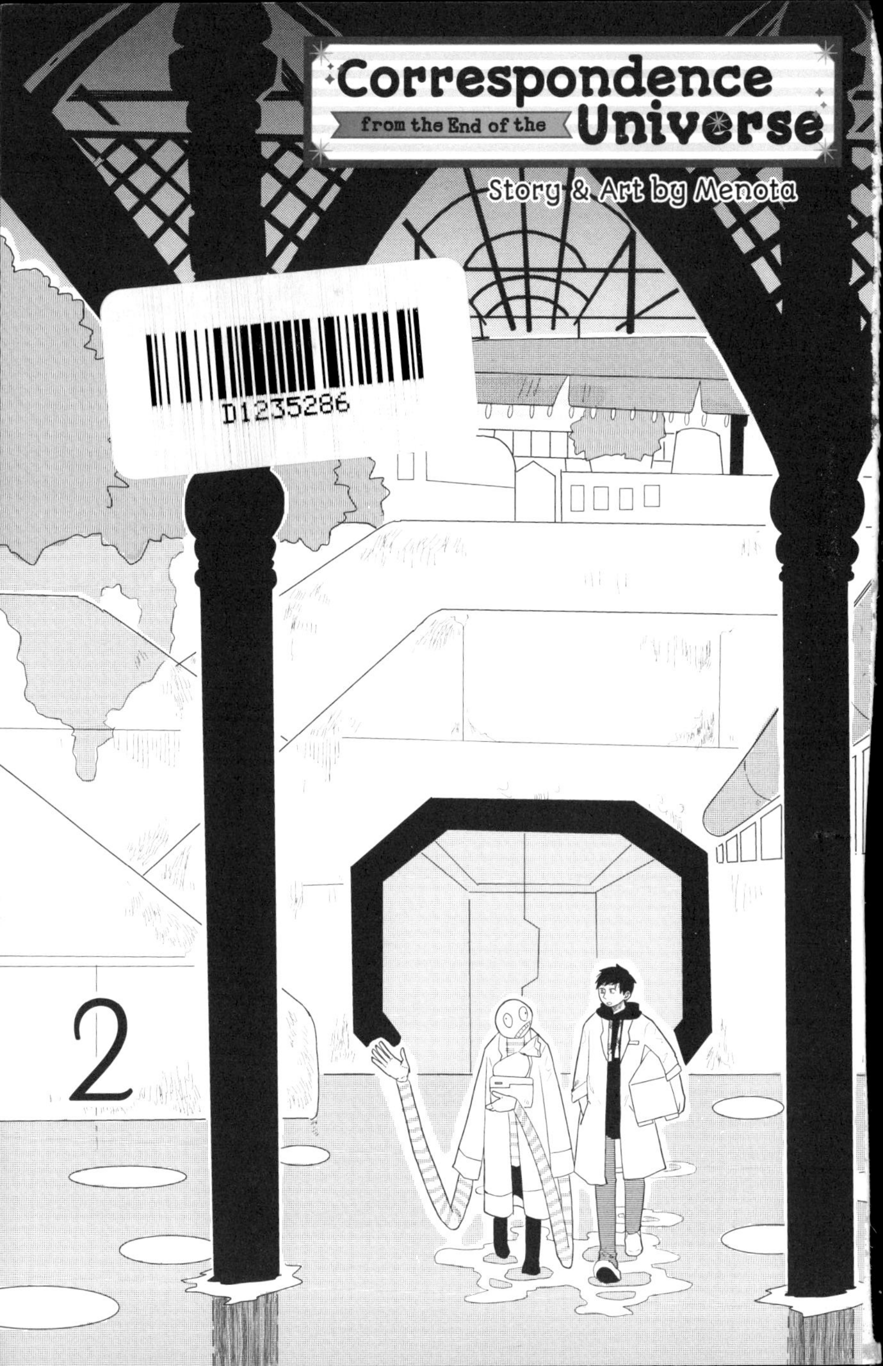
Correspondence
from the End of the
Universe
Story & Art by Menota
2

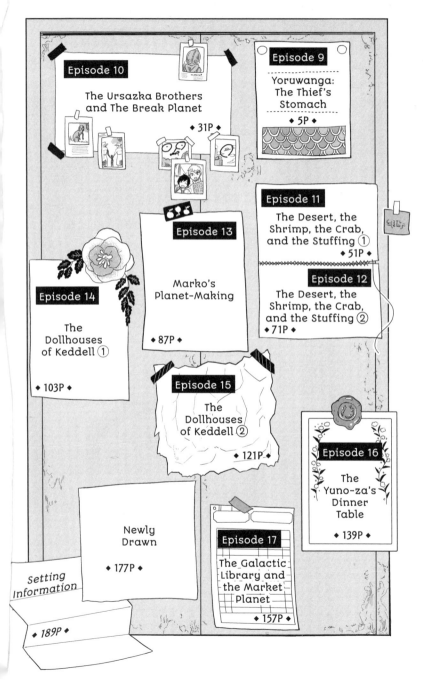

Character Introduction

The Director

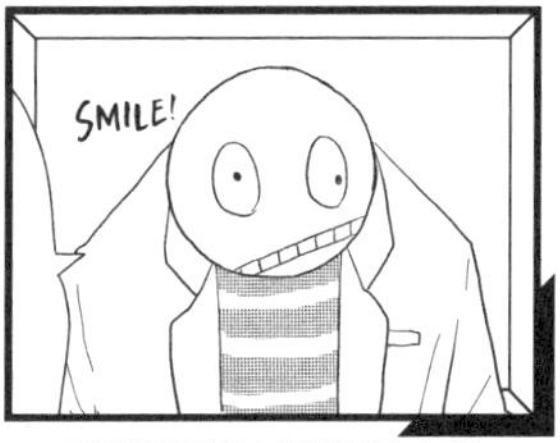
SMILE!

AN ALIEN FROM AKUZU NO. 4. TO PRONOUNCE HIS REAL NAME REQUIRES TWO TONGUES. LAID BACK, BUT RELIABLE. HIS TENURE WILL BE THE LONGEST.

Marko Rono-wavich Ursazka

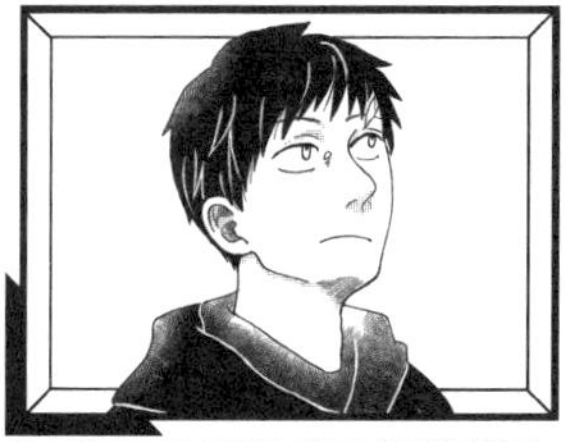

AN EARTHLING. AFTER GRADUATING FROM UNIVERSITY, HE PLANNED TO TRAVEL THE WORLD WITH HIS OLDER ROMANTIC PARTNER. EARNEST NO MATTER WHAT. BORN IN RUSSIA.

Nanagi

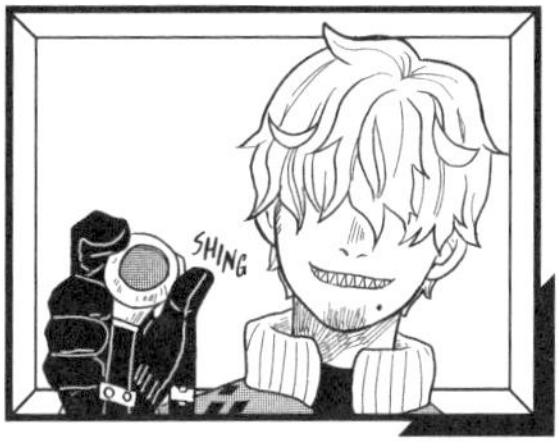
SHING

FROM THE PLANET DA-KOKOBA. HIS RACE LOOKS JUST LIKE HUMANS. HIS MANNER OF SPEECH IS A BIT ROUGH, BUT HE'S GOT A COMPANIONABLE PERSONALITY.

Fiitzii

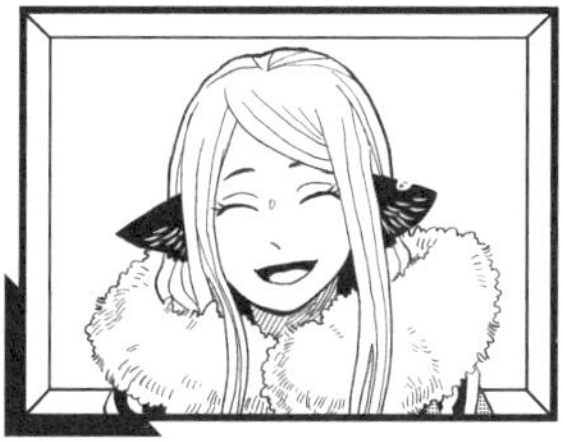

FROM THE PLANET SOLFE. FROM A PLANET THAT PRODUCES HEALTHCARE WORKERS. HER HANDS ARE HORNWORM-LIKE. SHE'S AS LAID BACK AS THE DIRECTOR.

Rayzoltalpa

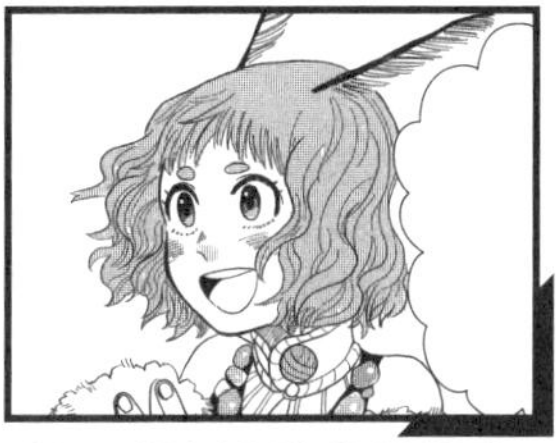

AN ALIEN FROM KIARA, OF A RACE THAT EATS ORE AND ROCKS. A MISCHIEVOUS GIRL FULL OF CURIOSITY. HER ROOM IS CONNECTED TO MOSLY VIA A MIRROR.

Mauu

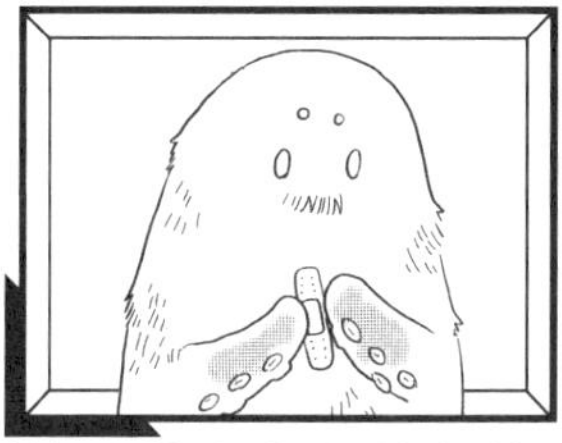

AN ALIEN FROM THE PLANET RONOUTOGI. A JUVENILE CLONE OF THE INDIVIDUAL WHO LIVES THERE. COMPASSIONATE AND GENTLE. HIS FRIEND NUU DIED IN AN ACCIDENT.

Summary

MARKO IS A RUSSIAN YOUTH WHO PLANNED TO TRAVEL THE WORLD WITH HIS PARTNER AFTER GRADUATING FROM UNIVERSITY. BEFORE THEY COULD DEPART, MARKO WAS ABDUCTED AND TRANSPORTED TO THE PLANET MOSLY, AN UNKNOWN WORLD FAR AWAY FROM EARTH. THERE, MARKO LEARNED THAT HE'D BEEN CONSCRIPTED AS A STAFF MEMBER OF THE INSTITUTE THAT CONTROLS THE OPERATIONS OF SPACE, THE BUREAU OF END MANAGEMENT, WHERE HE MUST CARRY OUT A TEN-YEAR MISSION. HORRIFIED BY THE TERMS OF HIS SERVICE, MARKO CONSTRUCTED AN ELABORATE PLAN TO RETURN TO EARTH, WHERE HIS PARTNER IS WAITING. NOT ONLY DID HIS PLAN FAIL, BUT MARKO WAS LEFT UNCONSCIOUS AND CAME TO WITH A GAPING HOLE IN HIS CHEST...

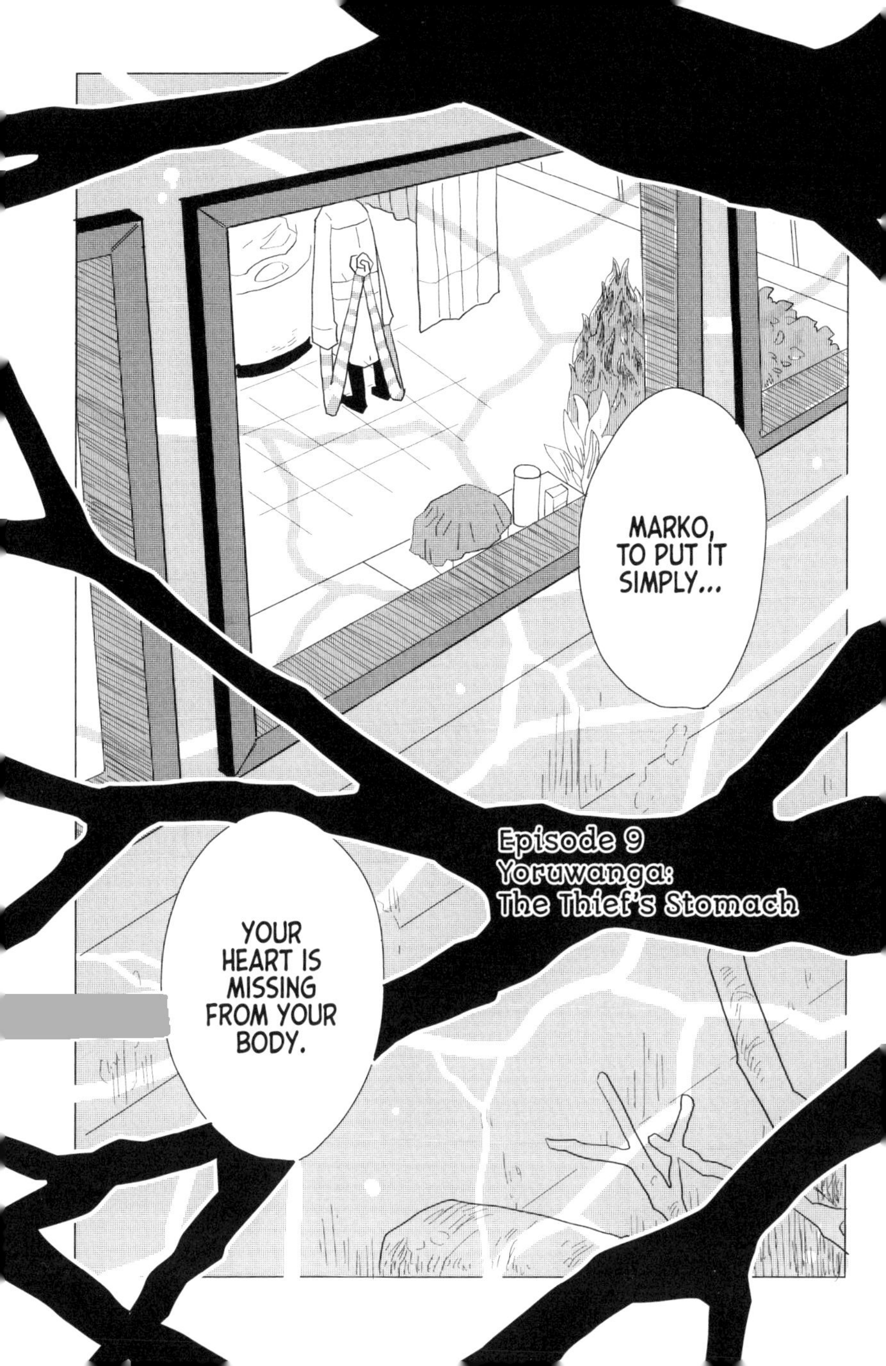
MARKO, TO PUT IT SIMPLY...
Episode 9
Yoruwanga:
The Thief's Stomach
YOUR HEART IS MISSING FROM YOUR BODY.

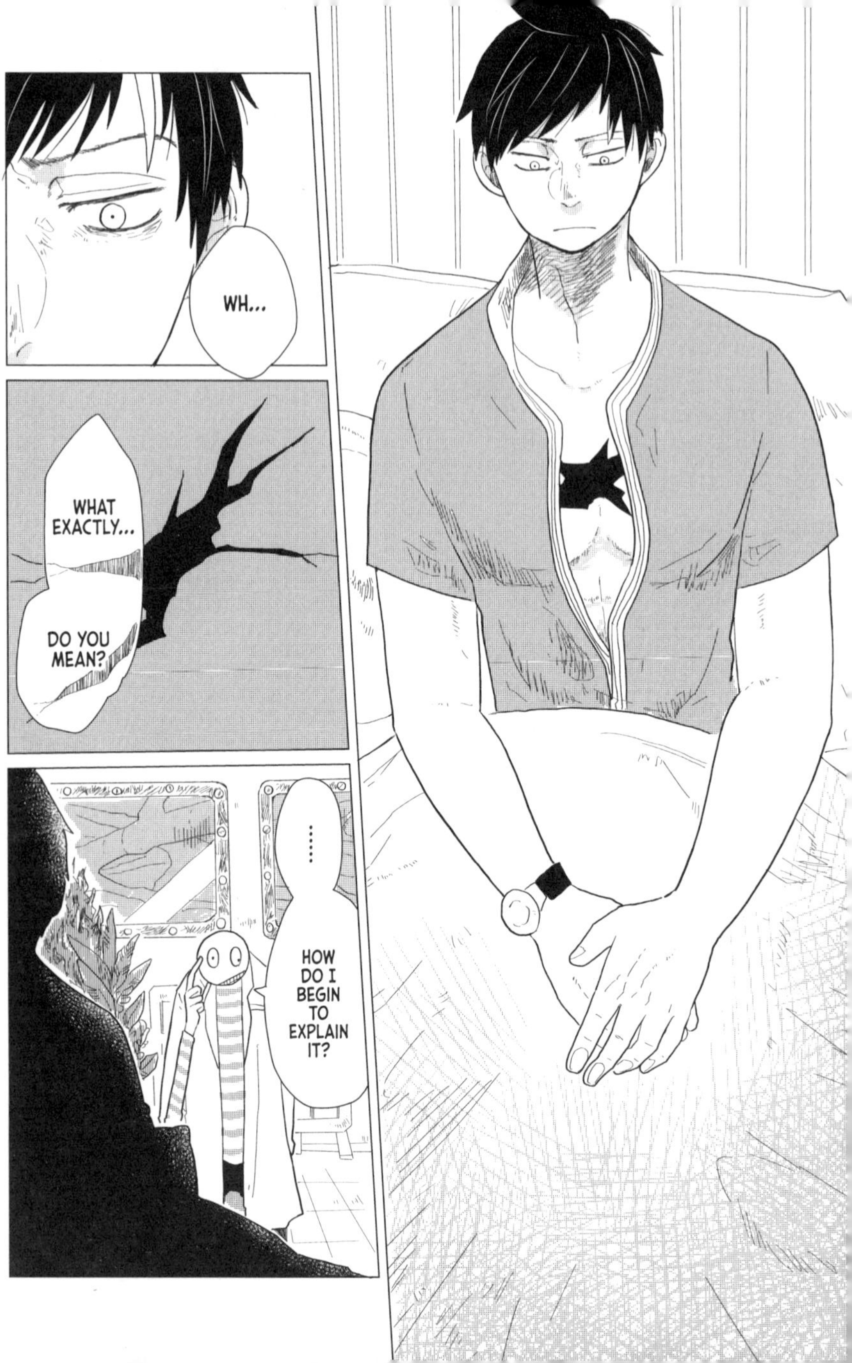
WH...
WHAT EXACTLY...
DO YOU MEAN?
......
HOW DO I BEGIN TO EXPLAIN IT?

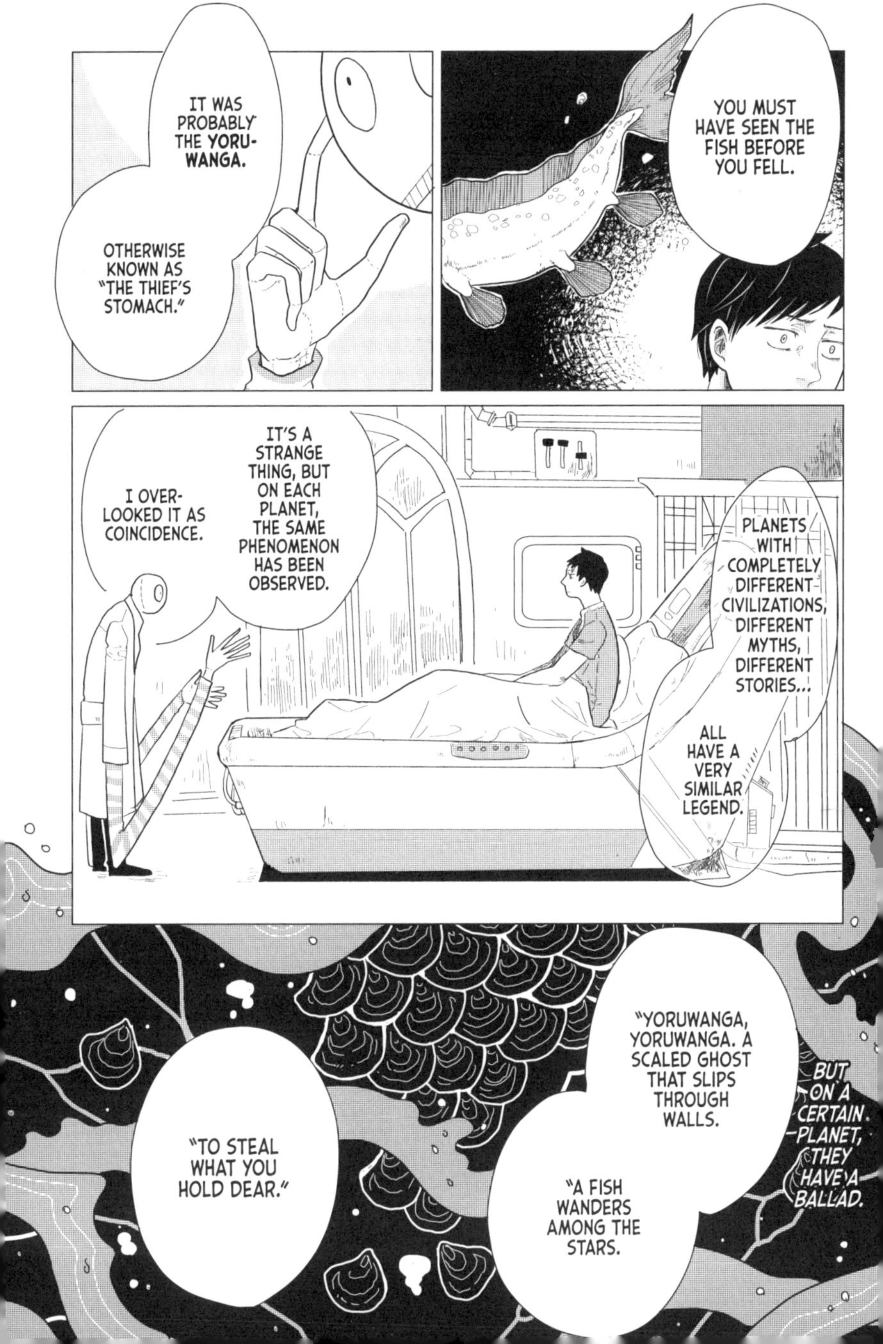
YOU MUST HAVE SEEN THE FISH BEFORE YOU FELL.
IT WAS PROBABLY THE **YORUWANGA.**
OTHERWISE KNOWN AS "THE THIEF'S STOMACH."
PLANETS WITH COMPLETELY DIFFERENT CIVILIZATIONS, DIFFERENT MYTHS, DIFFERENT STORIES...
ALL HAVE A VERY SIMILAR LEGEND.
IT'S A STRANGE THING, BUT ON EACH PLANET, THE SAME PHENOMENON HAS BEEN OBSERVED.
I OVER-LOOKED IT AS COINCIDENCE.
BUT ON A CERTAIN PLANET, THEY HAVE A BALLAD.
"YORUWANGA, YORUWANGA. A SCALED GHOST THAT SLIPS THROUGH WALLS.
"A FISH WANDERS AMONG THE STARS.
"TO STEAL WHAT YOU HOLD DEAR."

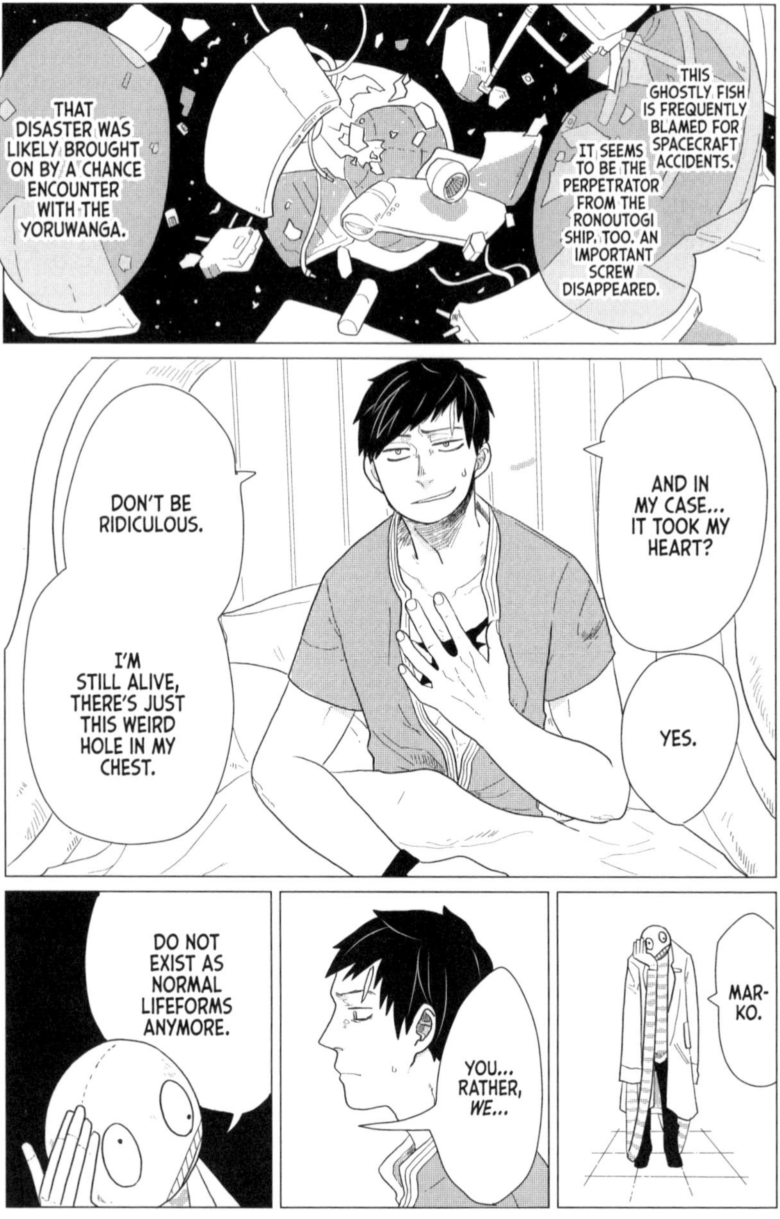
THIS GHOSTLY FISH IS FREQUENTLY BLAMED FOR SPACECRAFT ACCIDENTS.
IT SEEMS TO BE THE PERPETRATOR FROM THE RONOUTOGI SHIP, TOO. AN IMPORTANT SCREW DISAPPEARED.
THAT DISASTER WAS LIKELY BROUGHT ON BY A CHANCE ENCOUNTER WITH THE YORUWANGA.
AND IN MY CASE... IT TOOK MY HEART?
YES.
DON'T BE RIDICULOUS.
I'M STILL ALIVE, THERE'S JUST THIS WEIRD HOLE IN MY CHEST.
MAR-KO.
YOU... RATHER, *WE*...
DO NOT EXIST AS NORMAL LIFEFORMS ANYMORE.

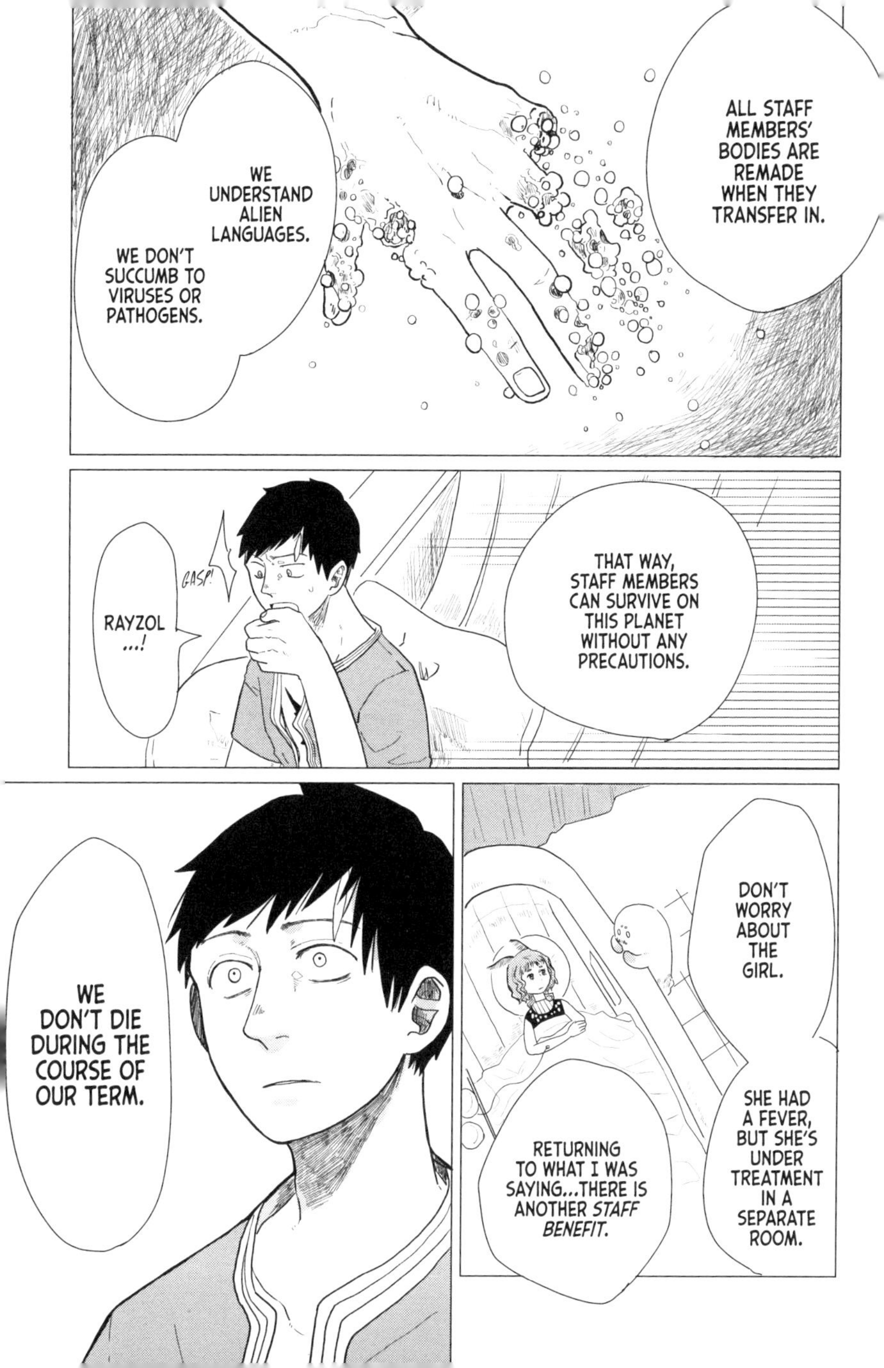
ALL STAFF MEMBERS' BODIES ARE REMADE WHEN THEY TRANSFER IN.
WE UNDERSTAND ALIEN LANGUAGES.
WE DON'T SUCCUMB TO VIRUSES OR PATHOGENS.
THAT WAY, STAFF MEMBERS CAN SURVIVE ON THIS PLANET WITHOUT ANY PRECAUTIONS.
GASP!
RAYZOL ...!
DON'T WORRY ABOUT THE GIRL.
SHE HAD A FEVER, BUT SHE'S UNDER TREATMENT IN A SEPARATE ROOM.
RETURNING TO WHAT I WAS SAYING...THERE IS ANOTHER *STAFF BENEFIT*.
WE DON'T DIE DURING THE COURSE OF OUR TERM.

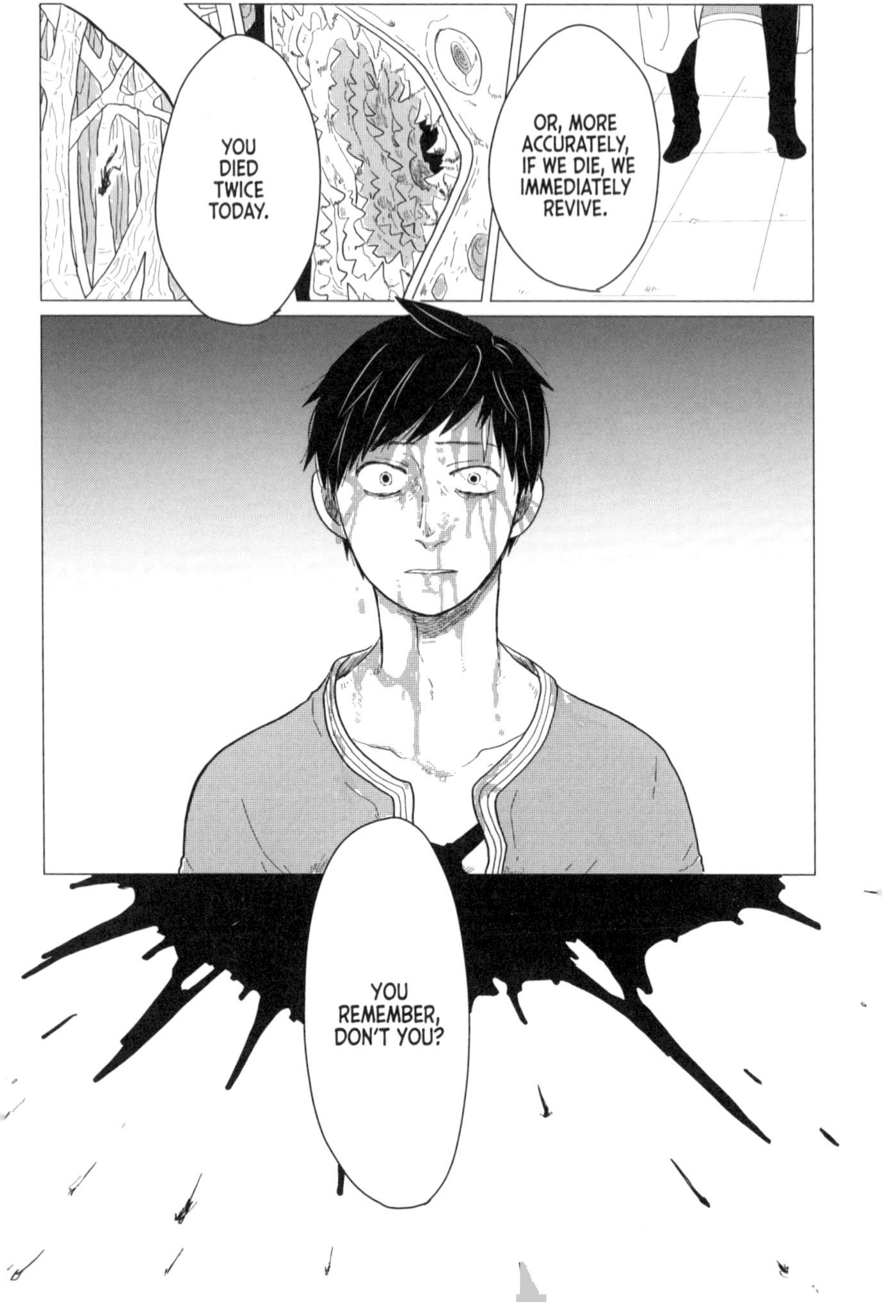
OR, MORE ACCURATELY, IF WE DIE, WE IMMEDIATELY REVIVE.
YOU DIED TWICE TODAY.
YOU REMEMBER, DON'T YOU?

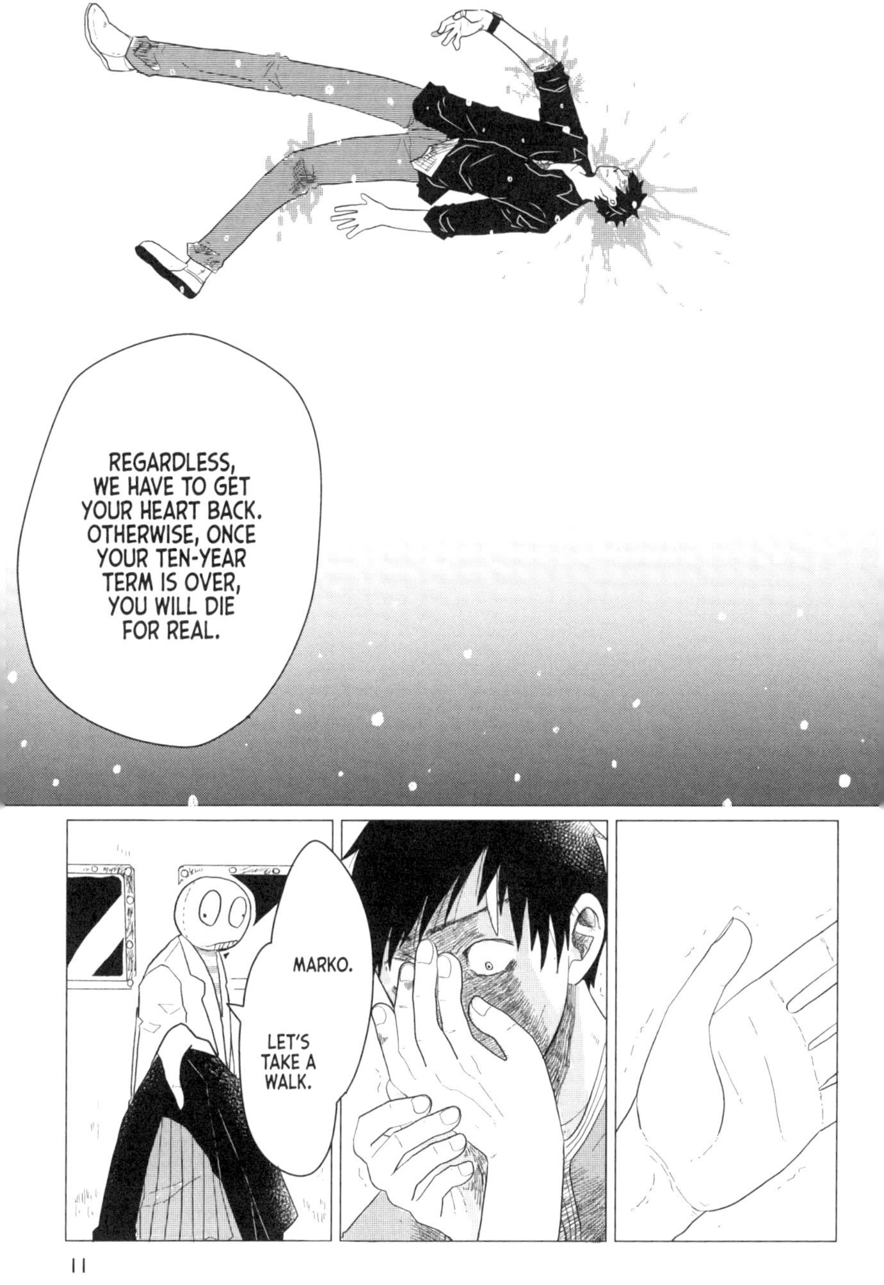
REGARDLESS, WE HAVE TO GET YOUR HEART BACK. OTHERWISE, ONCE YOUR TEN-YEAR TERM IS OVER, YOU WILL DIE FOR REAL.
MARKO.
LET'S TAKE A WALK.

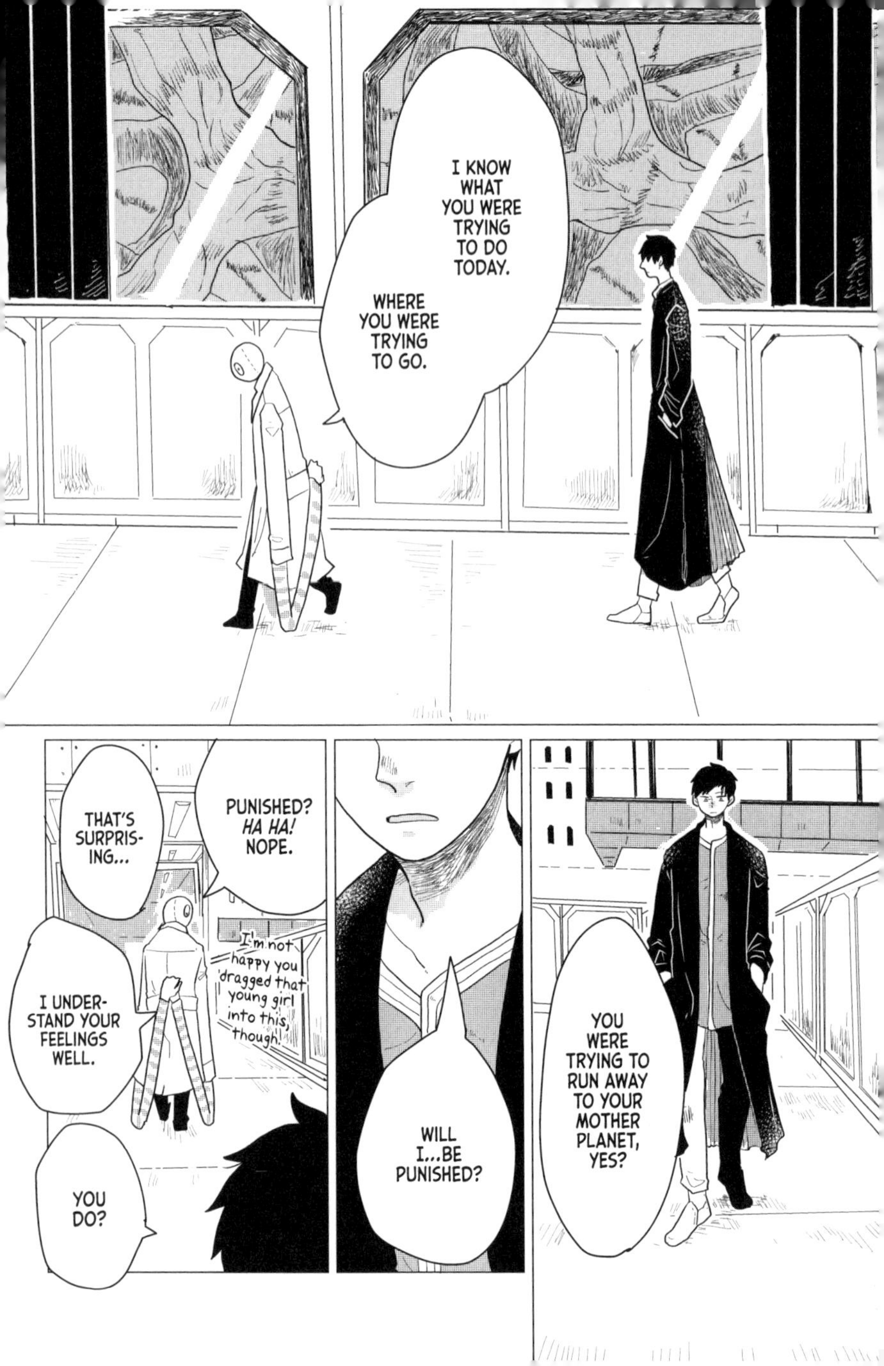
I KNOW WHAT YOU WERE TRYING TO DO TODAY.
WHERE YOU WERE TRYING TO GO.
YOU WERE TRYING TO RUN AWAY TO YOUR MOTHER PLANET, YES?
WILL I...BE PUNISHED?
PUNISHED? *HA HA!* NOPE.
THAT'S SURPRIS-ING...
I'm not happy you dragged that young girl into this, though.
I UNDER-STAND YOUR FEELINGS WELL.
YOU DO?

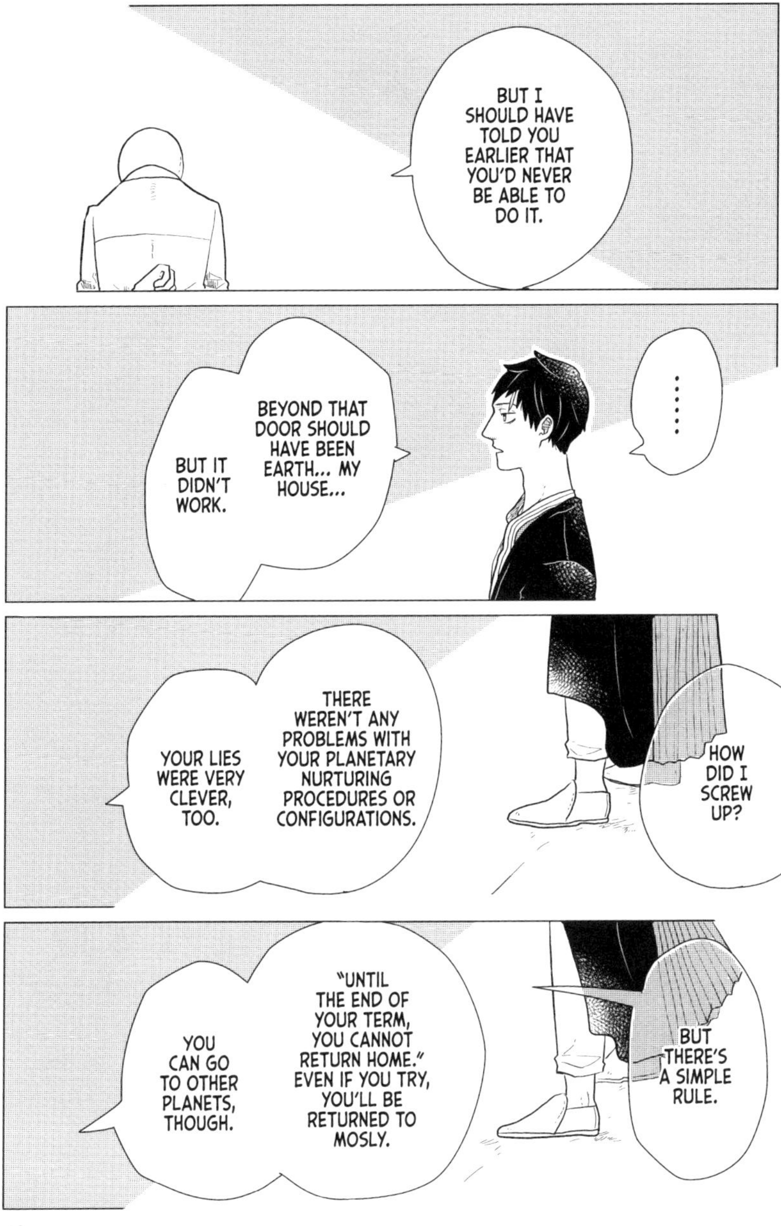
BUT I SHOULD HAVE TOLD YOU EARLIER THAT YOU'D NEVER BE ABLE TO DO IT.
......
BEYOND THAT DOOR SHOULD HAVE BEEN EARTH... MY HOUSE...
BUT IT DIDN'T WORK.
HOW DID I SCREW UP?
THERE WEREN'T ANY PROBLEMS WITH YOUR PLANETARY NURTURING PROCEDURES OR CONFIGURATIONS.
YOUR LIES WERE VERY CLEVER, TOO.
BUT THERE'S A SIMPLE RULE.
"UNTIL THE END OF YOUR TERM, YOU CANNOT RETURN HOME." EVEN IF YOU TRY, YOU'LL BE RETURNED TO MOSLY.
YOU CAN GO TO OTHER PLANETS, THOUGH.

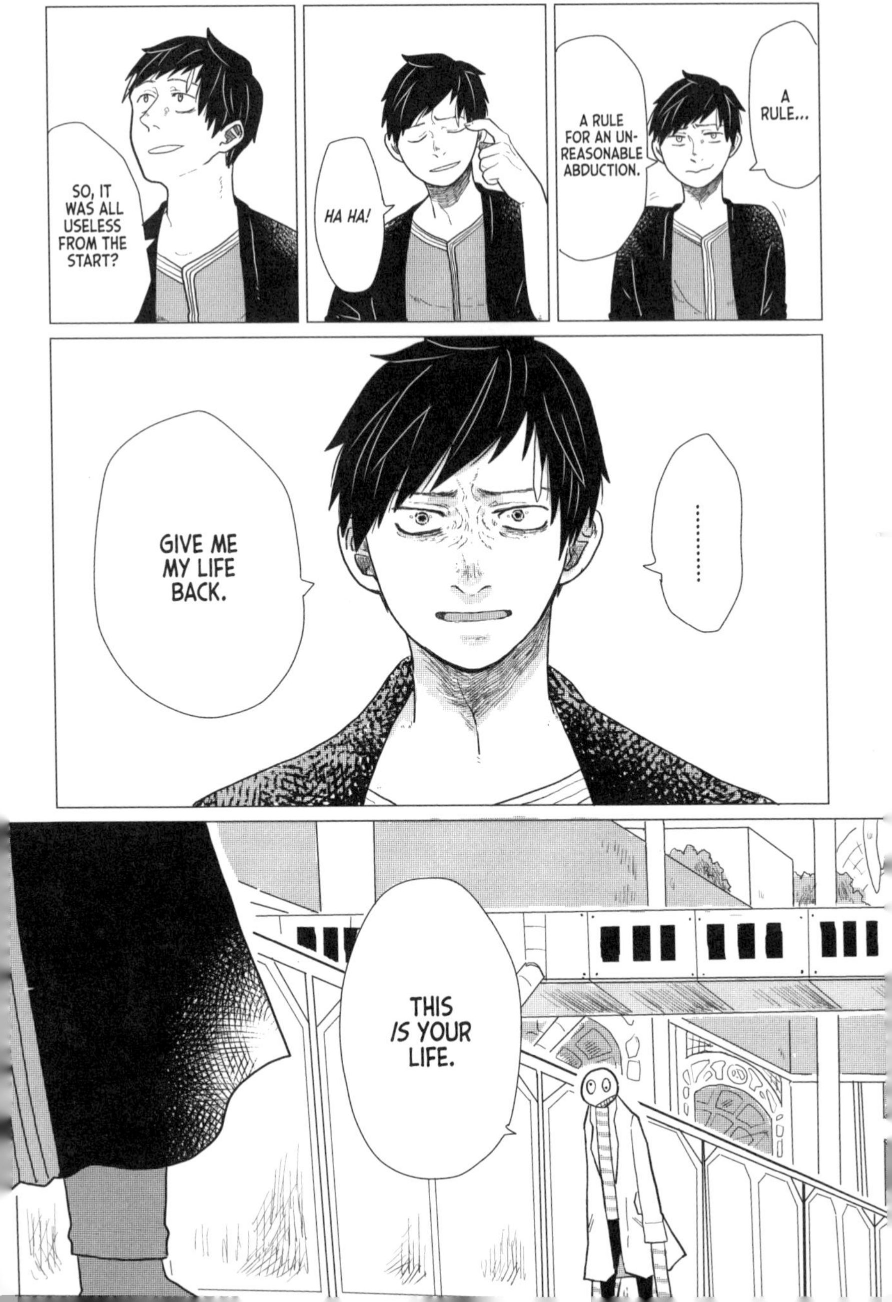
A RULE...
A RULE FOR AN UN-REASONABLE ABDUCTION.
HA HA!
SO, IT WAS ALL USELESS FROM THE START?
......
GIVE ME MY LIFE BACK.
THIS *IS* YOUR LIFE.

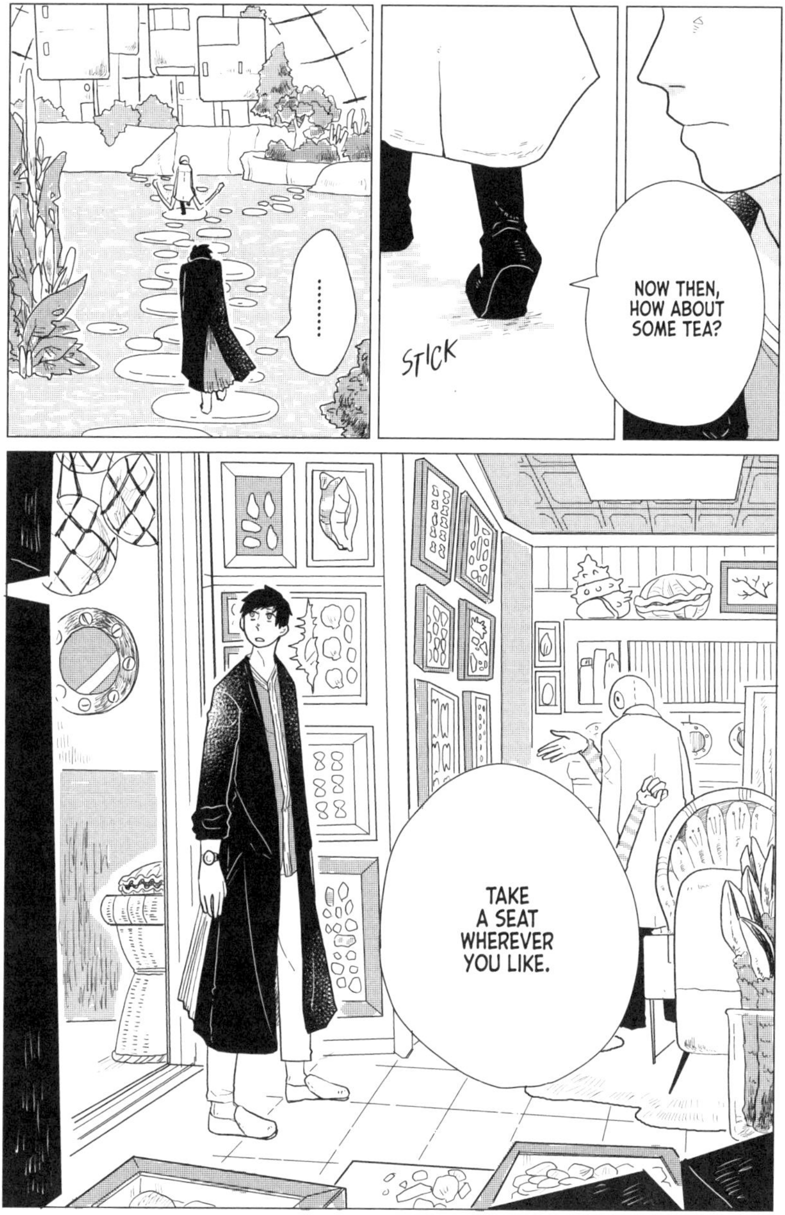
NOW THEN, HOW ABOUT SOME TEA?
STICK
......
TAKE A SEAT WHEREVER YOU LIKE.

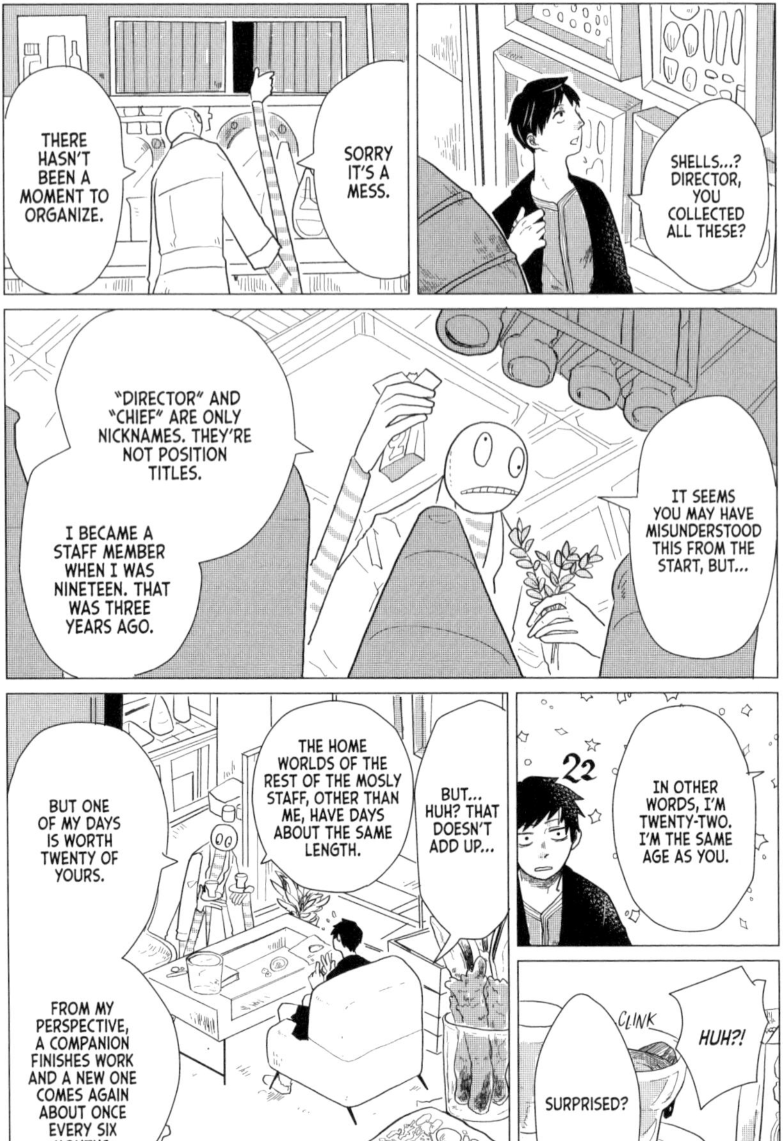
SHELLS...? DIRECTOR, YOU COLLECTED ALL THESE?
SORRY IT'S A MESS.
THERE HASN'T BEEN A MOMENT TO ORGANIZE.
IT SEEMS YOU MAY HAVE MISUNDERSTOOD THIS FROM THE START, BUT...
"DIRECTOR" AND "CHIEF" ARE ONLY NICKNAMES. THEY'RE NOT POSITION TITLES.
I BECAME A STAFF MEMBER WHEN I WAS NINETEEN. THAT WAS THREE YEARS AGO.
22
IN OTHER WORDS, I'M TWENTY-TWO. I'M THE SAME AGE AS YOU.
HUH?!
CLINK
SURPRISED?
BUT... HUH? THAT DOESN'T ADD UP...
THE HOME WORLDS OF THE REST OF THE MOSLY STAFF, OTHER THAN ME, HAVE DAYS ABOUT THE SAME LENGTH.
BUT ONE OF MY DAYS IS WORTH TWENTY OF YOURS.
FROM MY PERSPECTIVE, A COMPANION FINISHES WORK AND A NEW ONE COMES AGAIN ABOUT ONCE EVERY SIX MONTHS.

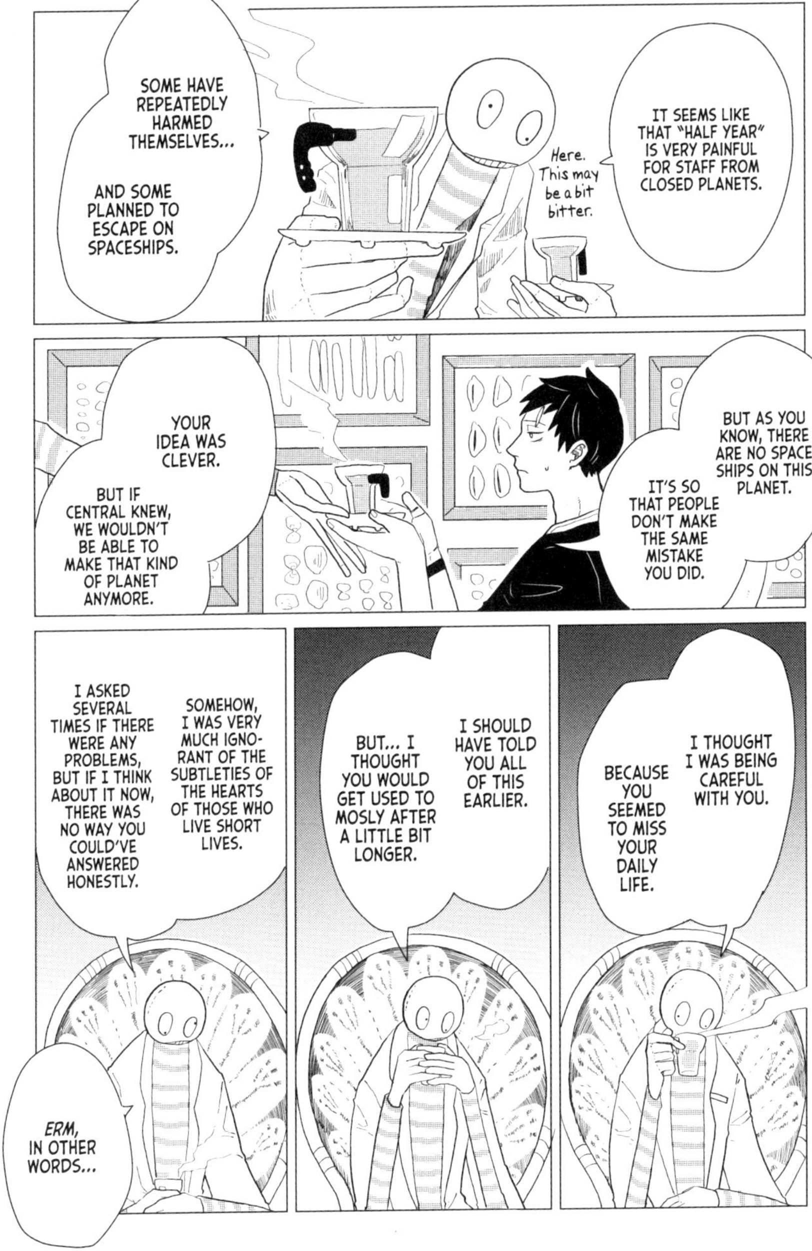
IT SEEMS LIKE THAT "HALF YEAR" IS VERY PAINFUL FOR STAFF FROM CLOSED PLANETS.
Here. This may be a bit bitter.
SOME HAVE REPEATEDLY HARMED THEMSELVES...
AND SOME PLANNED TO ESCAPE ON SPACESHIPS.
BUT AS YOU KNOW, THERE ARE NO SPACESHIPS ON THIS PLANET.
IT'S SO THAT PEOPLE DON'T MAKE THE SAME MISTAKE YOU DID.
YOUR IDEA WAS CLEVER.
BUT IF CENTRAL KNEW, WE WOULDN'T BE ABLE TO MAKE THAT KIND OF PLANET ANYMORE.
I THOUGHT I WAS BEING CAREFUL WITH YOU.
BECAUSE YOU SEEMED TO MISS YOUR DAILY LIFE.
I SHOULD HAVE TOLD YOU ALL OF THIS EARLIER.
BUT... I THOUGHT YOU WOULD GET USED TO MOSLY AFTER A LITTLE BIT LONGER.
SOMEHOW, I WAS VERY MUCH IGNORANT OF THE SUBTLETIES OF THE HEARTS OF THOSE WHO LIVE SHORT LIVES.
I ASKED SEVERAL TIMES IF THERE WERE ANY PROBLEMS, BUT IF I THINK ABOUT IT NOW, THERE WAS NO WAY YOU COULD'VE ANSWERED HONESTLY.
ERM, IN OTHER WORDS...

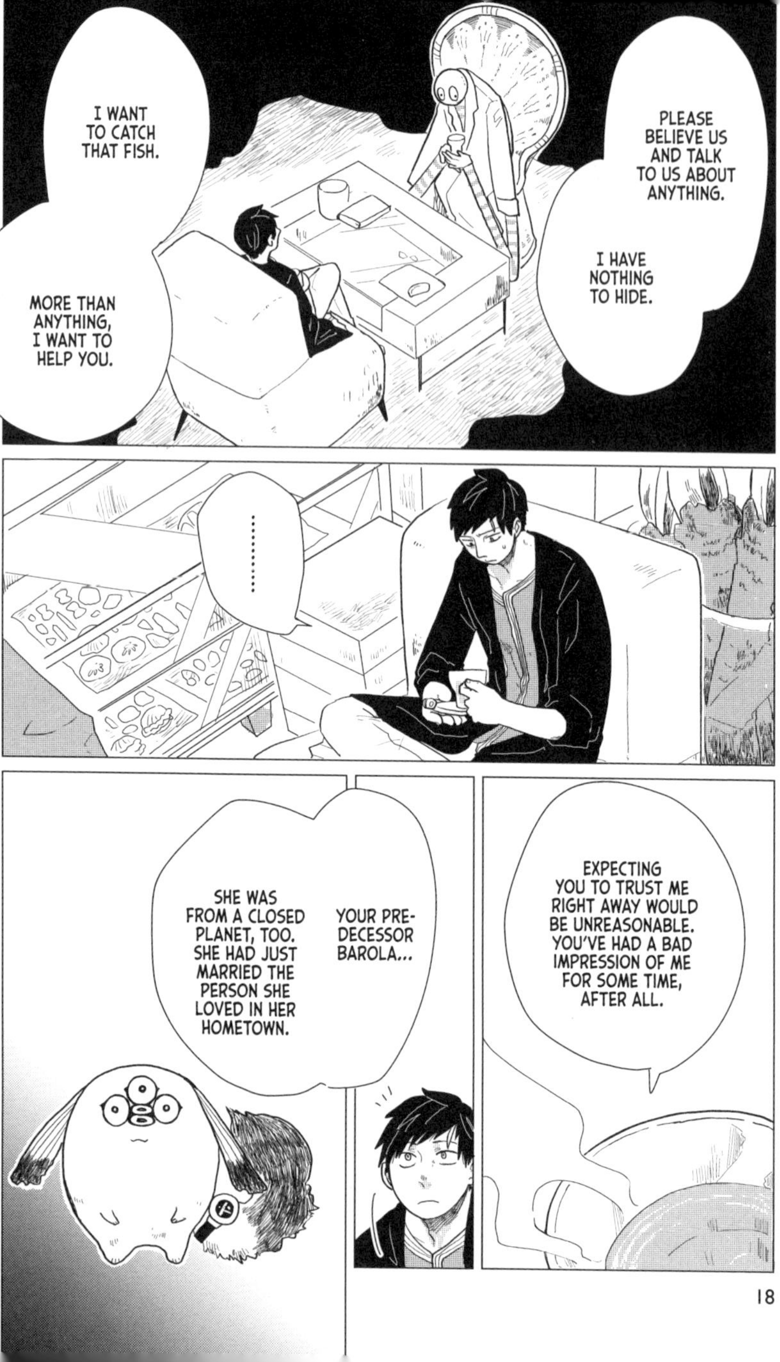
PLEASE BELIEVE US AND TALK TO US ABOUT ANYTHING.
I HAVE NOTHING TO HIDE.
I WANT TO CATCH THAT FISH.
MORE THAN ANYTHING, I WANT TO HELP YOU.
....
EXPECTING YOU TO TRUST ME RIGHT AWAY WOULD BE UNREASONABLE. YOU'VE HAD A BAD IMPRESSION OF ME FOR SOME TIME, AFTER ALL.
YOUR PRE-DECESSOR BAROLA...
SHE WAS FROM A CLOSED PLANET, TOO. SHE HAD JUST MARRIED THE PERSON SHE LOVED IN HER HOMETOWN.

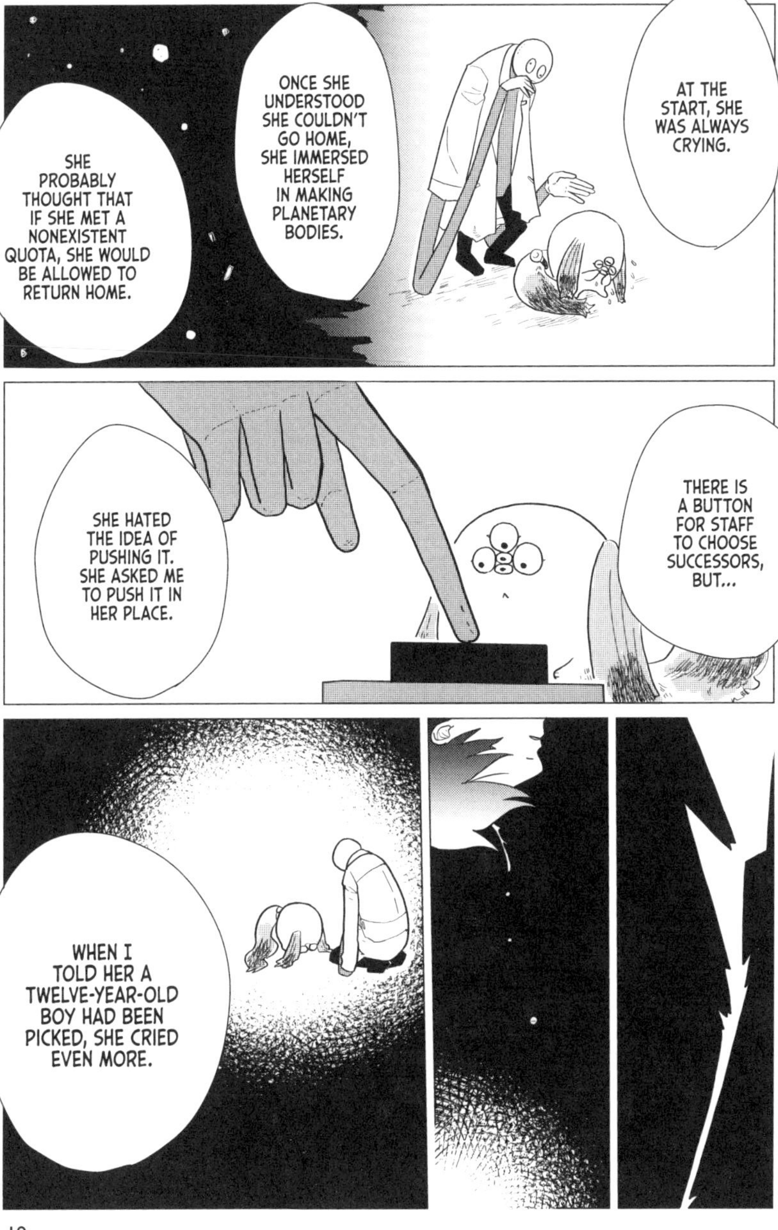
AT THE START, SHE WAS ALWAYS CRYING.
ONCE SHE UNDERSTOOD SHE COULDN'T GO HOME, SHE IMMERSED HERSELF IN MAKING PLANETARY BODIES.
SHE PROBABLY THOUGHT THAT IF SHE MET A NONEXISTENT QUOTA, SHE WOULD BE ALLOWED TO RETURN HOME.
THERE IS A BUTTON FOR STAFF TO CHOOSE SUCCESSORS, BUT...
SHE HATED THE IDEA OF PUSHING IT. SHE ASKED ME TO PUSH IT IN HER PLACE.
WHEN I TOLD HER A TWELVE-YEAR-OLD BOY HAD BEEN PICKED, SHE CRIED EVEN MORE.

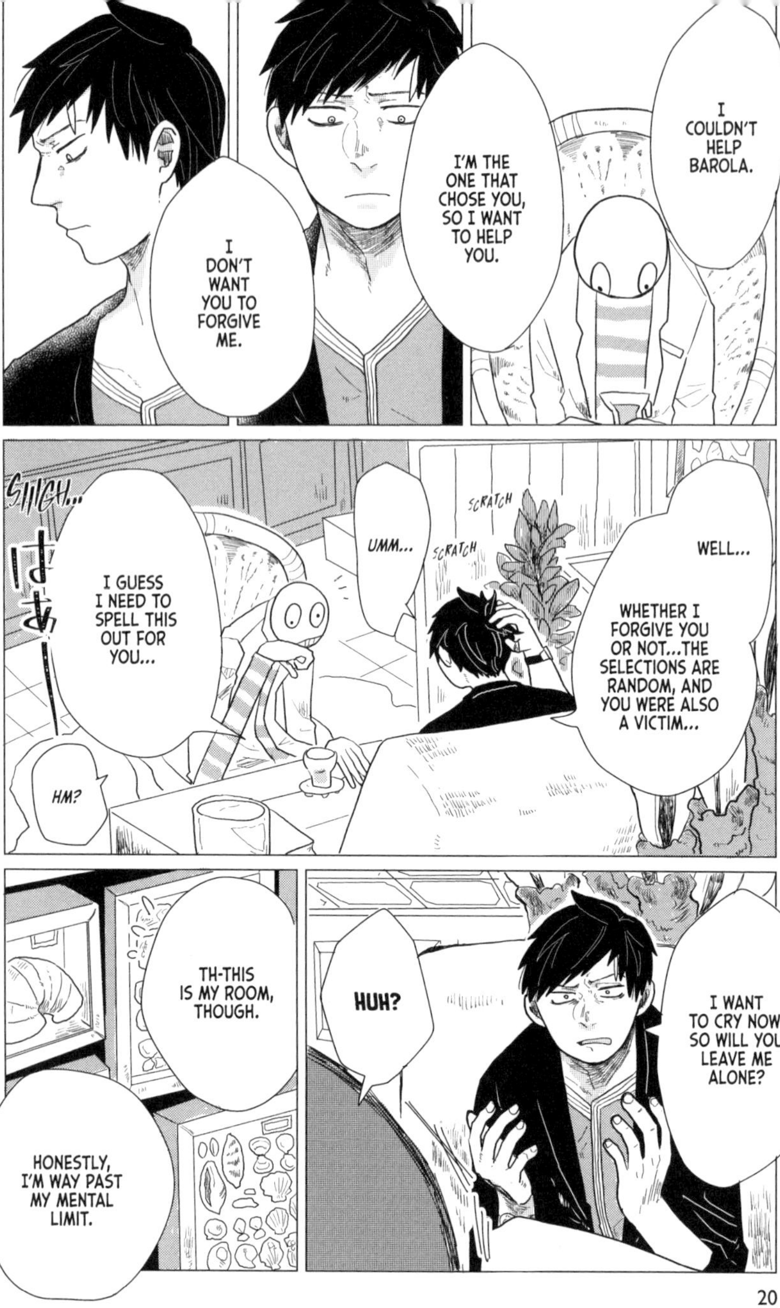
I COULDN'T HELP BAROLA.
I'M THE ONE THAT CHOSE YOU, SO I WANT TO HELP YOU.
I DON'T WANT YOU TO FORGIVE ME.
WELL...
WHETHER I FORGIVE YOU OR NOT...THE SELECTIONS ARE RANDOM, AND YOU WERE ALSO A VICTIM...
SCRATCH
SCRATCH
UMM...
I GUESS I NEED TO SPELL THIS OUT FOR YOU...
SIIGH...
はぁ
HM?
I WANT TO CRY NOW, SO WILL YOU LEAVE ME ALONE?
HUH?
TH-THIS IS MY ROOM, THOUGH.
HONESTLY, I'M WAY PAST MY MENTAL LIMIT.

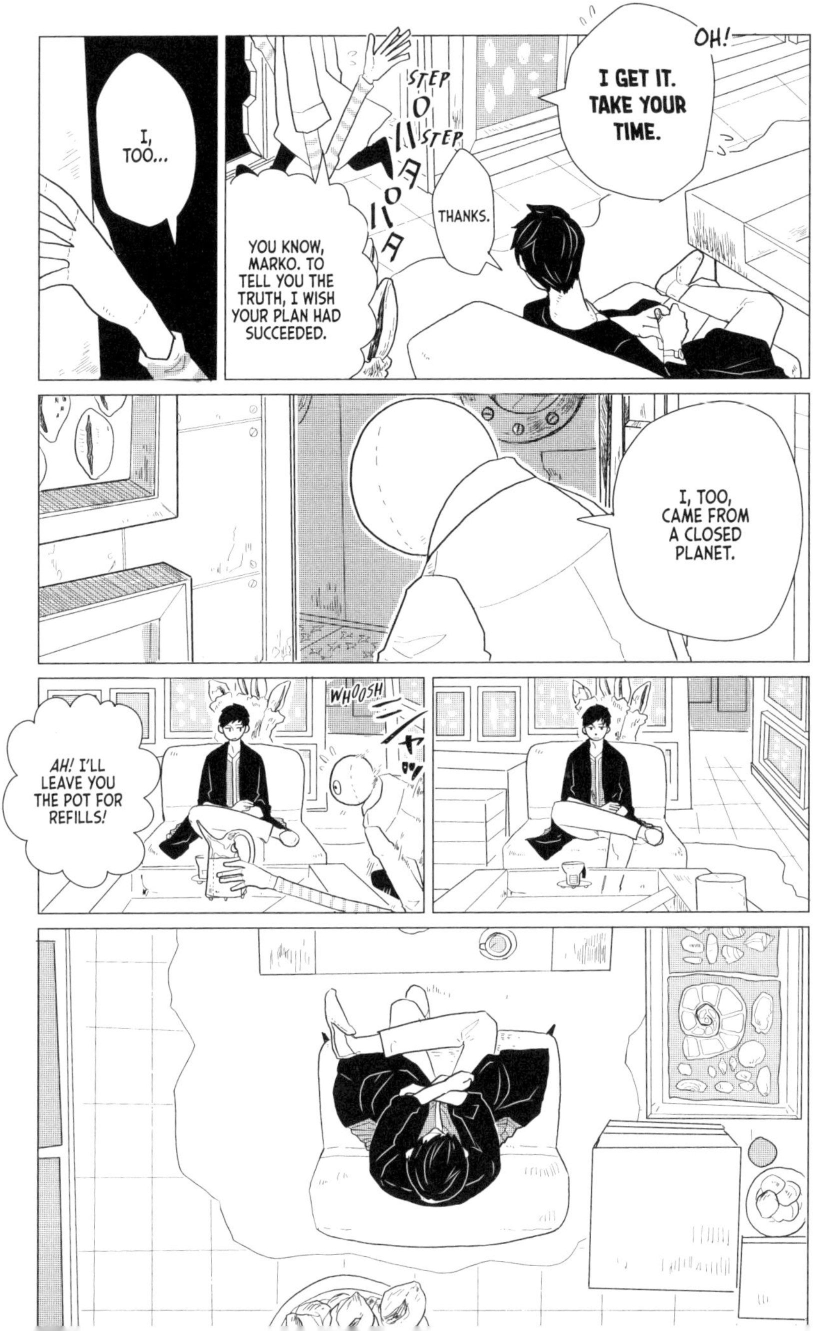
OH!
I GET IT. TAKE YOUR TIME.
STEP
STEP
THANKS.
YOU KNOW, MARKO. TO TELL YOU THE TRUTH, I WISH YOUR PLAN HAD SUCCEEDED.
I, TOO...
I, TOO, CAME FROM A CLOSED PLANET.
WHOOSH
AH! I'LL LEAVE YOU THE POT FOR REFILLS!

CLUNK
SLIDE
"PLEASE STAY WITH ME FOREVER.
"I DON'T WANT TO LEAVE YOU ON YOUR OWN.
"AND I...
"I WILL MAKE YOU HAPPY, SO..."
U...
UGH...
DAMN IT...!

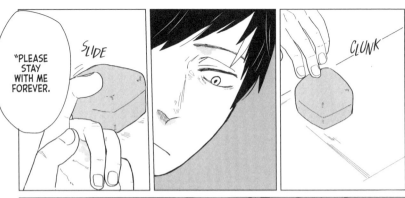

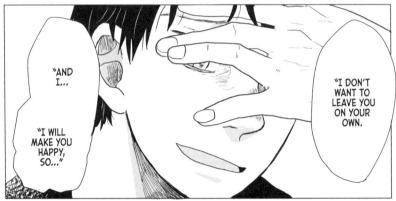

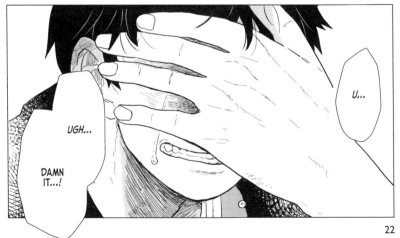

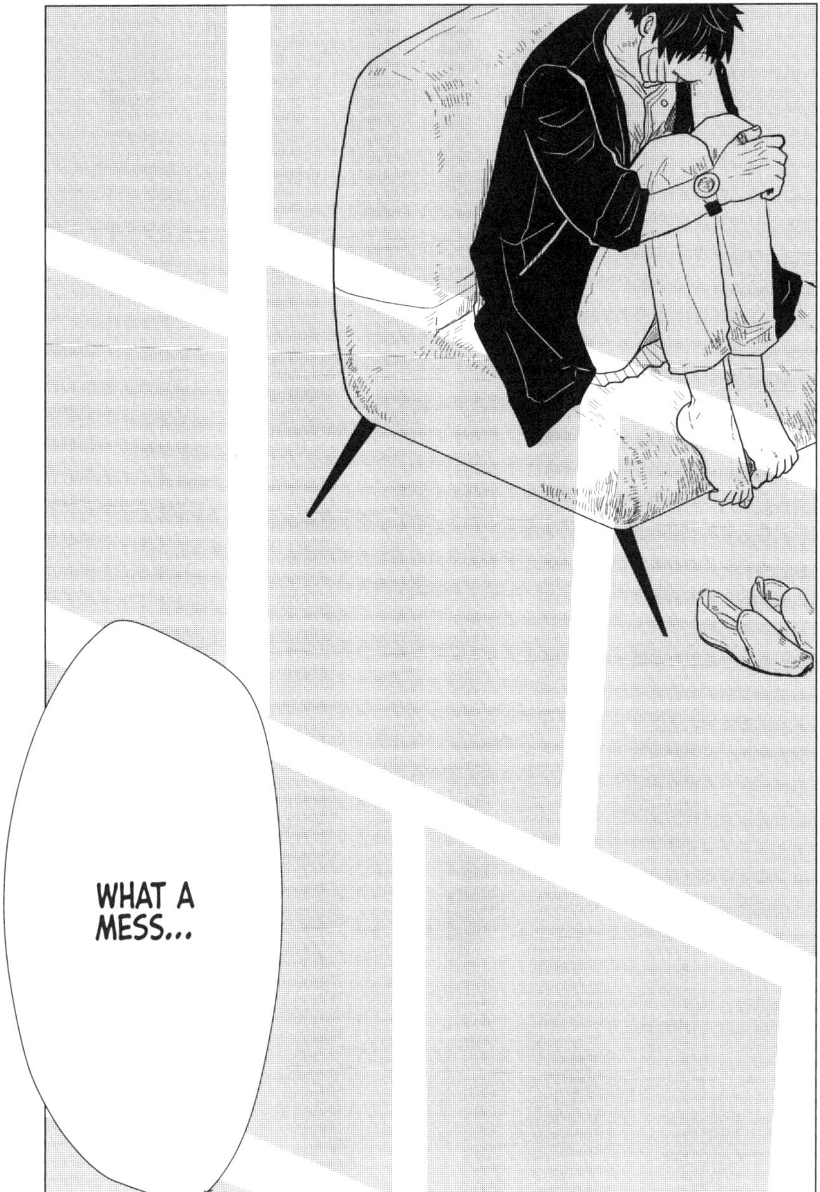
WHAT A MESS...

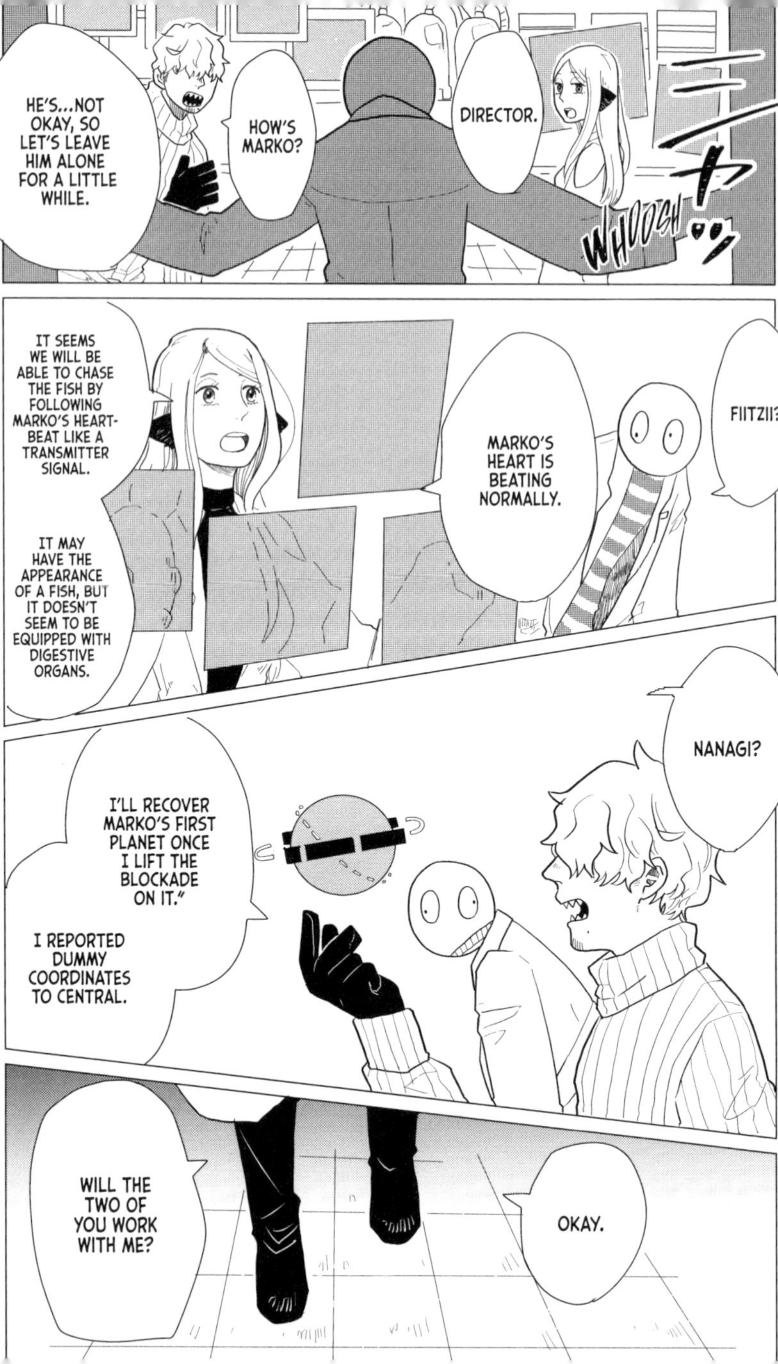
WHOOSH
DIRECTOR.
HOW'S MARKO?
HE'S...NOT OKAY, SO LET'S LEAVE HIM ALONE FOR A LITTLE WHILE.
FIITZII?
MARKO'S HEART IS BEATING NORMALLY.
IT SEEMS WE WILL BE ABLE TO CHASE THE FISH BY FOLLOWING MARKO'S HEART-BEAT LIKE A TRANSMITTER SIGNAL.
IT MAY HAVE THE APPEARANCE OF A FISH, BUT IT DOESN'T SEEM TO BE EQUIPPED WITH DIGESTIVE ORGANS.
NANAGI?
I'LL RECOVER MARKO'S FIRST PLANET ONCE I LIFT THE BLOCKADE ON IT."
I REPORTED DUMMY COORDINATES TO CENTRAL.
WILL THE TWO OF YOU WORK WITH ME?
OKAY.

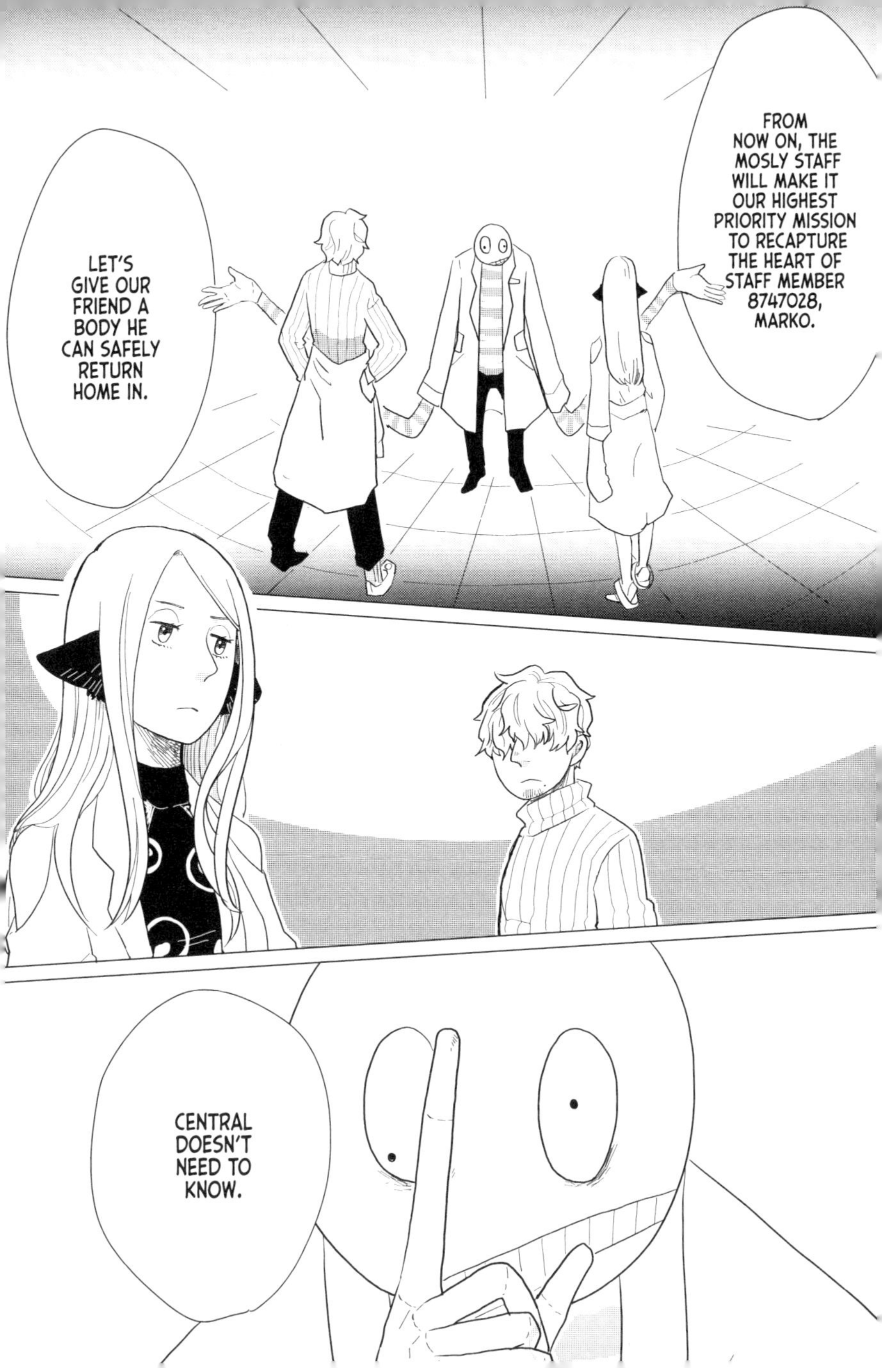
FROM NOW ON, THE MOSLY STAFF WILL MAKE IT OUR HIGHEST PRIORITY MISSION TO RECAPTURE THE HEART OF STAFF MEMBER 8747028, MARKO.
LET'S GIVE OUR FRIEND A BODY HE CAN SAFELY RETURN HOME IN.
CENTRAL DOESN'T NEED TO KNOW.

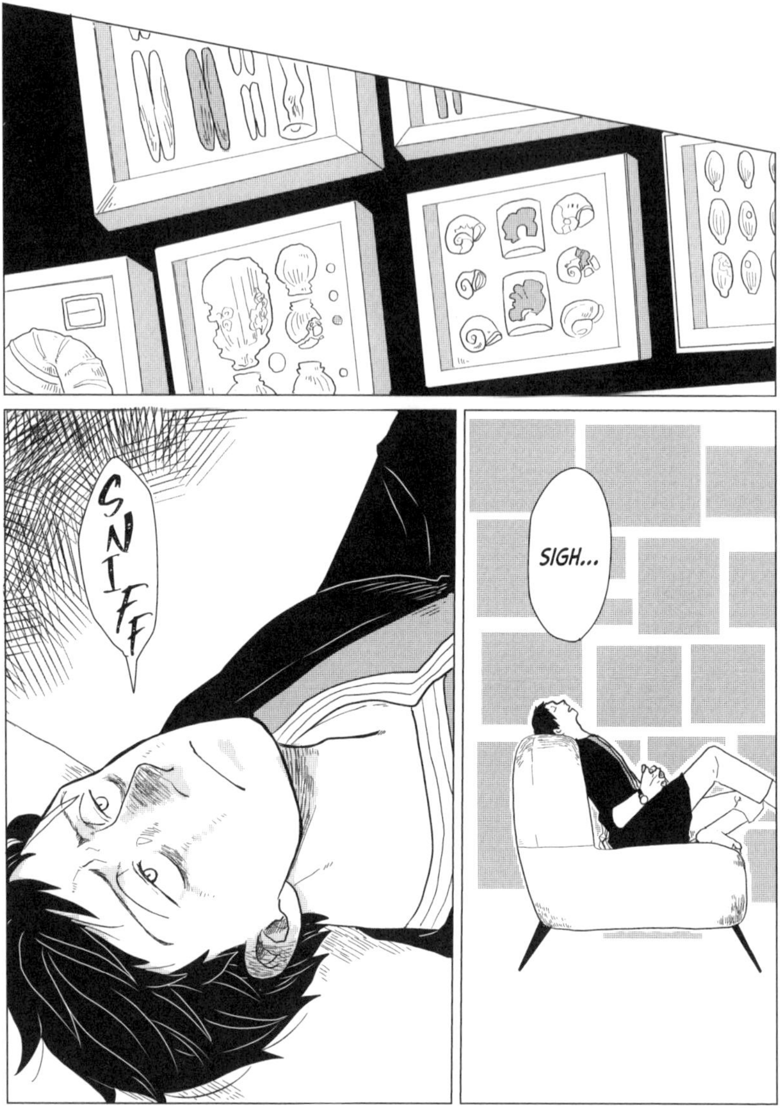
SIGH...
SNIFF

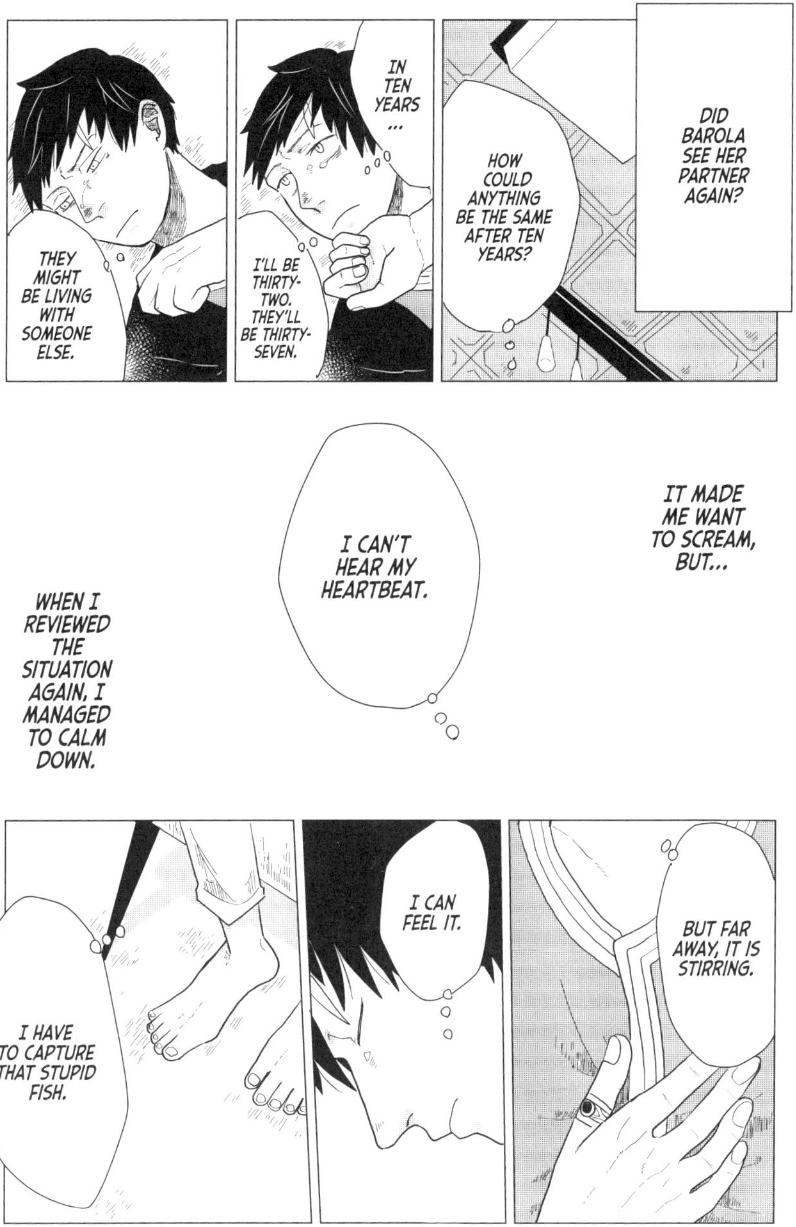
DID BAROLA SEE HER PARTNER AGAIN?
HOW COULD ANYTHING BE THE SAME AFTER TEN YEARS?
IN TEN YEARS ...
I'LL BE THIRTY-TWO. THEY'LL BE THIRTY-SEVEN.
THEY MIGHT BE LIVING WITH SOMEONE ELSE.
IT MADE ME WANT TO SCREAM, BUT...
I CAN'T HEAR MY HEARTBEAT.
WHEN I REVIEWED THE SITUATION AGAIN, I MANAGED TO CALM DOWN.
BUT FAR AWAY, IT IS STIRRING.
I CAN FEEL IT.
I HAVE TO CAPTURE THAT STUPID FISH.

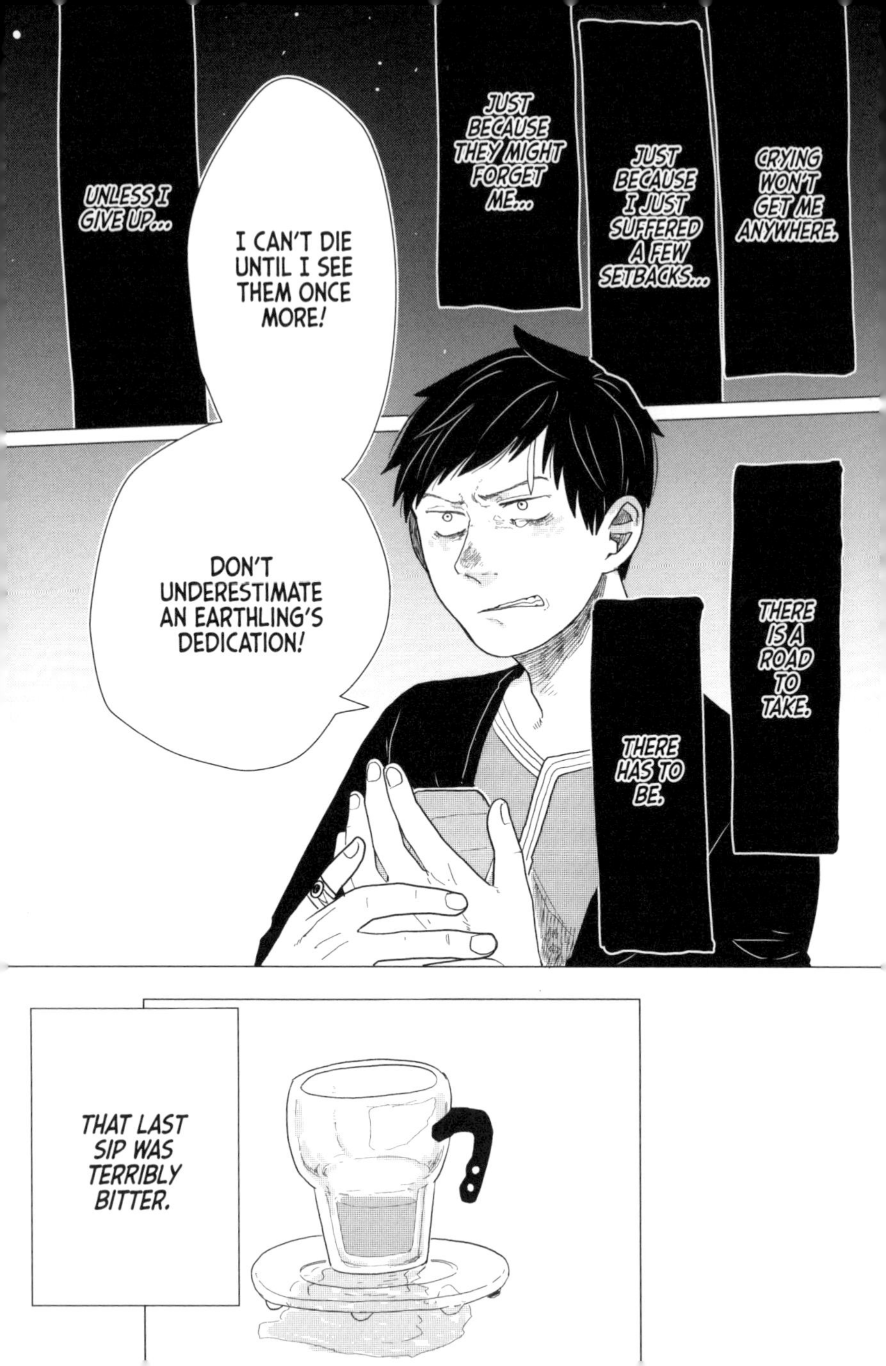
CRYING WON'T GET ME ANYWHERE.
JUST BECAUSE I JUST SUFFERED A FEW SETBACKS...
JUST BECAUSE THEY MIGHT FORGET ME...
UNLESS I GIVE UP...
I CAN'T DIE UNTIL I SEE THEM ONCE MORE!
THERE IS A ROAD TO TAKE.
THERE HAS TO BE.
DON'T UNDERESTIMATE AN EARTHLING'S DEDICATION!
THAT LAST SIP WAS TERRIBLY BITTER.

Ruikano Tea

- RELAXES AND REMEDIES MOTION SICKNESS.

- TASTES SIMILAR TO MATÉ.

- TENDS TO BE BITTER BECAUSE EVEN A SMALL VOLUME OF LEAVES MAKES A STRONG INFUSION.

- ORIGINALLY THESE WERE DIPPED TO ONE'S DESIRED STRENGTH IN HOT WATER TO BE DRUNK.

Episode 10
The Ursazka Brothers and the Break Planet

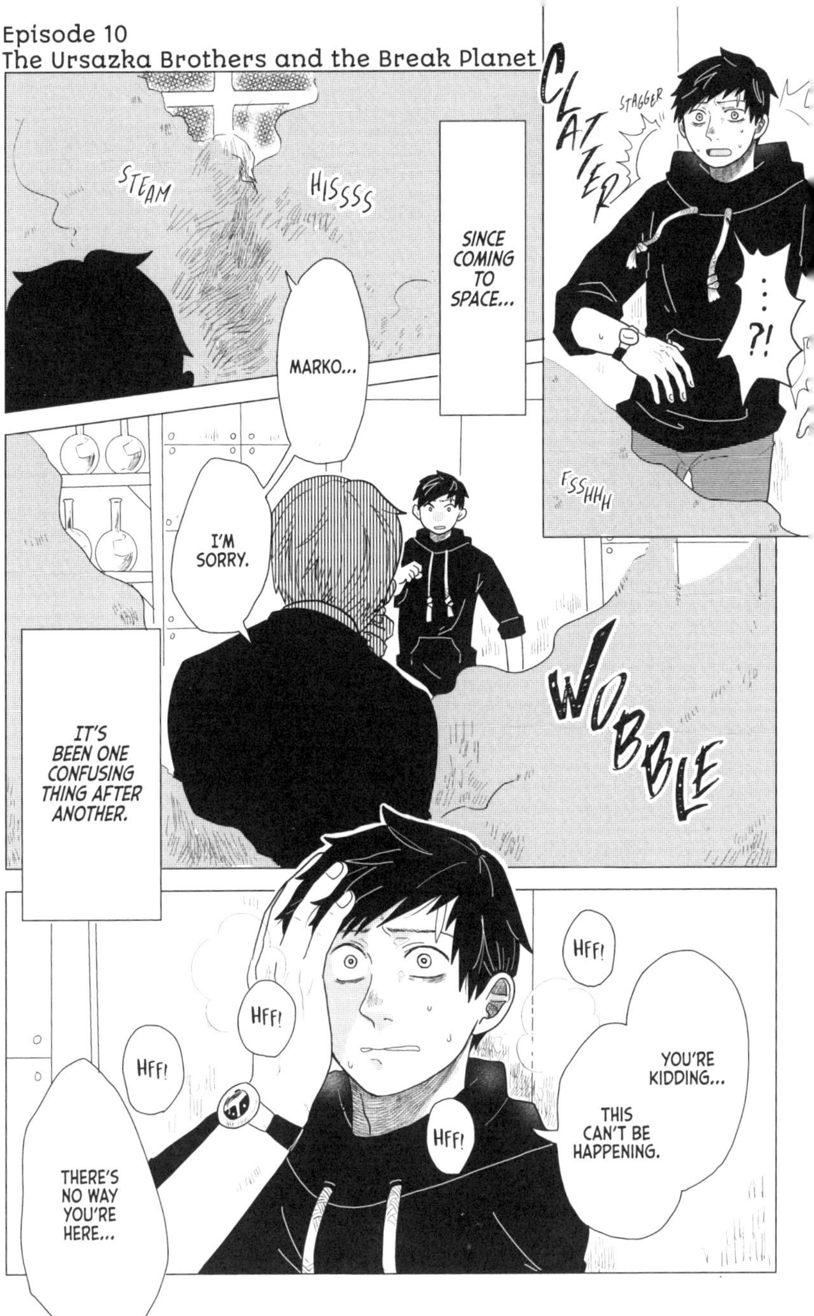
CLATTER
STAGGER
...
?!
FSSHHH
SINCE COMING TO SPACE...
HISSSS
STEAM
MARKO...
I'M SORRY.
WOBBLE
IT'S BEEN ONE CONFUSING THING AFTER ANOTHER.
HFF!
YOU'RE KIDDING...
THIS CAN'T BE HAPPENING.
HFF!
HFF!
HFF!
THERE'S NO WAY YOU'RE HERE...

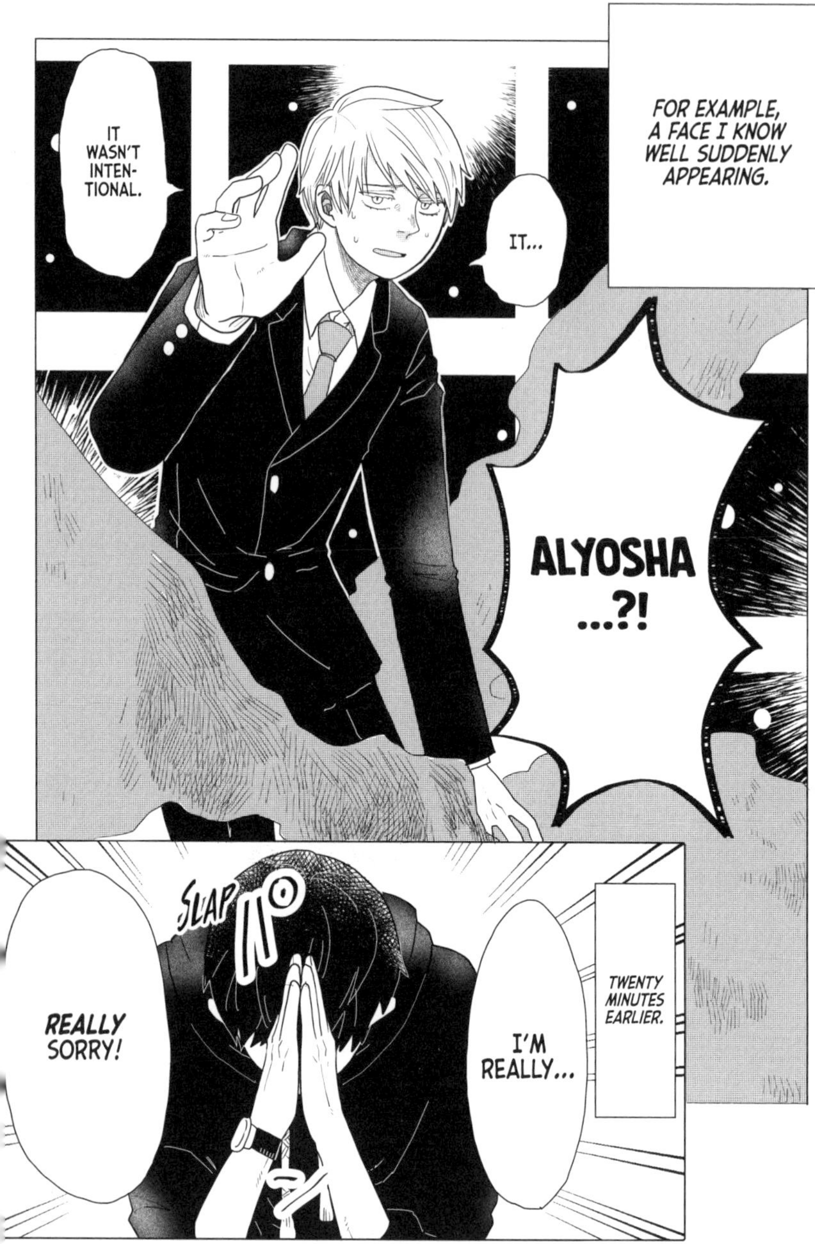
FOR EXAMPLE, A FACE I KNOW WELL SUDDENLY APPEARING.
ALYOSHA ...?!
IT...
IT WASN'T INTEN-TIONAL.
TWENTY MINUTES EARLIER.
I'M REALLY...
SLAP
REALLY SORRY!

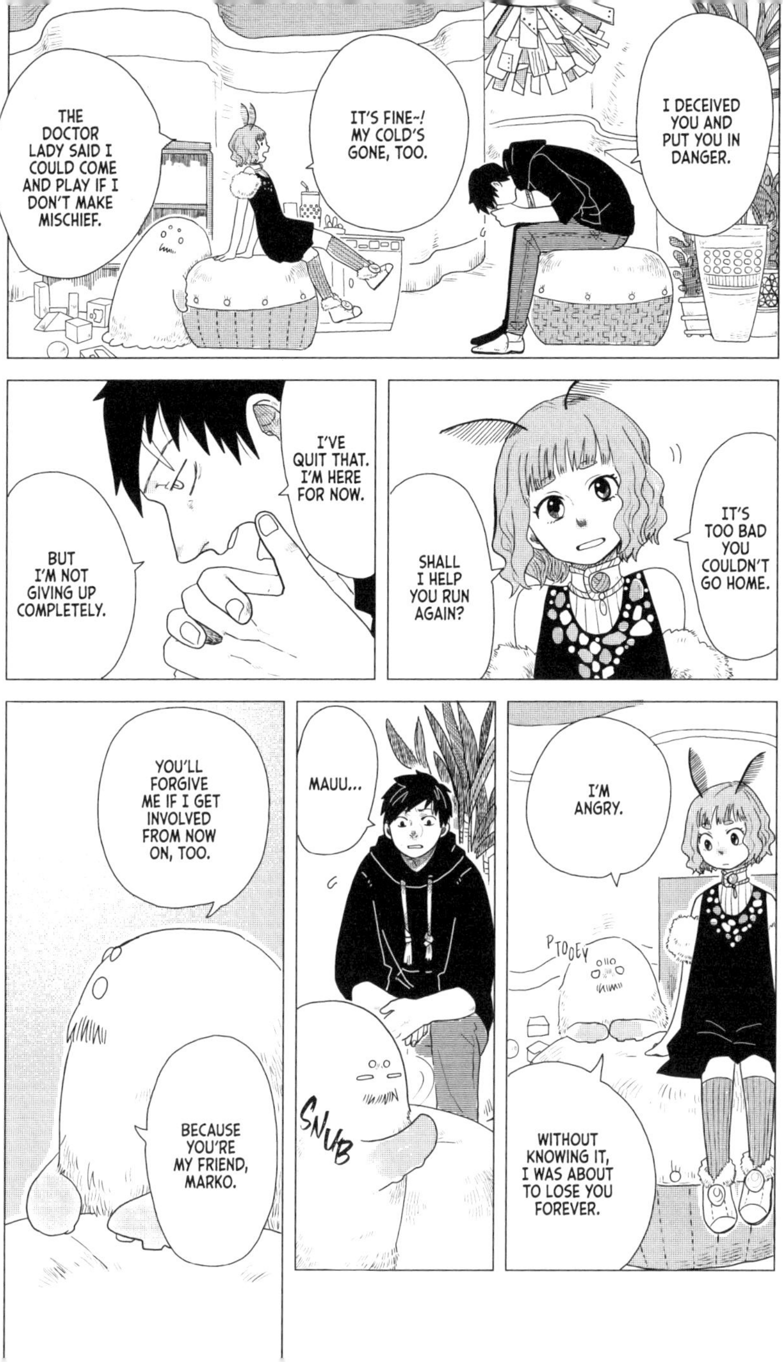
I DECEIVED YOU AND PUT YOU IN DANGER.
IT'S FINE~! MY COLD'S GONE, TOO.
THE DOCTOR LADY SAID I COULD COME AND PLAY IF I DON'T MAKE MISCHIEF.
IT'S TOO BAD YOU COULDN'T GO HOME.
SHALL I HELP YOU RUN AGAIN?
I'VE QUIT THAT. I'M HERE FOR NOW.
BUT I'M NOT GIVING UP COMPLETELY.
I'M ANGRY.
PTOOEY
WITHOUT KNOWING IT, I WAS ABOUT TO LOSE YOU FOREVER.
MAUU...
SNUB
YOU'LL FORGIVE ME IF I GET INVOLVED FROM NOW ON, TOO.
BECAUSE YOU'RE MY FRIEND, MARKO.

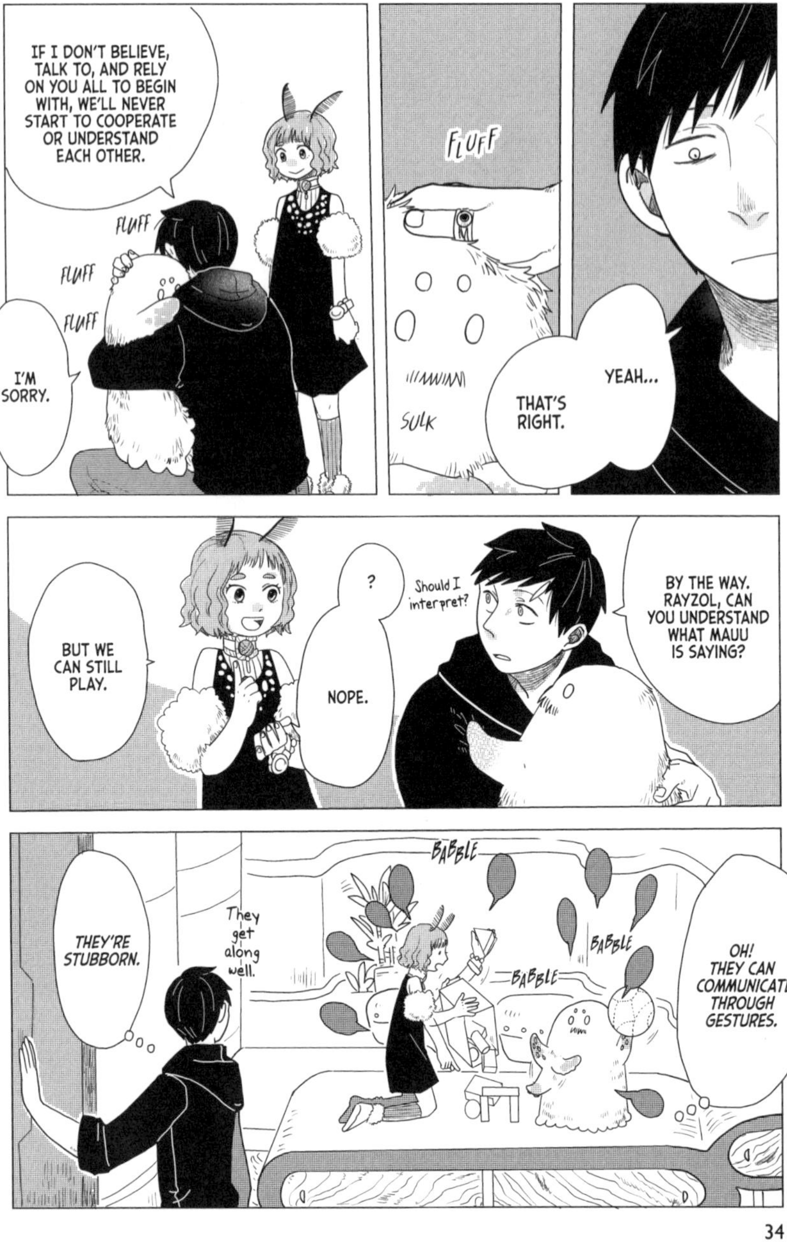
YEAH...
THAT'S RIGHT.
FLUFF
SULK
IF I DON'T BELIEVE, TALK TO, AND RELY ON YOU ALL TO BEGIN WITH, WE'LL NEVER START TO COOPERATE OR UNDERSTAND EACH OTHER.
FLUFF
FLUFF
FLUFF
I'M SORRY.
BY THE WAY. RAYZOL, CAN YOU UNDERSTAND WHAT MAUU IS SAYING?
Should I interpret?
?
NOPE.
BUT WE CAN STILL PLAY.
OH! THEY CAN COMMUNICATE THROUGH GESTURES.
BABBLE
BABBLE
BABBLE
They get along well.
THEY'RE STUBBORN.

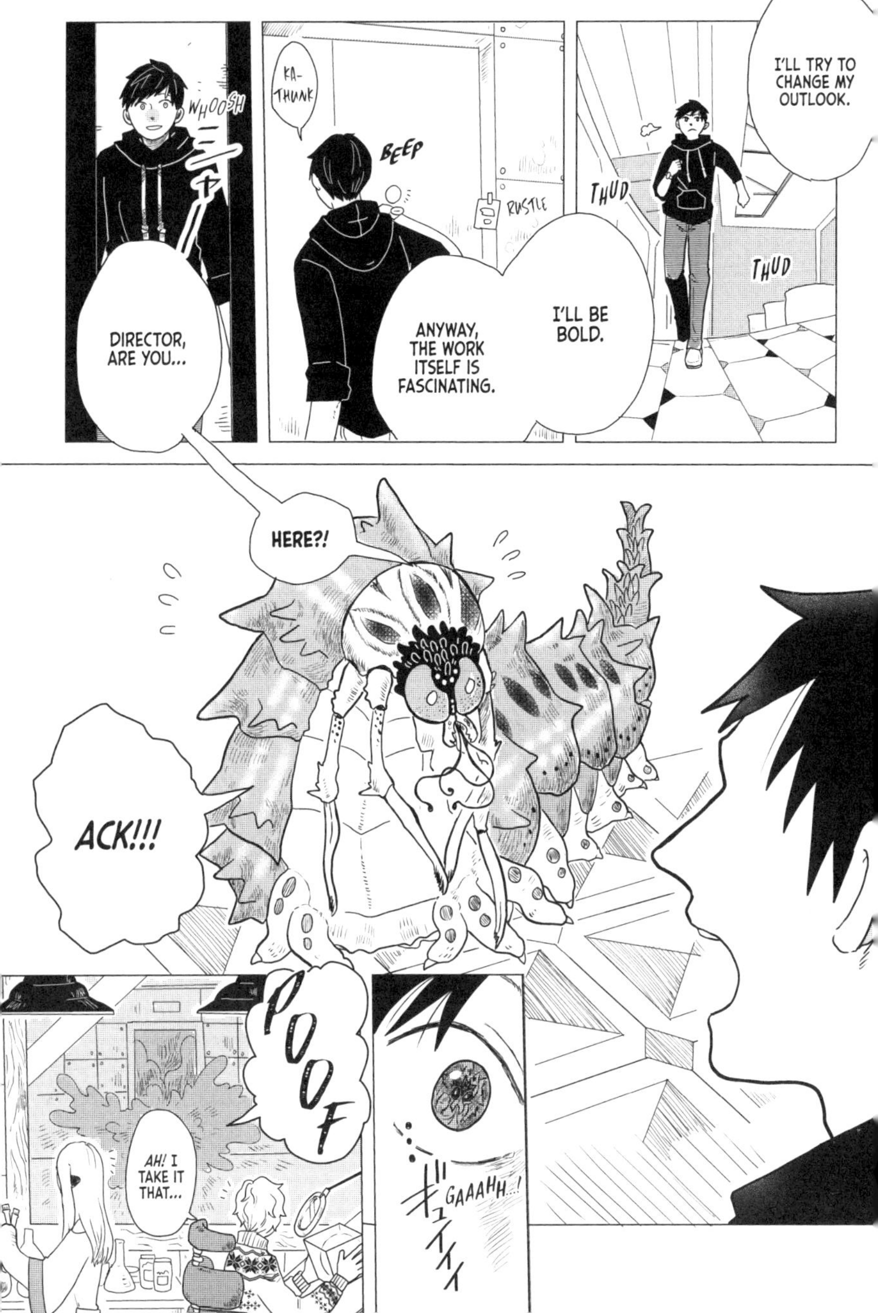
I'LL TRY TO CHANGE MY OUTLOOK.
THUD
THUD
I'LL BE BOLD.
KA-THUNK
BEEP
RUSTLE
ANYWAY, THE WORK ITSELF IS FASCINATING.
WHOOSH
DIRECTOR, ARE YOU...
HERE?!
ACK!!!
GAAAHH..!
POOF
AH! I TAKE IT THAT...

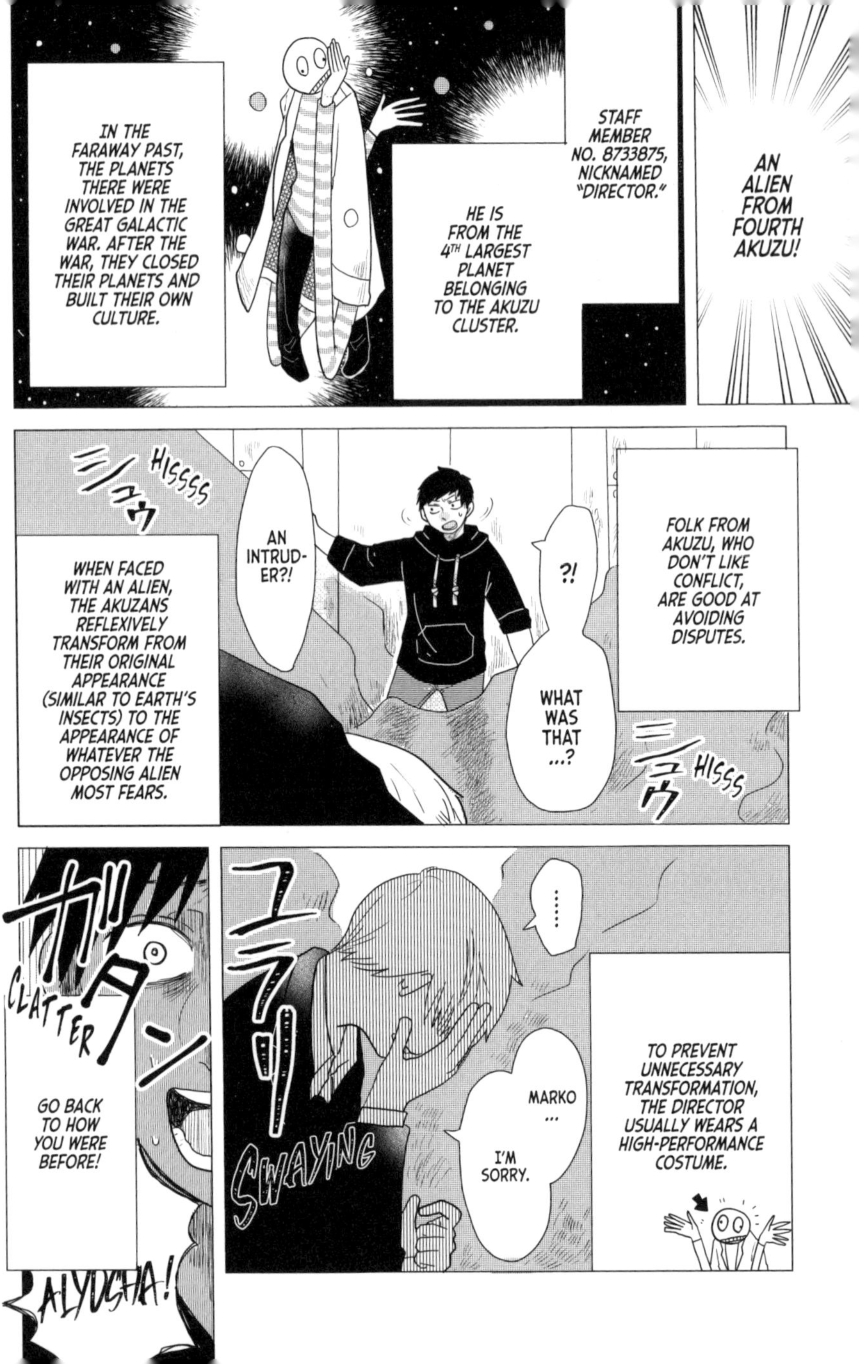
AN ALIEN FROM FOURTH AKUZU!
STAFF MEMBER NO. 8733875, NICKNAMED "DIRECTOR."
HE IS FROM THE 4TH LARGEST PLANET BELONGING TO THE AKUZU CLUSTER.
IN THE FARAWAY PAST, THE PLANETS THERE WERE INVOLVED IN THE GREAT GALACTIC WAR. AFTER THE WAR, THEY CLOSED THEIR PLANETS AND BUILT THEIR OWN CULTURE.
FOLK FROM AKUZU, WHO DON'T LIKE CONFLICT, ARE GOOD AT AVOIDING DISPUTES.
?!
WHAT WAS THAT ...?
HISSS
AN INTRUDER?!
HISSSSS
WHEN FACED WITH AN ALIEN, THE AKUZANS REFLEXIVELY TRANSFORM FROM THEIR ORIGINAL APPEARANCE (SIMILAR TO EARTH'S INSECTS) TO THE APPEARANCE OF WHATEVER THE OPPOSING ALIEN MOST FEARS.
......
TO PREVENT UNNECESSARY TRANSFORMATION, THE DIRECTOR USUALLY WEARS A HIGH-PERFORMANCE COSTUME.
MARKO ...
I'M SORRY.
SWAYING
CLATTER
GO BACK TO HOW YOU WERE BEFORE!
ALYOSHA!

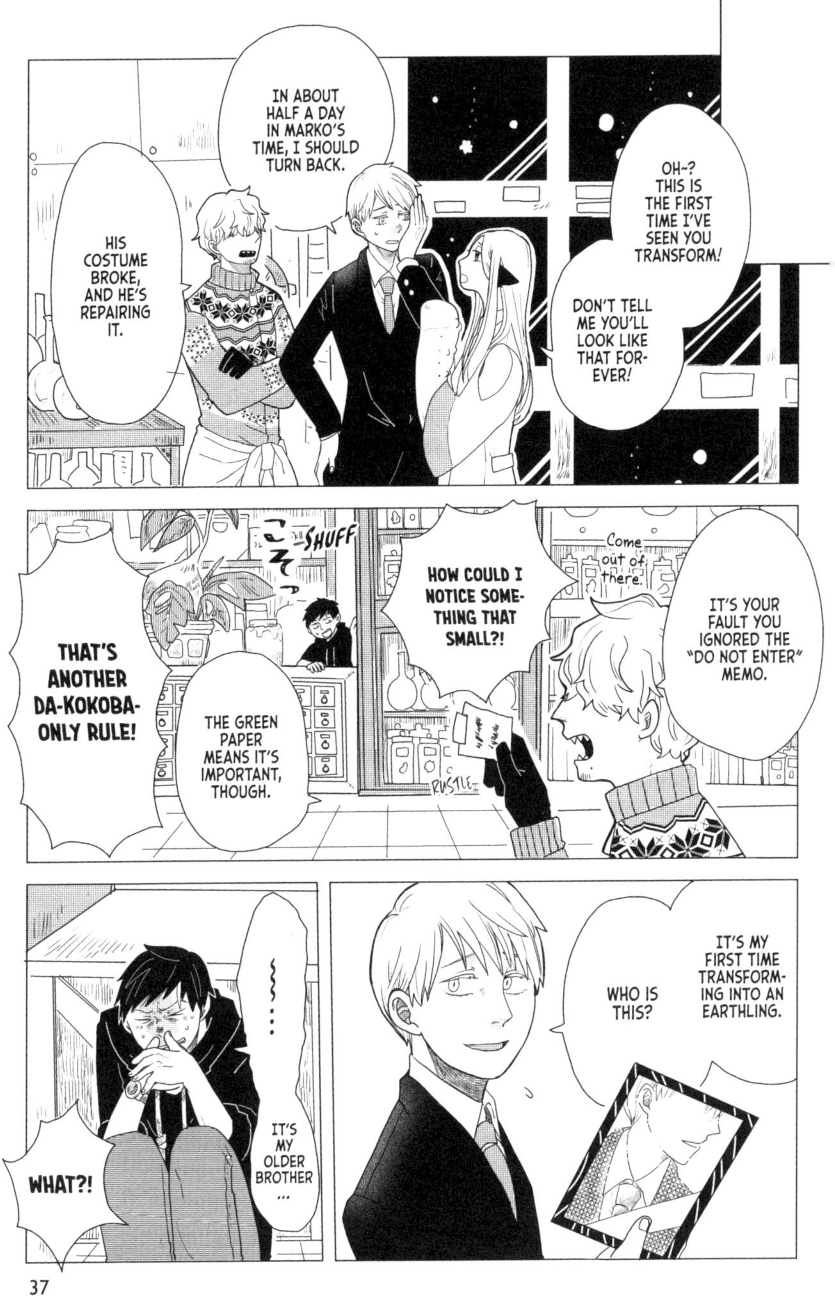
OH~? THIS IS THE FIRST TIME I'VE SEEN YOU TRANSFORM!
DON'T TELL ME YOU'LL LOOK LIKE THAT FOR-EVER!
IN ABOUT HALF A DAY IN MARKO'S TIME, I SHOULD TURN BACK.
HIS COSTUME BROKE, AND HE'S REPAIRING IT.
IT'S YOUR FAULT YOU IGNORED THE "DO NOT ENTER" MEMO.
Come out of there.
HOW COULD I NOTICE SOME-THING THAT SMALL?!
SHUFF
RUSTLE
THE GREEN PAPER MEANS IT'S IMPORTANT, THOUGH.
THAT'S ANOTHER DA-KOKOBA-ONLY RULE!
IT'S MY FIRST TIME TRANSFORM-ING INTO AN EARTHLING.
WHO IS THIS?
......
IT'S MY OLDER BROTHER...
WHAT?!

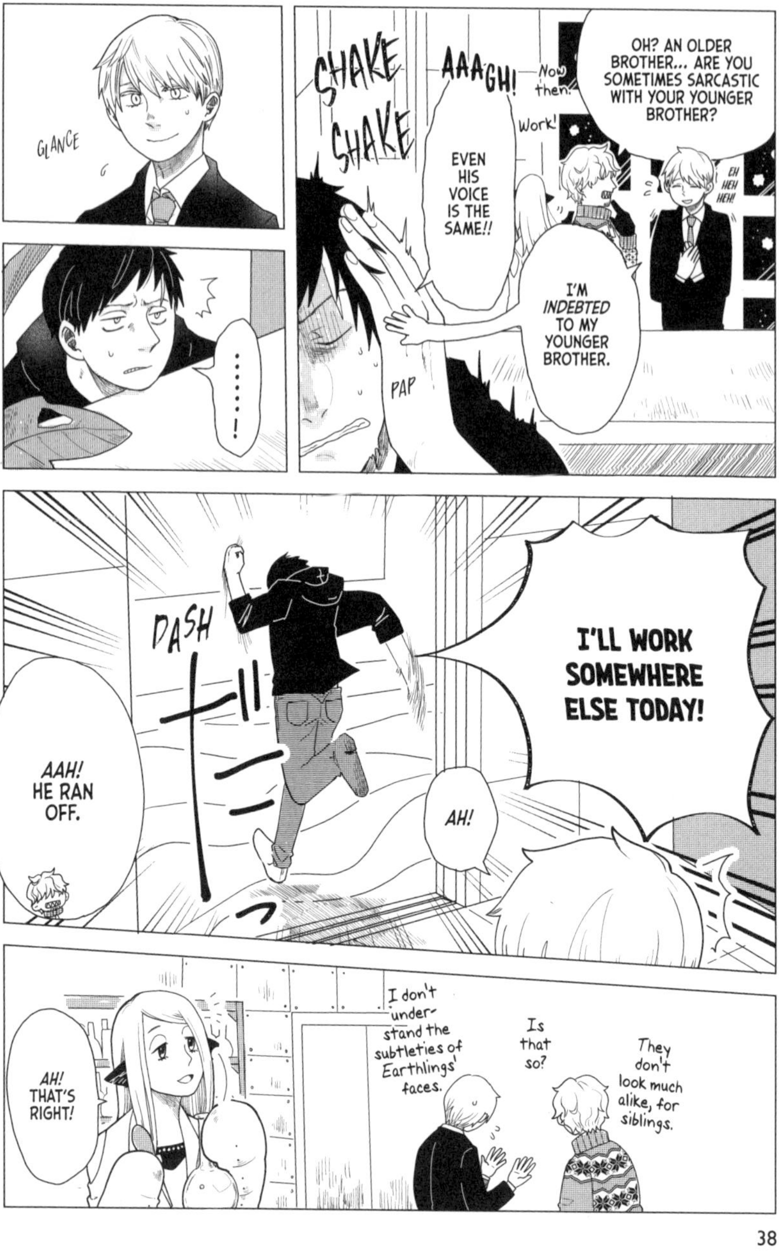
OH? AN OLDER BROTHER... ARE YOU SOMETIMES SARCASTIC WITH YOUR YOUNGER BROTHER?
EH HEH HEH!
Now then!
Work!
AAAGH!
SHAKE SHAKE
EVEN HIS VOICE IS THE SAME!!
I'M *INDEBTED* TO MY YOUNGER BROTHER.
PAP
GLANCE
......!
I'LL WORK SOMEWHERE ELSE TODAY!
AH!
DASH
AAH! HE RAN OFF.
They don't look much alike, for siblings.
Is that so?
I don't under-stand the subtleties of Earthlings' faces.
AH! THAT'S RIGHT!

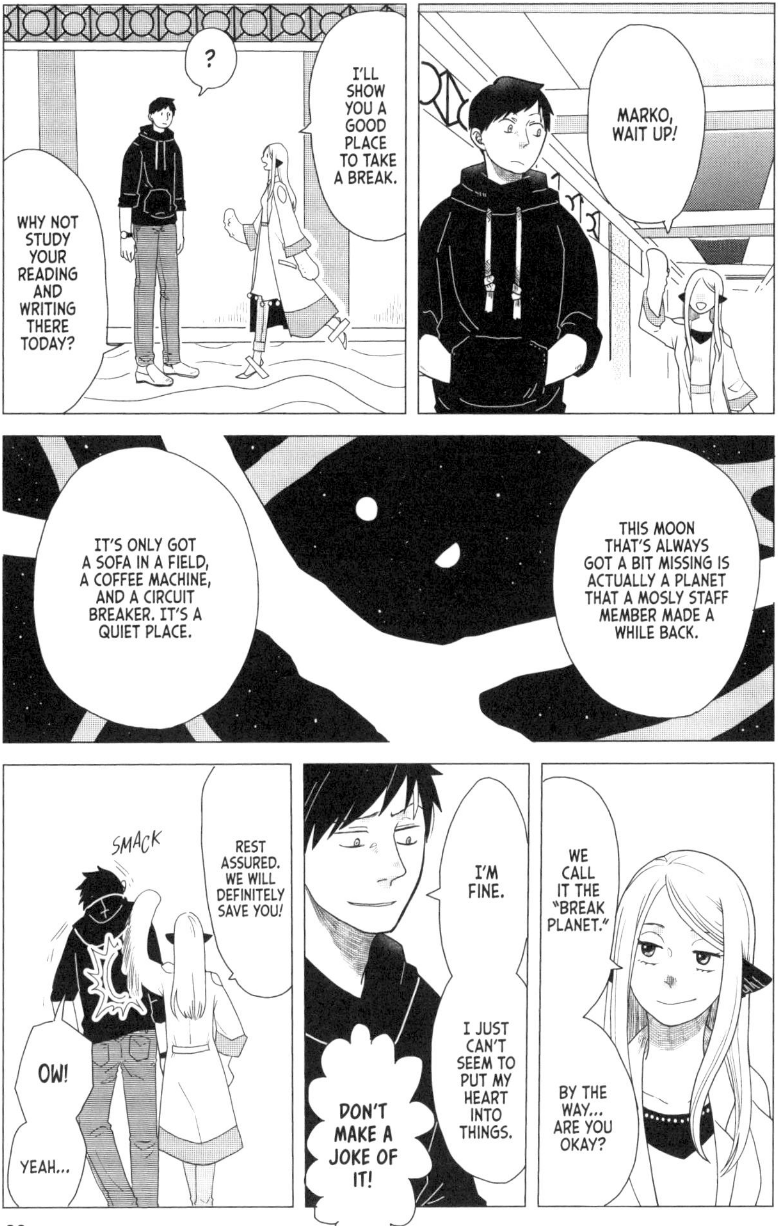
MARKO, WAIT UP!
I'LL SHOW YOU A GOOD PLACE TO TAKE A BREAK.
?
WHY NOT STUDY YOUR READING AND WRITING THERE TODAY?
THIS MOON THAT'S ALWAYS GOT A BIT MISSING IS ACTUALLY A PLANET THAT A MOSLY STAFF MEMBER MADE A WHILE BACK.
IT'S ONLY GOT A SOFA IN A FIELD, A COFFEE MACHINE, AND A CIRCUIT BREAKER. IT'S A QUIET PLACE.
WE CALL IT THE "BREAK PLANET."
BY THE WAY... ARE YOU OKAY?
I'M FINE.
I JUST CAN'T SEEM TO PUT MY HEART INTO THINGS.
DON'T MAKE A JOKE OF IT!
REST ASSURED. WE WILL DEFINITELY SAVE YOU!
SMACK
OW!
YEAH...

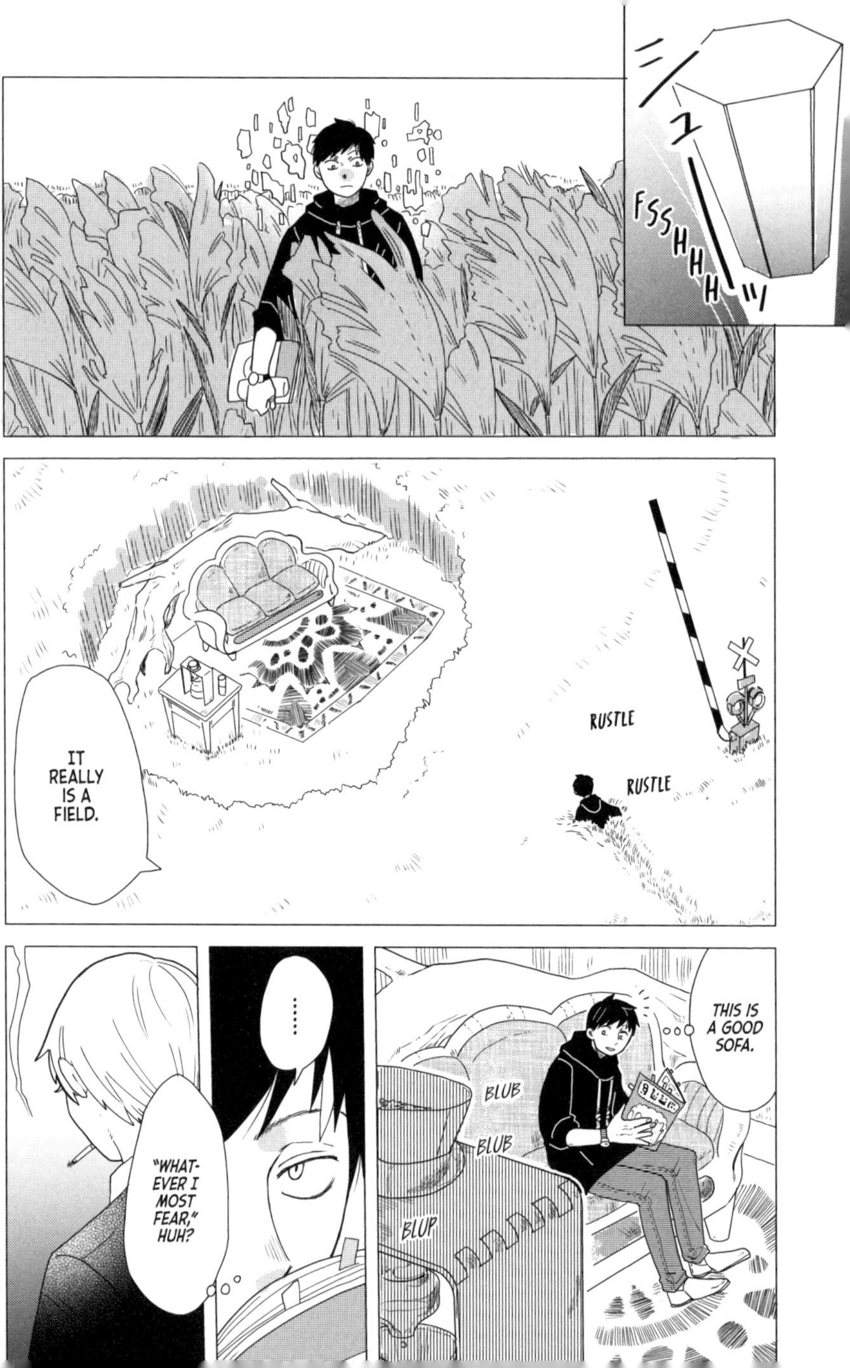
FSSHHH
RUSTLE
RUSTLE
IT REALLY IS A FIELD.
THIS IS A GOOD SOFA.
BLUB
BLUB
BLUP
......
"WHATEVER I MOST FEAR," HUH?

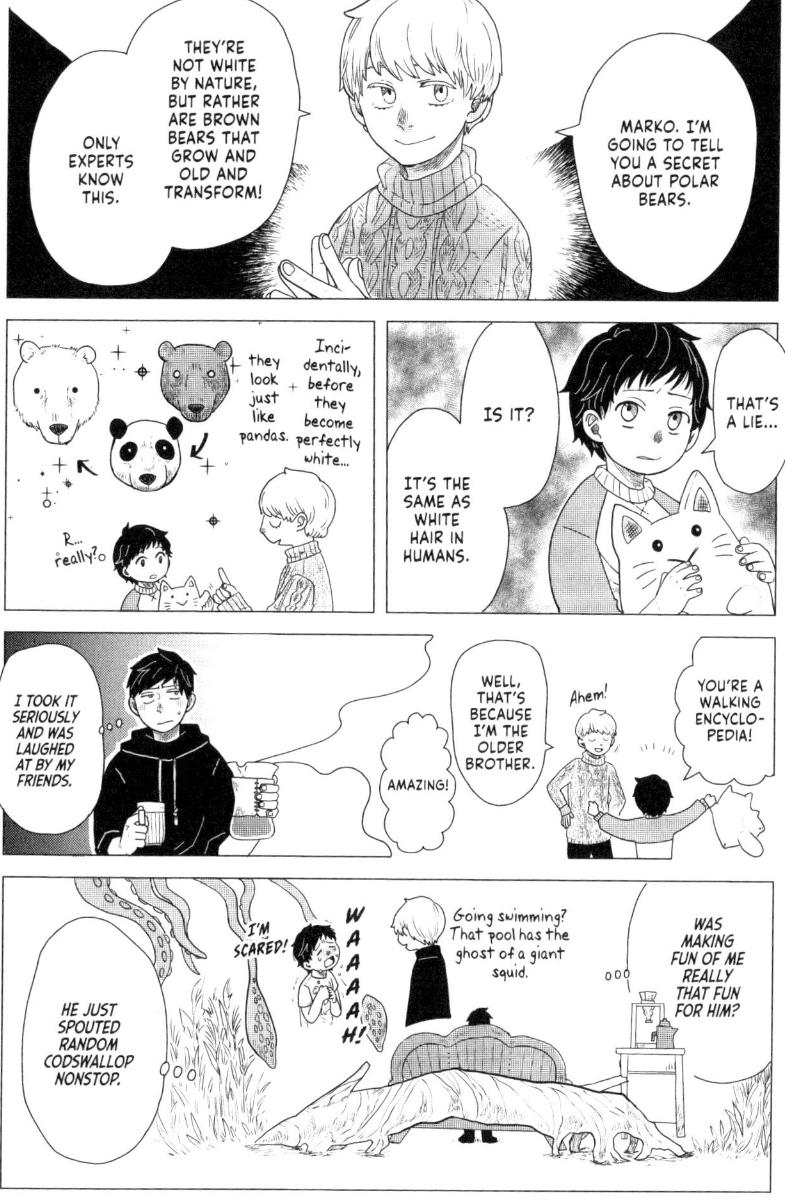

MARKO. I'M GOING TO TELL YOU A SECRET ABOUT POLAR BEARS.
THEY'RE NOT WHITE BY NATURE, BUT RATHER ARE BROWN BEARS THAT GROW AND OLD AND TRANSFORM!
ONLY EXPERTS KNOW THIS.
THAT'S A LIE...
IS IT?
IT'S THE SAME AS WHITE HAIR IN HUMANS.
Inci-dentally, before they become perfectly white...
they look just like pandas.
R... really?
YOU'RE A WALKING ENCYCLO-PEDIA!
Ahem!
WELL, THAT'S BECAUSE I'M THE OLDER BROTHER.
AMAZING!
I TOOK IT SERIOUSLY AND WAS LAUGHED AT BY MY FRIENDS.
WAS MAKING FUN OF ME REALLY THAT FUN FOR HIM?
Going swimming? That pool has the ghost of a giant squid.
WAAAAAH!
I'M SCARED!
HE JUST SPOUTED RANDOM CODSWALLOP NONSTOP.

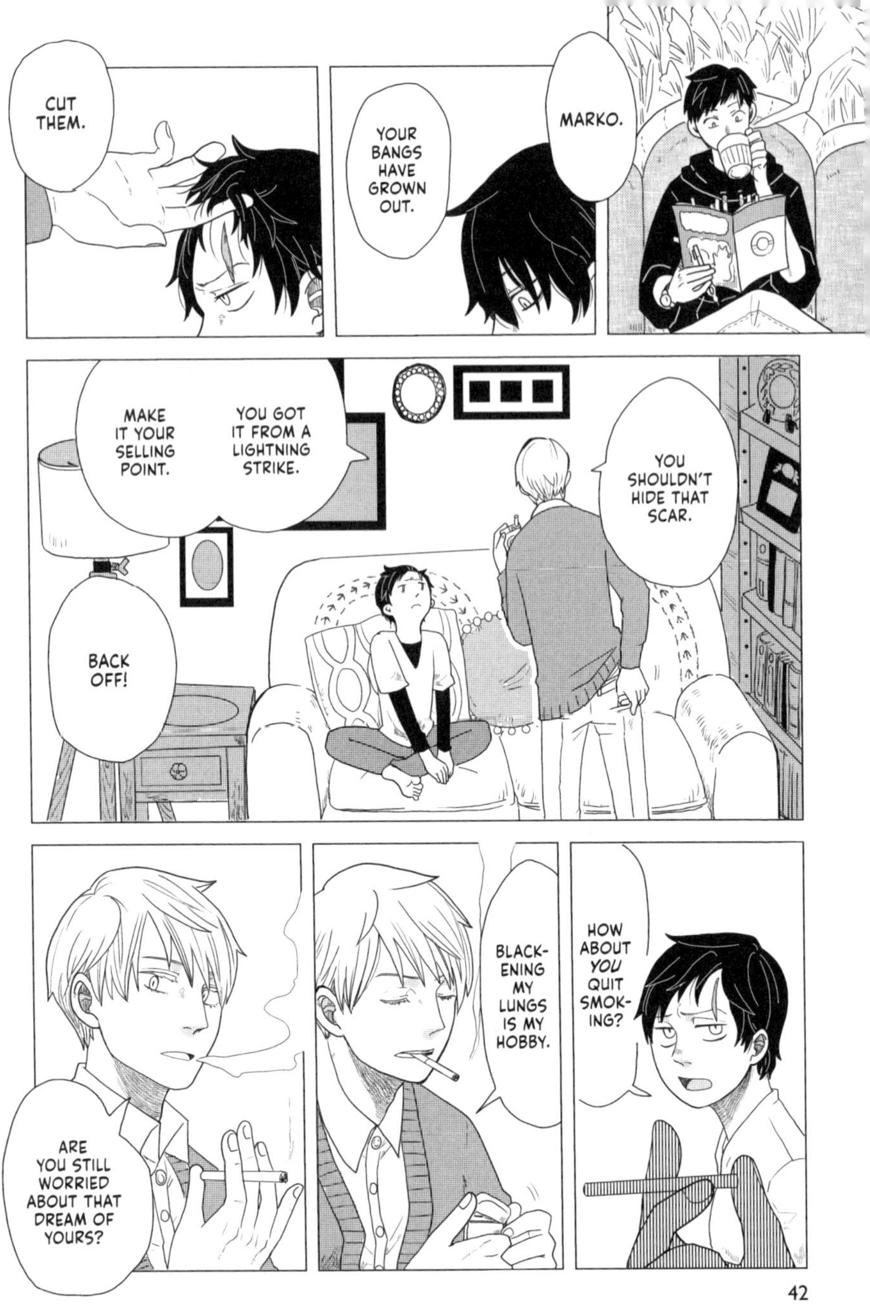
MARKO.
YOUR BANGS HAVE GROWN OUT.
CUT THEM.
YOU SHOULDN'T HIDE THAT SCAR.
YOU GOT IT FROM A LIGHTNING STRIKE.
MAKE IT YOUR SELLING POINT.
BACK OFF!
HOW ABOUT *YOU* QUIT SMOKING?
BLACK-ENING MY LUNGS IS MY HOBBY.
ARE YOU STILL WORRIED ABOUT THAT DREAM OF YOURS?

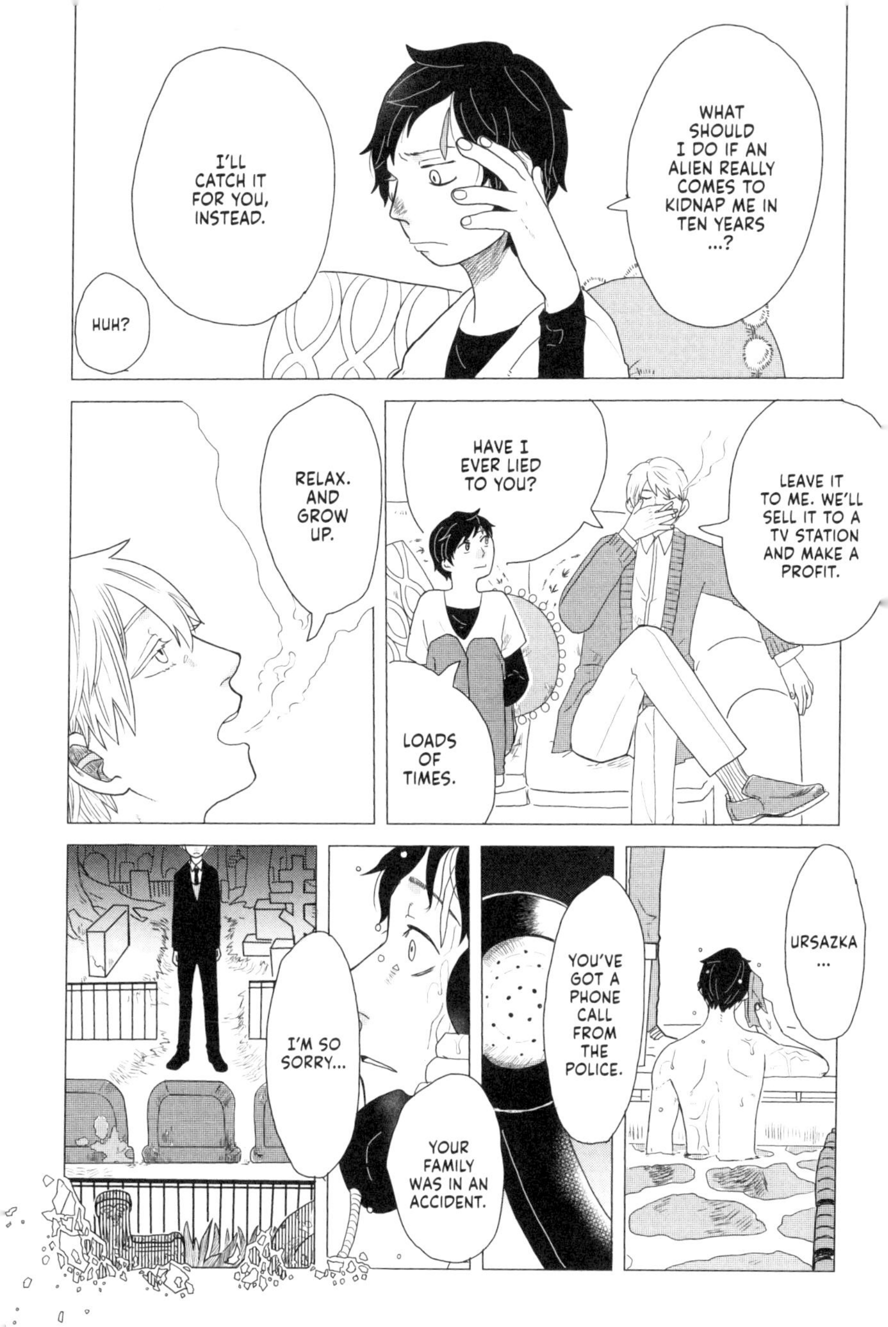
WHAT SHOULD I DO IF AN ALIEN REALLY COMES TO KIDNAP ME IN TEN YEARS ...?
I'LL CATCH IT FOR YOU, INSTEAD.
HUH?
LEAVE IT TO ME. WE'LL SELL IT TO A TV STATION AND MAKE A PROFIT.
HAVE I EVER LIED TO YOU?
LOADS OF TIMES.
RELAX. AND GROW UP.
URSAZKA ...
YOU'VE GOT A PHONE CALL FROM THE POLICE.
YOUR FAMILY WAS IN AN ACCIDENT.
I'M SO SORRY...

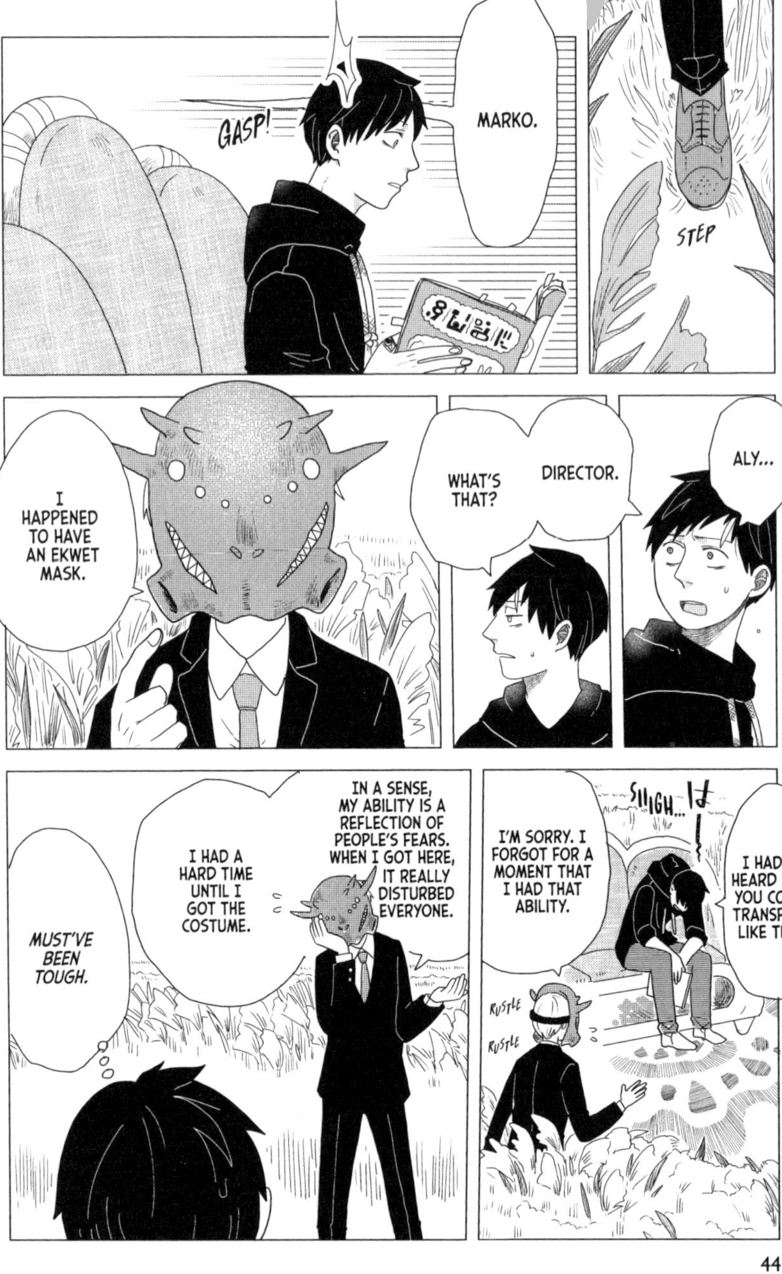
STEP
MARKO.
GASP!
ALY...
DIRECTOR.
WHAT'S THAT?
I HAPPENED TO HAVE AN EKWET MASK.
I HADN'T HEARD THAT YOU COULD TRANSFORM LIKE THAT.
SIIGH...
I'M SORRY. I FORGOT FOR A MOMENT THAT I HAD THAT ABILITY.
RUSTLE
RUSTLE
IN A SENSE, MY ABILITY IS A REFLECTION OF PEOPLE'S FEARS. WHEN I GOT HERE, IT REALLY DISTURBED EVERYONE.
I HAD A HARD TIME UNTIL I GOT THE COSTUME.
MUST'VE BEEN TOUGH.

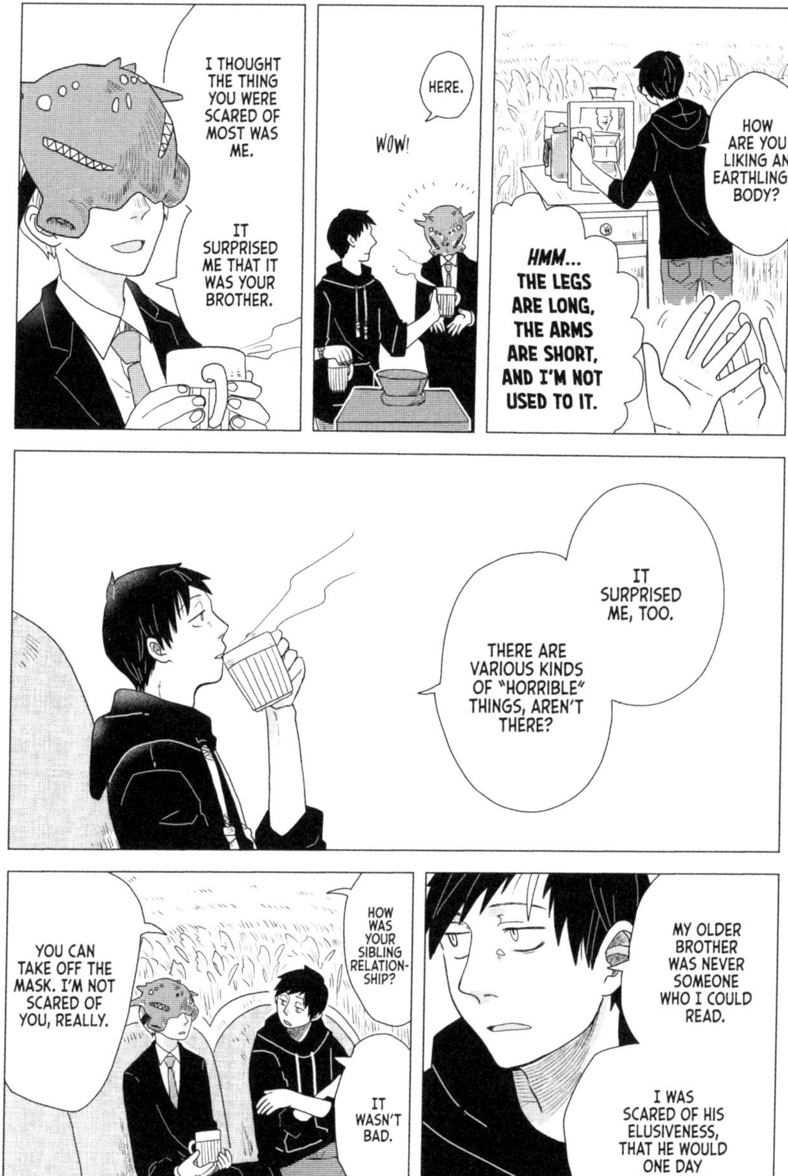

HOW ARE YOU LIKING AN EARTHLING'S BODY?
HMM... THE LEGS ARE LONG, THE ARMS ARE SHORT, AND I'M NOT USED TO IT.
HERE.
WOW!
I THOUGHT THE THING YOU WERE SCARED OF MOST WAS ME.
IT SURPRISED ME THAT IT WAS YOUR BROTHER.
IT SURPRISED ME, TOO.
THERE ARE VARIOUS KINDS OF "HORRIBLE" THINGS, AREN'T THERE?
MY OLDER BROTHER WAS NEVER SOMEONE WHO I COULD READ.
I WAS SCARED OF HIS ELUSIVENESS, THAT HE WOULD ONE DAY DISAPPEAR.
HOW WAS YOUR SIBLING RELATION-SHIP?
YOU CAN TAKE OFF THE MASK. I'M NOT SCARED OF YOU, REALLY.
IT WASN'T BAD.

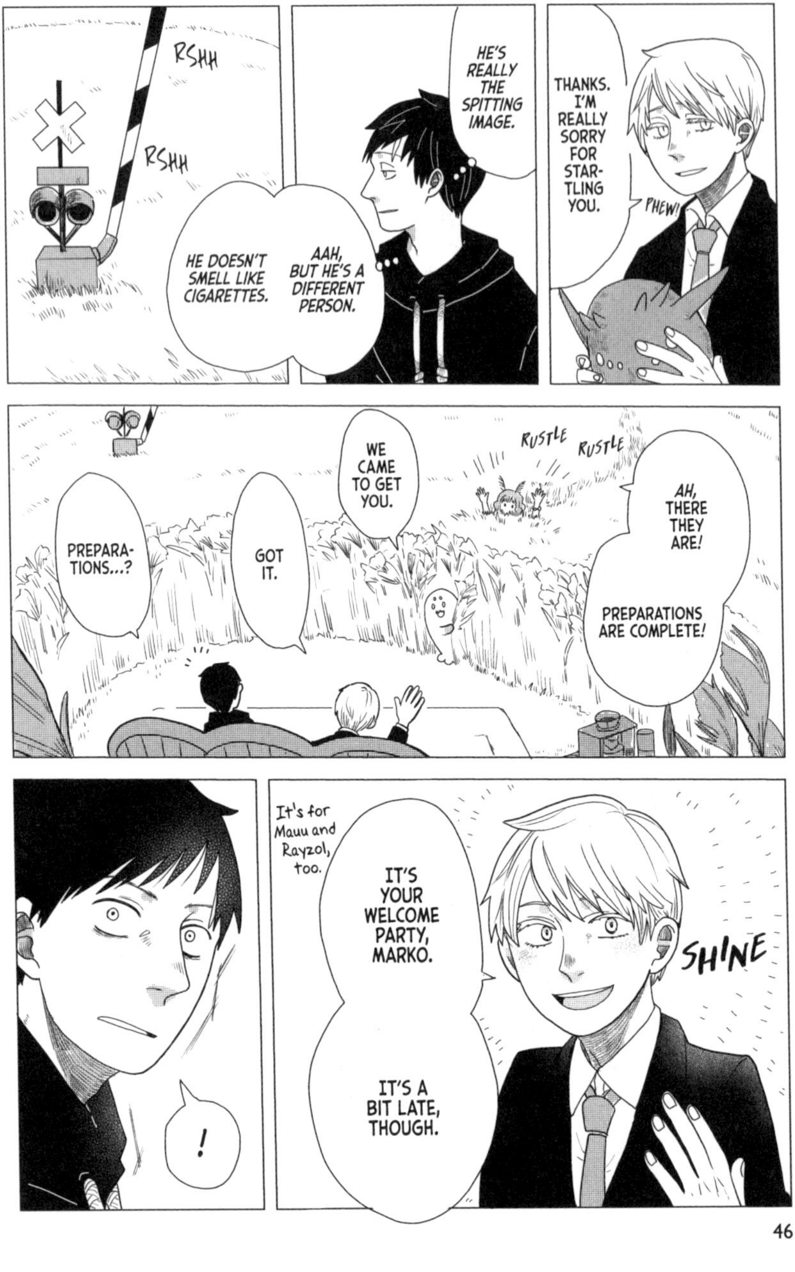

THANKS. I'M REALLY SORRY FOR STAR-TLING YOU.
PHEW!
HE'S REALLY THE SPITTING IMAGE.
AAH, BUT HE'S A DIFFERENT PERSON.
HE DOESN'T SMELL LIKE CIGARETTES.
RSHH
RSHH
RUSTLE RUSTLE
AH, THERE THEY ARE!
PREPARATIONS ARE COMPLETE!
WE CAME TO GET YOU.
GOT IT.
PREPARA-TIONS...?
SHINE
IT'S YOUR WELCOME PARTY, MARKO.
IT'S A BIT LATE, THOUGH.
It's for Mauu and Rayzol, too.
!

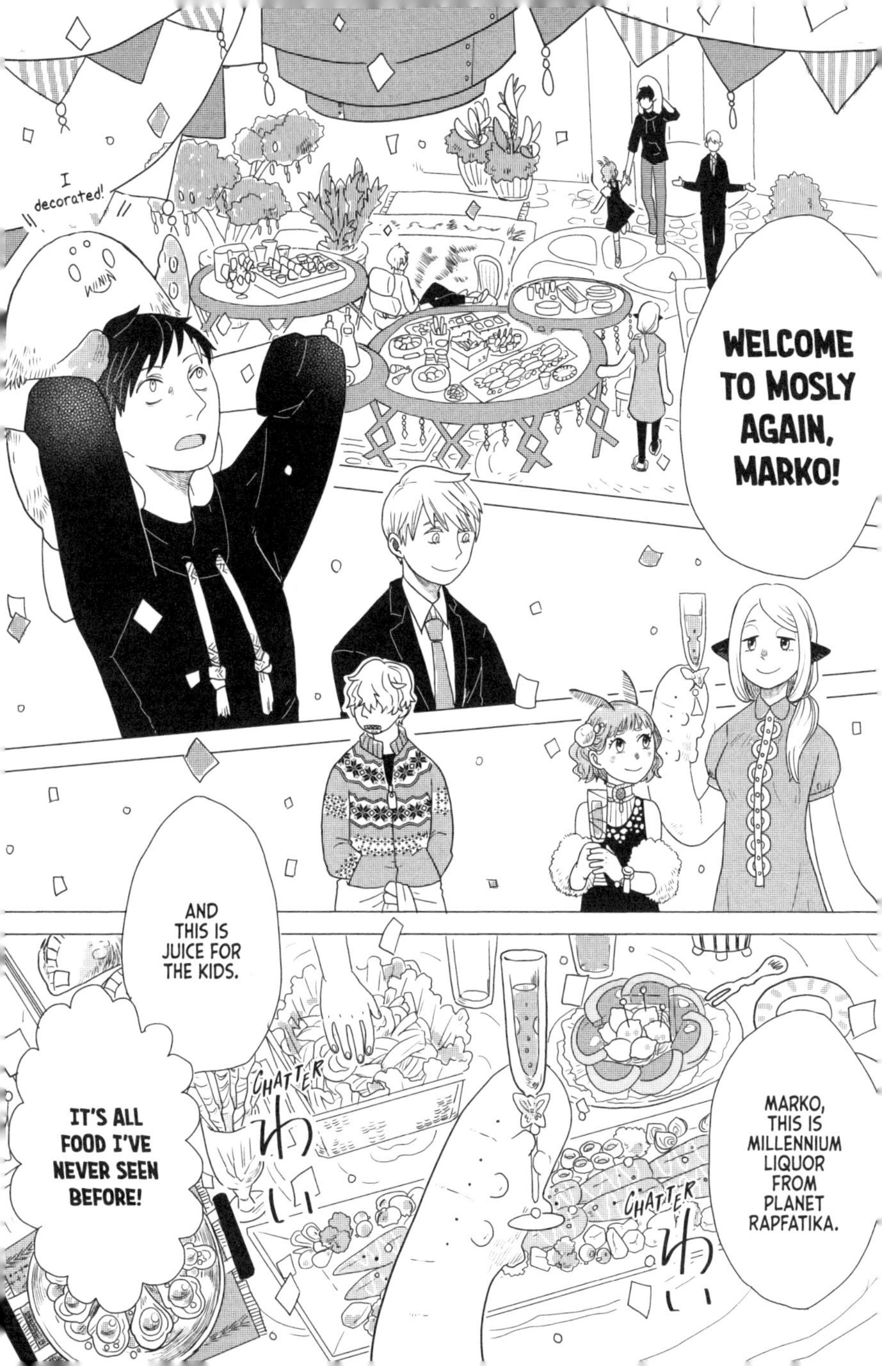
WELCOME TO MOSLY AGAIN, MARKO!
I decorated!
MARKO, THIS IS MILLENNIUM LIQUOR FROM PLANET RAPFATIKA.
CHATTER
AND THIS IS JUICE FOR THE KIDS.
CHATTER
IT'S ALL FOOD I'VE NEVER SEEN BEFORE!

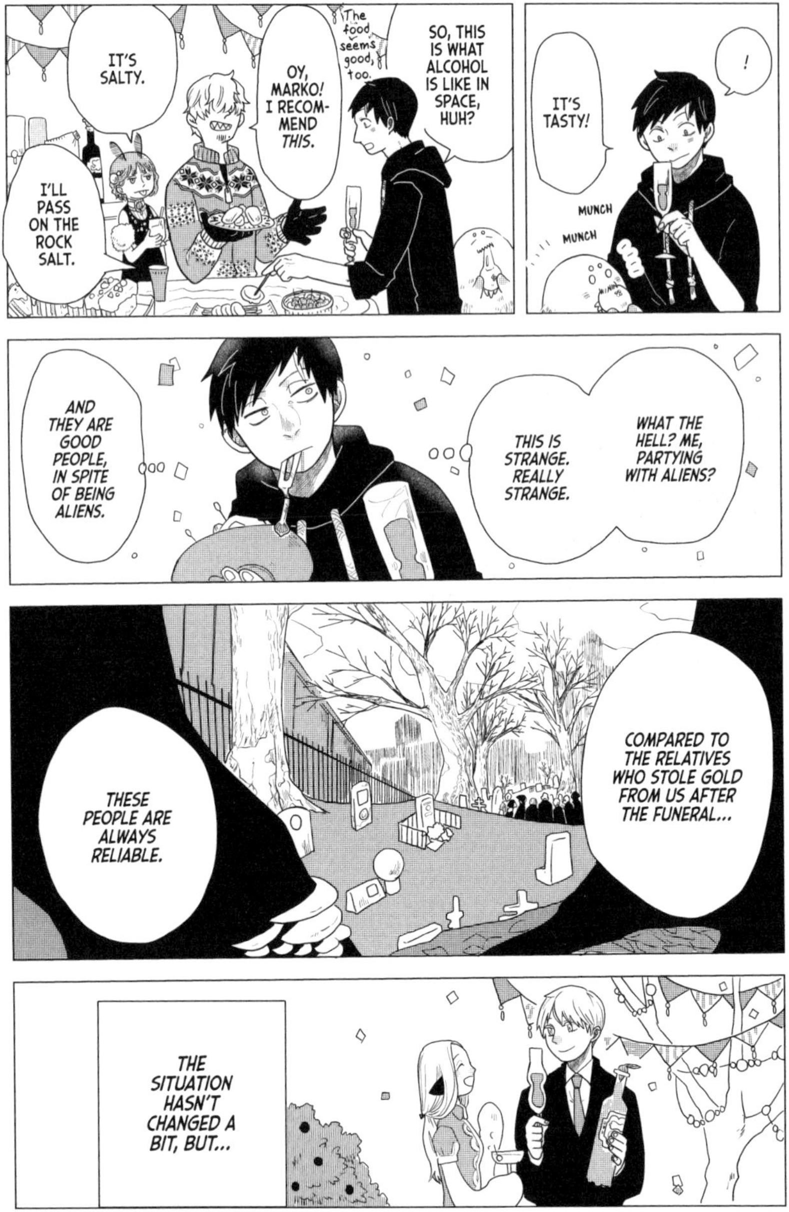
!
IT'S TASTY!
MUNCH
MUNCH
SO, THIS IS WHAT ALCOHOL IS LIKE IN SPACE, HUH?
The food seems good, too.
OY, MARKO! I RECOMMEND THIS.
IT'S SALTY.
I'LL PASS ON THE ROCK SALT.
WHAT THE HELL? ME, PARTYING WITH ALIENS?
THIS IS STRANGE. REALLY STRANGE.
AND THEY ARE GOOD PEOPLE, IN SPITE OF BEING ALIENS.
COMPARED TO THE RELATIVES WHO STOLE GOLD FROM US AFTER THE FUNERAL...
THESE PEOPLE ARE ALWAYS RELIABLE.
THE SITUATION HASN'T CHANGED A BIT, BUT...

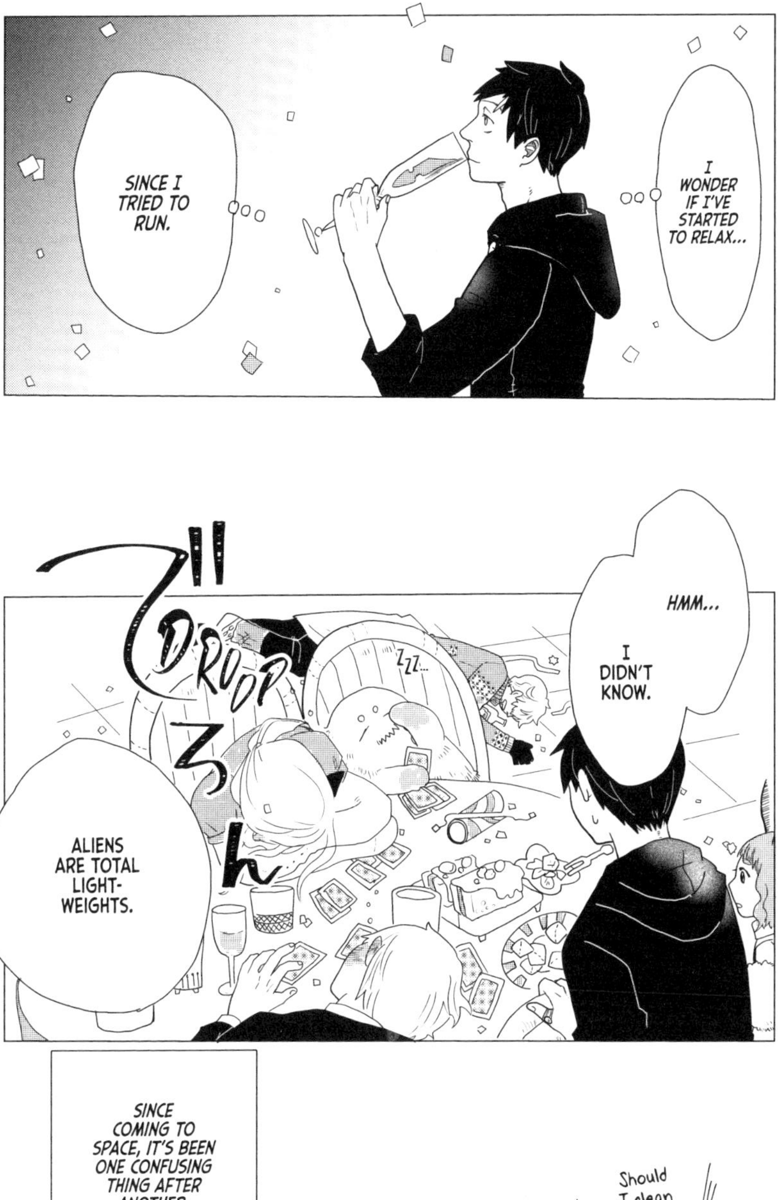
I WONDER IF I'VE STARTED TO RELAX...
SINCE I TRIED TO RUN.
HMM...
I DIDN'T KNOW.
ZZZ...
DROOP
ALIENS ARE TOTAL LIGHT-WEIGHTS.
Should I clean this up...?
SINCE COMING TO SPACE, IT'S BEEN ONE CONFUSING THING AFTER ANOTHER.

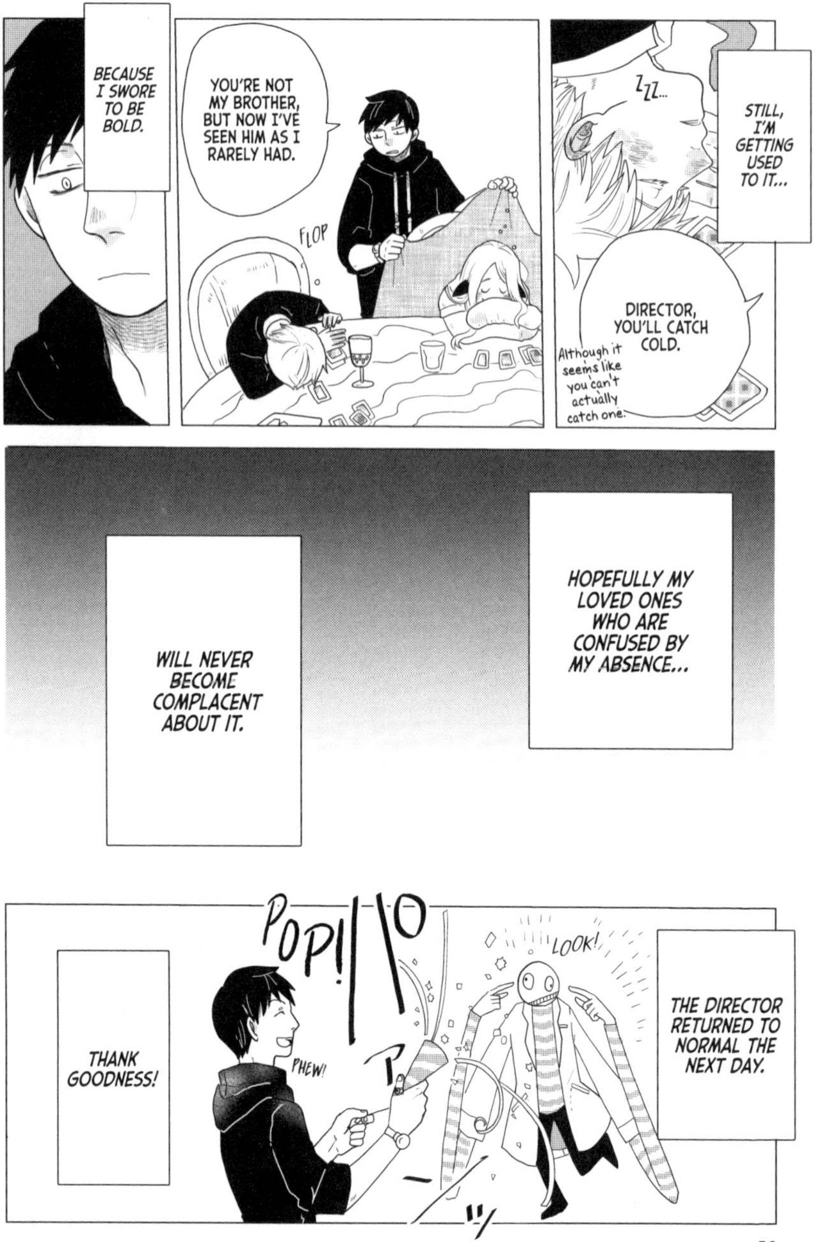
STILL, I'M GETTING USED TO IT...
Zzz...
DIRECTOR, YOU'LL CATCH COLD.
Although it seems like you can't actually catch one.
YOU'RE NOT MY BROTHER, BUT NOW I'VE SEEN HIM AS I RARELY HAD.
FLOP
BECAUSE I SWORE TO BE BOLD.
HOPEFULLY MY LOVED ONES WHO ARE CONFUSED BY MY ABSENCE...
WILL NEVER BECOME COMPLACENT ABOUT IT.
THE DIRECTOR RETURNED TO NORMAL THE NEXT DAY.
LOOK!
POP!!
PHEW!
THANK GOODNESS!

Episode 11: The Desert, the Shrimp, the Crab, and the Stuffing ①

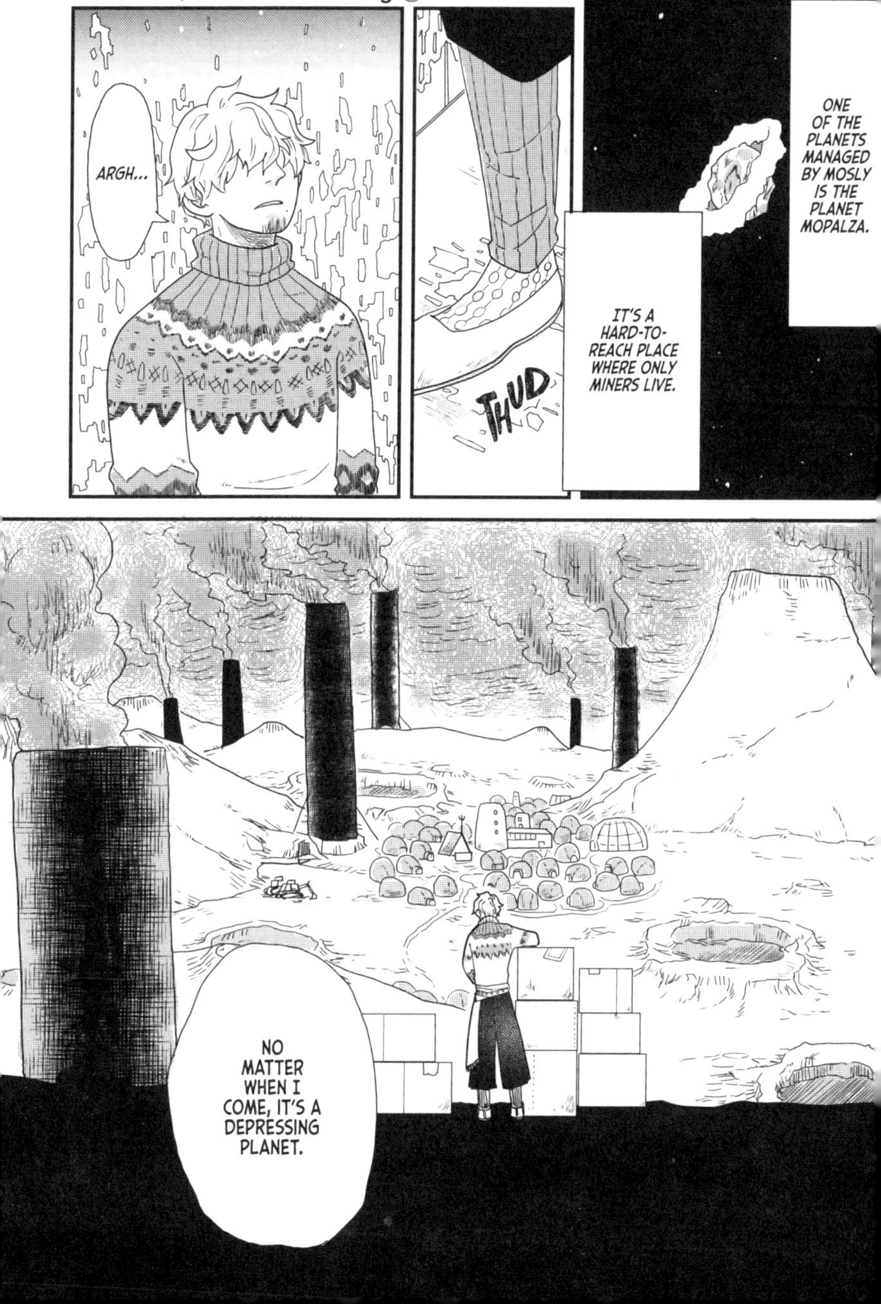

ONE OF THE PLANETS MANAGED BY MOSLY IS THE PLANET MOPALZA.
IT'S A HARD-TO-REACH PLACE WHERE ONLY MINERS LIVE.
THUD
ARGH...
NO MATTER WHEN I COME, IT'S A DEPRESSING PLANET.

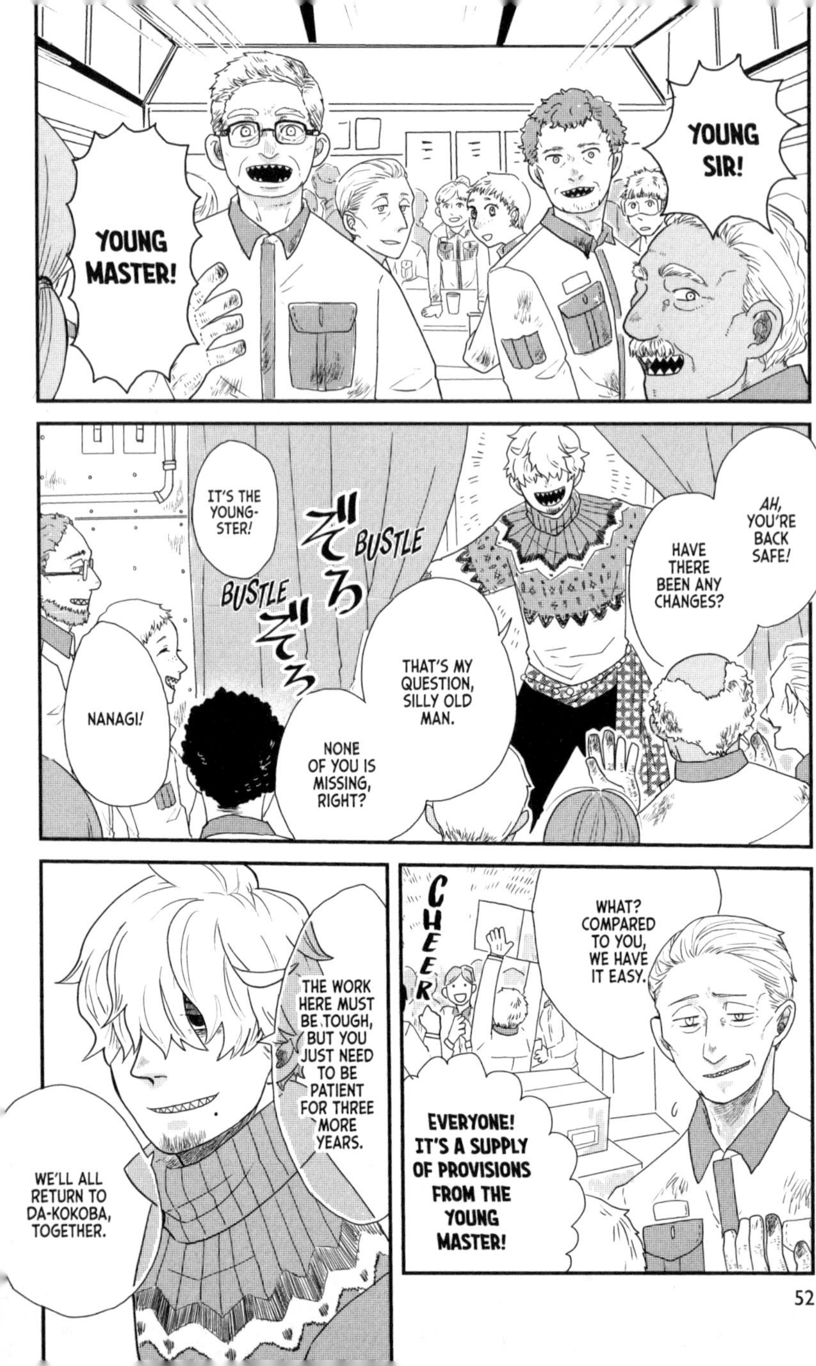
YOUNG SIR!
YOUNG MASTER!
AH, YOU'RE BACK SAFE!
HAVE THERE BEEN ANY CHANGES?
IT'S THE YOUNG-STER!
ぞろ BUSTLE
BUSTLE ぞろ
THAT'S MY QUESTION, SILLY OLD MAN.
NONE OF YOU IS MISSING, RIGHT?
NANAGI!
WHAT? COMPARED TO YOU, WE HAVE IT EASY.
CHEER
EVERYONE! IT'S A SUPPLY OF PROVISIONS FROM THE YOUNG MASTER!
THE WORK HERE MUST BE TOUGH, BUT YOU JUST NEED TO BE PATIENT FOR THREE MORE YEARS.
WE'LL ALL RETURN TO DA-KOKOBA, TOGETHER.

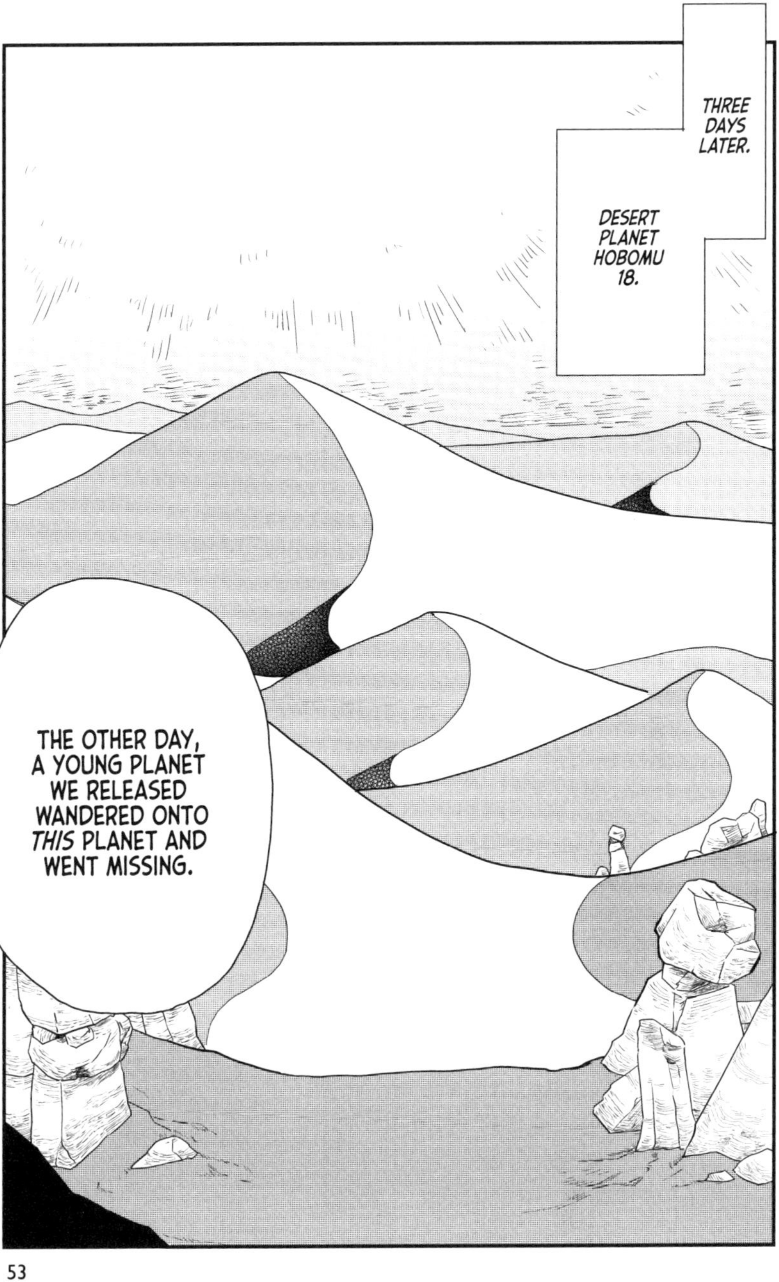
THREE DAYS LATER.
DESERT PLANET HOBOMU 18.
THE OTHER DAY, A YOUNG PLANET WE RELEASED WANDERED ONTO *THIS* PLANET AND WENT MISSING.

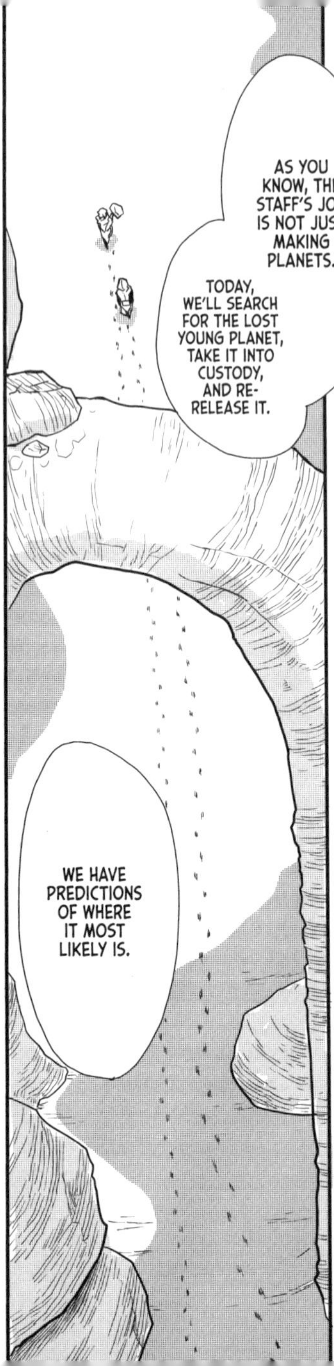
AS YOU KNOW, THE STAFF'S JOB IS NOT JUST MAKING PLANETS.
TODAY, WE'LL SEARCH FOR THE LOST YOUNG PLANET, TAKE IT INTO CUSTODY, AND RE-RELEASE IT.
WE HAVE PREDICTIONS OF WHERE IT MOST LIKELY IS.

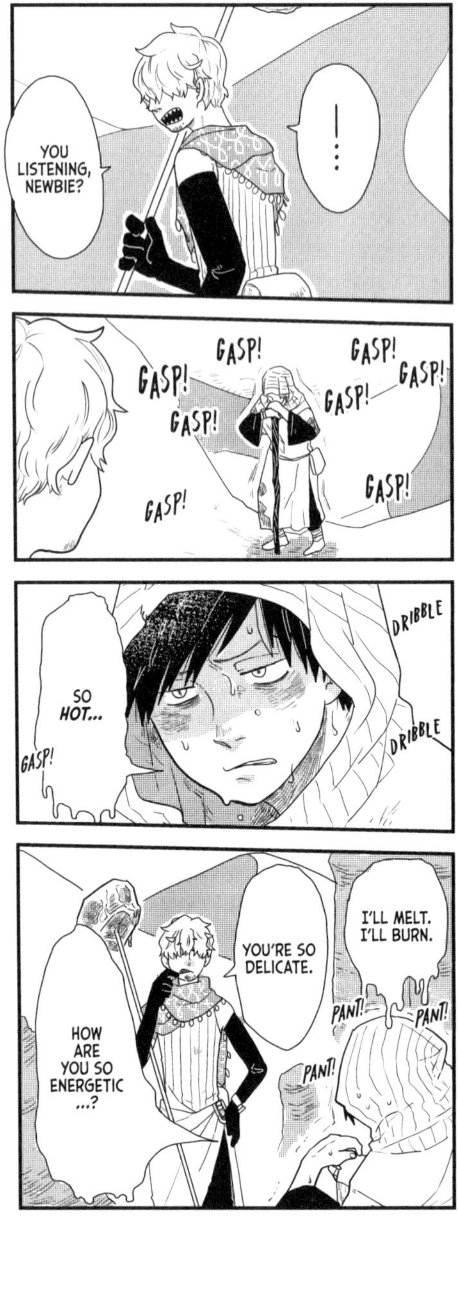
!...
YOU LISTENING, NEWBIE?
GASP!
GASP!
GASP!
GASP!
GASP!
GASP!
GASP!
GASP!
DRIBBLE
DRIBBLE
SO HOT...
GASP!
I'LL MELT. I'LL BURN.
PANT!
PANT!
YOU'RE SO DELICATE.
PANT!
HOW ARE YOU SO ENERGETIC ...?

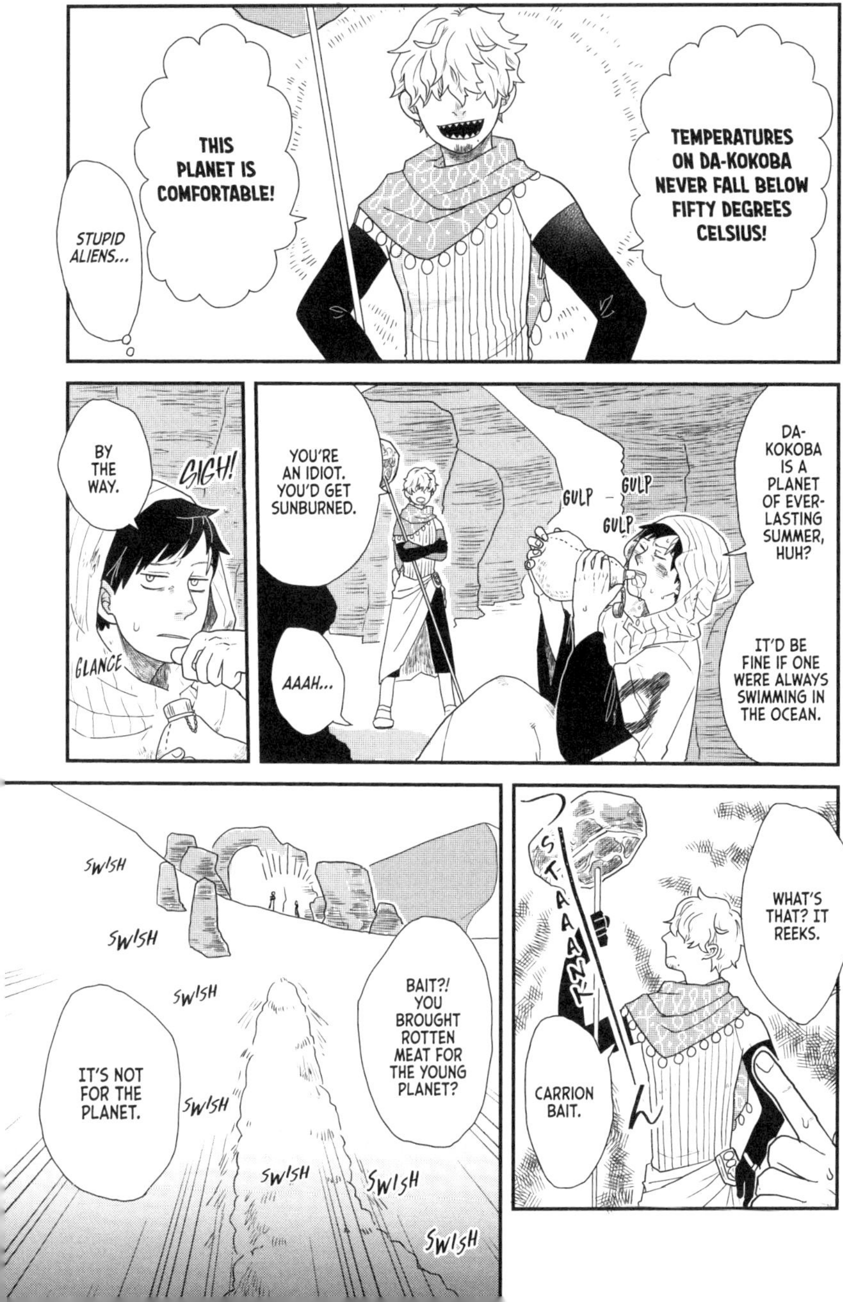
TEMPERATURES ON DA-KOKOBA NEVER FALL BELOW FIFTY DEGREES CELSIUS!
THIS PLANET IS COMFORTABLE!
STUPID ALIENS...
DA-KOKOBA IS A PLANET OF EVER-LASTING SUMMER, HUH?
GULP
GULP
GULP
IT'D BE FINE IF ONE WERE ALWAYS SWIMMING IN THE OCEAN.
YOU'RE AN IDIOT. YOU'D GET SUNBURNED.
AAAH...
SIGH!
BY THE WAY.
GLANCE
WHAT'S THAT? IT REEKS.
STAAAAN!
CARRION BAIT.
BAIT?! YOU BROUGHT ROTTEN MEAT FOR THE YOUNG PLANET?
SWISH
SWISH
SWISH
IT'S NOT FOR THE PLANET.
SWISH
SWISH
SWISH
SWISH

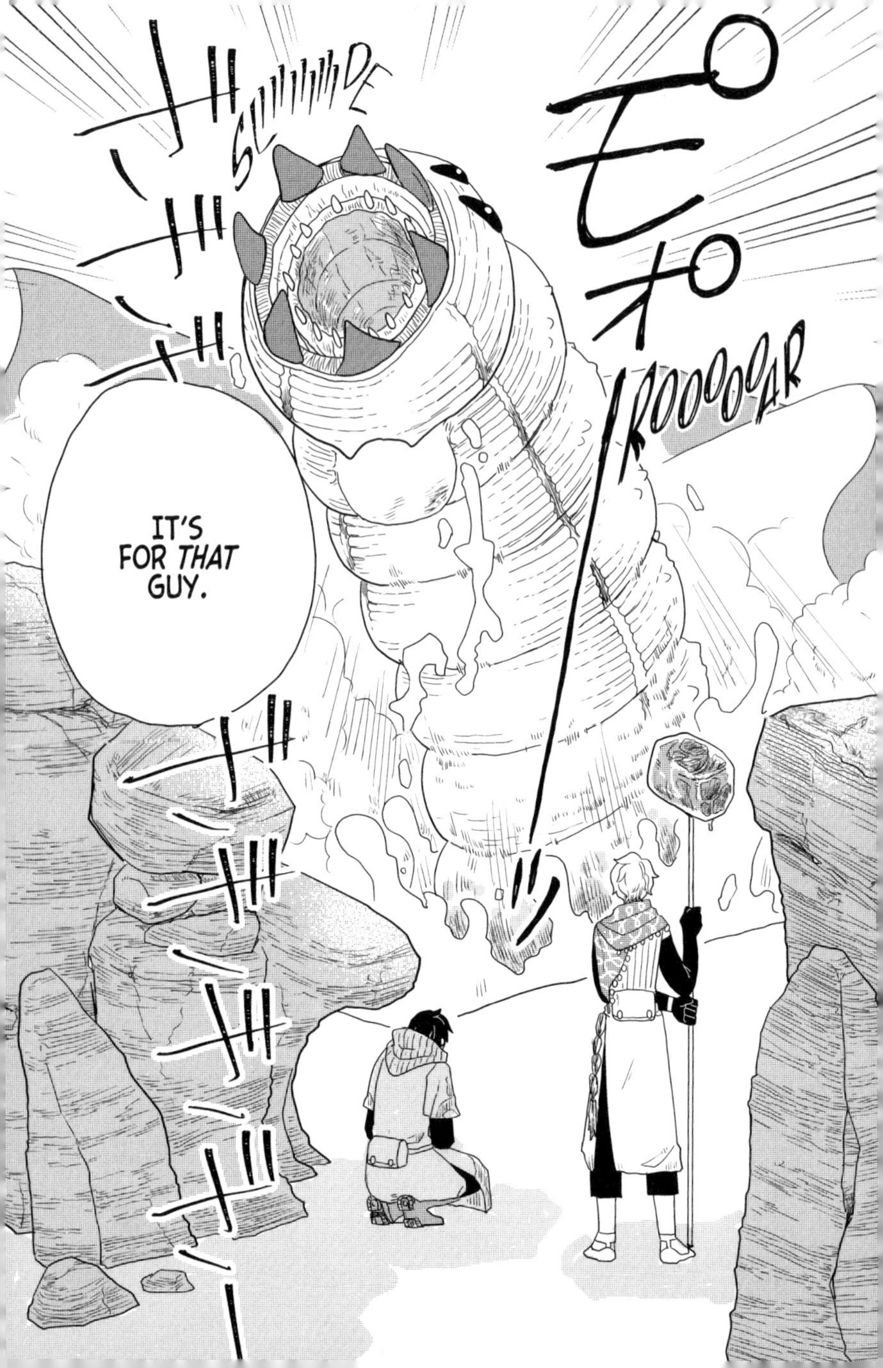
ROOOOOAR
SLIIIIIIIDE
IT'S FOR *THAT* GUY.

MON...

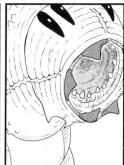

HE'S BIGGER THAN I EXPECTED.

HUH?

SHIVER

MONGOLIAN DEATH WORM*...

UNIDENTIFIED MYSTERIOUS ANIMALS

CRYPTID ENTHUSIAST!

IT REALLY EXISTS...!

*A UMA (Unidentified Mysterious Animal) that lives in the Gobi Desert. It is similar in appearance to earthworms and hornworms, with a body length of 0.5~1.5 meters.

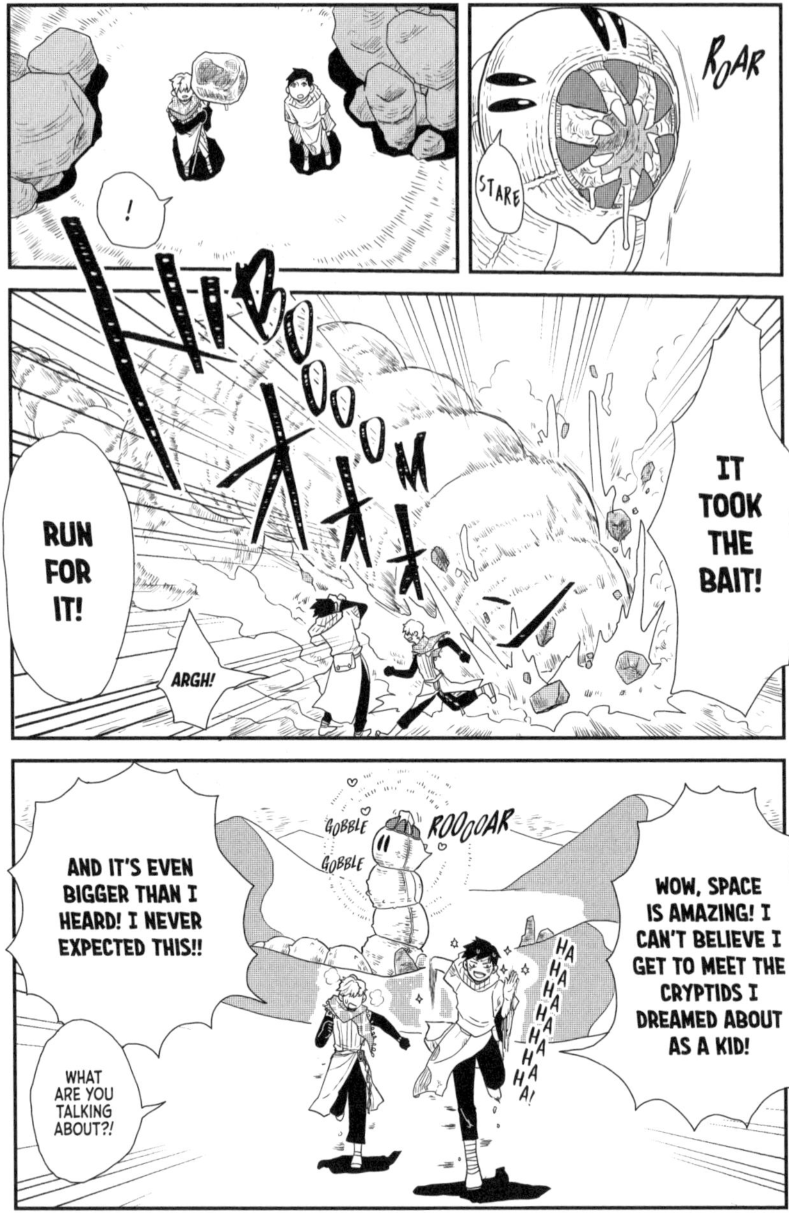
ROAR
STARE
!
IT TOOK THE BAIT!
BOOOOOM
RUN FOR IT!
ARGH!
WOW, SPACE IS AMAZING! I CAN'T BELIEVE I GET TO MEET THE CRYPTIDS I DREAMED ABOUT AS A KID!
HA HA HA HA HA HA HA!
ROOOOAR
GOBBLE GOBBLE
AND IT'S EVEN BIGGER THAN I HEARD! I NEVER EXPECTED THIS!!
WHAT ARE YOU TALKING ABOUT?!

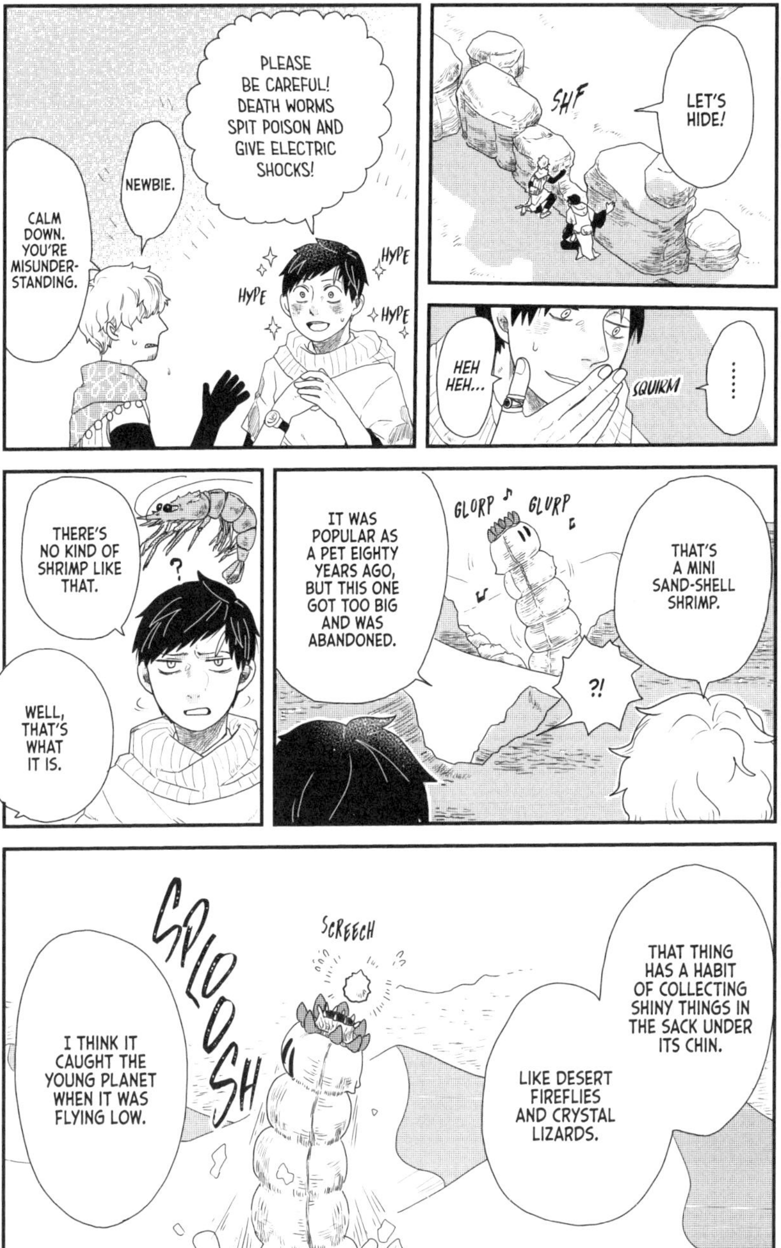
LET'S HIDE!
SHF
......
SQUIRM
HEH HEH...
PLEASE BE CAREFUL! DEATH WORMS SPIT POISON AND GIVE ELECTRIC SHOCKS!
HYPE
HYPE
HYPE
NEWBIE.
CALM DOWN. YOU'RE MISUNDER-STANDING.
THAT'S A MINI SAND-SHELL SHRIMP.
?!
GLURP
GLORP
IT WAS POPULAR AS A PET EIGHTY YEARS AGO, BUT THIS ONE GOT TOO BIG AND WAS ABANDONED.
THERE'S NO KIND OF SHRIMP LIKE THAT.
?
WELL, THAT'S WHAT IT IS.
THAT THING HAS A HABIT OF COLLECTING SHINY THINGS IN THE SACK UNDER ITS CHIN.
LIKE DESERT FIREFLIES AND CRYSTAL LIZARDS.
SCREECH
SPLOOOSH
I THINK IT CAUGHT THE YOUNG PLANET WHEN IT WAS FLYING LOW.

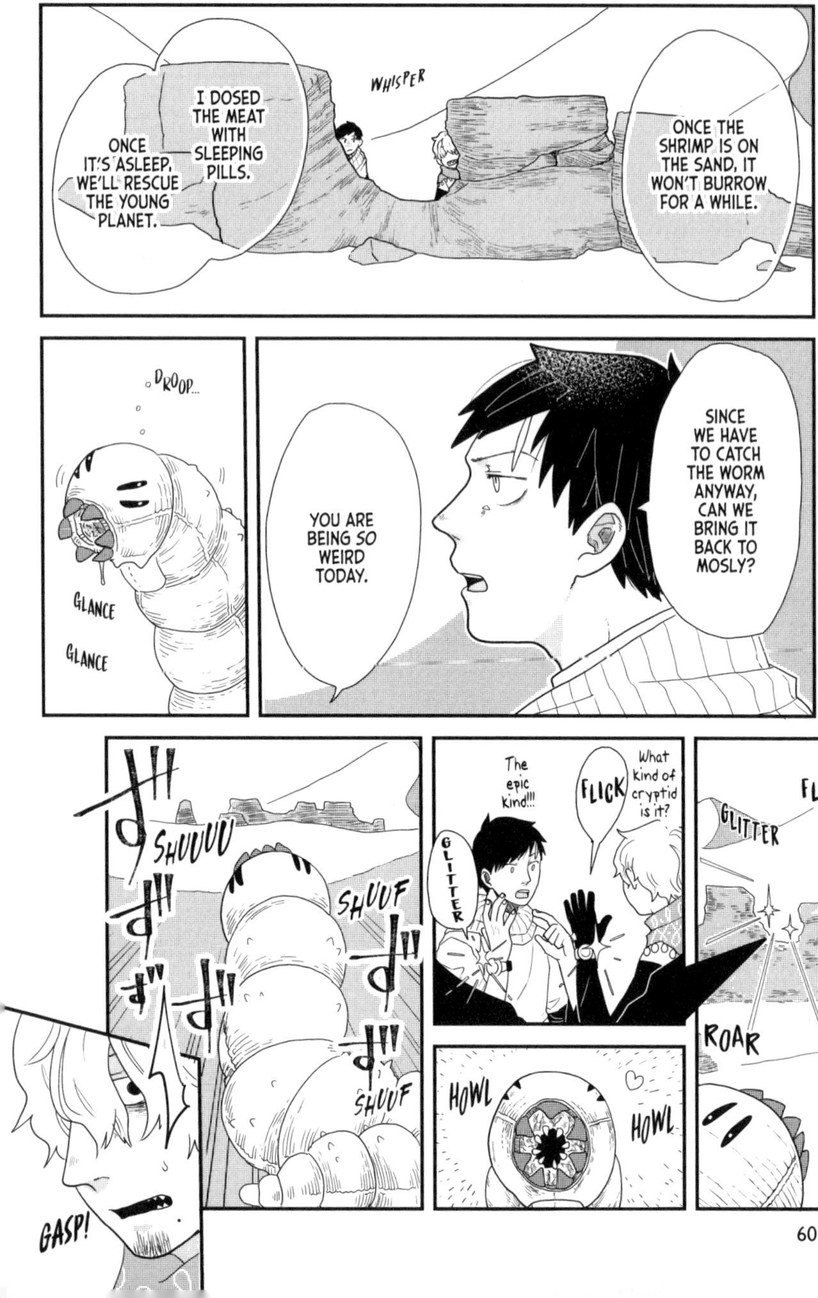
ONCE THE SHRIMP IS ON THE SAND, IT WON'T BURROW FOR A WHILE.
WHISPER
I DOSED THE MEAT WITH SLEEPING PILLS.
ONCE IT'S ASLEEP, WE'LL RESCUE THE YOUNG PLANET.
SINCE WE HAVE TO CATCH THE WORM ANYWAY, CAN WE BRING IT BACK TO MOSLY?
YOU ARE BEING SO WEIRD TODAY.
DROOP...
GLANCE
GLANCE
FLICK
GLITTER
ROAR
What kind of cryptid is it?
FLICK
The epic kind!!!
GLITTER
HOWL
HOWL
SHUUUU
SHUUF
SHUUF
GASP!

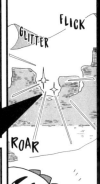

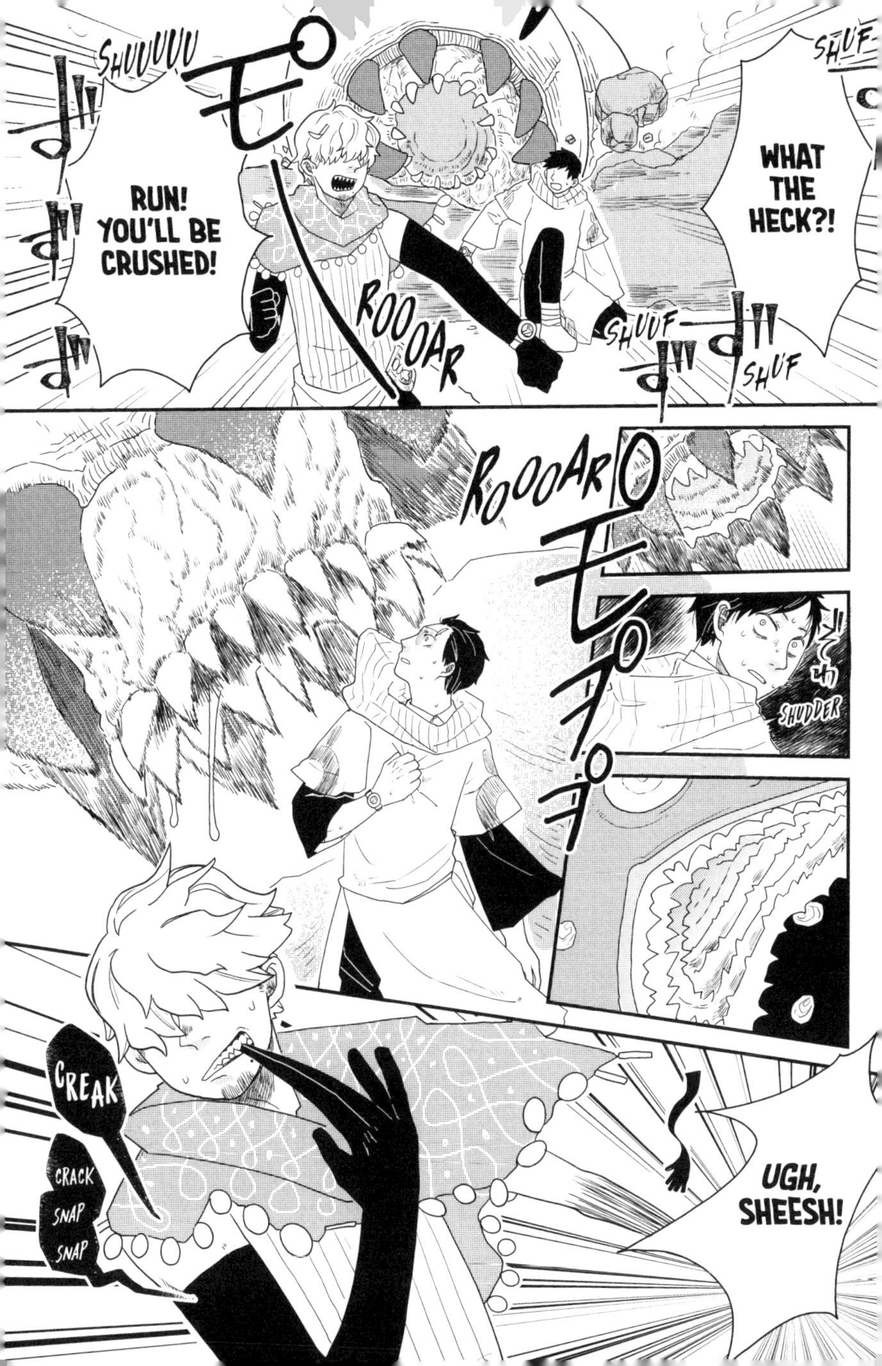
SHUF
WHAT THE HECK?!
SHUUUUU
RUN! YOU'LL BE CRUSHED!
ROOOAR
SHUUF
SHUF
ROOOAR
SHUDDER
UGH, SHEESH!
CREAK
CRACK
SNAP
SNAP

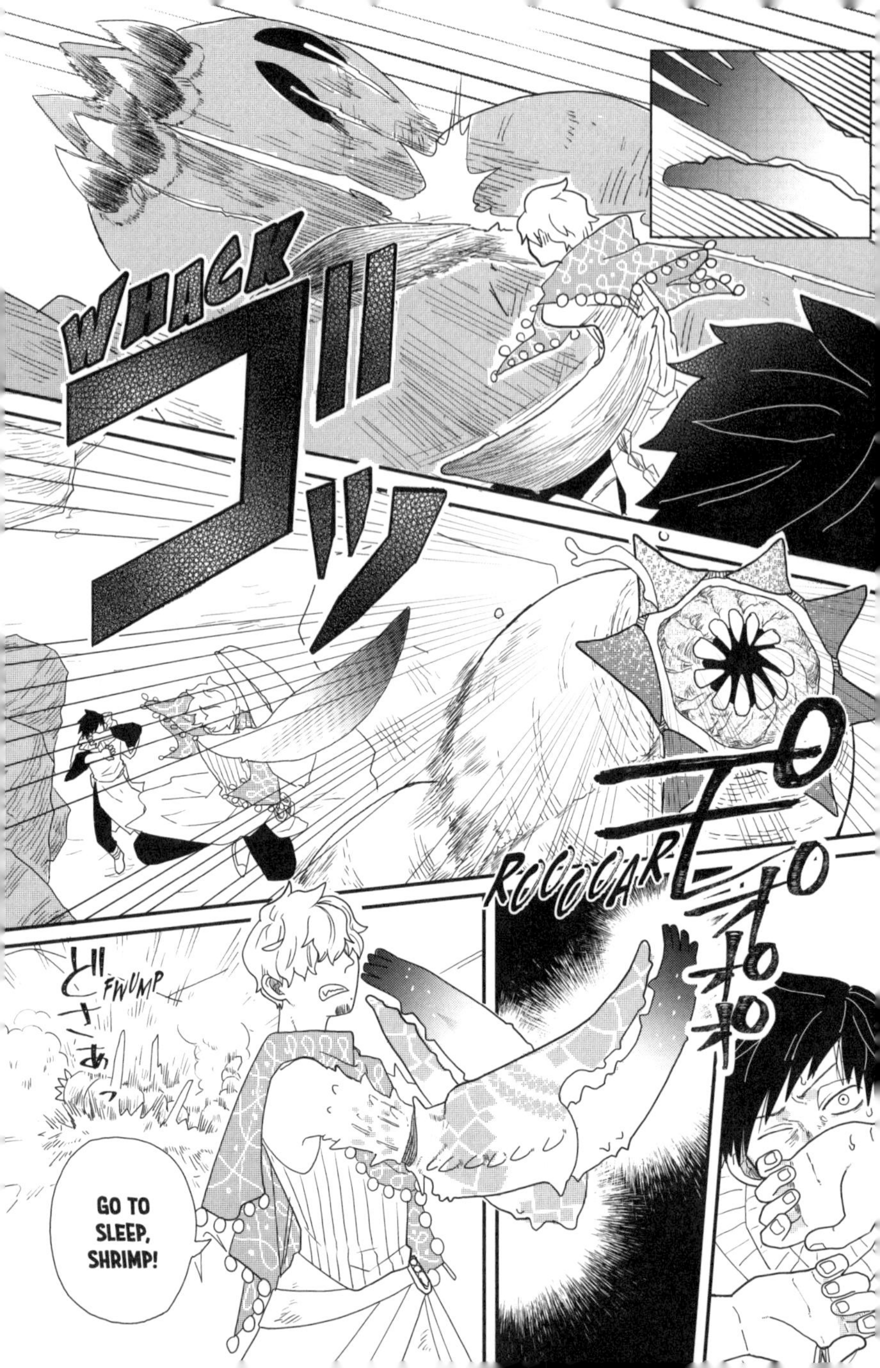
WHACK
ゴッ
ROOOOAR
FWUMP
GO TO SLEEP, SHRIMP!

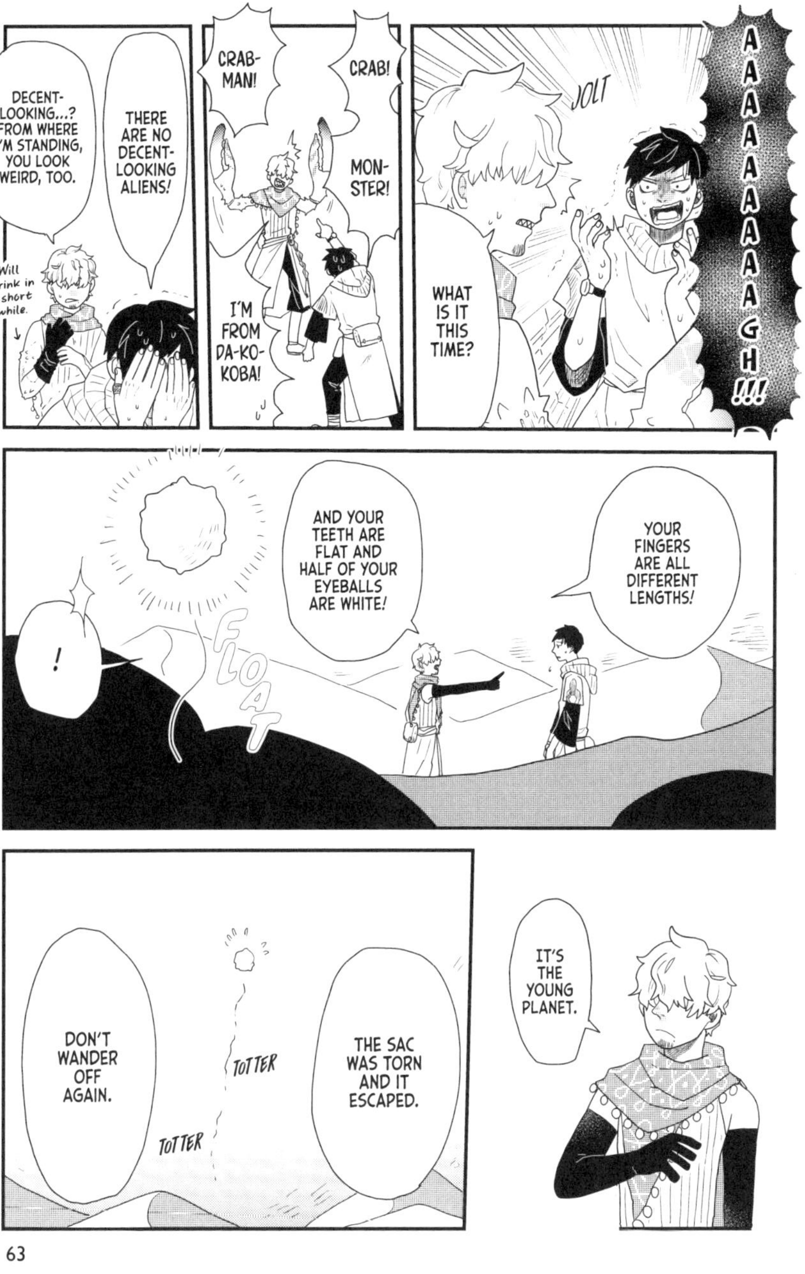
AAAAAAAAAAAGH!!!
JOLT
WHAT IS IT THIS TIME?
CRAB!
CRAB-MAN!
MON-STER!
I'M FROM DA-KO-KOBA!
THERE ARE NO DECENT-LOOKING ALIENS!
DECENT-LOOKING...? FROM WHERE I'M STANDING, YOU LOOK WEIRD, TOO.
Will shrink in a short while.
YOUR FINGERS ARE ALL DIFFERENT LENGTHS!
AND YOUR TEETH ARE FLAT AND HALF OF YOUR EYEBALLS ARE WHITE!
FLOAT
!
IT'S THE YOUNG PLANET.
THE SAC WAS TORN AND IT ESCAPED.
TOTTER
TOTTER
DON'T WANDER OFF AGAIN.

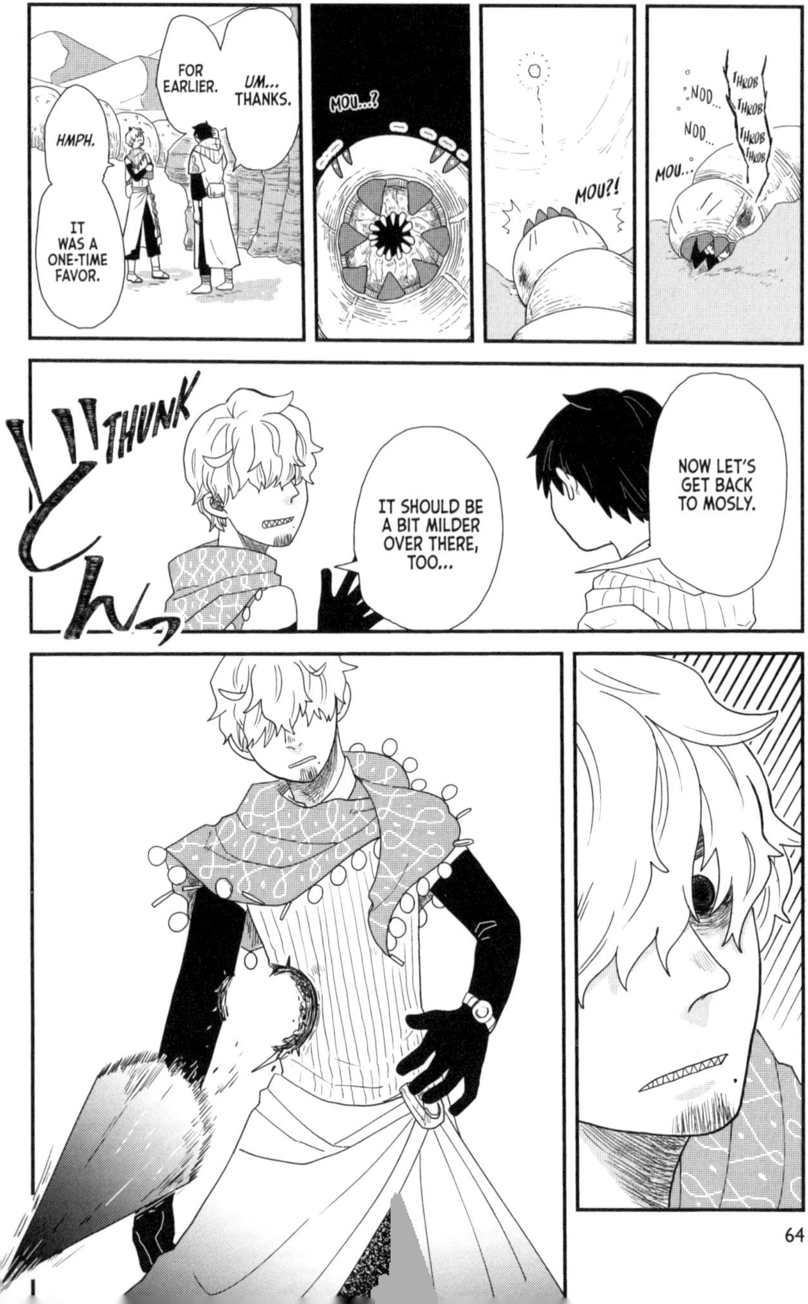
NOD... NOD...
MOU...
THROB THROB THROB THROB
MOU?!
MOU...?
UM... THANKS.
FOR EARLIER.
HMPH.
IT WAS A ONE-TIME FAVOR.
NOW LET'S GET BACK TO MOSLY.
IT SHOULD BE A BIT MILDER OVER THERE, TOO...
THUNK

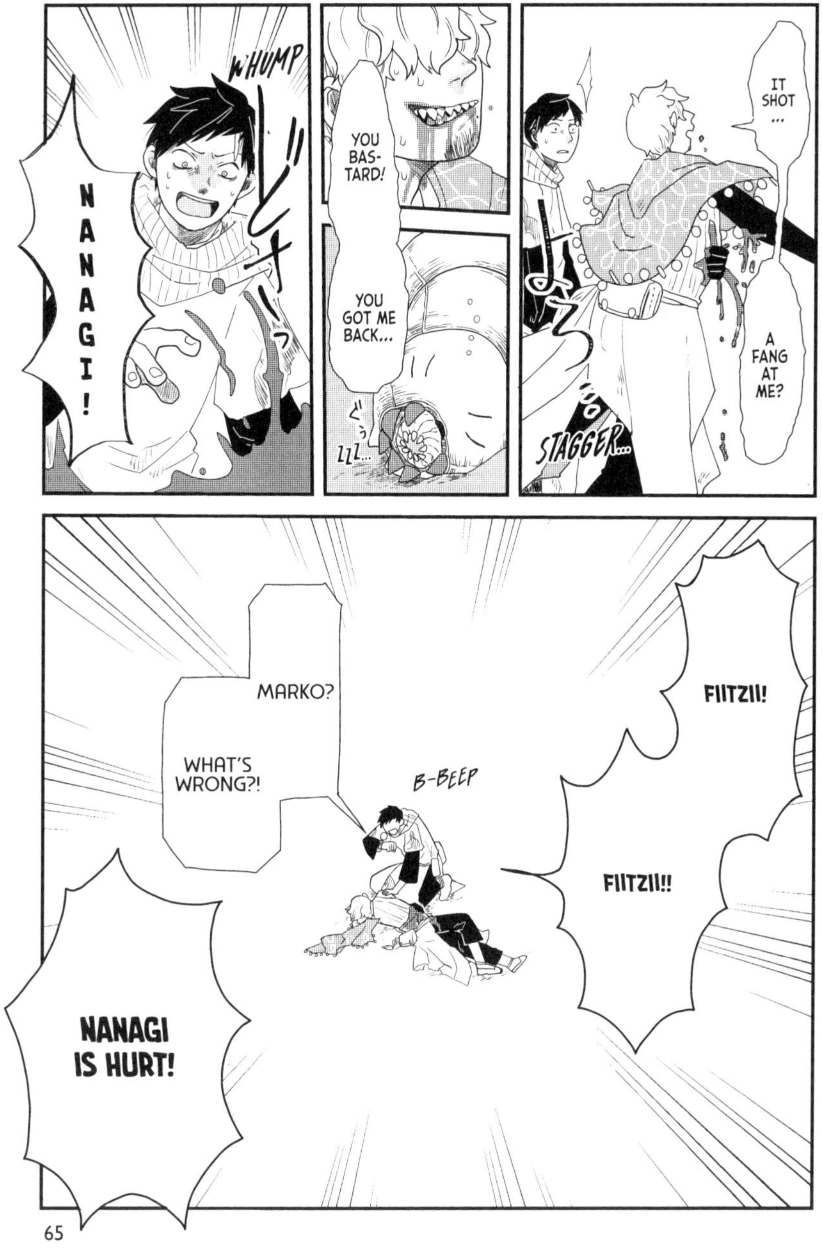
IT SHOT ...
A FANG AT ME?
STAGGER...
YOU BASTARD!
YOU GOT ME BACK...
ZZZ...
WHUMP
NANAGI!
FIITZII!
FIITZII!!
B-BEEP
MARKO?
WHAT'S WRONG?!
NANAGI IS HURT!

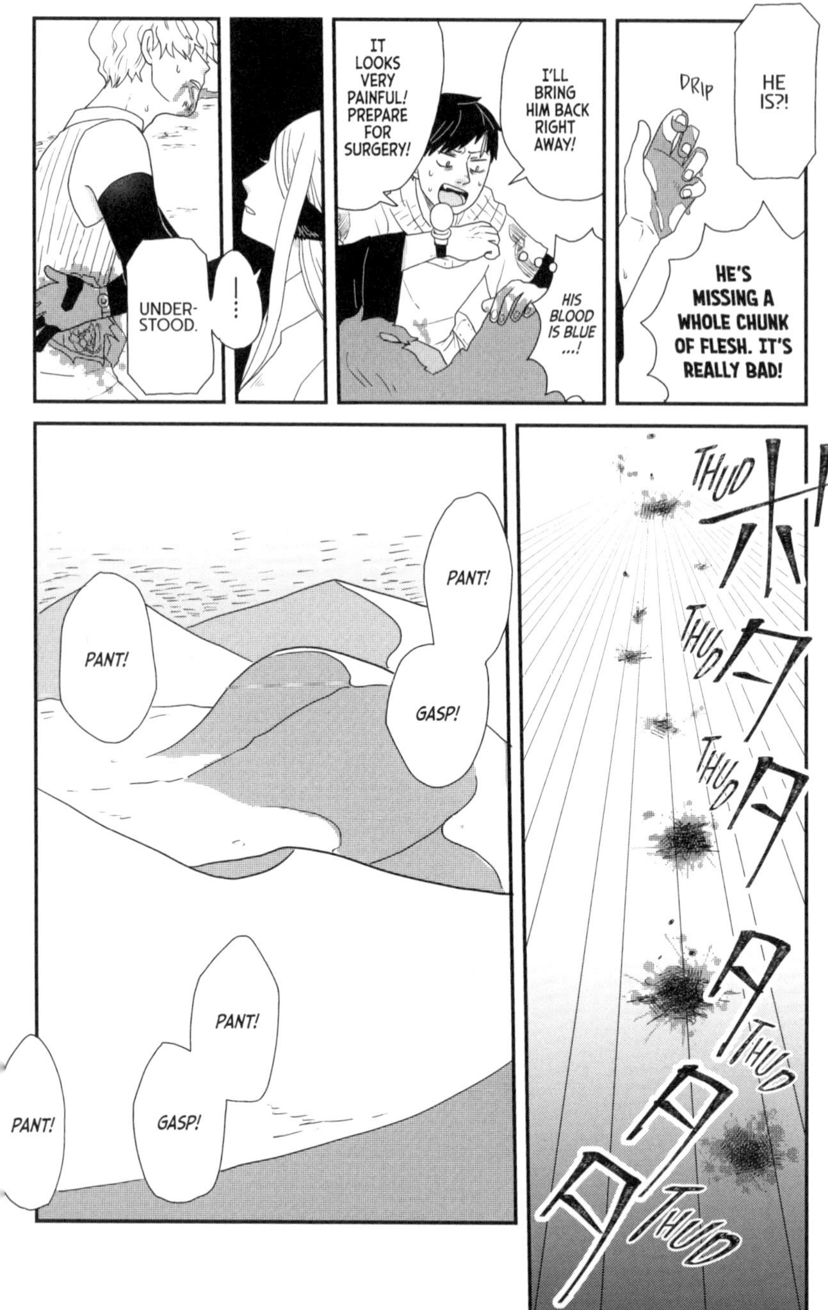
HE IS?!
DRIP
HE'S MISSING A WHOLE CHUNK OF FLESH. IT'S REALLY BAD!
I'LL BRING HIM BACK RIGHT AWAY!
IT LOOKS VERY PAINFUL! PREPARE FOR SURGERY!
HIS BLOOD IS BLUE ...!
...!
UNDER-STOOD.
THUD
THUD
THUD
THUD
THUD
PANT!
PANT!
GASP!
PANT!
GASP!
PANT!

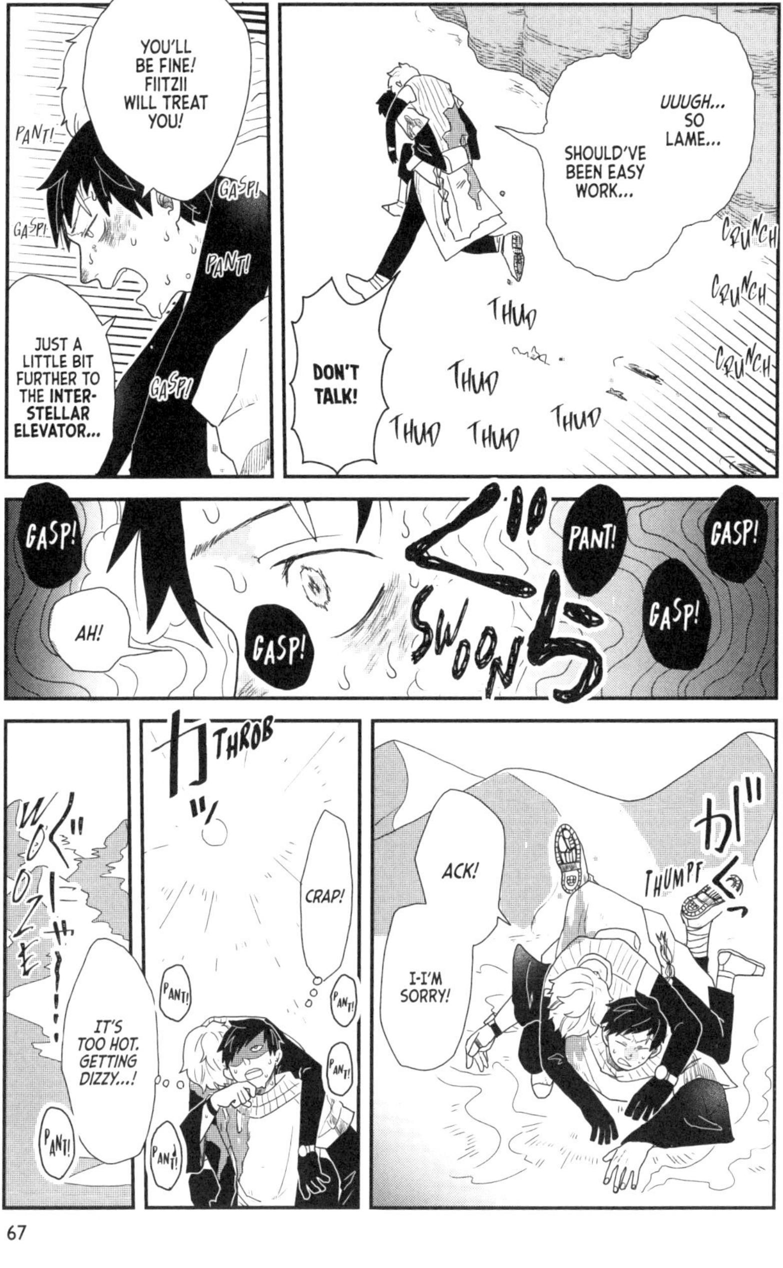
UUUGH... SO LAME...
SHOULD'VE BEEN EASY WORK...
CRUNCH
CRUNCH
CRUNCH
DON'T TALK!
THUD
THUD
THUD
THUD
THUD
YOU'LL BE FINE! FIITZII WILL TREAT YOU!
PANT!
GASP!
GASP!
PANT!
JUST A LITTLE BIT FURTHER TO THE INTER-STELLAR ELEVATOR...
GASP!
GASP!
PANT!
GASP!
SWOON
GASP!
GASP!
AH!
THUMPF
ACK!
I-I'M SORRY!
THROB
CRAP!
PANT!
PANT!
PANT!
PANT!
WOOZE
IT'S TOO HOT. GETTING DIZZY...!
PANT!

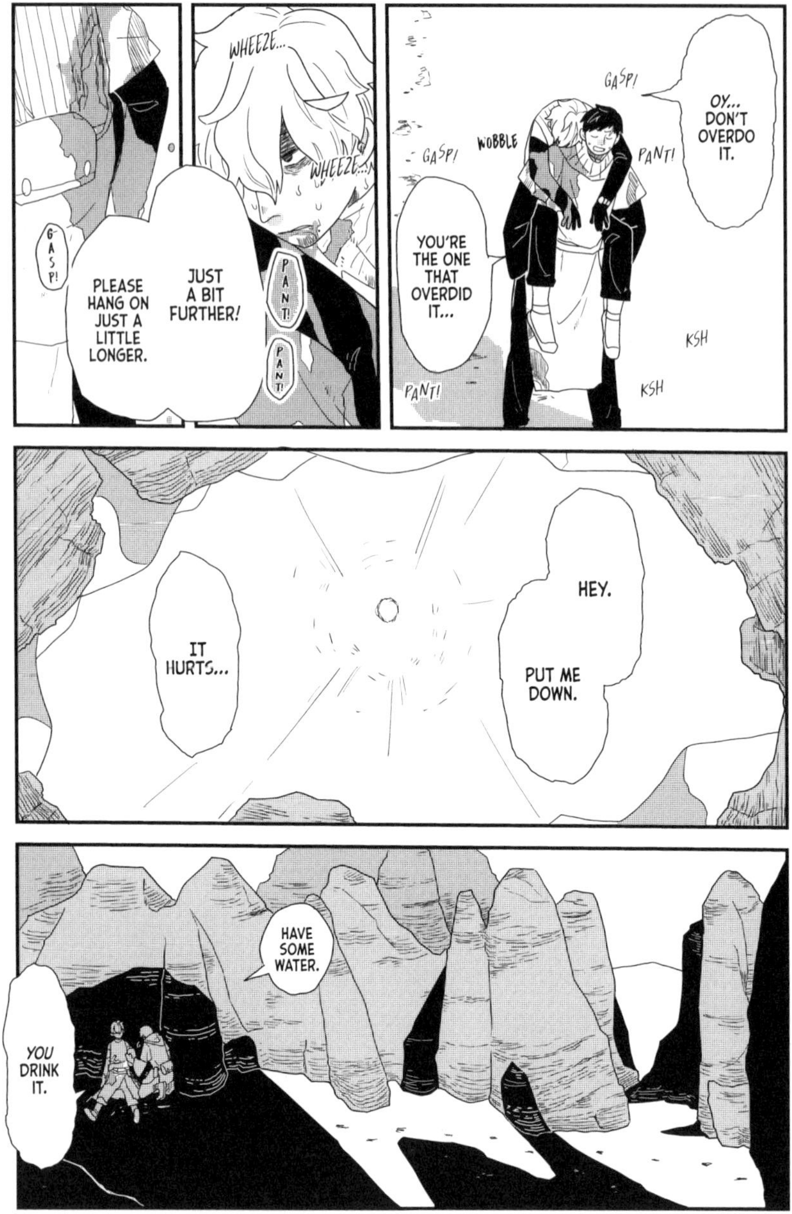
GASP!
OY... DON'T OVERDO IT.
WOBBLE
PANT!
GASP!
YOU'RE THE ONE THAT OVERDID IT...
KSH
KSH
PANT!
WHEEZE...
WHEEZE...
JUST A BIT FURTHER!
PANT!
PANT!
PLEASE HANG ON JUST A LITTLE LONGER.
GASP!
HEY.
PUT ME DOWN.
IT HURTS...
HAVE SOME WATER.
YOU DRINK IT.

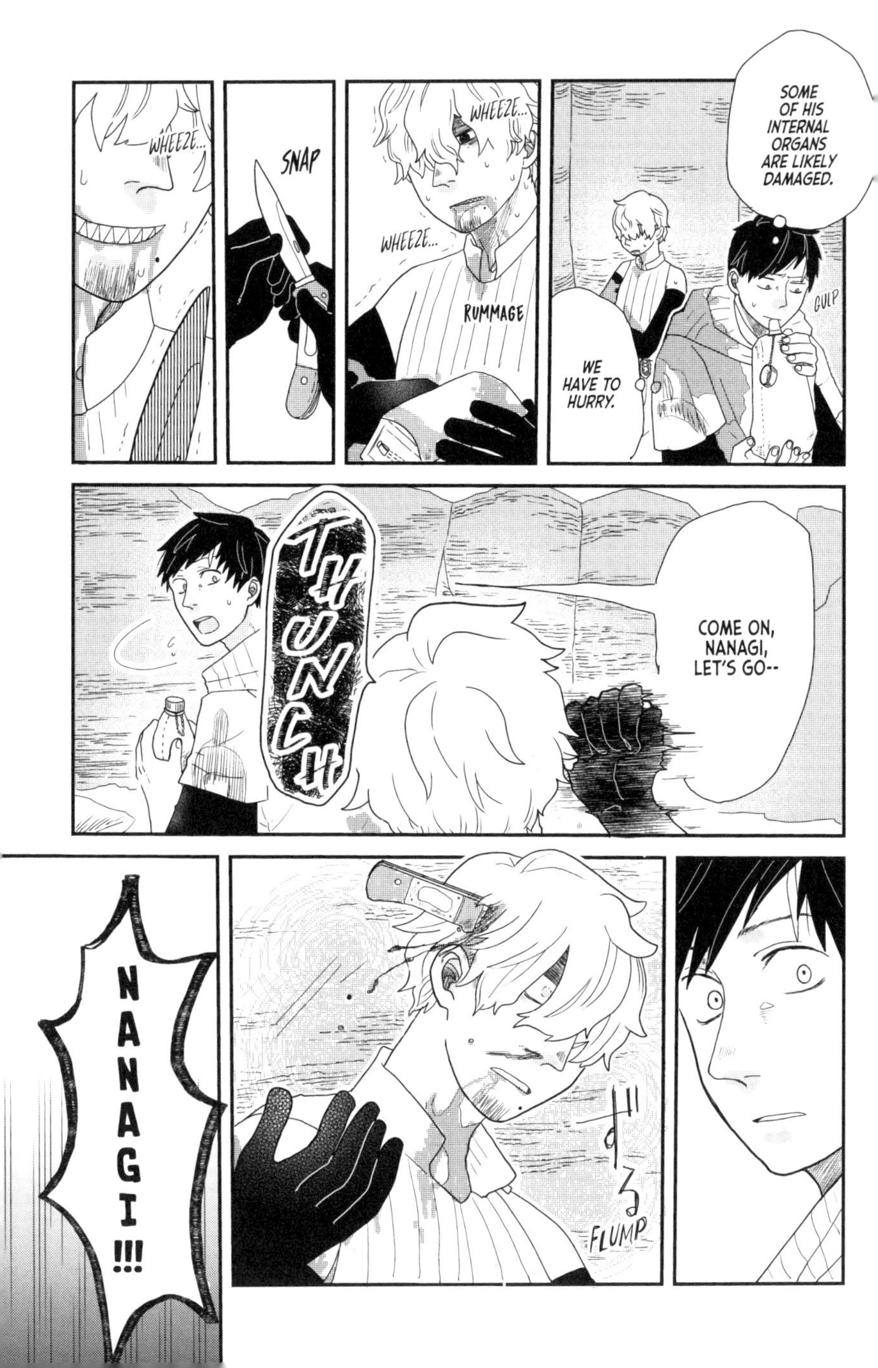
SOME OF HIS INTERNAL ORGANS ARE LIKELY DAMAGED.
GULP
WE HAVE TO HURRY.
WHEEZE...
WHEEZE...
RUMMAGE
SNAP
WHEEZE...
COME ON, NANAGI, LET'S GO--
THUNCH
FLUMP
NANAGI!!!

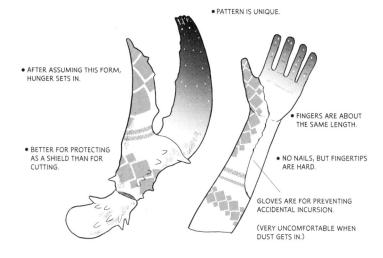

• PATTERN IS UNIQUE.

• AFTER ASSUMING THIS FORM, HUNGER SETS IN.

• BETTER FOR PROTECTING AS A SHIELD THAN FOR CUTTING.

• FINGERS ARE ABOUT THE SAME LENGTH.

• NO NAILS, BUT FINGERTIPS ARE HARD.

GLOVES ARE FOR PREVENTING ACCIDENTAL INCURSION.

(VERY UNCOMFORTABLE WHEN DUST GETS IN.)

Episode 12: The Desert, the Shrimp, the Crab, and the Stuffing ②

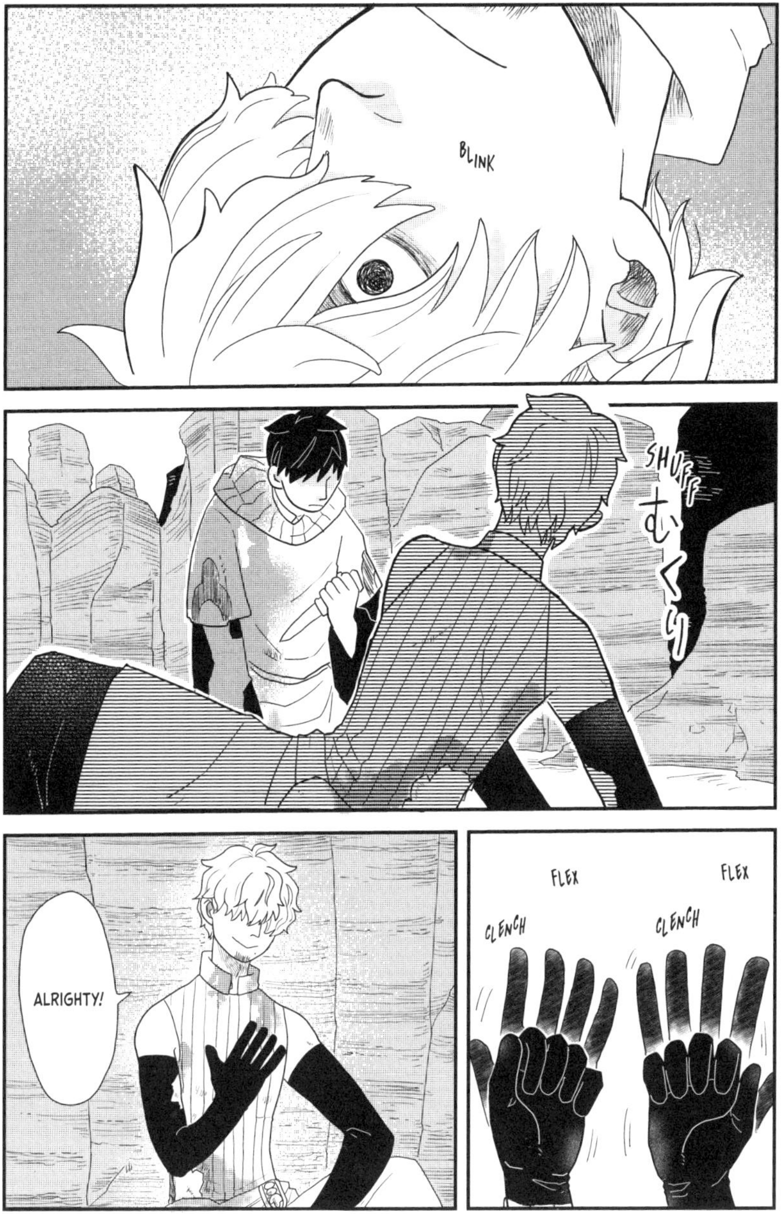
BLINK
SHUFF
むくり
FLEX
FLEX
CLENCH
CLENCH
ALRIGHTY!

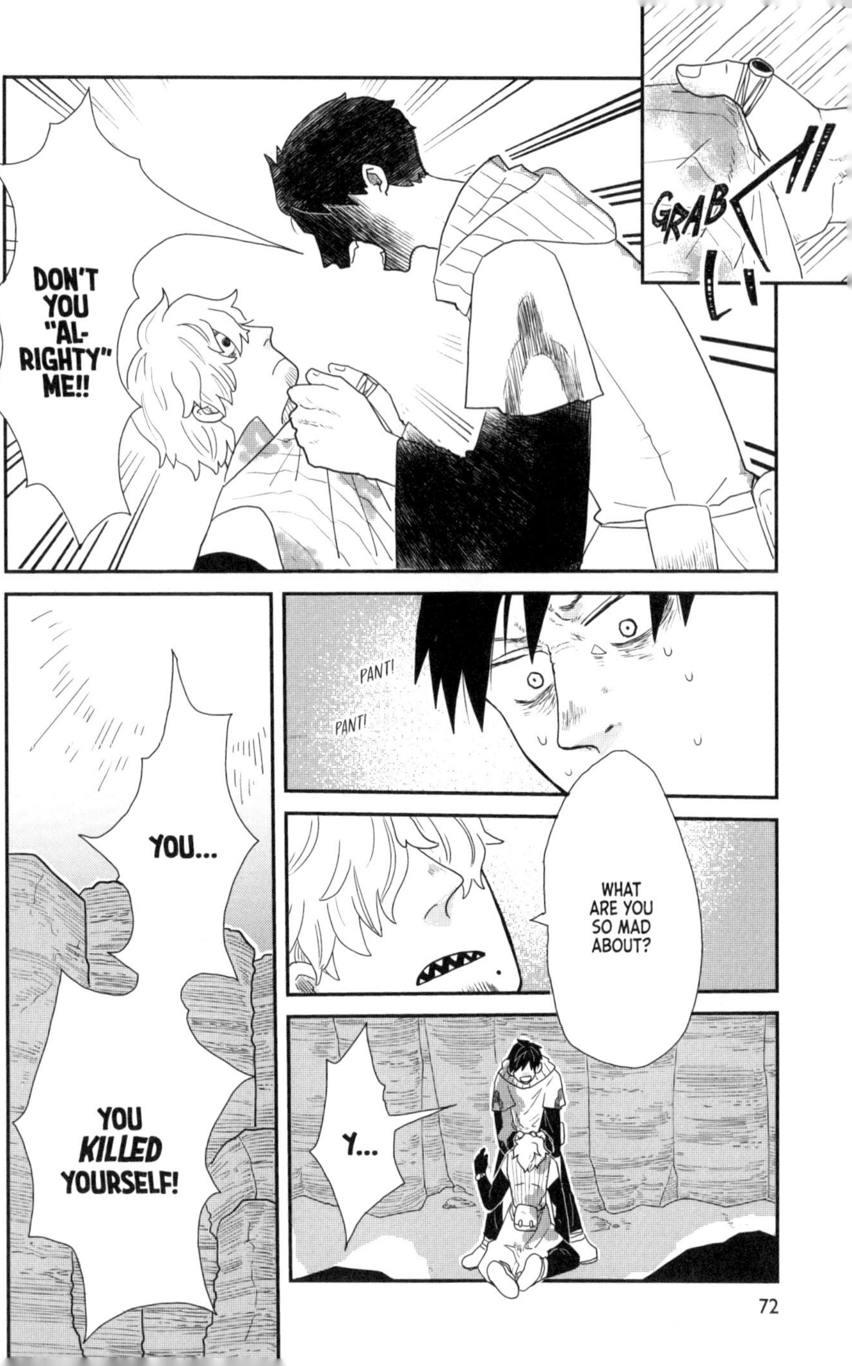
GRAB
DON'T YOU "AL-RIGHTY" ME!!
PANT!
PANT!
WHAT ARE YOU SO MAD ABOUT?
Y...
YOU...
YOU *KILLED* YOURSELF!

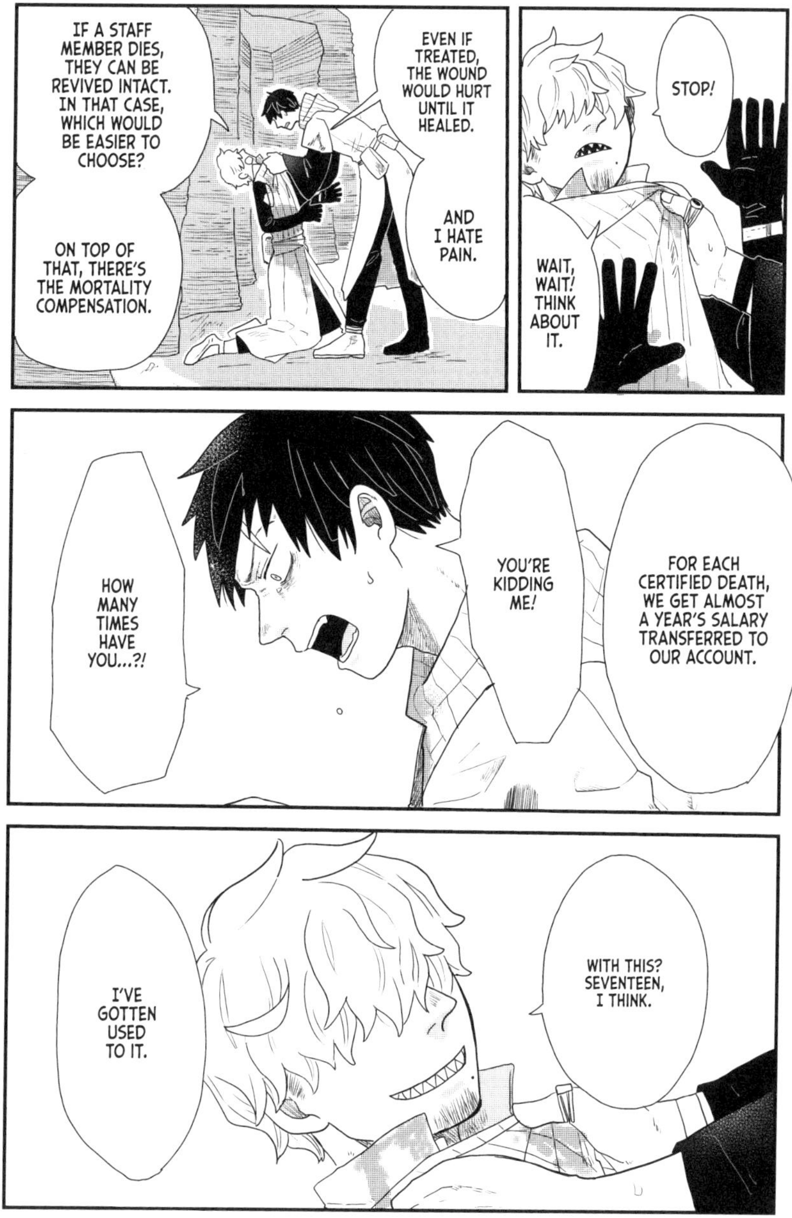
STOP!
WAIT, WAIT! THINK ABOUT IT.
EVEN IF TREATED, THE WOUND WOULD HURT UNTIL IT HEALED.
AND I HATE PAIN.
IF A STAFF MEMBER DIES, THEY CAN BE REVIVED INTACT. IN THAT CASE, WHICH WOULD BE EASIER TO CHOOSE?
ON TOP OF THAT, THERE'S THE MORTALITY COMPENSATION.
FOR EACH CERTIFIED DEATH, WE GET ALMOST A YEAR'S SALARY TRANSFERRED TO OUR ACCOUNT.
YOU'RE KIDDING ME!
HOW MANY TIMES HAVE YOU...?!
WITH THIS? SEVENTEEN, I THINK.
I'VE GOTTEN USED TO IT.

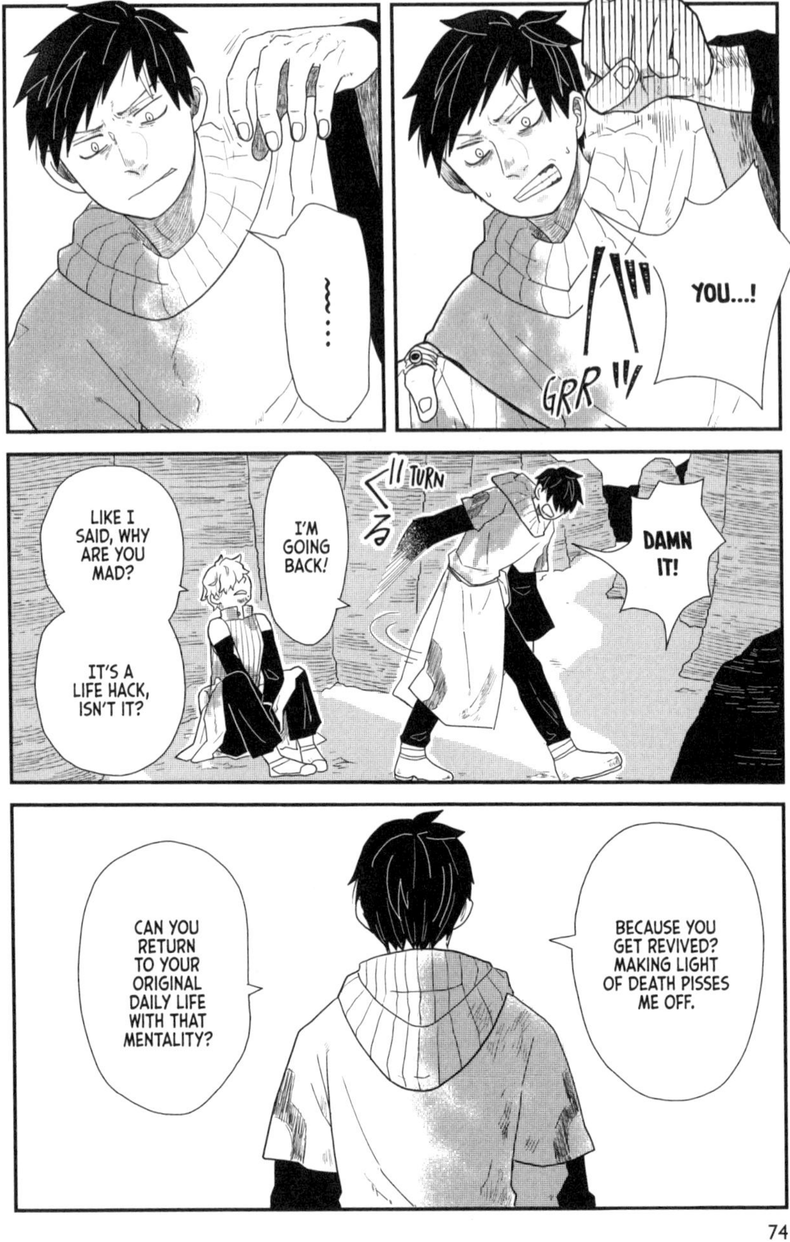
GRR
YOU...!
~...
DAMN IT!
TURN
I'M GOING BACK!
LIKE I SAID, WHY ARE YOU MAD?
IT'S A LIFE HACK, ISN'T IT?
BECAUSE YOU GET REVIVED? MAKING LIGHT OF DEATH PISSES ME OFF.
CAN YOU RETURN TO YOUR ORIGINAL DAILY LIFE WITH THAT MENTALITY?

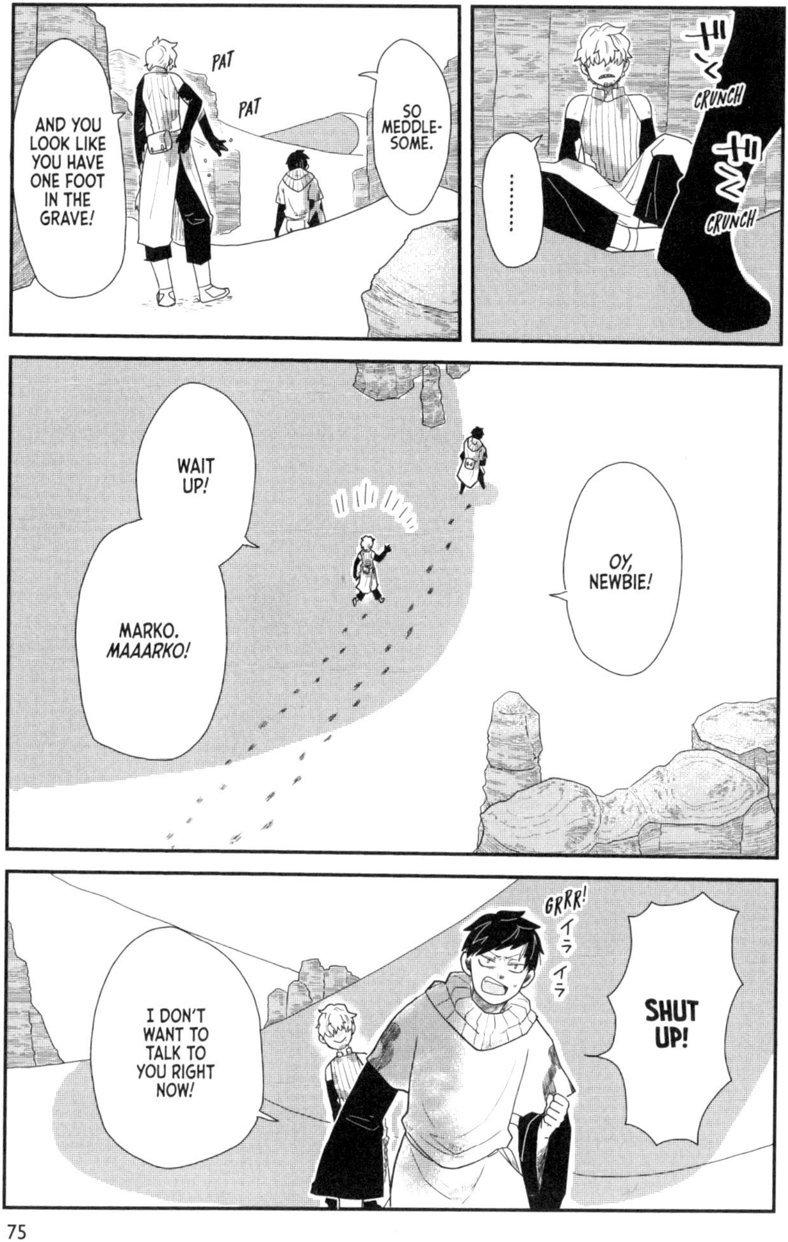
CRUNCH
CRUNCH
......
SO MEDDLESOME.
PAT
PAT
AND YOU LOOK LIKE YOU HAVE ONE FOOT IN THE GRAVE!
OY, NEWBIE!
WAIT UP!
MARKO. MAAARKO!
GRRR!
イラ イラ
SHUT UP!
I DON'T WANT TO TALK TO YOU RIGHT NOW!

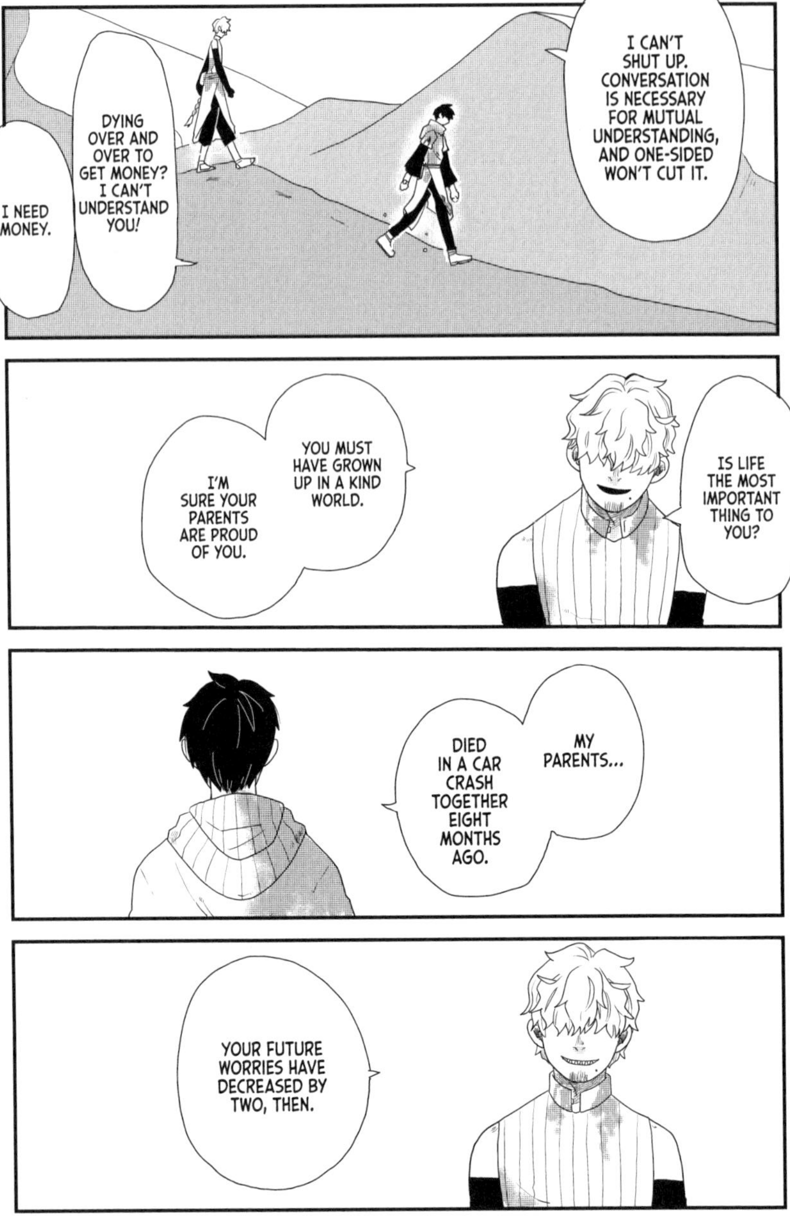
I CAN'T SHUT UP. CONVERSATION IS NECESSARY FOR MUTUAL UNDERSTANDING, AND ONE-SIDED WON'T CUT IT.
DYING OVER AND OVER TO GET MONEY? I CAN'T UNDERSTAND YOU!
I NEED MONEY.
IS LIFE THE MOST IMPORTANT THING TO YOU?
YOU MUST HAVE GROWN UP IN A KIND WORLD.
I'M SURE YOUR PARENTS ARE PROUD OF YOU.
MY PARENTS...
DIED IN A CAR CRASH TOGETHER EIGHT MONTHS AGO.
YOUR FUTURE WORRIES HAVE DECREASED BY TWO, THEN.

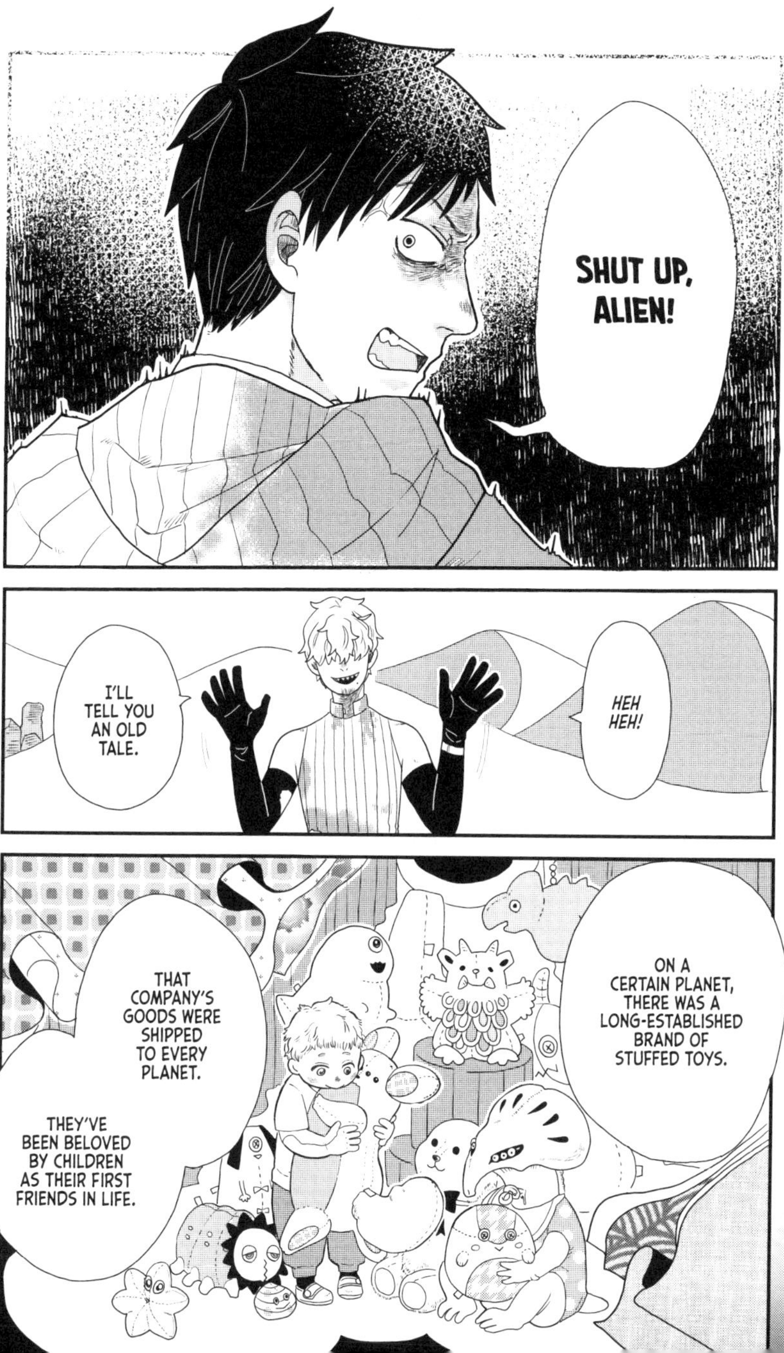
SHUT UP, ALIEN!
HEH HEH!
I'LL TELL YOU AN OLD TALE.
ON A CERTAIN PLANET, THERE WAS A LONG-ESTABLISHED BRAND OF STUFFED TOYS.
THAT COMPANY'S GOODS WERE SHIPPED TO EVERY PLANET.
THEY'VE BEEN BELOVED BY CHILDREN AS THEIR FIRST FRIENDS IN LIFE.

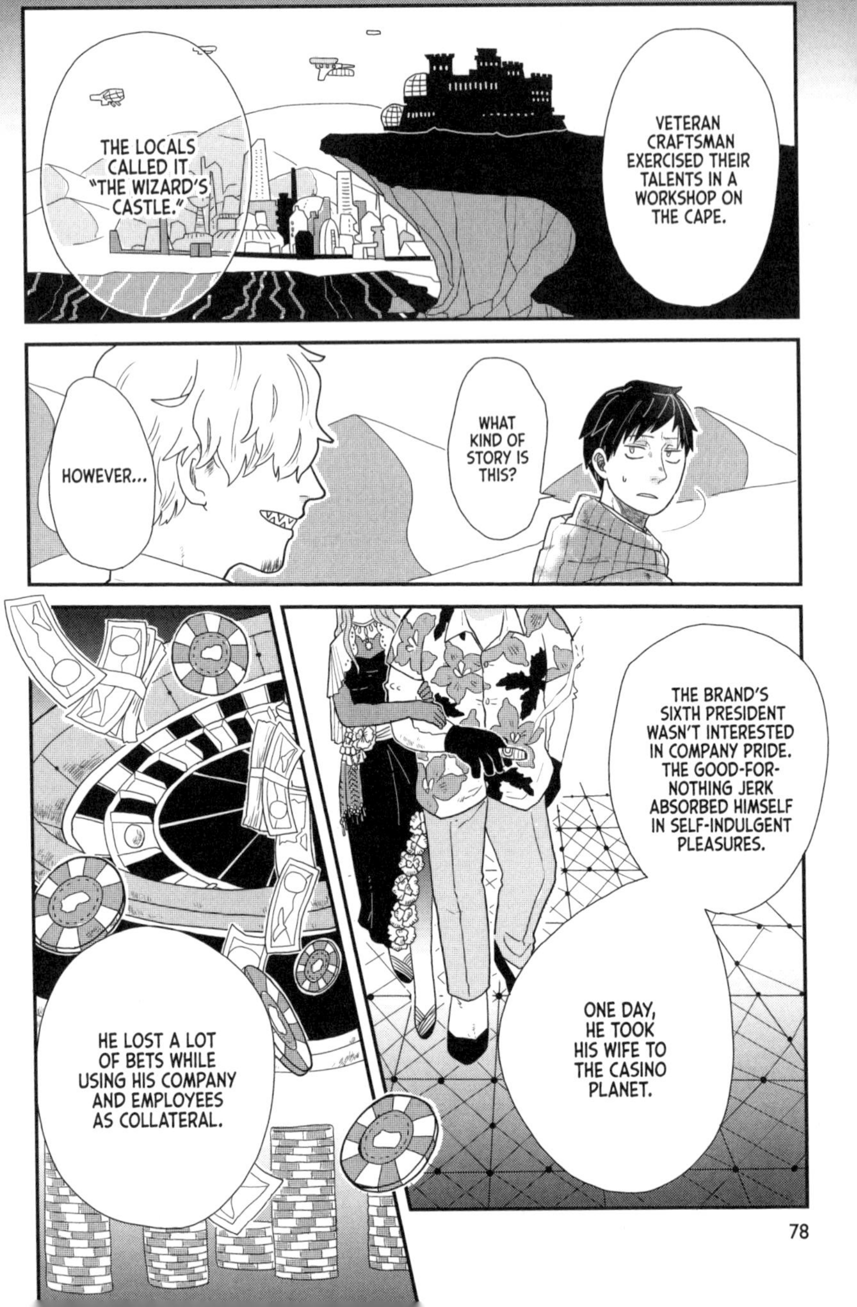
VETERAN CRAFTSMAN EXERCISED THEIR TALENTS IN A WORKSHOP ON THE CAPE.
THE LOCALS CALLED IT "THE WIZARD'S CASTLE."
WHAT KIND OF STORY IS THIS?
HOWEVER...
THE BRAND'S SIXTH PRESIDENT WASN'T INTERESTED IN COMPANY PRIDE. THE GOOD-FOR-NOTHING JERK ABSORBED HIMSELF IN SELF-INDULGENT PLEASURES.
ONE DAY, HE TOOK HIS WIFE TO THE CASINO PLANET.
HE LOST A LOT OF BETS WHILE USING HIS COMPANY AND EMPLOYEES AS COLLATERAL.

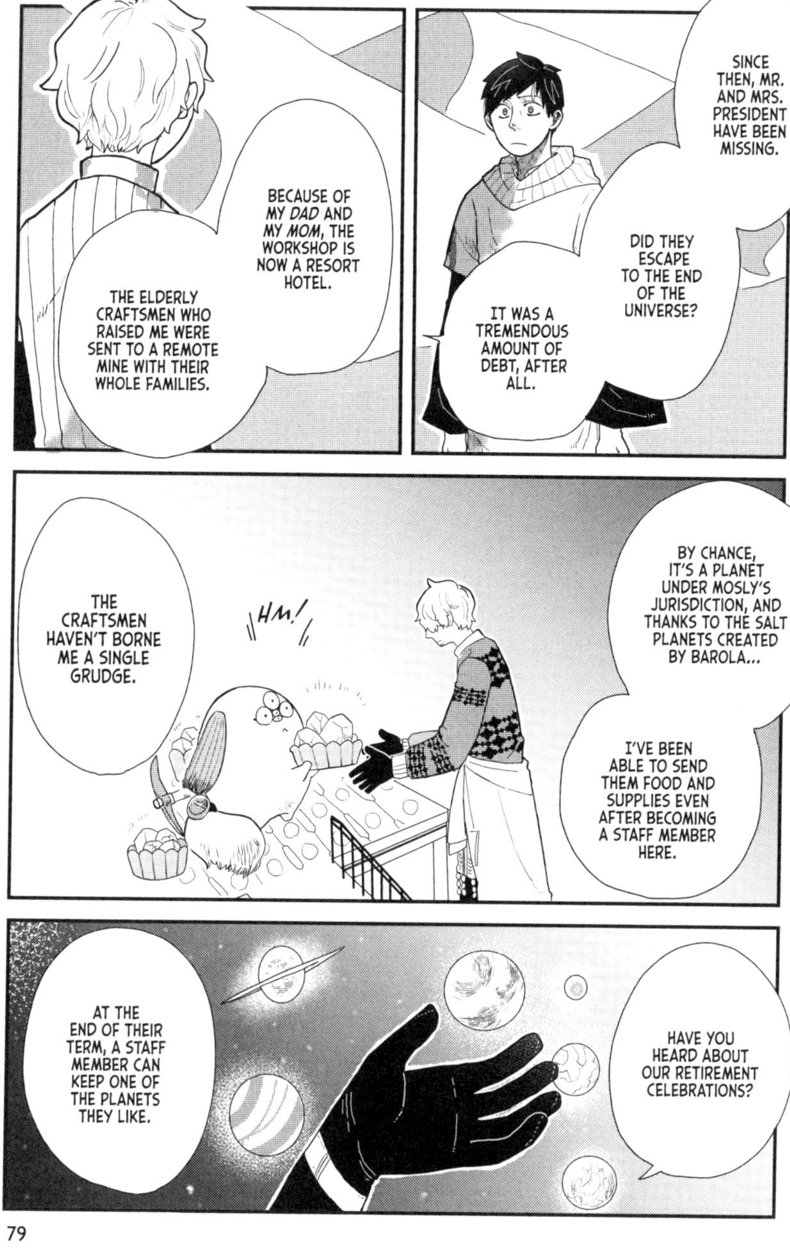
SINCE THEN, MR. AND MRS. PRESIDENT HAVE BEEN MISSING.
DID THEY ESCAPE TO THE END OF THE UNIVERSE?
IT WAS A TREMENDOUS AMOUNT OF DEBT, AFTER ALL.
BECAUSE OF MY *DAD* AND MY *MOM*, THE WORKSHOP IS NOW A RESORT HOTEL.
THE ELDERLY CRAFTSMEN WHO RAISED ME WERE SENT TO A REMOTE MINE WITH THEIR WHOLE FAMILIES.
BY CHANCE, IT'S A PLANET UNDER MOSLY'S JURISDICTION, AND THANKS TO THE SALT PLANETS CREATED BY BAROLA...
I'VE BEEN ABLE TO SEND THEM FOOD AND SUPPLIES EVEN AFTER BECOMING A STAFF MEMBER HERE.
HM!
THE CRAFTSMEN HAVEN'T BORNE ME A SINGLE GRUDGE.
HAVE YOU HEARD ABOUT OUR RETIREMENT CELEBRATIONS?
AT THE END OF THEIR TERM, A STAFF MEMBER CAN KEEP ONE OF THE PLANETS THEY LIKE.

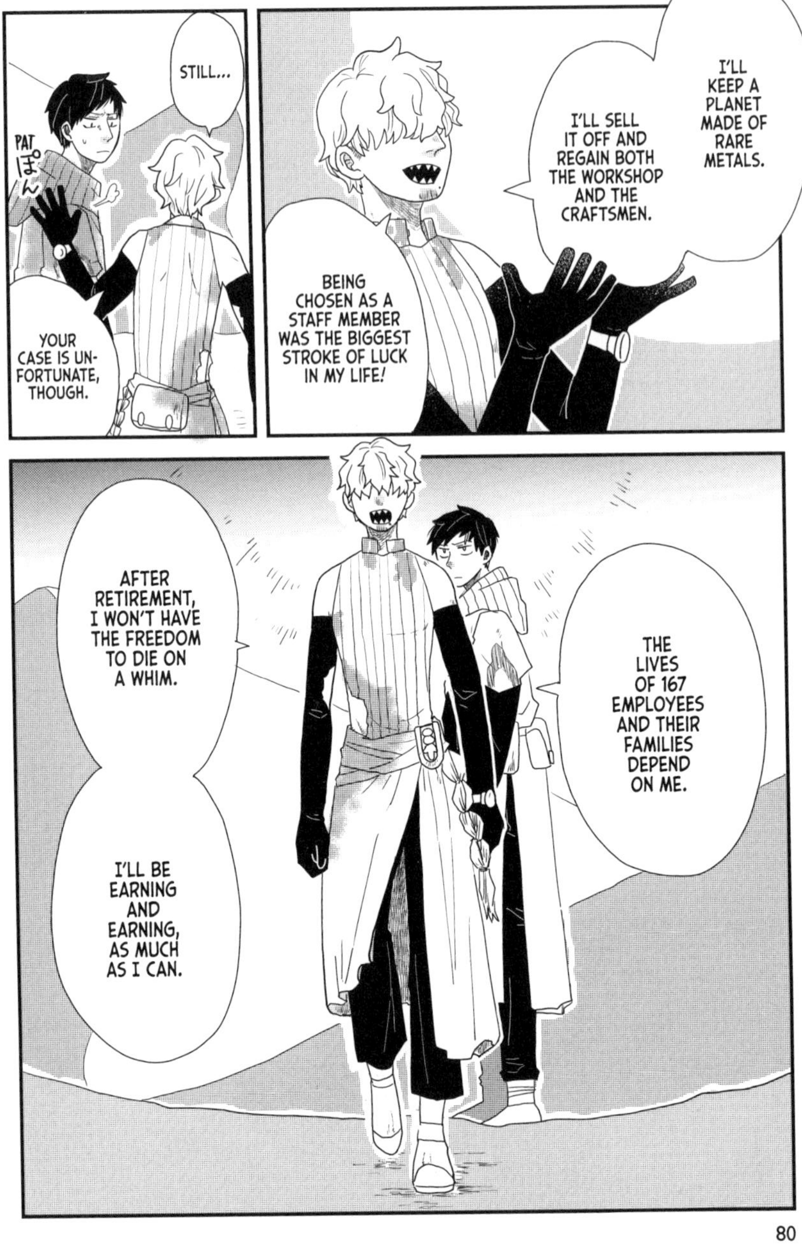
I'LL KEEP A PLANET MADE OF RARE METALS.
I'LL SELL IT OFF AND REGAIN BOTH THE WORKSHOP AND THE CRAFTSMEN.
BEING CHOSEN AS A STAFF MEMBER WAS THE BIGGEST STROKE OF LUCK IN MY LIFE!
STILL...
PAT ぽん
YOUR CASE IS UN-FORTUNATE, THOUGH.
THE LIVES OF 167 EMPLOYEES AND THEIR FAMILIES DEPEND ON ME.
AFTER RETIREMENT, I WON'T HAVE THE FREEDOM TO DIE ON A WHIM.
I'LL BE EARNING AND EARNING, AS MUCH AS I CAN.

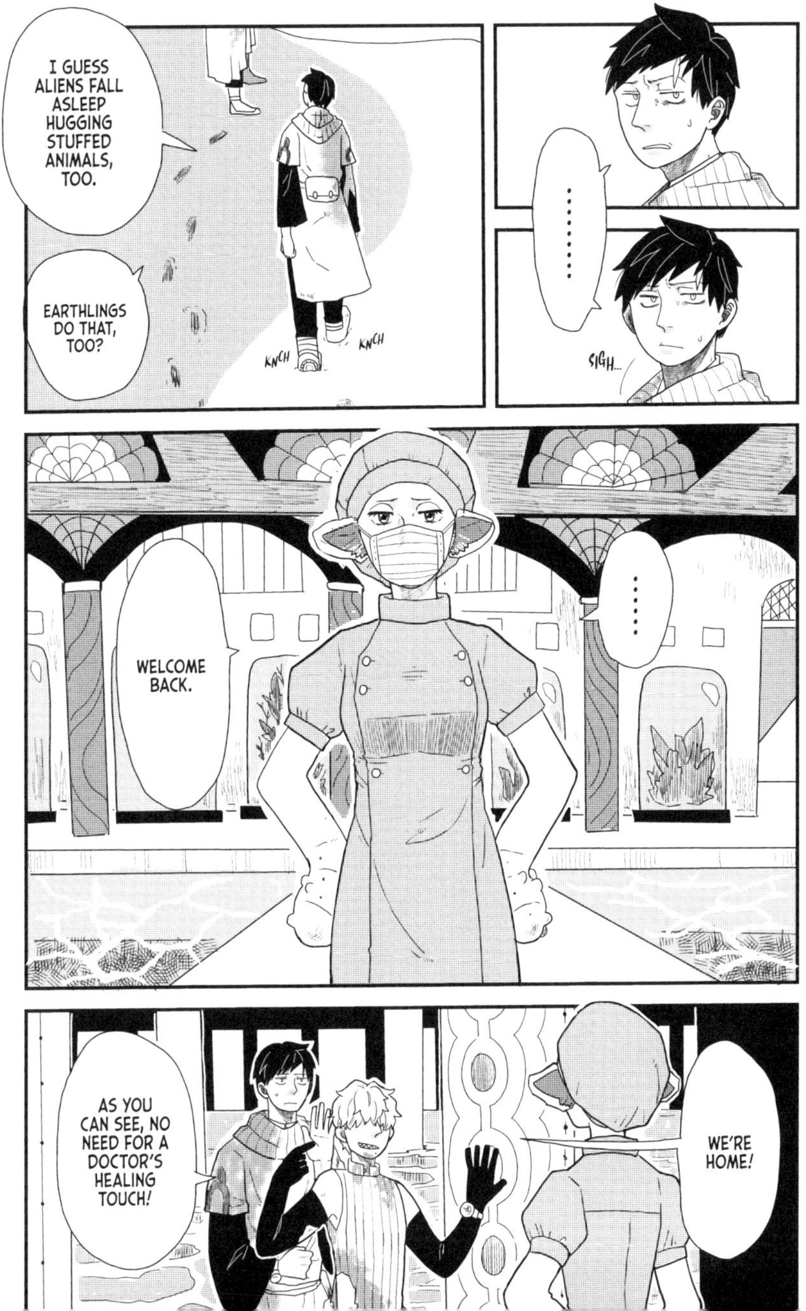
......
SIGH...
I GUESS ALIENS FALL ASLEEP HUGGING STUFFED ANIMALS, TOO.
EARTHLINGS DO THAT, TOO?
KNCH
KNCH
......
WELCOME BACK.
WE'RE HOME!
AS YOU CAN SEE, NO NEED FOR A DOCTOR'S HEALING TOUCH!

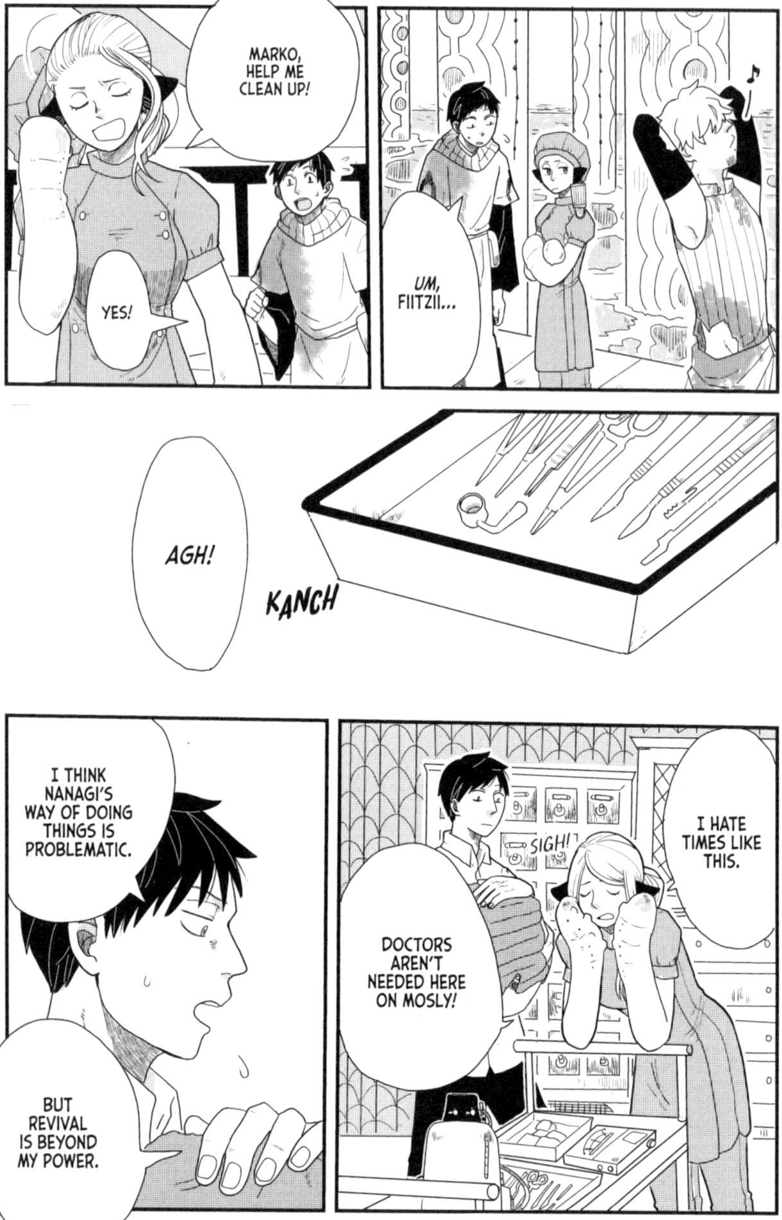
UM, FIITZII...
MARKO, HELP ME CLEAN UP!
YES!
KANCH
AGH!
I HATE TIMES LIKE THIS.
SIGH!
DOCTORS AREN'T NEEDED HERE ON MOSLY!
I THINK NANAGI'S WAY OF DOING THINGS IS PROBLEMATIC.
BUT REVIVAL IS BEYOND MY POWER.

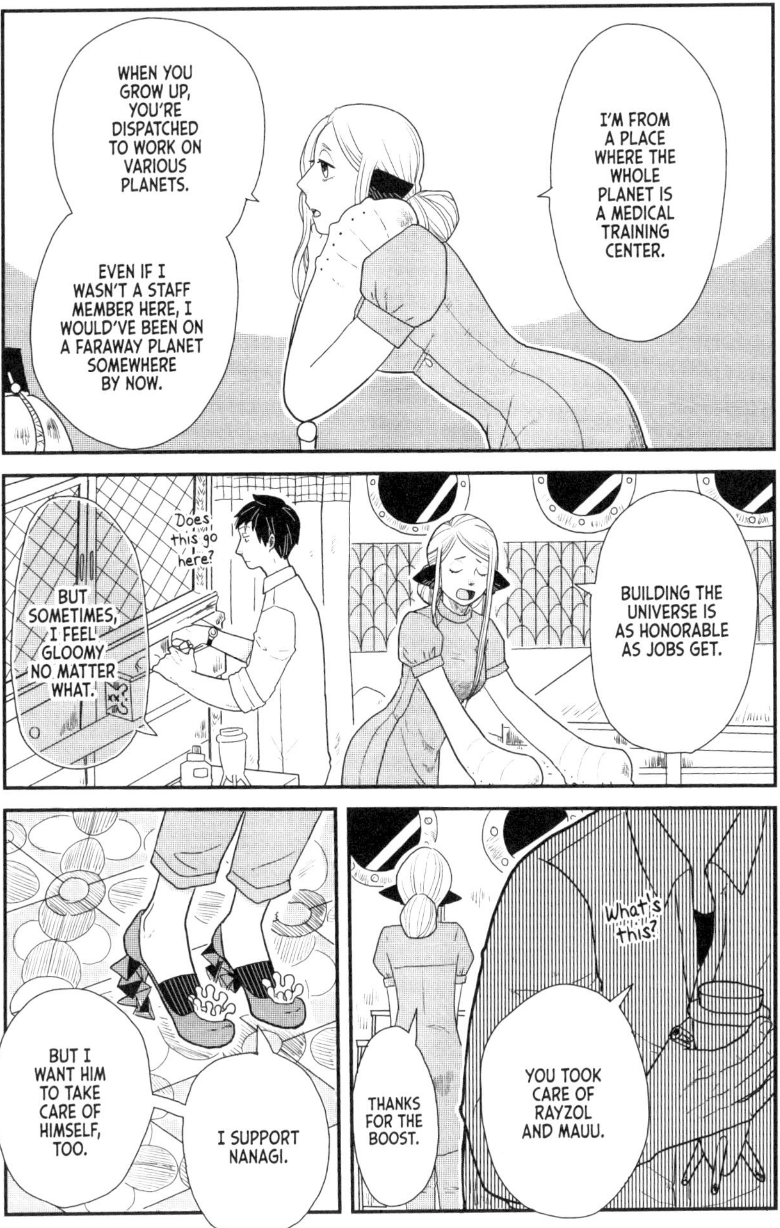
I'M FROM A PLACE WHERE THE WHOLE PLANET IS A MEDICAL TRAINING CENTER.
WHEN YOU GROW UP, YOU'RE DISPATCHED TO WORK ON VARIOUS PLANETS.
EVEN IF I WASN'T A STAFF MEMBER HERE, I WOULD'VE BEEN ON A FARAWAY PLANET SOMEWHERE BY NOW.
BUILDING THE UNIVERSE IS AS HONORABLE AS JOBS GET.
Does this go here?
BUT SOMETIMES, I FEEL GLOOMY NO MATTER WHAT.
What's this?
YOU TOOK CARE OF RAYZOL AND MAUU.
THANKS FOR THE BOOST.
I SUPPORT NANAGI.
BUT I WANT HIM TO TAKE CARE OF HIMSELF, TOO.

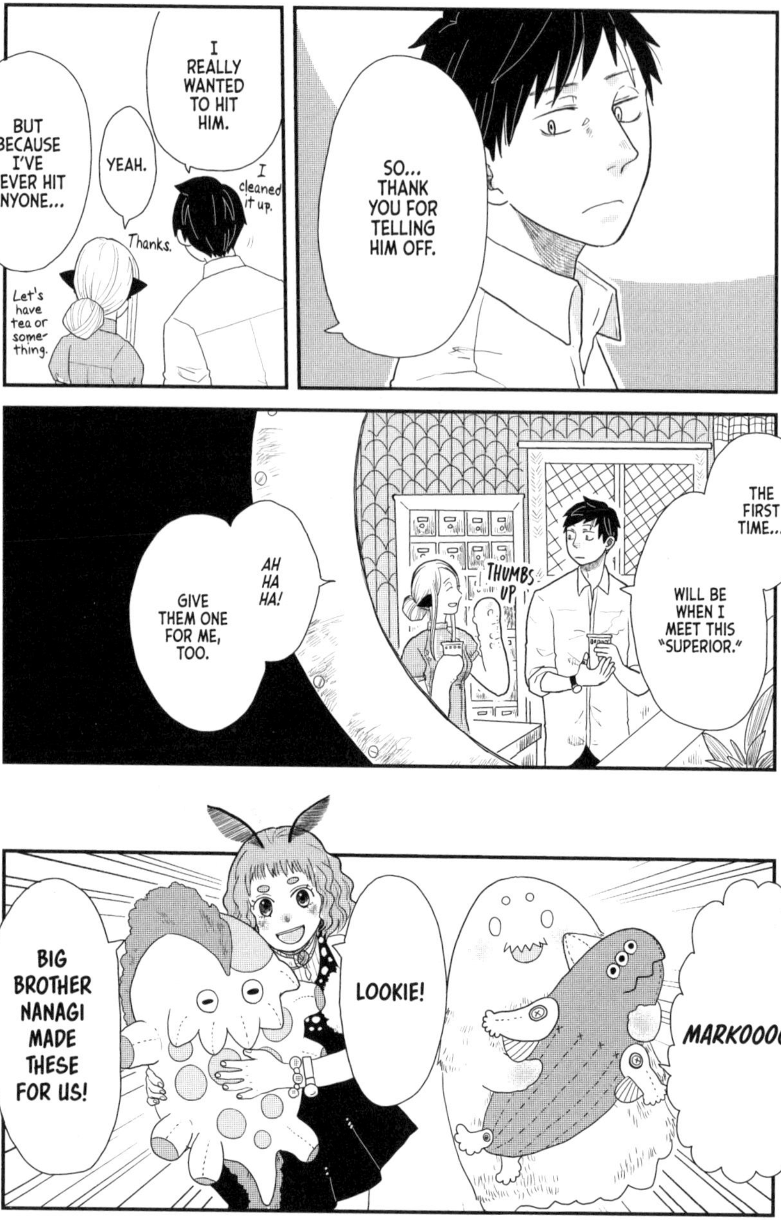
SO... THANK YOU FOR TELLING HIM OFF.
I REALLY WANTED TO HIT HIM.
I cleaned it up.
YEAH.
BUT BECAUSE I'VE NEVER HIT ANYONE...
Thanks.
Let's have tea or something.
THE FIRST TIME...
WILL BE WHEN I MEET THIS "SUPERIOR."
THUMBS UP
AH HA HA!
GIVE THEM ONE FOR ME, TOO.
MARKOOOO!
LOOKIE!
BIG BROTHER NANAGI MADE THESE FOR US!

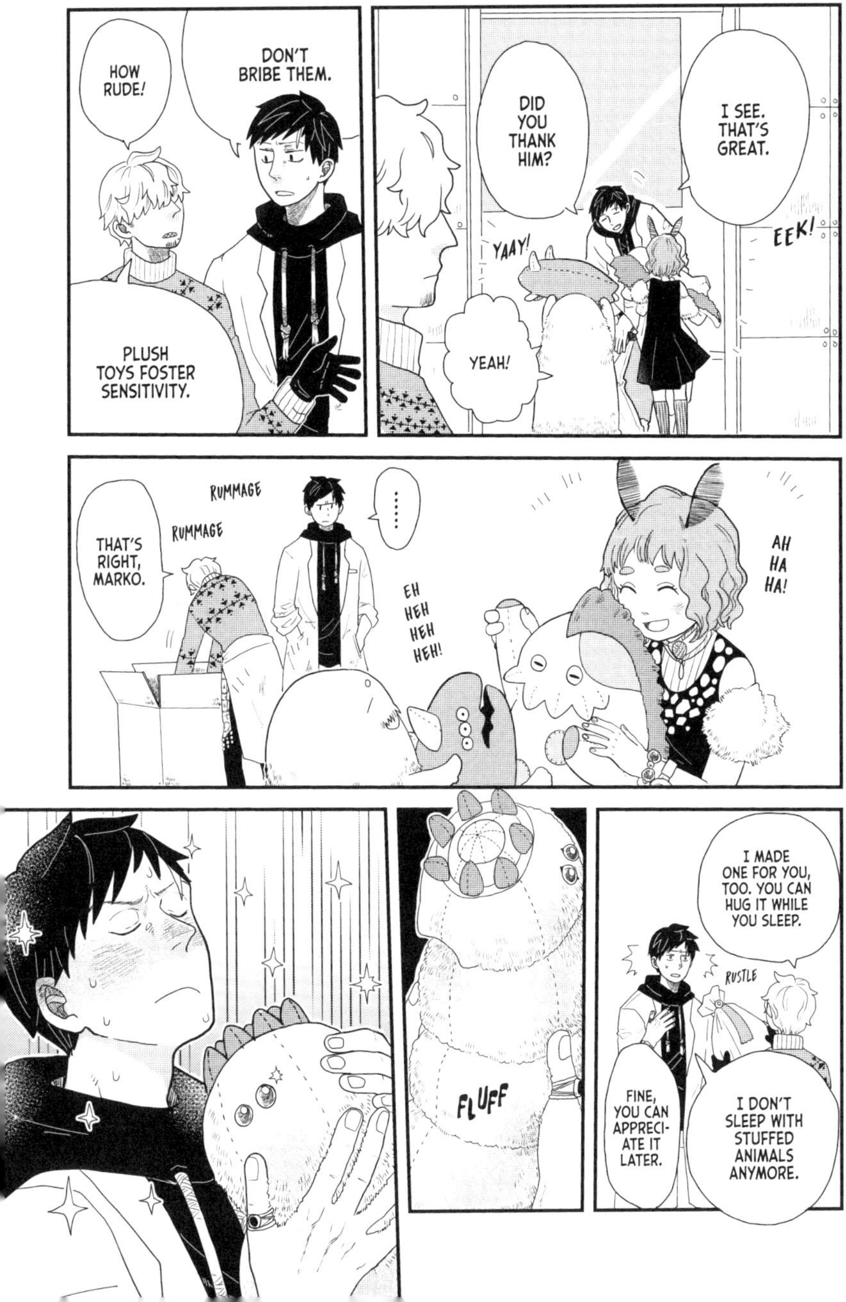
I SEE. THAT'S GREAT.
EEK!
DID YOU THANK HIM?
YAAY!
YEAH!
DON'T BRIBE THEM.
HOW RUDE!
PLUSH TOYS FOSTER SENSITIVITY.
AH HA HA!
EH HEH HEH HEH!
......
RUMMAGE
RUMMAGE
THAT'S RIGHT, MARKO.
I MADE ONE FOR YOU, TOO. YOU CAN HUG IT WHILE YOU SLEEP.
RUSTLE
I DON'T SLEEP WITH STUFFED ANIMALS ANYMORE.
FINE, YOU CAN APPRECI-ATE IT LATER.
FLUFF

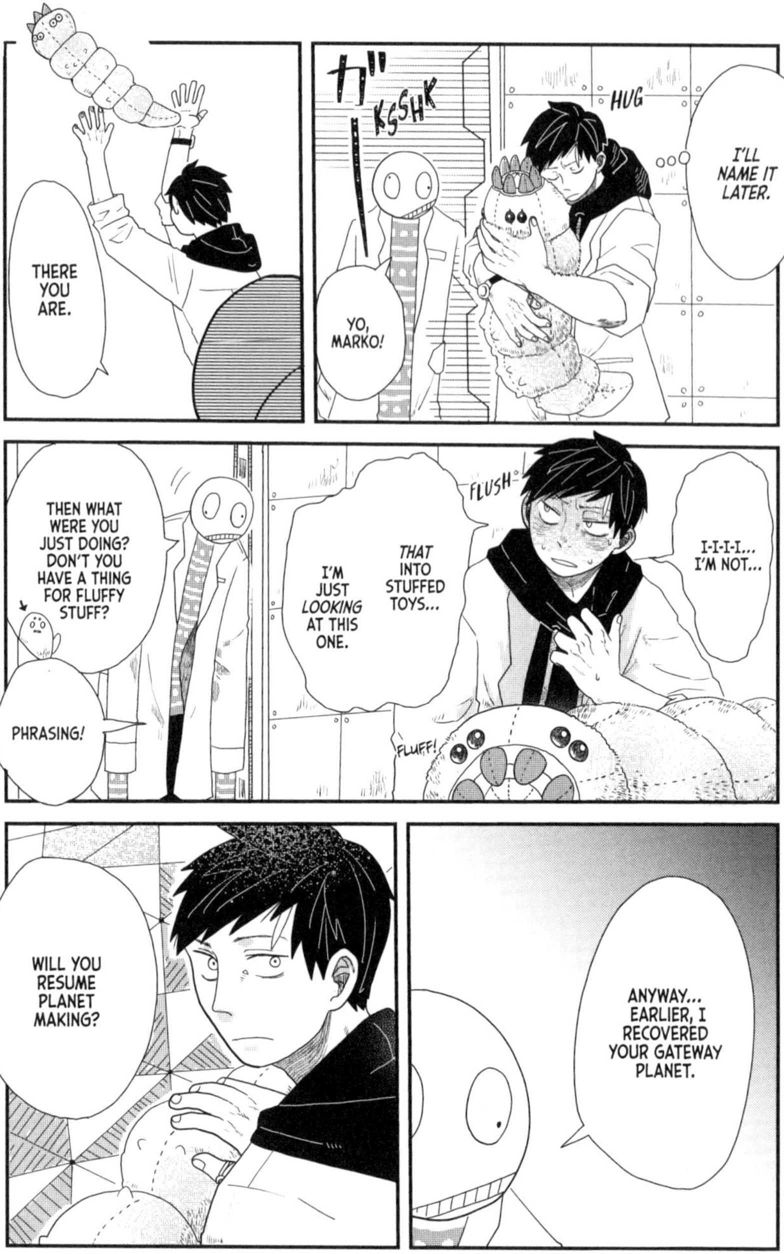
HUG
I'LL NAME IT LATER.
ガ
KSSHK
YO, MARKO!
THERE YOU ARE.
I-I-I-I... I'M NOT...
FLUSH
THAT INTO STUFFED TOYS...
I'M JUST *LOOKING* AT THIS ONE.
FLUFF!
THEN WHAT WERE YOU JUST DOING? DON'T YOU HAVE A THING FOR FLUFFY STUFF?
PHRASING!
ANYWAY... EARLIER, I RECOVERED YOUR GATEWAY PLANET.
WILL YOU RESUME PLANET MAKING?

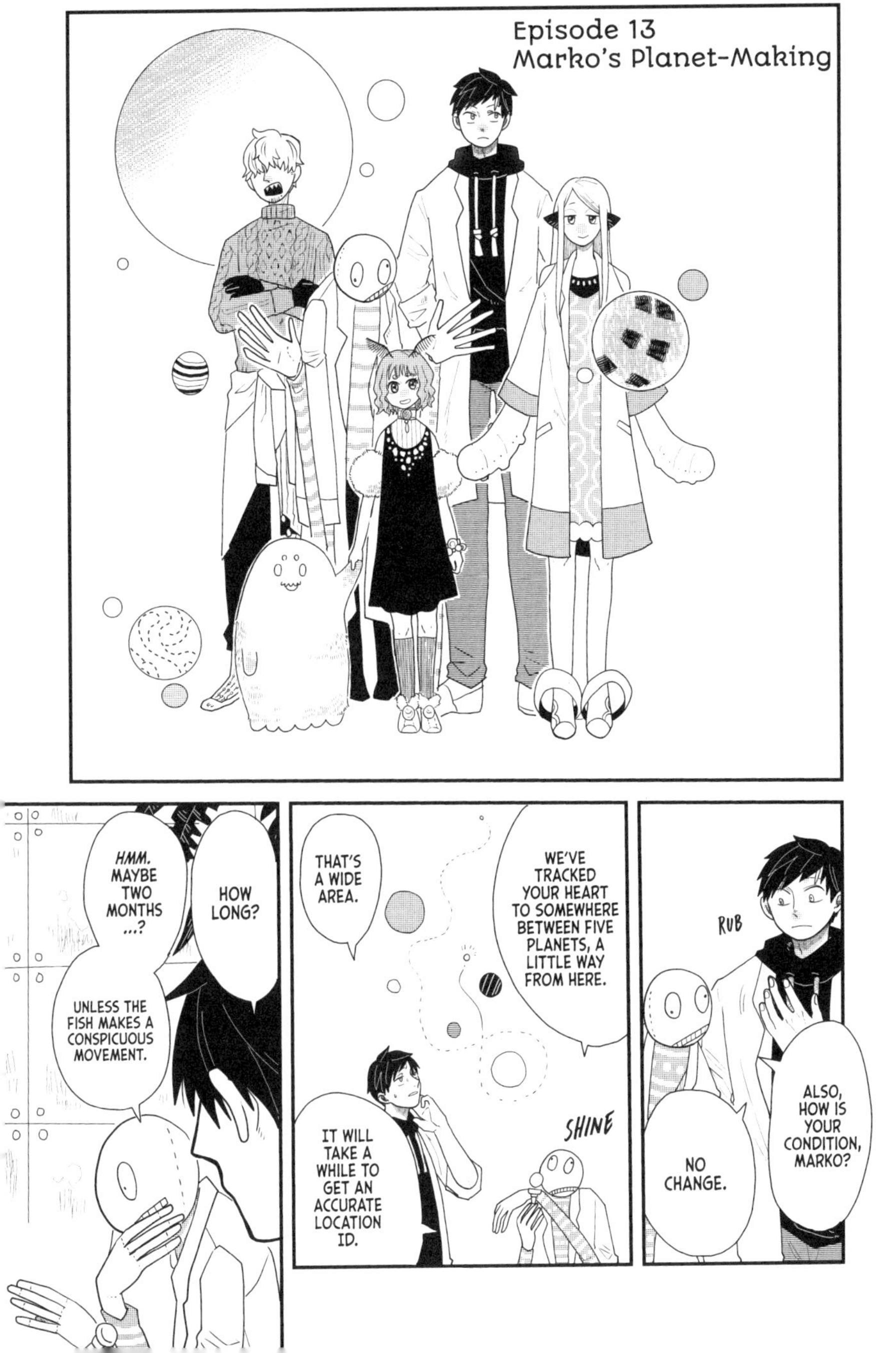
Episode 13
Marko's Planet-Making
ALSO, HOW IS YOUR CONDITION, MARKO?
NO CHANGE.
RUB
WE'VE TRACKED YOUR HEART TO SOMEWHERE BETWEEN FIVE PLANETS, A LITTLE WAY FROM HERE.
THAT'S A WIDE AREA.
SHINE
IT WILL TAKE A WHILE TO GET AN ACCURATE LOCATION ID.
HOW LONG?
HMM. MAYBE TWO MONTHS ...?
UNLESS THE FISH MAKES A CONSPICUOUS MOVEMENT.

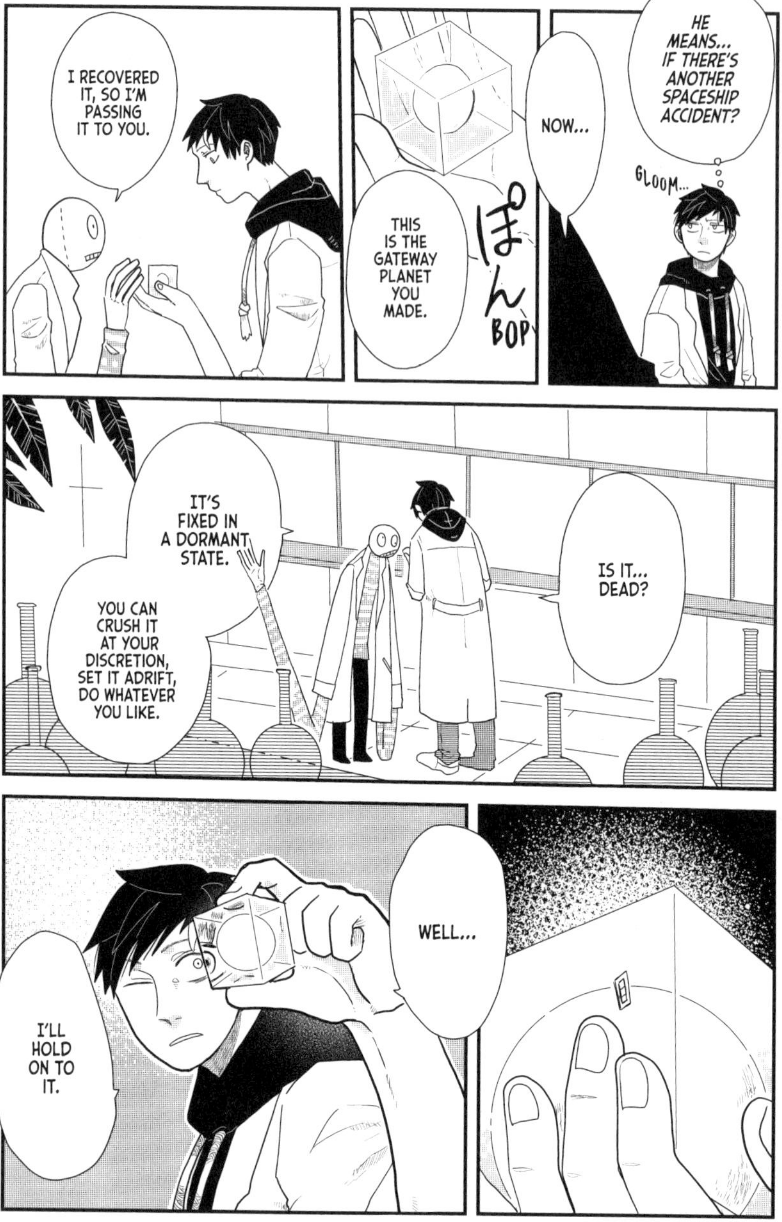
HE MEANS... IF THERE'S ANOTHER SPACESHIP ACCIDENT?
GLOOM...
NOW...
THIS IS THE GATEWAY PLANET YOU MADE.
ぽん
BOP
I RECOVERED IT, SO I'M PASSING IT TO YOU.
IS IT... DEAD?
IT'S FIXED IN A DORMANT STATE.
YOU CAN CRUSH IT AT YOUR DISCRETION, SET IT ADRIFT, DO WHATEVER YOU LIKE.
WELL...
I'LL HOLD ON TO IT.

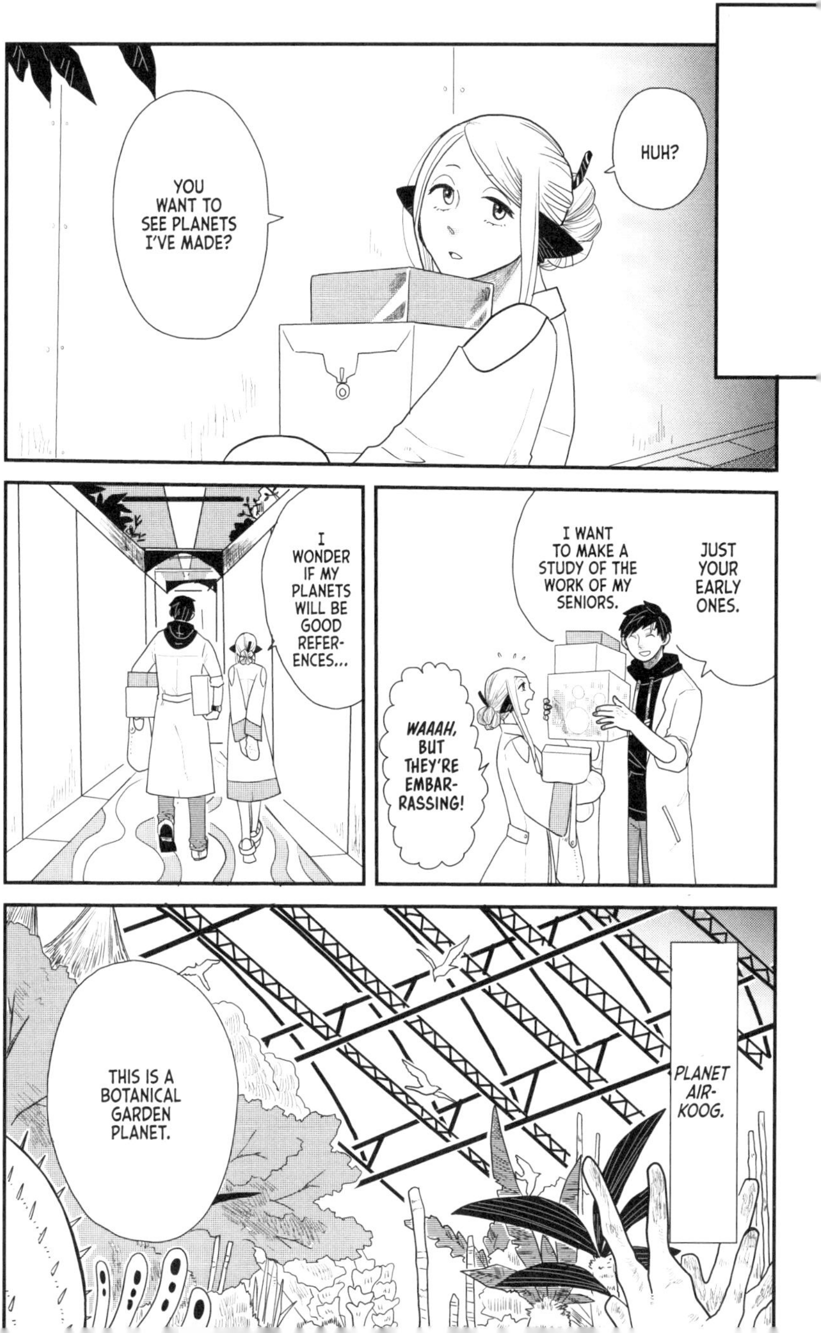
HUH?
YOU WANT TO SEE PLANETS I'VE MADE?
JUST YOUR EARLY ONES.
I WANT TO MAKE A STUDY OF THE WORK OF MY SENIORS.
WAAAH, BUT THEY'RE EMBARRASSING!
I WONDER IF MY PLANETS WILL BE GOOD REFERENCES...
PLANET AIR-KOOG.
THIS IS A BOTANICAL GARDEN PLANET.

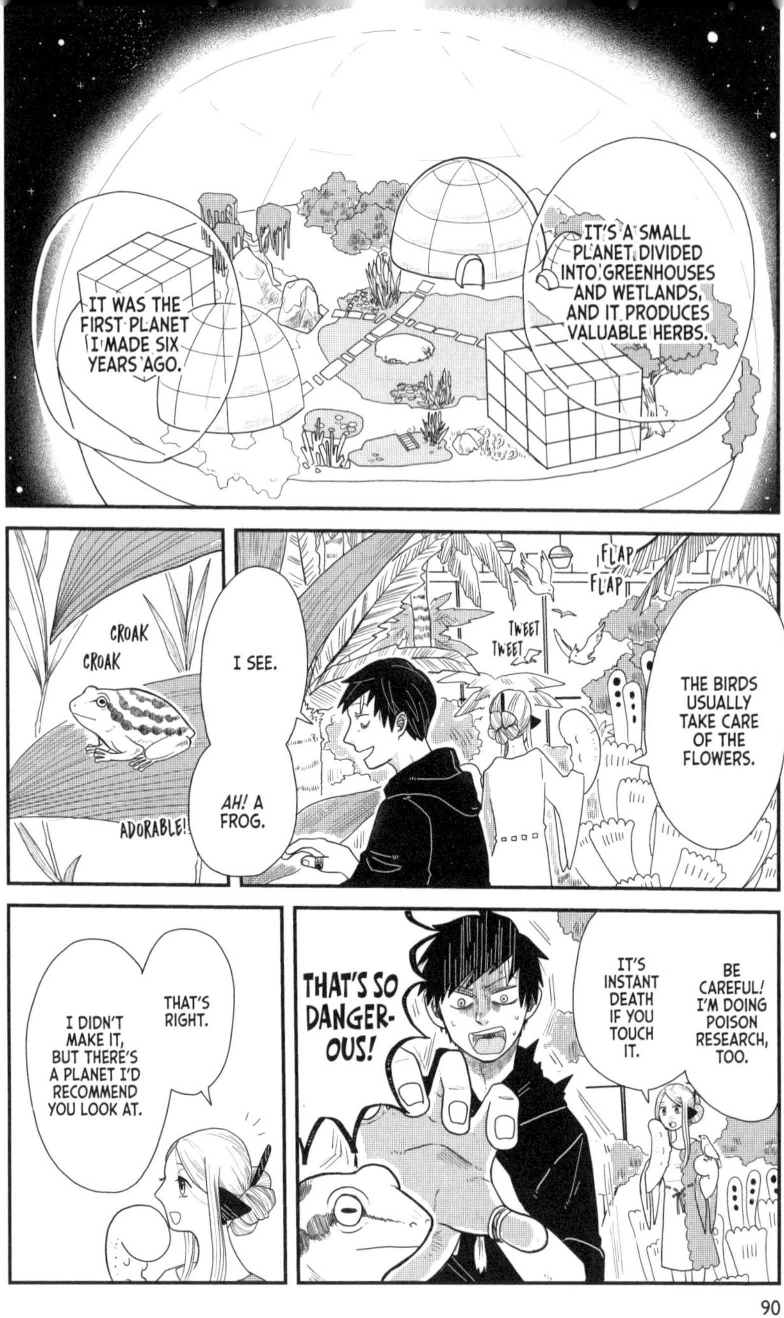
IT'S A SMALL PLANET DIVIDED INTO GREENHOUSES AND WETLANDS, AND IT PRODUCES VALUABLE HERBS.
IT WAS THE FIRST PLANET I MADE SIX YEARS AGO.
FLAP
FLAP
TWEET
TWEET
THE BIRDS USUALLY TAKE CARE OF THE FLOWERS.
I SEE.
AH! A FROG.
CROAK
CROAK
ADORABLE!
BE CAREFUL! I'M DOING POISON RESEARCH, TOO.
IT'S INSTANT DEATH IF YOU TOUCH IT.
THAT'S SO DANGER-OUS!
THAT'S RIGHT.
I DIDN'T MAKE IT, BUT THERE'S A PLANET I'D RECOMMEND YOU LOOK AT.

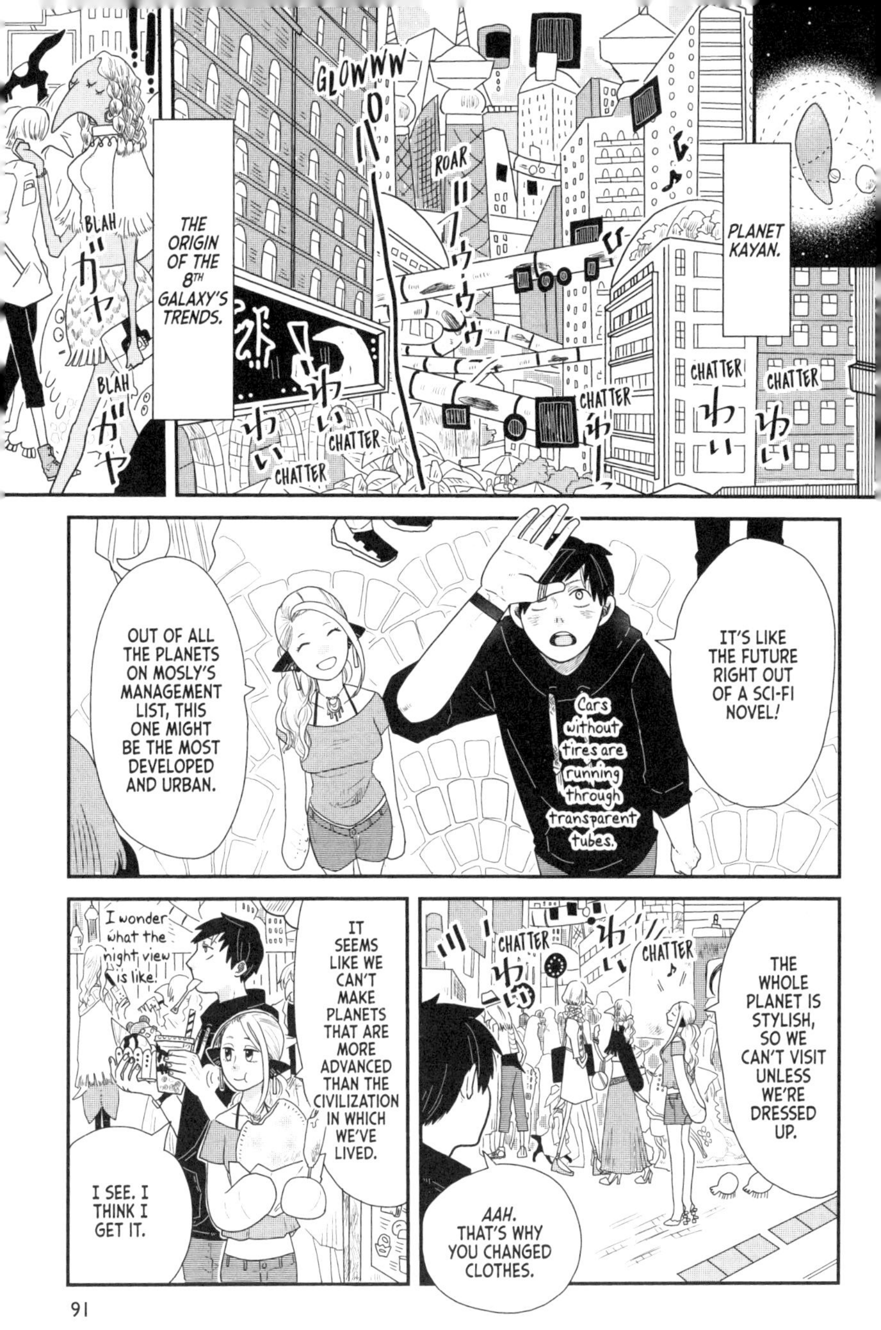
PLANET KAYAN.
CHATTER
CHATTER
CHATTER
ROAR
GLOWWW
CHATTER
CHATTER
THE ORIGIN OF THE 8TH GALAXY'S TRENDS.
BLAH
BLAH
IT'S LIKE THE FUTURE RIGHT OUT OF A SCI-FI NOVEL!
Cars without tires are running through transparent tubes.
OUT OF ALL THE PLANETS ON MOSLY'S MANAGEMENT LIST, THIS ONE MIGHT BE THE MOST DEVELOPED AND URBAN.
THE WHOLE PLANET IS STYLISH, SO WE CAN'T VISIT UNLESS WE'RE DRESSED UP.
CHATTER
CHATTER
AAH. THAT'S WHY YOU CHANGED CLOTHES.
IT SEEMS LIKE WE CAN'T MAKE PLANETS THAT ARE MORE ADVANCED THAN THE CIVILIZATION IN WHICH WE'VE LIVED.
I wonder what the night view is like.
I SEE. I THINK I GET IT.

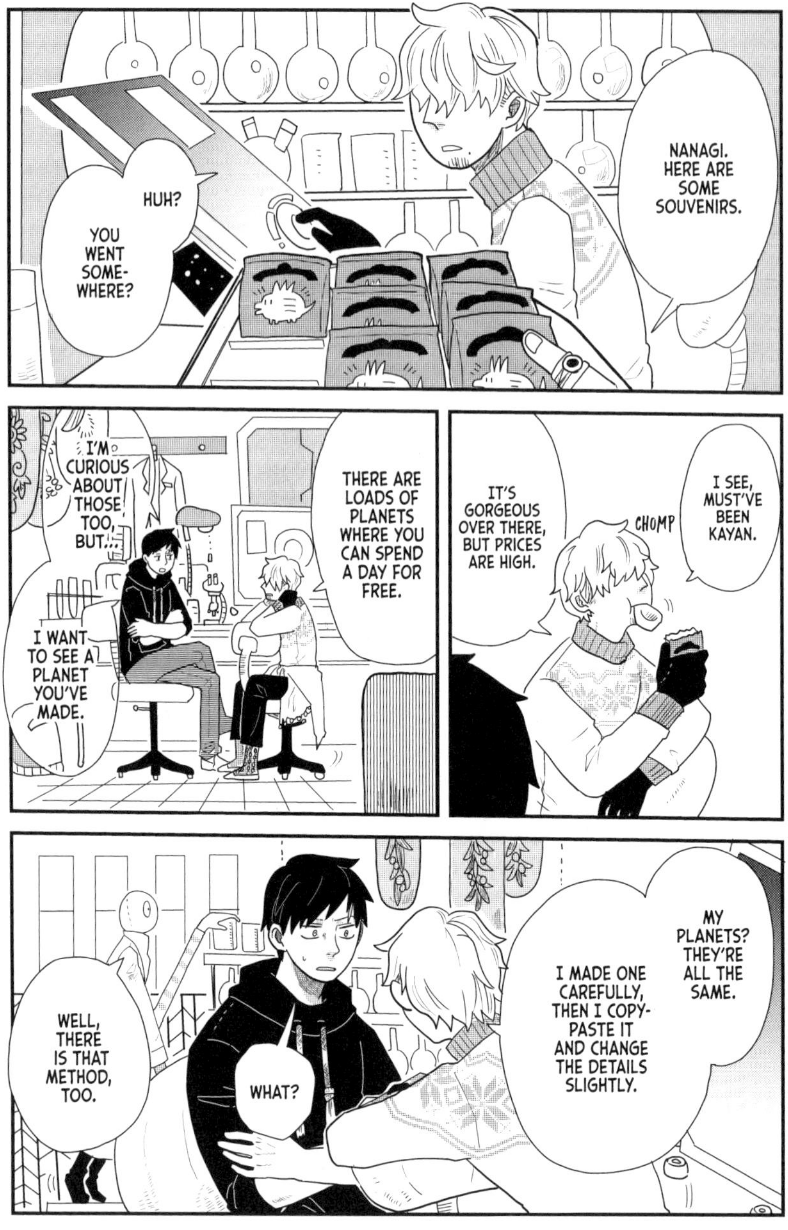
NANAGI. HERE ARE SOME SOUVENIRS.
HUH?
YOU WENT SOME-WHERE?
I SEE, MUST'VE BEEN KAYAN.
CHOMP
IT'S GORGEOUS OVER THERE, BUT PRICES ARE HIGH.
THERE ARE LOADS OF PLANETS WHERE YOU CAN SPEND A DAY FOR FREE.
I'M CURIOUS ABOUT THOSE TOO, BUT...
I WANT TO SEE A PLANET YOU'VE MADE.
MY PLANETS? THEY'RE ALL THE SAME.
I MADE ONE CAREFULLY, THEN I COPY-PASTE IT AND CHANGE THE DETAILS SLIGHTLY.
WHAT?
WELL, THERE IS THAT METHOD, TOO.

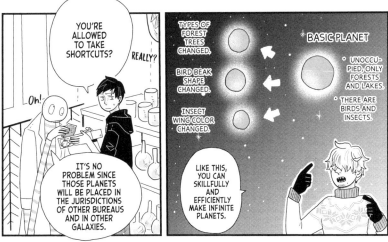

BASIC PLANET
• UNOCCUPIED, ONLY FORESTS AND LAKES.
• THERE ARE BIRDS AND INSECTS.
TYPES OF FOREST TREES CHANGED.
BIRD BEAK SHAPE CHANGED.
INSECT WING COLOR CHANGED.
LIKE THIS, YOU CAN SKILLFULLY AND EFFICIENTLY MAKE INFINITE PLANETS.
YOU'RE ALLOWED TO TAKE SHORTCUTS?
REALLY?
Oh!
IT'S NO PROBLEM SINCE THOSE PLANETS WILL BE PLACED IN THE JURISDICTIONS OF OTHER BUREAUS AND IN OTHER GALAXIES.
WHAT'S A PLANET YOU'D RECOMMEND CHECKING OUT, DIRECTOR?
HUH?
ME?!
THERE IS A 120-TAA-LONG SANDY BEACH ON PLANET NOETEHRA (※1 TAA = 3 KM).
You can pick up shellfish.
THE O-46 SPRING-SUMMER PLANET IS FAMOUS FOR ITS RADEN-LIKE TRADITIONAL CRAFTS.
FALL-WINTER PLANET
SPRING-SUMMER PLANET
THE PLANET KOGAE HOLDS A SHELLFISH EXPO ONCE EVERY YEAR.
SMILE
SMILE
SMILE

※Raden is a decorative technique involving putting thinly sliced mother-of-pearl onto the surface of lacquerware and such to create a beautiful iridescent luster.

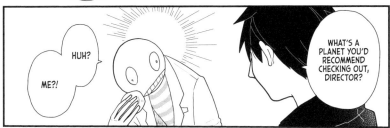

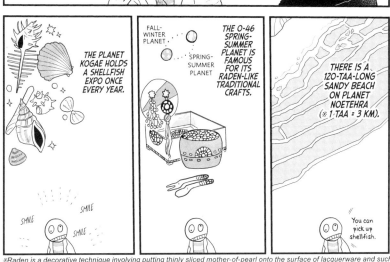

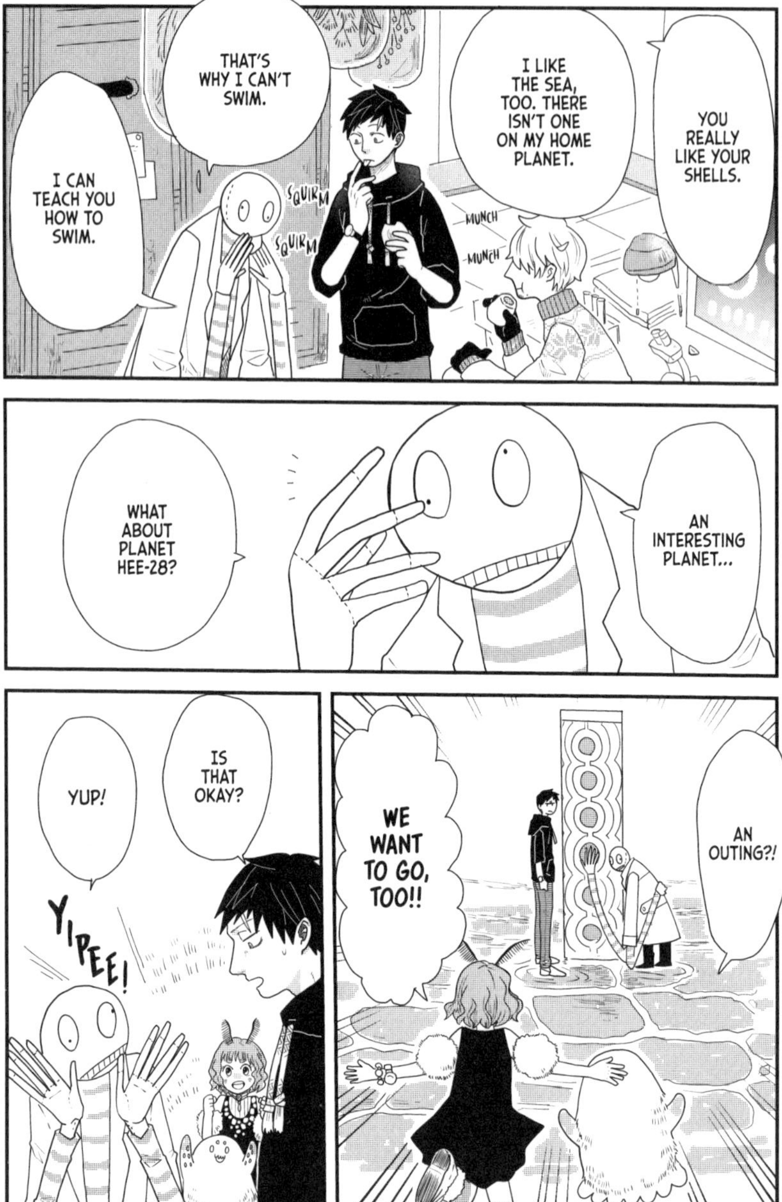
YOU REALLY LIKE YOUR SHELLS.
I LIKE THE SEA, TOO. THERE ISN'T ONE ON MY HOME PLANET.
MUNCH
MUNCH
THAT'S WHY I CAN'T SWIM.
SQUIRM
SQUIRM
I CAN TEACH YOU HOW TO SWIM.
AN INTERESTING PLANET...
WHAT ABOUT PLANET HEE-28?
AN OUTING?!
WE WANT TO GO, TOO!!
IS THAT OKAY?
YUP!
YIPEE!

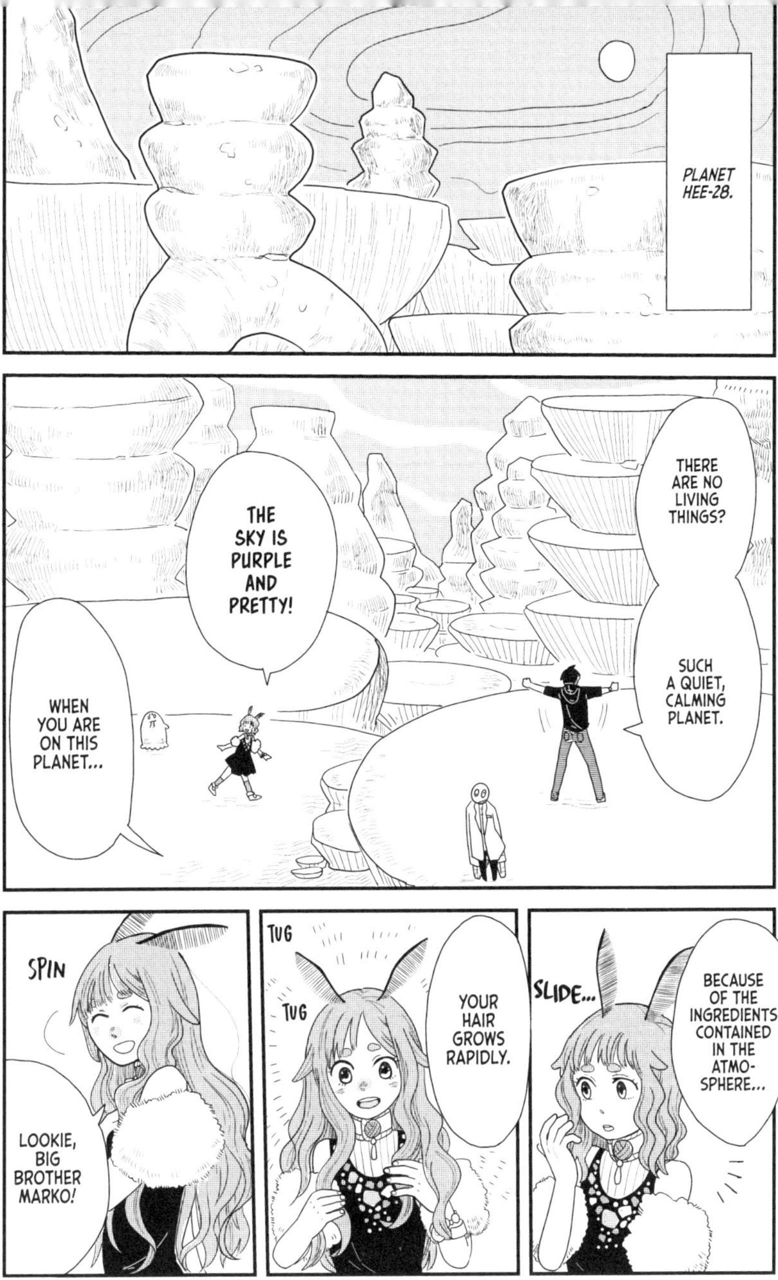
PLANET HEE-28.
THERE ARE NO LIVING THINGS?
SUCH A QUIET, CALMING PLANET.
THE SKY IS PURPLE AND PRETTY!
WHEN YOU ARE ON THIS PLANET...
BECAUSE OF THE INGREDIENTS CONTAINED IN THE ATMOSPHERE...
SLIDE...
YOUR HAIR GROWS RAPIDLY.
TUG
TUG
SPIN
LOOKIE, BIG BROTHER MARKO!

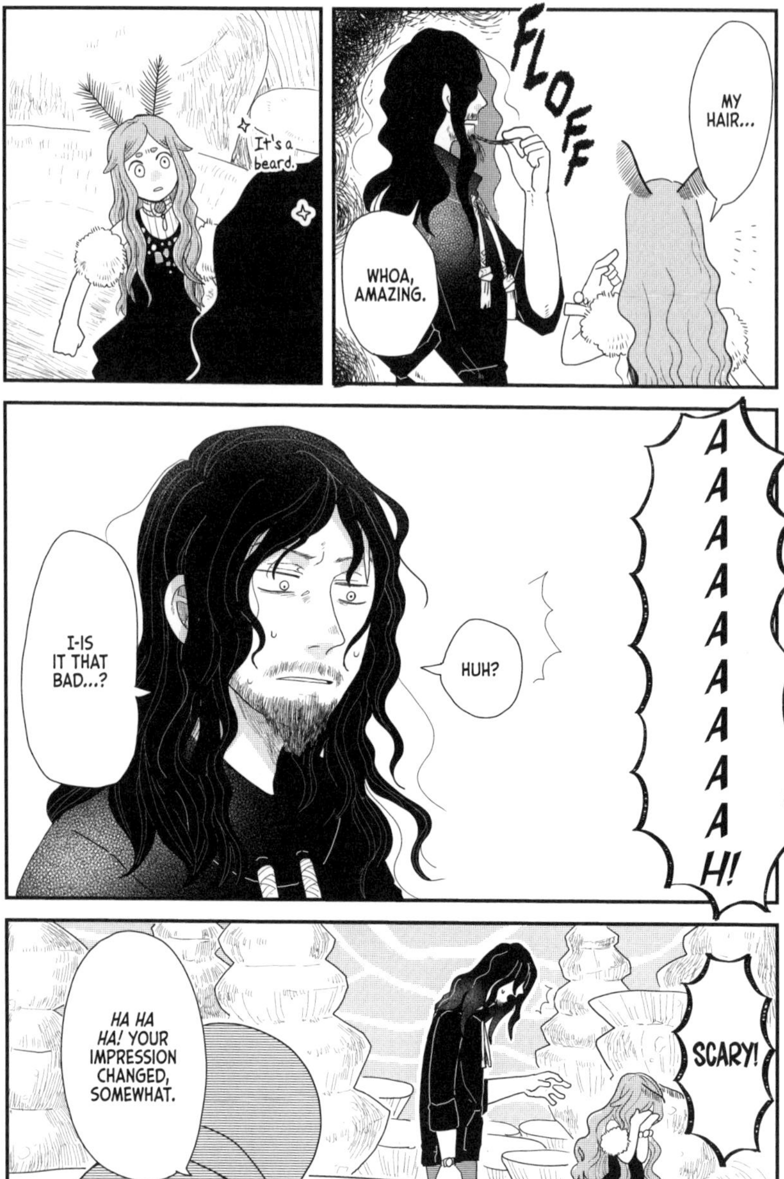
MY HAIR...
FLOFF
WHOA, AMAZING.
It's a beard.
AAAAAAAAAH!
HUH?
I-IS IT THAT BAD...?
SCARY!
HA HA HA! YOUR IMPRESSION CHANGED, SOMEWHAT.

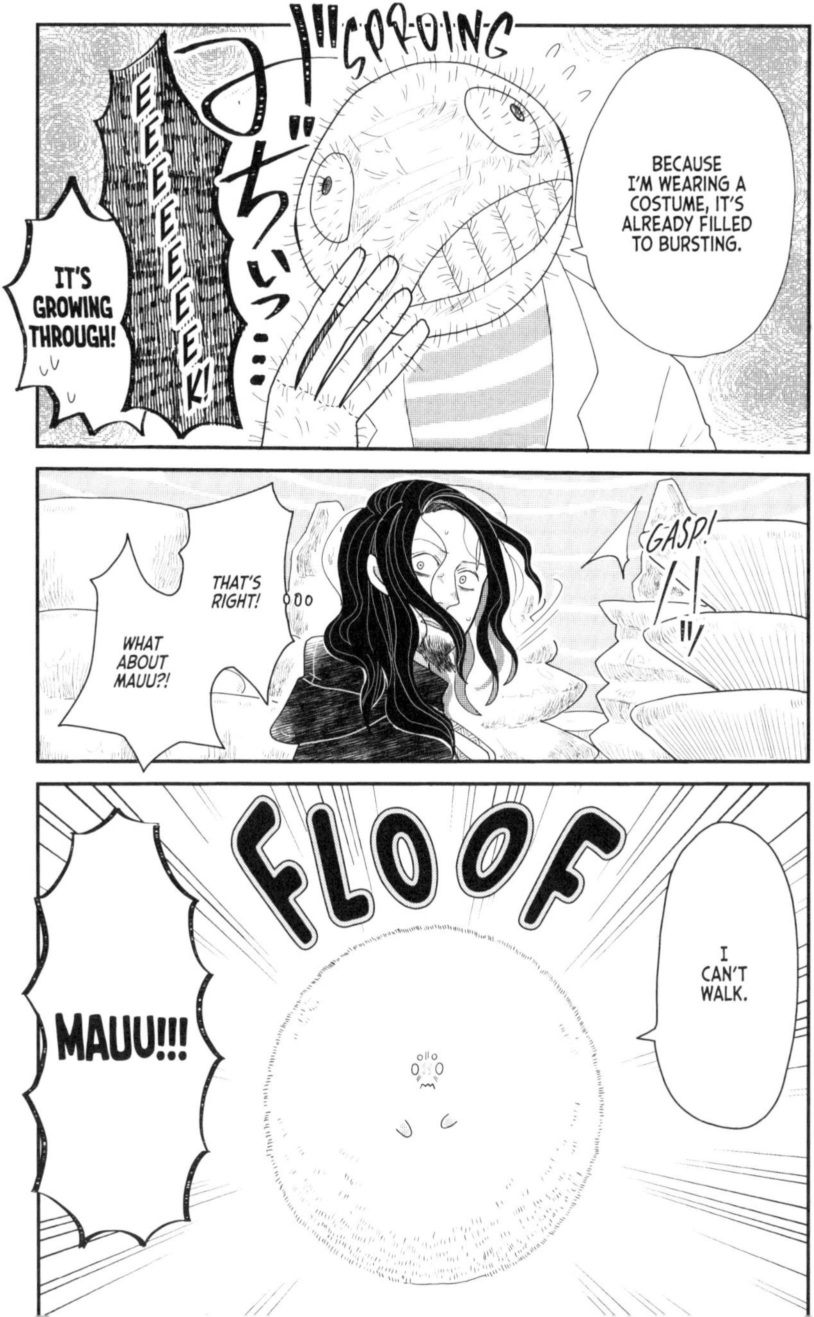
BECAUSE I'M WEARING A COSTUME, IT'S ALREADY FILLED TO BURSTING.
SPROING
EEEEEEEEK!
IT'S GROWING THROUGH!
GASP!
THAT'S RIGHT!
WHAT ABOUT MAUU?!
I CAN'T WALK.
FLOOF
MAUU!!!

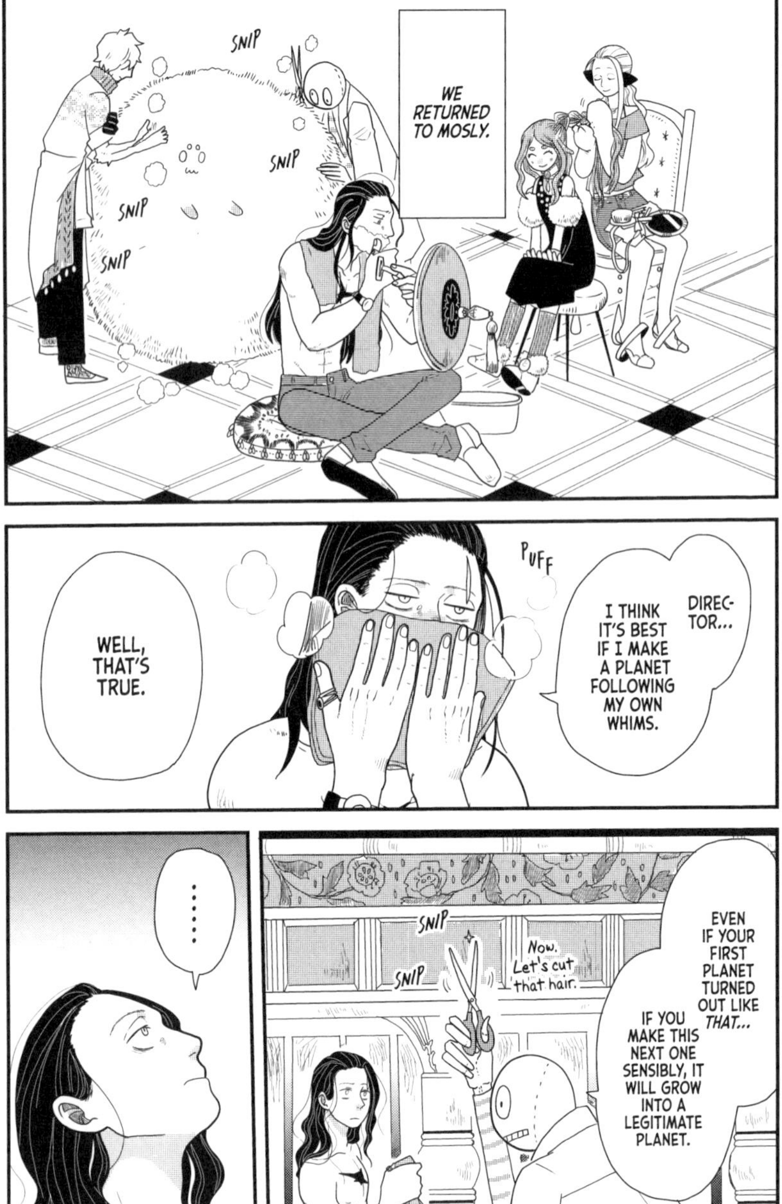
WE RETURNED TO MOSLY.
SNIP
SNIP
SNIP
SNIP
DIRECTOR...
I THINK IT'S BEST IF I MAKE A PLANET FOLLOWING MY OWN WHIMS.
PUFF
WELL, THAT'S TRUE.
EVEN IF YOUR FIRST PLANET TURNED OUT LIKE *THAT*...
IF YOU MAKE THIS NEXT ONE SENSIBLY, IT WILL GROW INTO A LEGITIMATE PLANET.
Now. Let's cut that hair.
SNIP
SNIP
......

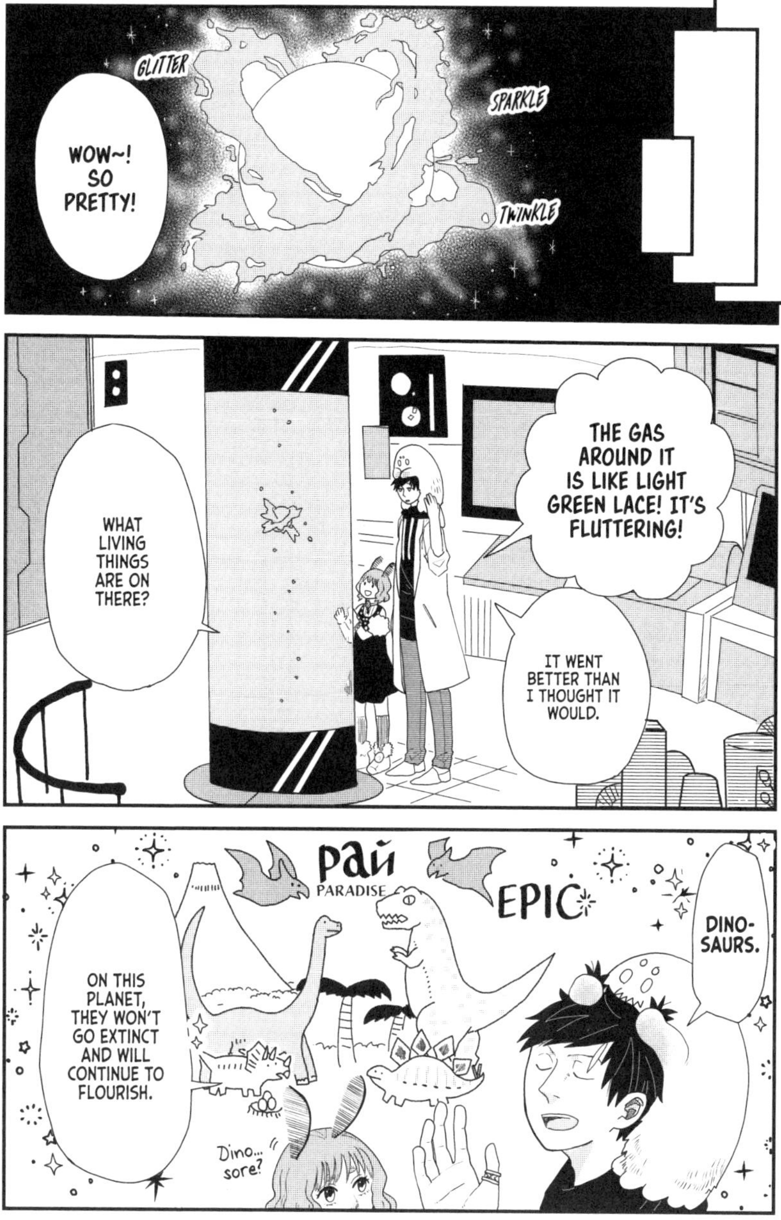
SPARKLE
GLITTER
TWINKLE
WOW~! SO PRETTY!
THE GAS AROUND IT IS LIKE LIGHT GREEN LACE! IT'S FLUTTERING!
IT WENT BETTER THAN I THOUGHT IT WOULD.
WHAT LIVING THINGS ARE ON THERE?
DINO-SAURS.
EPIC
Paй
PARADISE
ON THIS PLANET, THEY WON'T GO EXTINCT AND WILL CONTINUE TO FLOURISH.
Dino... sore?

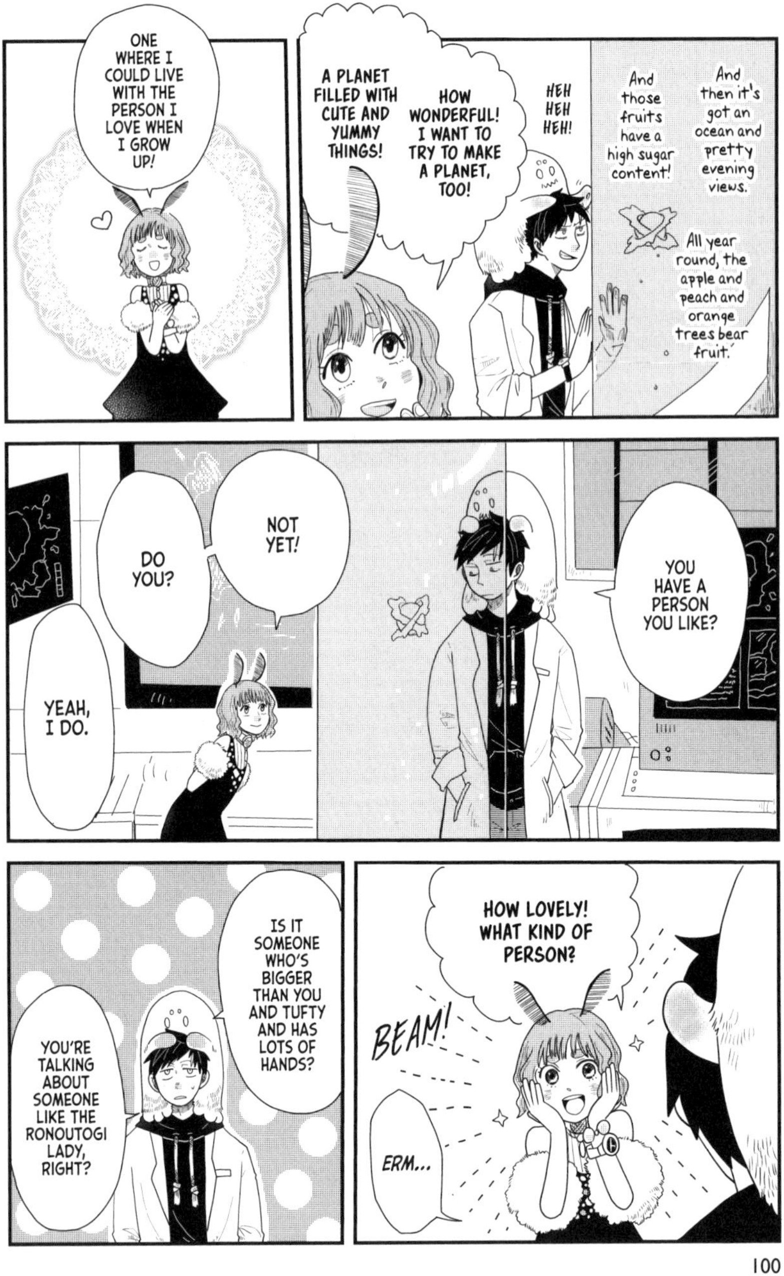
And then it's got an ocean and pretty evening views.
And those fruits have a high sugar content!
All year round, the apple and peach and orange trees bear fruit.
HEH HEH HEH!
HOW WONDERFUL! I WANT TO TRY TO MAKE A PLANET, TOO!
A PLANET FILLED WITH CUTE AND YUMMY THINGS!
ONE WHERE I COULD LIVE WITH THE PERSON I LOVE WHEN I GROW UP!
YOU HAVE A PERSON YOU LIKE?
NOT YET!
DO YOU?
YEAH, I DO.
HOW LOVELY! WHAT KIND OF PERSON?
BEAM!
ERM...
IS IT SOMEONE WHO'S BIGGER THAN YOU AND TUFTY AND HAS LOTS OF HANDS?
YOU'RE TALKING ABOUT SOMEONE LIKE THE RONOUTOGI LADY, RIGHT?

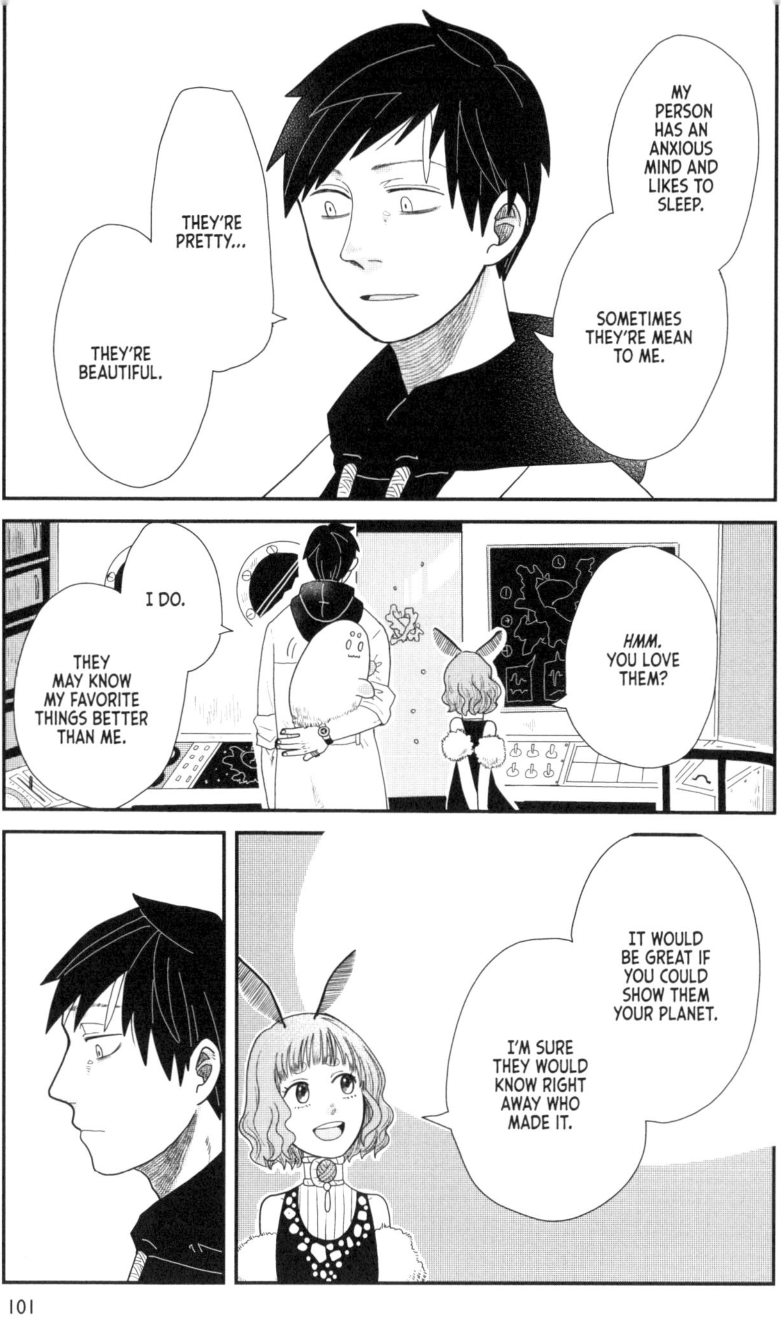
MY PERSON HAS AN ANXIOUS MIND AND LIKES TO SLEEP.
SOMETIMES THEY'RE MEAN TO ME.
THEY'RE PRETTY...
THEY'RE BEAUTIFUL.
HMM. YOU LOVE THEM?
I DO.
THEY MAY KNOW MY FAVORITE THINGS BETTER THAN ME.
IT WOULD BE GREAT IF YOU COULD SHOW THEM YOUR PLANET.
I'M SURE THEY WOULD KNOW RIGHT AWAY WHO MADE IT.

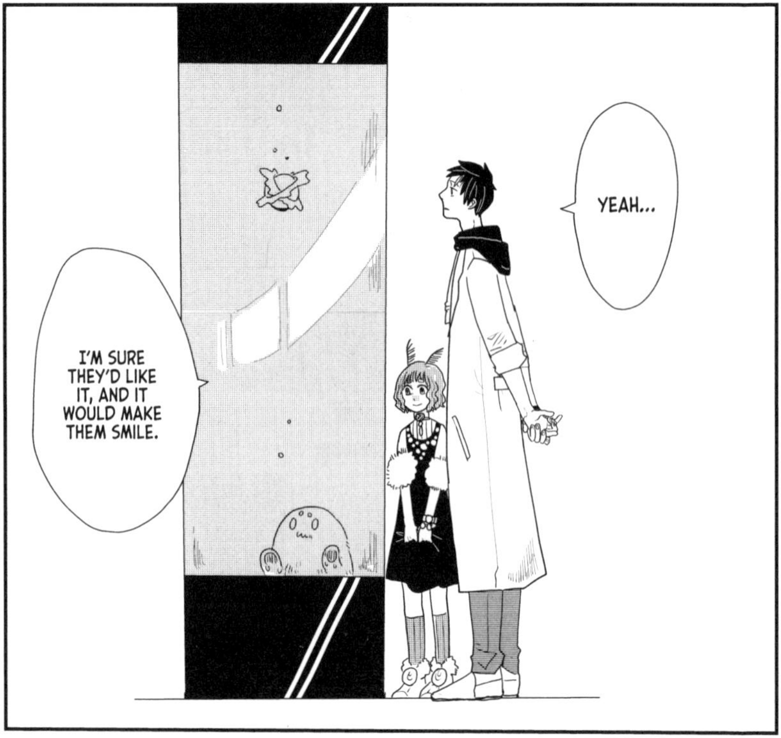
YEAH...
I'M SURE THEY'D LIKE IT, AND IT WOULD MAKE THEM SMILE.

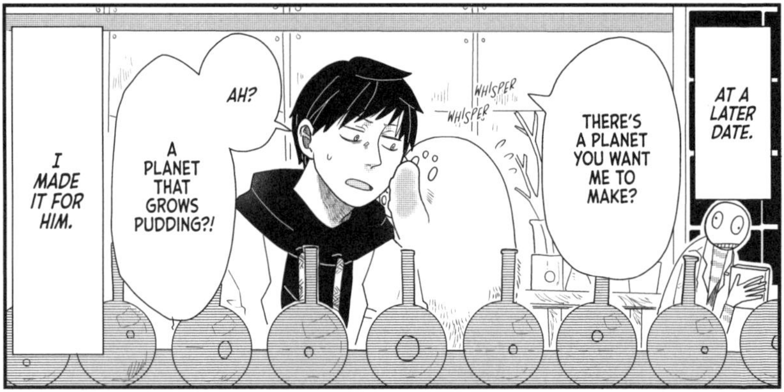
AT A LATER DATE.
THERE'S A PLANET YOU WANT ME TO MAKE?
WHISPER
WHISPER
AH? A PLANET THAT GROWS PUDDING?!
I MADE IT FOR HIM.

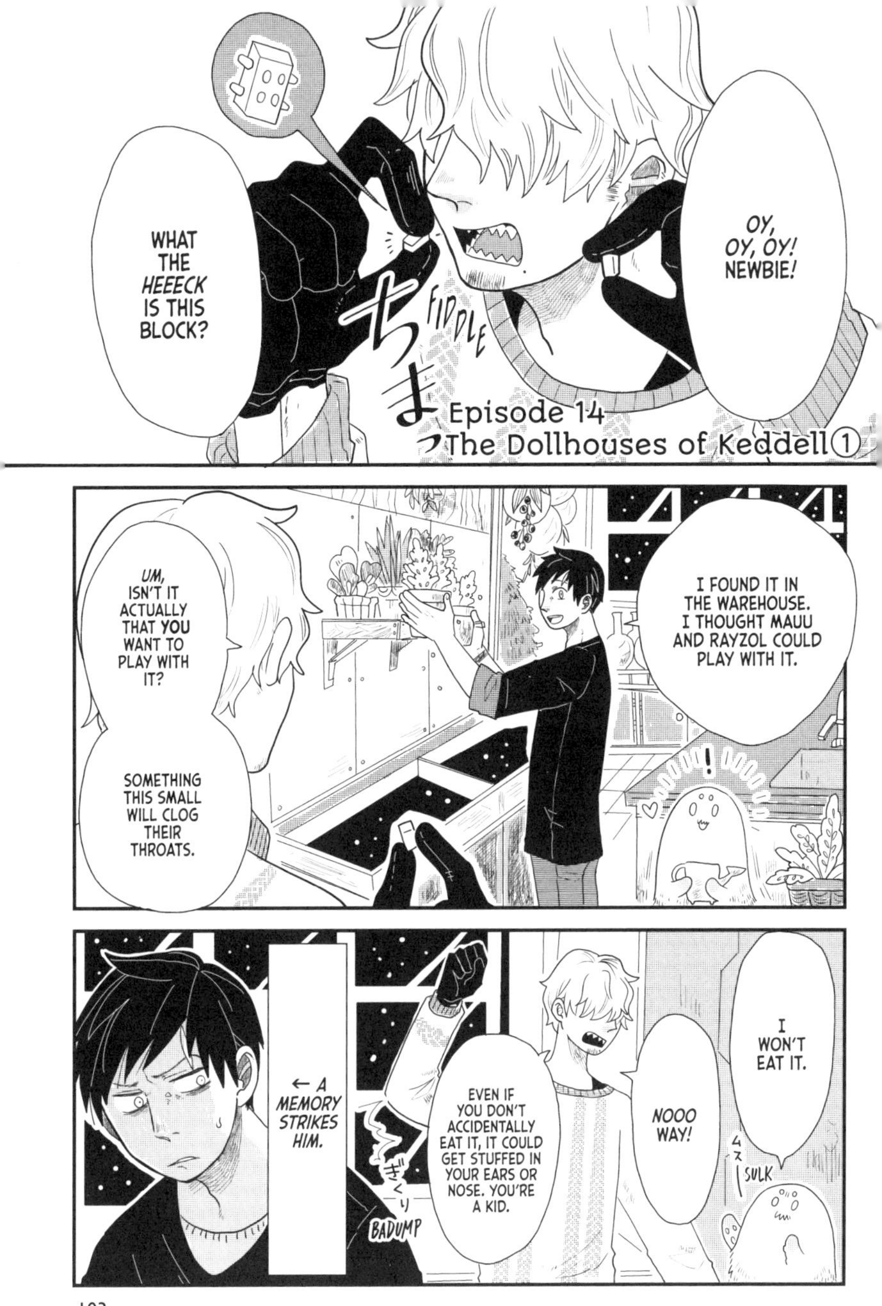
OY, OY, OY! NEWBIE!
WHAT THE *HEEECK* IS THIS BLOCK?
FIDDLE
Episode 14
The Dollhouses of Keddell ①
I FOUND IT IN THE WAREHOUSE. I THOUGHT MAUU AND RAYZOL COULD PLAY WITH IT.
UM, ISN'T IT ACTUALLY THAT **YOU** WANT TO PLAY WITH IT?
SOMETHING THIS SMALL WILL CLOG THEIR THROATS.
I WON'T EAT IT.
NOOO WAY!
SULK
EVEN IF YOU DON'T ACCIDENTALLY EAT IT, IT COULD GET STUFFED IN YOUR EARS OR NOSE. YOU'RE A KID.
BADUMP
← *A MEMORY STRIKES HIM.*

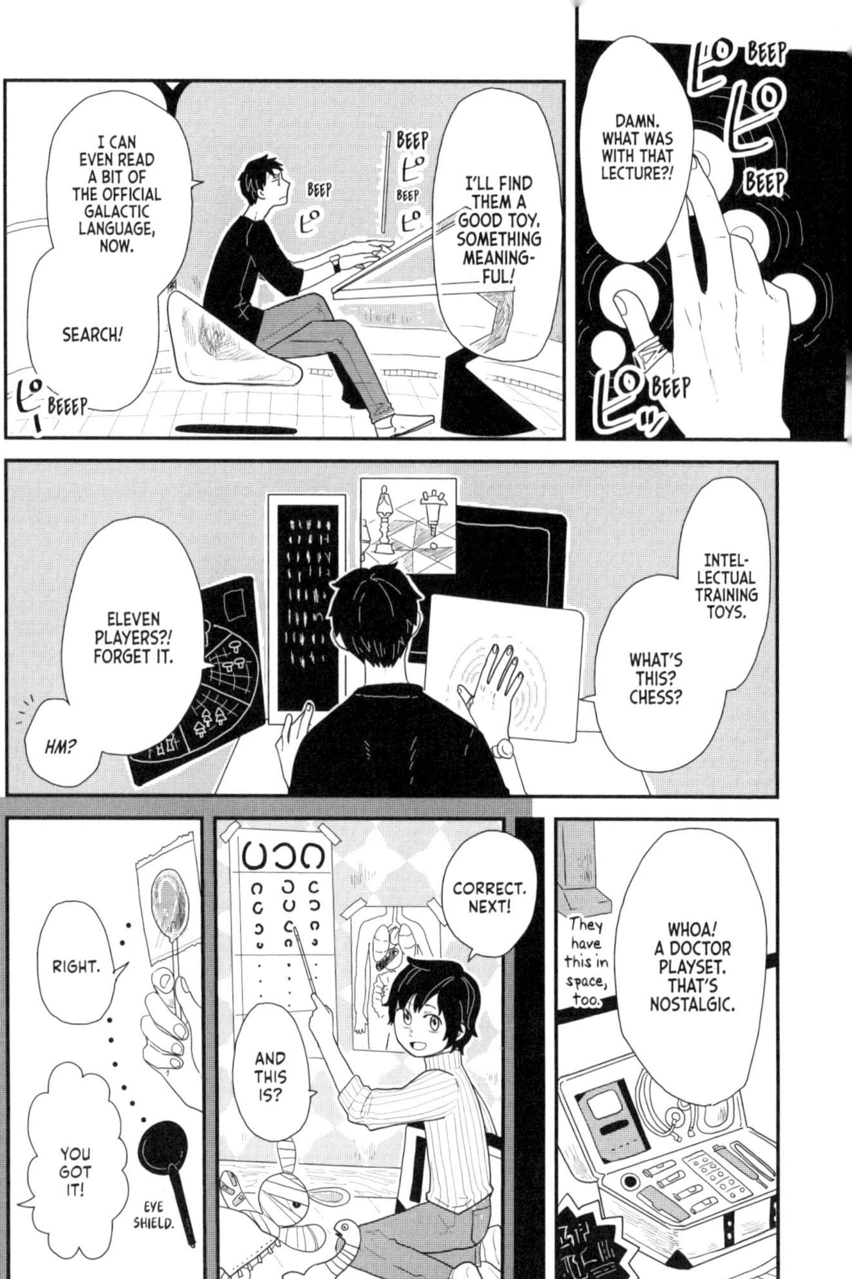

ピ BEEP
DAMN. WHAT WAS WITH THAT LECTURE?!
ピ BEEP
ピッ BEEP
I'LL FIND THEM A GOOD TOY. SOMETHING MEANING-FUL!
BEEP ピ
BEEP ピ
BEEP ピ
I CAN EVEN READ A BIT OF THE OFFICIAL GALACTIC LANGUAGE, NOW.
SEARCH!
ピー BEEEP
INTEL-LECTUAL TRAINING TOYS.
WHAT'S THIS? CHESS?
ELEVEN PLAYERS?! FORGET IT.
HM?
WHOA! A DOCTOR PLAYSET. THAT'S NOSTALGIC.
They have this in space, too.
CORRECT. NEXT!
AND THIS IS?
RIGHT.
YOU GOT IT!
EYE SHIELD.

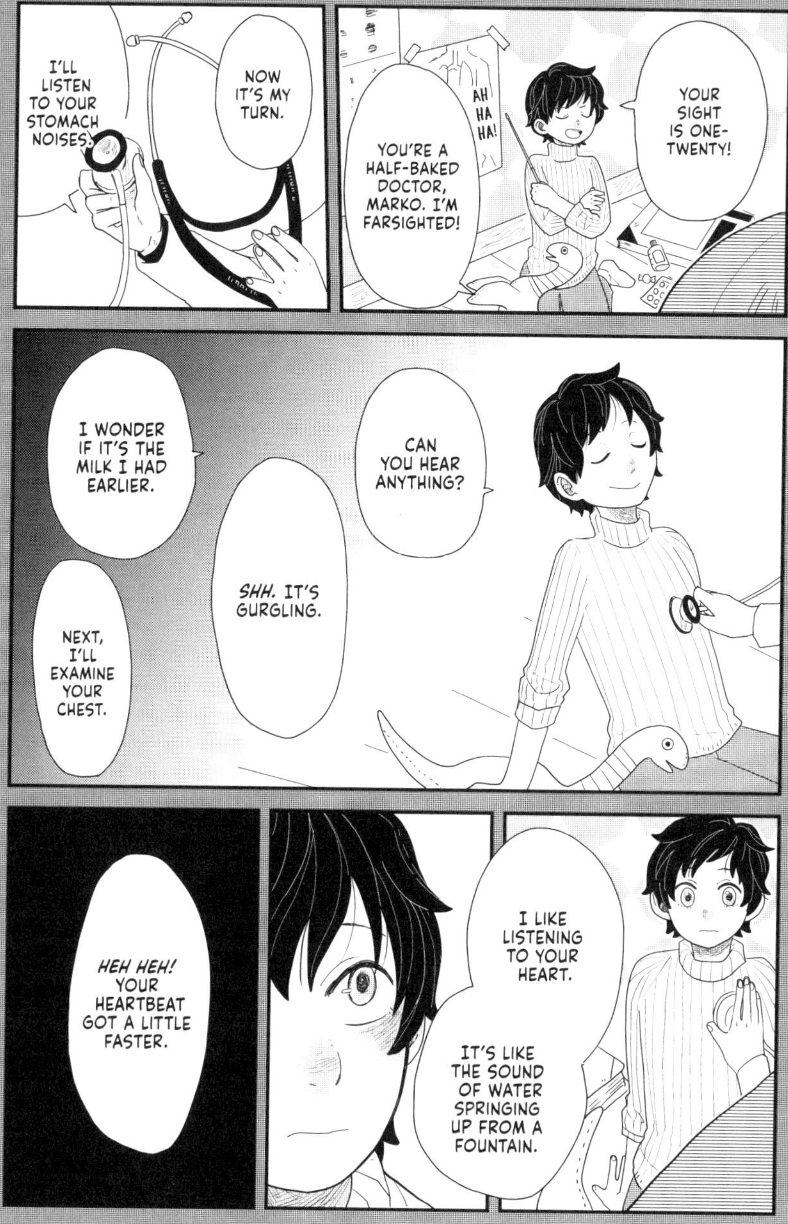
YOUR SIGHT IS ONE-TWENTY!
AH HA HA!
YOU'RE A HALF-BAKED DOCTOR, MARKO. I'M FARSIGHTED!
NOW IT'S MY TURN.
I'LL LISTEN TO YOUR STOMACH NOISES.
CAN YOU HEAR ANYTHING?
SHH. IT'S GURGLING.
I WONDER IF IT'S THE MILK I HAD EARLIER.
NEXT, I'LL EXAMINE YOUR CHEST.
I LIKE LISTENING TO YOUR HEART.
IT'S LIKE THE SOUND OF WATER SPRINGING UP FROM A FOUNTAIN.
HEH HEH! YOUR HEARTBEAT GOT A LITTLE FASTER.

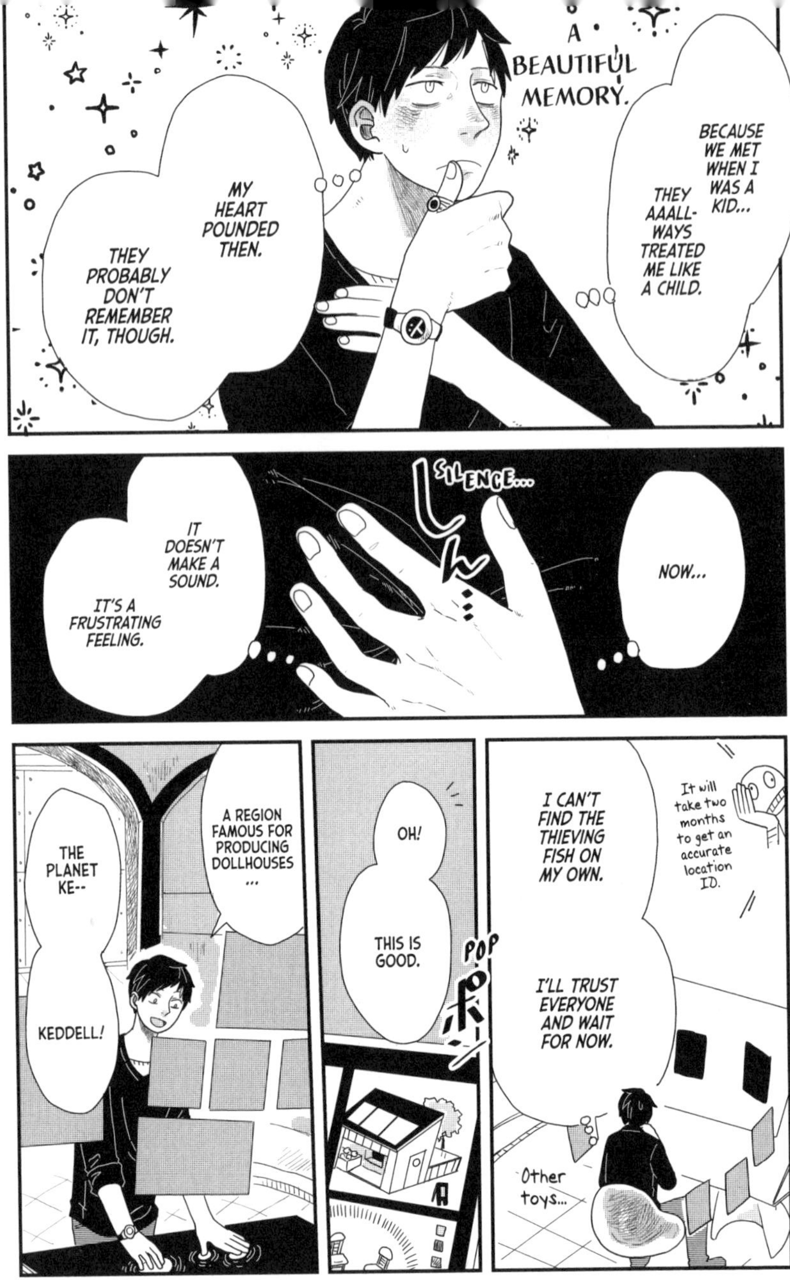
BECAUSE WE MET WHEN I WAS A KID...
THEY AAALL-WAYS TREATED ME LIKE A CHILD.
A BEAUTIFUL MEMORY.
MY HEART POUNDED THEN.
THEY PROBABLY DON'T REMEMBER IT, THOUGH.
NOW...
SILENCE...
IT DOESN'T MAKE A SOUND.
IT'S A FRUSTRATING FEELING.
I CAN'T FIND THE THIEVING FISH ON MY OWN.
It will take two months to get an accurate location ID.
I'LL TRUST EVERYONE AND WAIT FOR NOW.
Other toys...
OH!
THIS IS GOOD.
POP
A REGION FAMOUS FOR PRODUCING DOLLHOUSES...
THE PLANET KE--
KEDDELL!

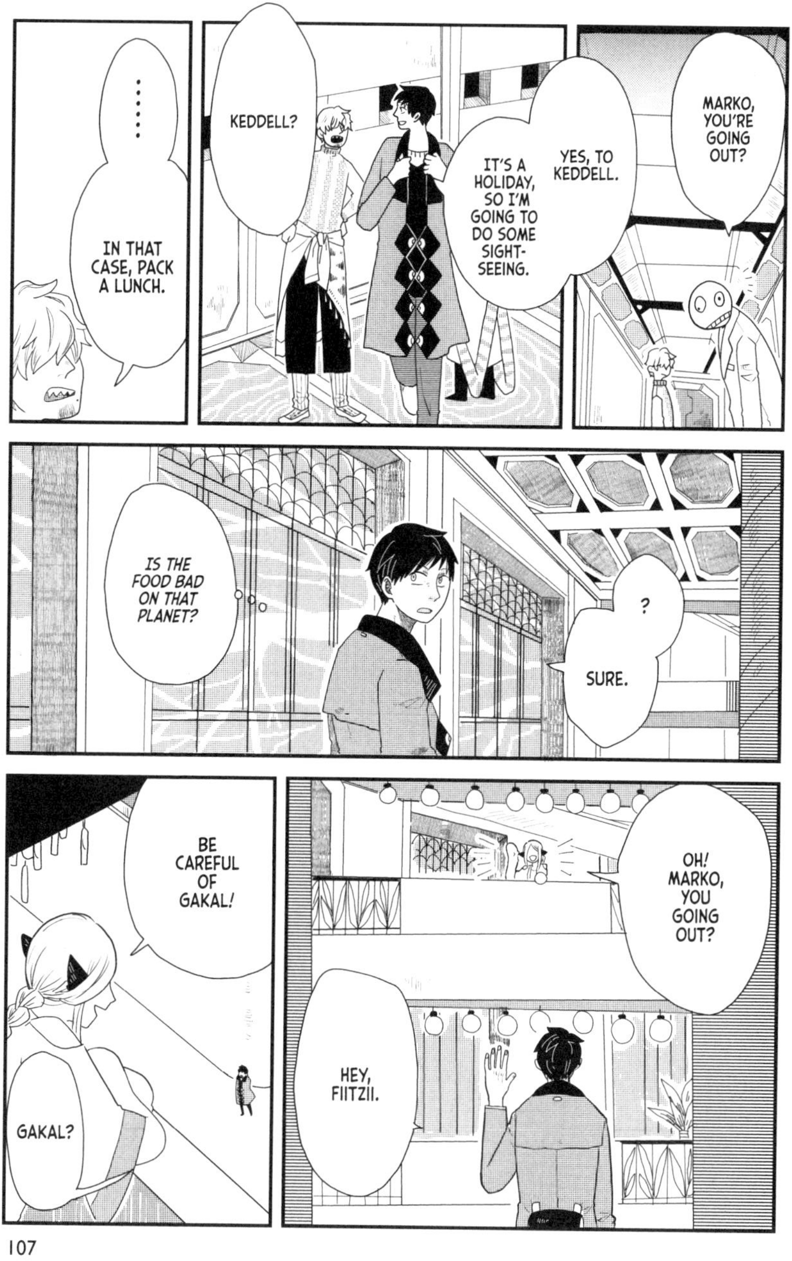
MARKO, YOU'RE GOING OUT?
YES, TO KEDDELL.
IT'S A HOLIDAY, SO I'M GOING TO DO SOME SIGHT-SEEING.
KEDDELL?
......
IN THAT CASE, PACK A LUNCH.
IS THE FOOD BAD ON THAT PLANET?
?
SURE.
OH! MARKO, YOU GOING OUT?
HEY, FIITZII.
BE CAREFUL OF GAKAL!
GAKAL?

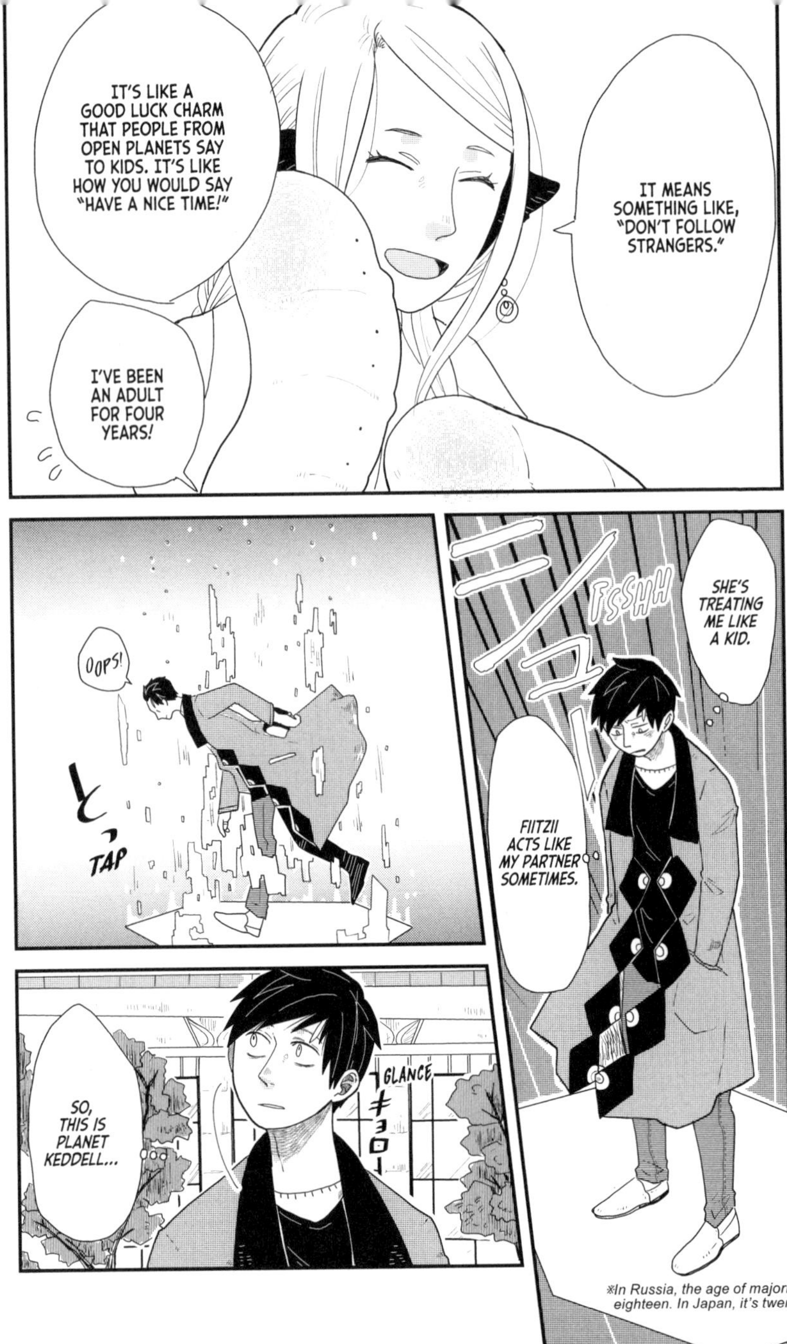
IT MEANS SOMETHING LIKE, "DON'T FOLLOW STRANGERS."
IT'S LIKE A GOOD LUCK CHARM THAT PEOPLE FROM OPEN PLANETS SAY TO KIDS. IT'S LIKE HOW YOU WOULD SAY "HAVE A NICE TIME!"
I'VE BEEN AN ADULT FOR FOUR YEARS!
FSSHH
SHE'S TREATING ME LIKE A KID.
FIITZII ACTS LIKE MY PARTNER SOMETIMES.
OOPS!
TAP
SO, THIS IS PLANET KEDDELL...
GLANCE
※In Russia, the age of majority is eighteen. In Japan, it's twenty.

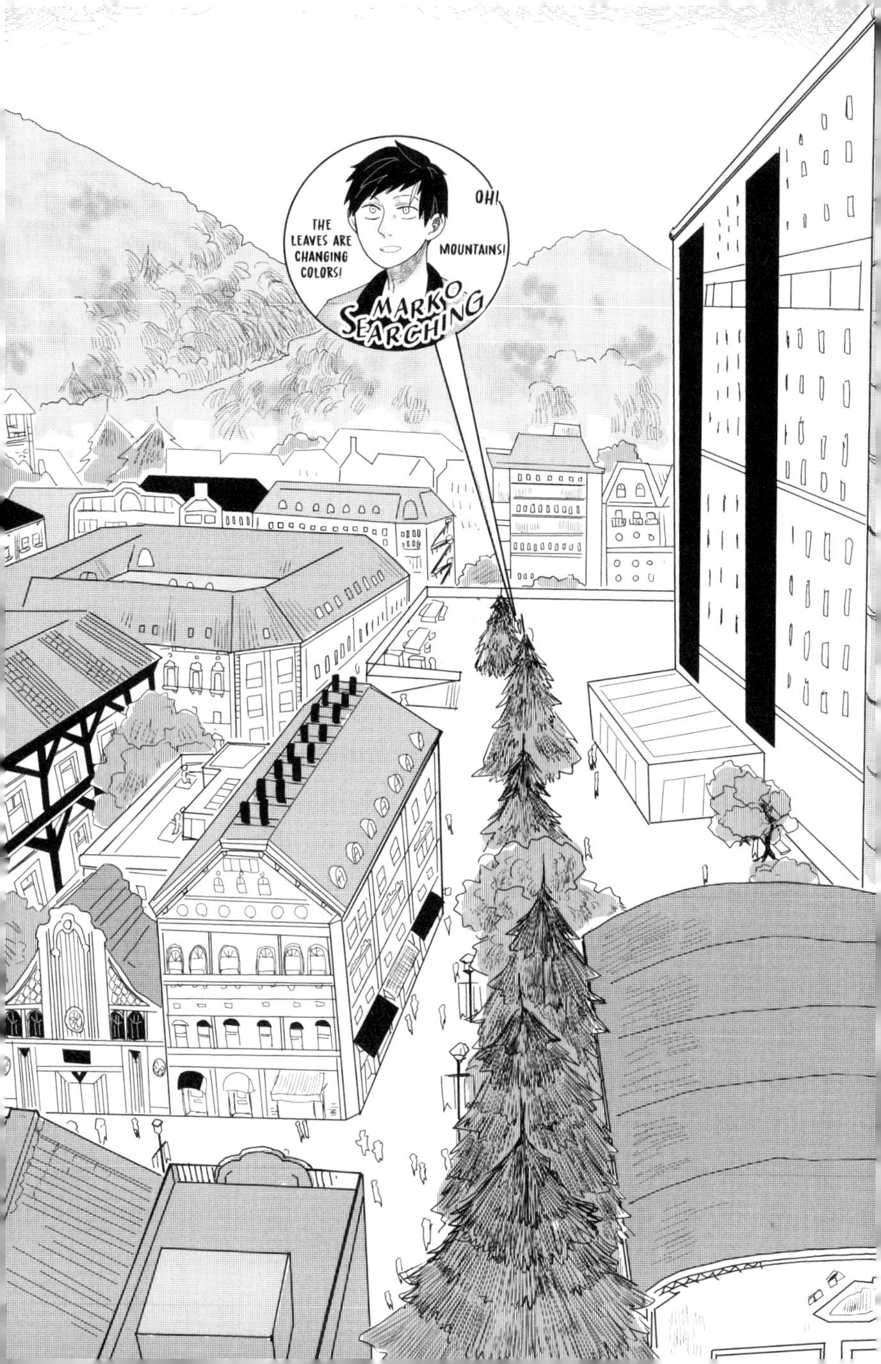
OH!
MOUNTAINS!
THE LEAVES ARE CHANGING COLORS!
MARKO SEARCHING

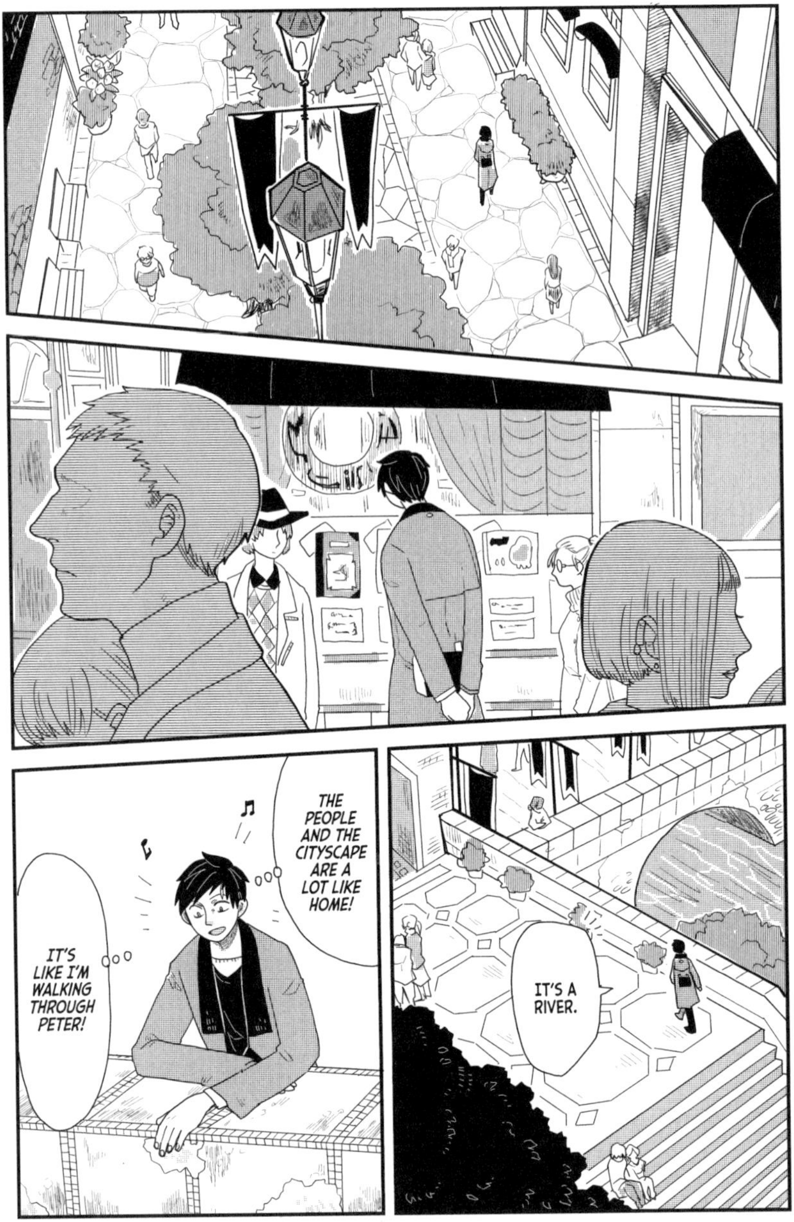
IT'S A RIVER.
THE PEOPLE AND THE CITYSCAPE ARE A LOT LIKE HOME!
IT'S LIKE I'M WALKING THROUGH PETER!

※Peter is a nickname for St. Petersburg.

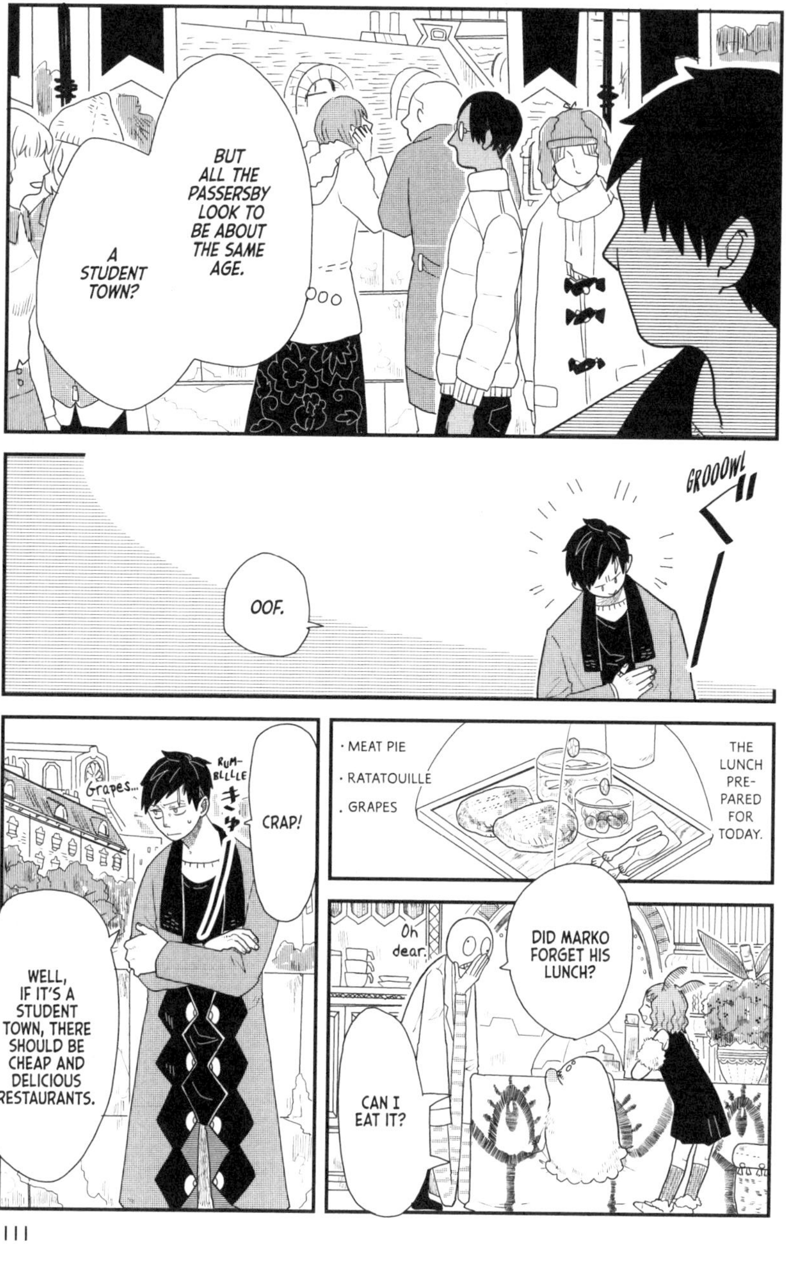
BUT ALL THE PASSERSBY LOOK TO BE ABOUT THE SAME AGE.
A STUDENT TOWN?
GROOOWL
OOF.
THE LUNCH PRE-PARED FOR TODAY.
· MEAT PIE
· RATATOUILLE
. GRAPES
DID MARKO FORGET HIS LUNCH?
Oh dear.
CAN I EAT IT?
CRAP!
RUM-BLLLLE
Grapes...
WELL, IF IT'S A STUDENT TOWN, THERE SHOULD BE CHEAP AND DELICIOUS RESTAURANTS.

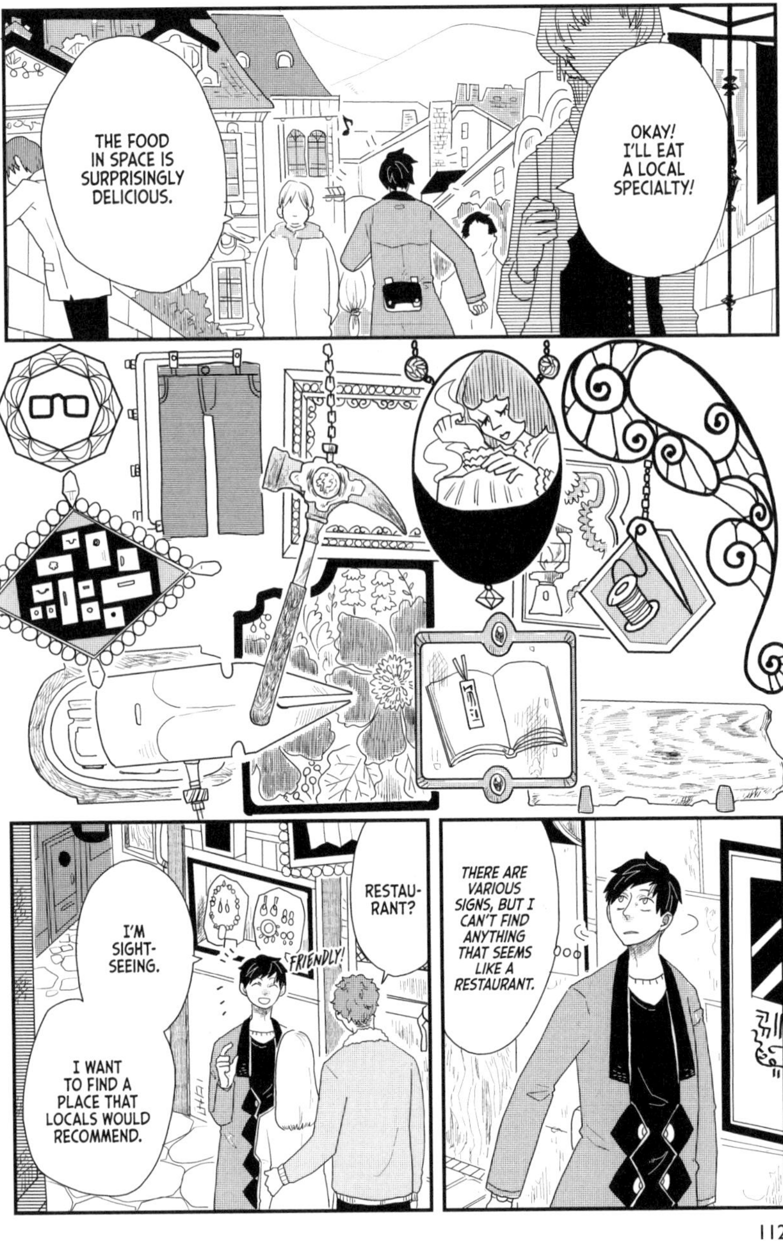
OKAY! I'LL EAT A LOCAL SPECIALTY!
THE FOOD IN SPACE IS SURPRISINGLY DELICIOUS.
THERE ARE VARIOUS SIGNS, BUT I CAN'T FIND ANYTHING THAT SEEMS LIKE A RESTAURANT.
RESTAU-RANT?
FRIENDLY!
I'M SIGHT-SEEING.
I WANT TO FIND A PLACE THAT LOCALS WOULD RECOMMEND.

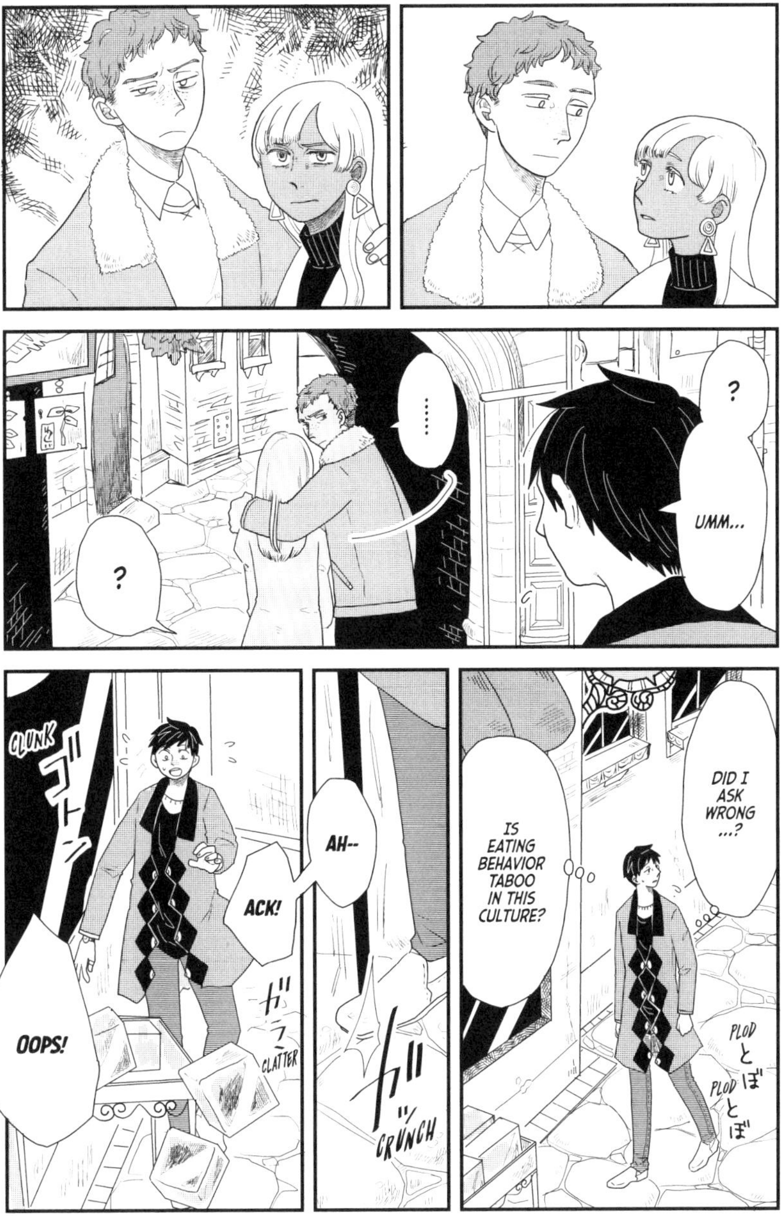
?
UMM...
......
?
DID I ASK WRONG ...?
IS EATING BEHAVIOR TABOO IN THIS CULTURE?
PLOD とぼ
PLOD とぼ
AH--
ガッ
CRUNCH
ガラ
CLATTER
ACK!
ゴトン
CLUNK
OOPS!

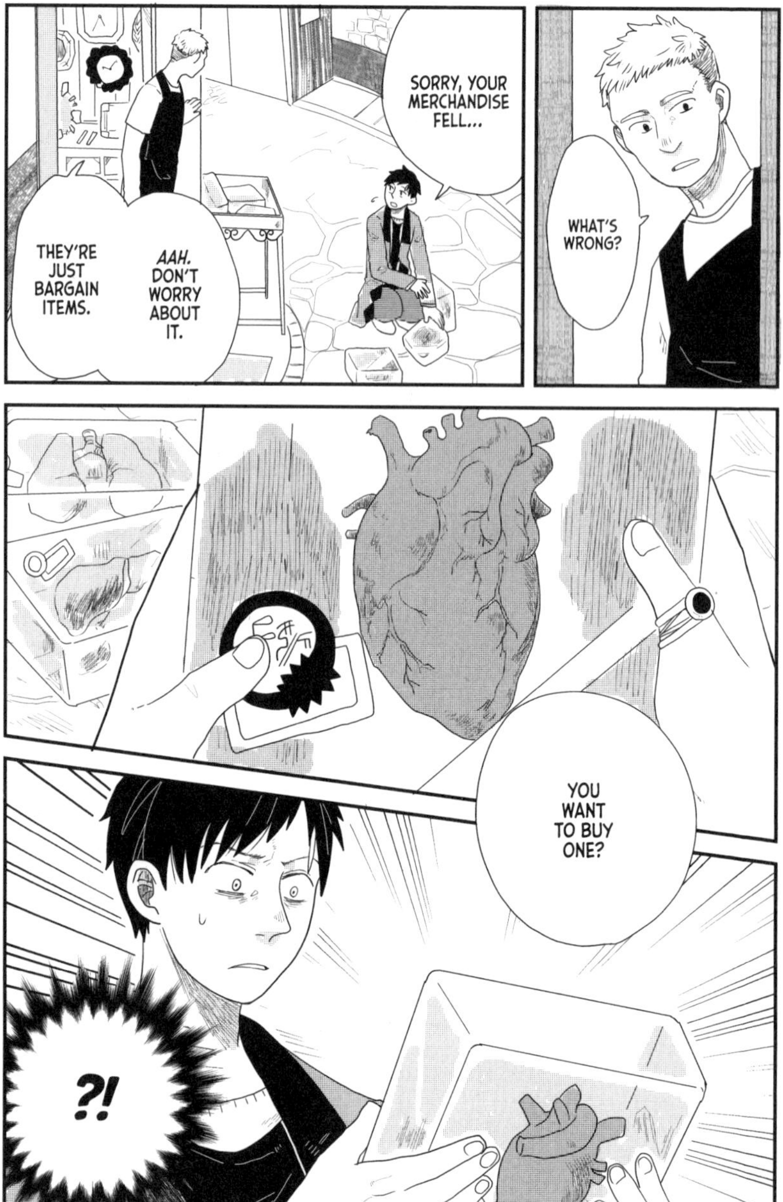
WHAT'S WRONG?
SORRY, YOUR MERCHANDISE FELL...
AAH. DON'T WORRY ABOUT IT.
THEY'RE JUST BARGAIN ITEMS.
YOU WANT TO BUY ONE?
?!

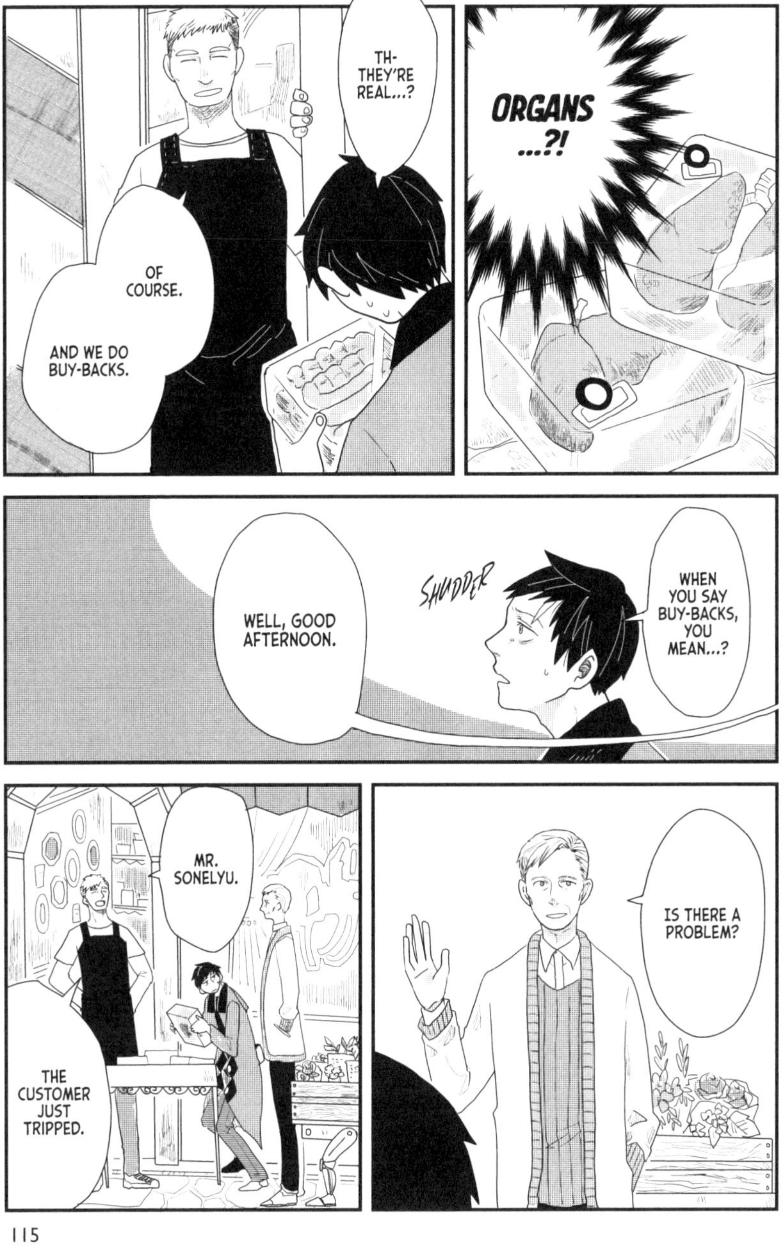
ORGANS ...?!
TH- THEY'RE REAL...?
OF COURSE.
AND WE DO BUY-BACKS.
WHEN YOU SAY BUY-BACKS, YOU MEAN...?
SHUDDER
WELL, GOOD AFTERNOON.
IS THERE A PROBLEM?
MR. SONELYU.
THE CUSTOMER JUST TRIPPED.

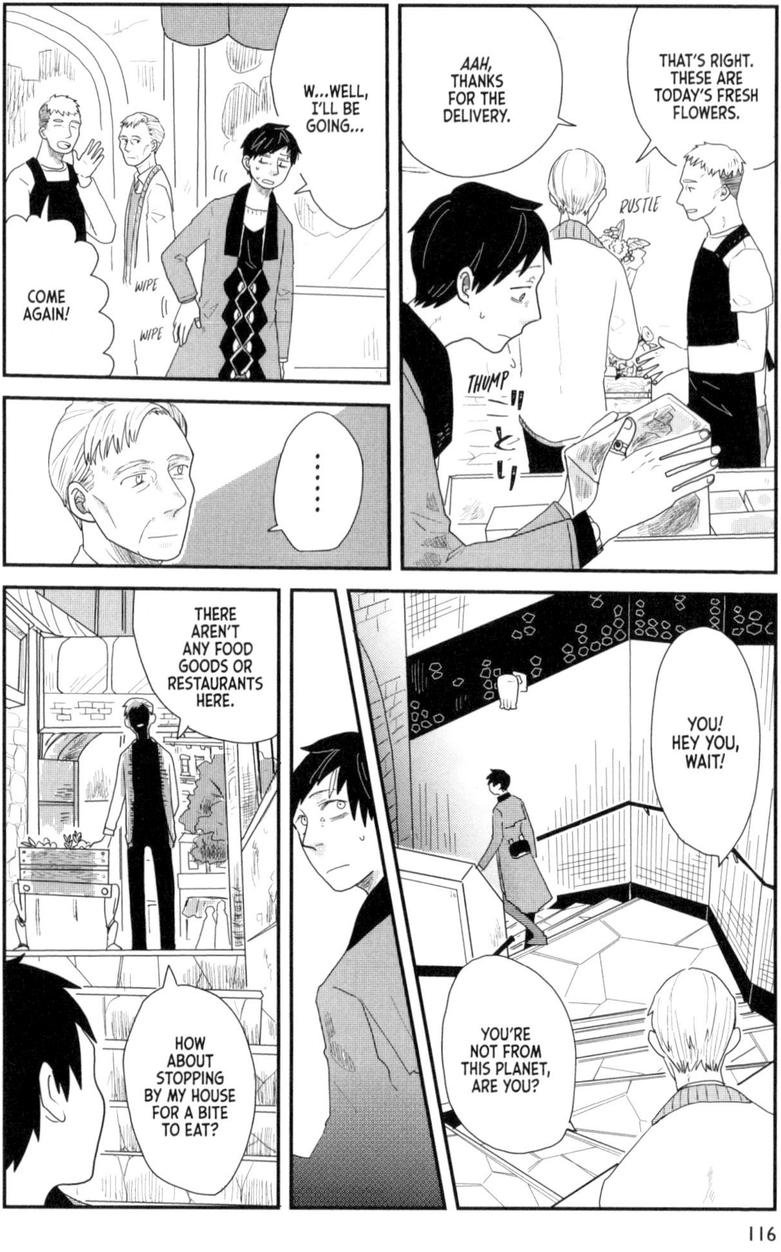
THAT'S RIGHT. THESE ARE TODAY'S FRESH FLOWERS.
AAH, THANKS FOR THE DELIVERY.
RUSTLE
THUMP
W...WELL, I'LL BE GOING...
COME AGAIN!
WIPE
WIPE
......
YOU! HEY YOU, WAIT!
YOU'RE NOT FROM THIS PLANET, ARE YOU?
THERE AREN'T ANY FOOD GOODS OR RESTAURANTS HERE.
HOW ABOUT STOPPING BY MY HOUSE FOR A BITE TO EAT?

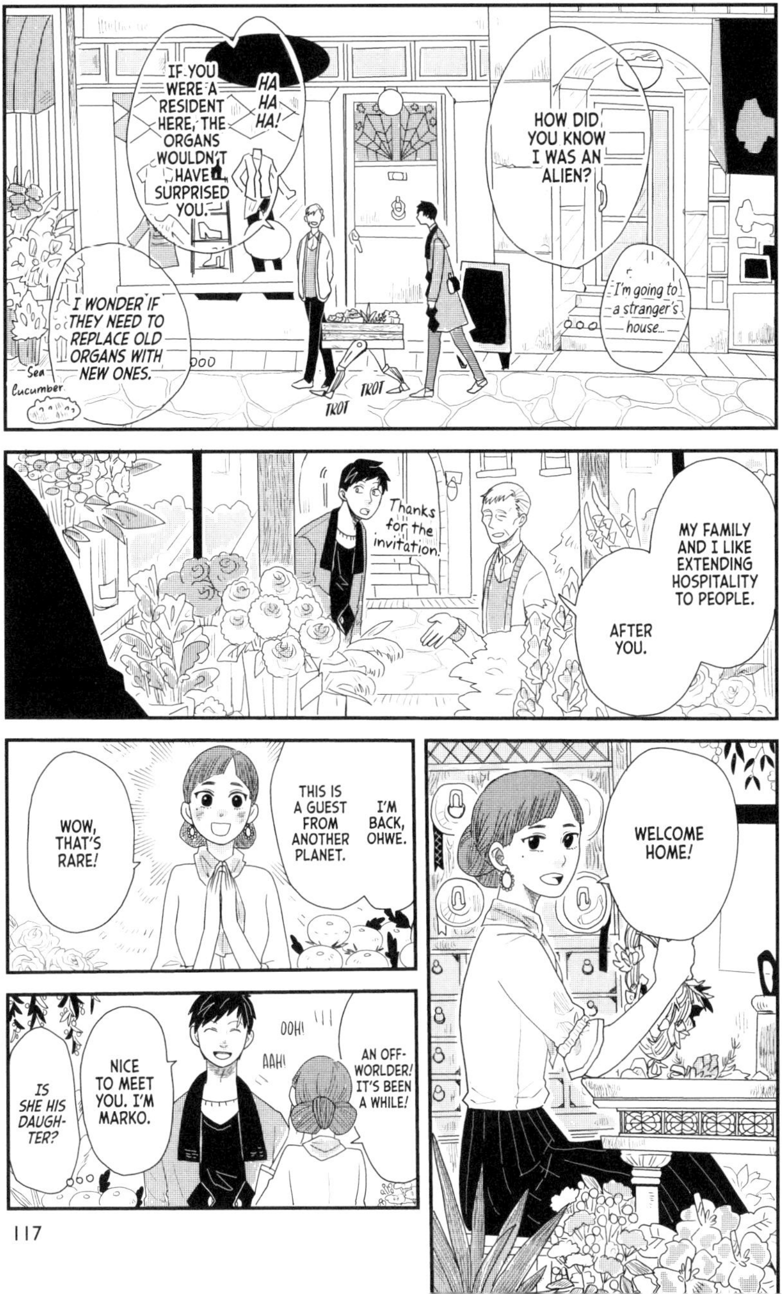
HOW DID YOU KNOW I WAS AN ALIEN?
I'm going to a stranger's house...
HA HA HA!
IF YOU WERE A RESIDENT HERE, THE ORGANS WOULDN'T HAVE SURPRISED YOU.
I WONDER IF THEY NEED TO REPLACE OLD ORGANS WITH NEW ONES.
Sea cucumber.
TROT
TROT
MY FAMILY AND I LIKE EXTENDING HOSPITALITY TO PEOPLE.
AFTER YOU.
Thanks for the invitation.
WELCOME HOME!
I'M BACK, OHWE.
THIS IS A GUEST FROM ANOTHER PLANET.
WOW, THAT'S RARE!
AN OFF-WORLDER! IT'S BEEN A WHILE!
OOH!
AAH!
NICE TO MEET YOU. I'M MARKO.
IS SHE HIS DAUGHTER?

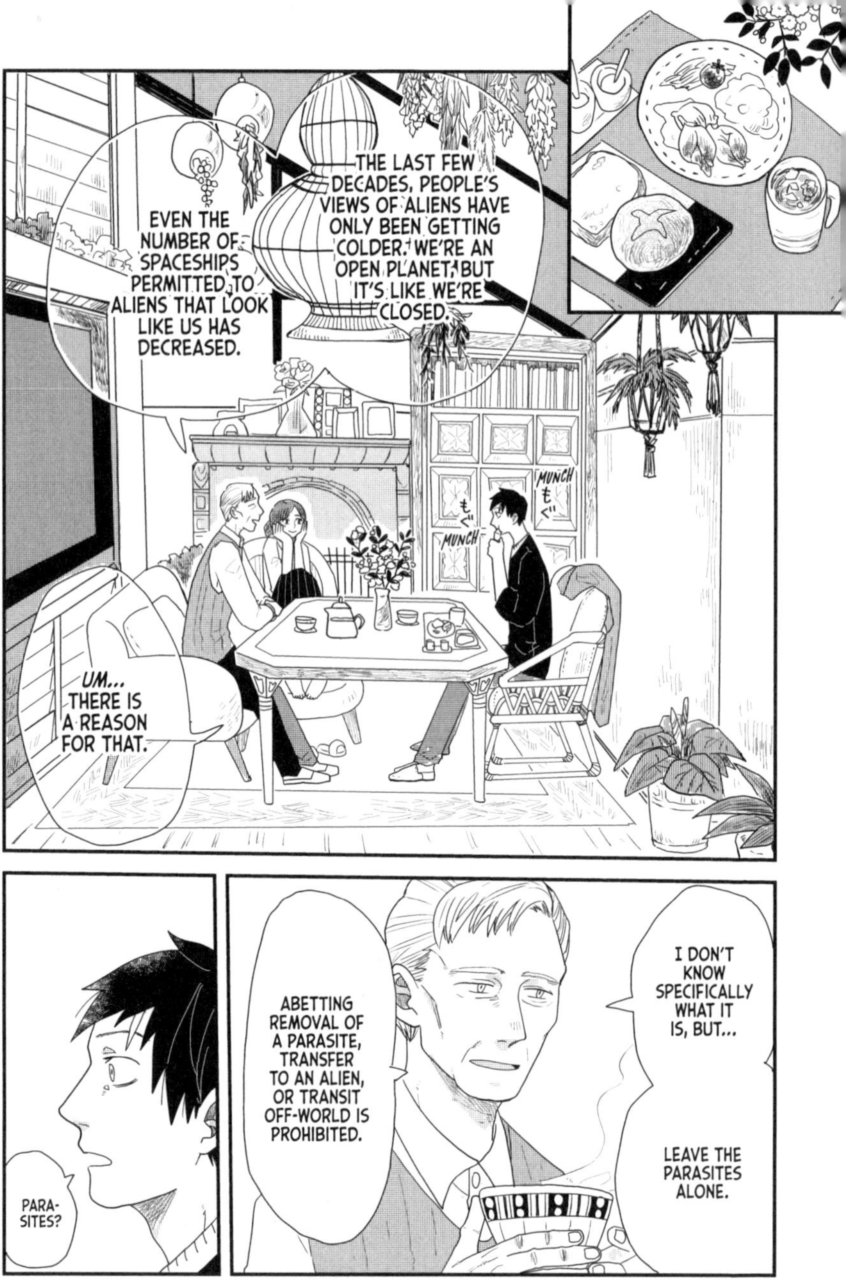
THE LAST FEW DECADES, PEOPLE'S VIEWS OF ALIENS HAVE ONLY BEEN GETTING COLDER. WE'RE AN OPEN PLANET, BUT IT'S LIKE WE'RE CLOSED.
EVEN THE NUMBER OF SPACESHIPS PERMITTED TO ALIENS THAT LOOK LIKE US HAS DECREASED.
MUNCH もぐ
もぐ MUNCH
UM... THERE IS A REASON FOR THAT.
I DON'T KNOW SPECIFICALLY WHAT IT IS, BUT...
LEAVE THE PARASITES ALONE.
ABETTING REMOVAL OF A PARASITE, TRANSFER TO AN ALIEN, OR TRANSIT OFF-WORLD IS PROHIBITED.
PARA-SITES?

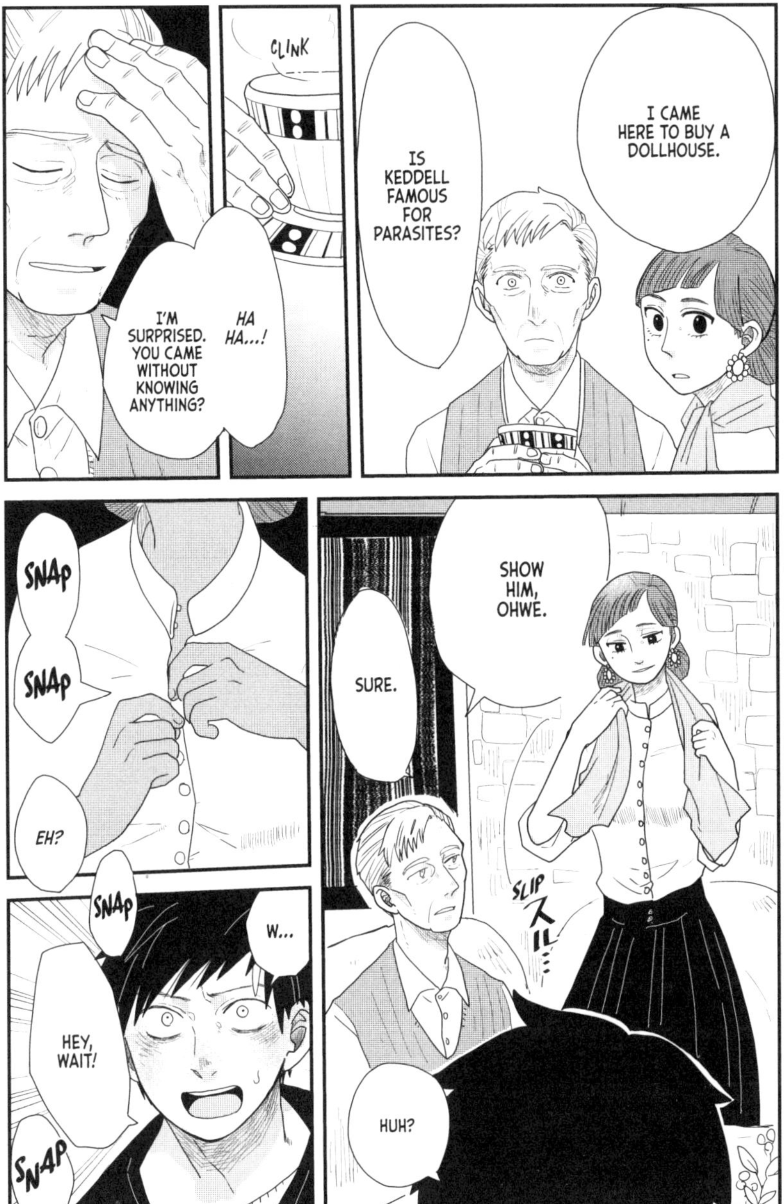
I CAME HERE TO BUY A DOLLHOUSE.
IS KEDDELL FAMOUS FOR PARASITES?
CLINK
HA HA...!
I'M SURPRISED. YOU CAME WITHOUT KNOWING ANYTHING?
SHOW HIM, OHWE.
SURE.
SLIP
スル
HUH?
SNAP
SNAP
EH?
SNAP
W...
HEY, WAIT!
SNAP

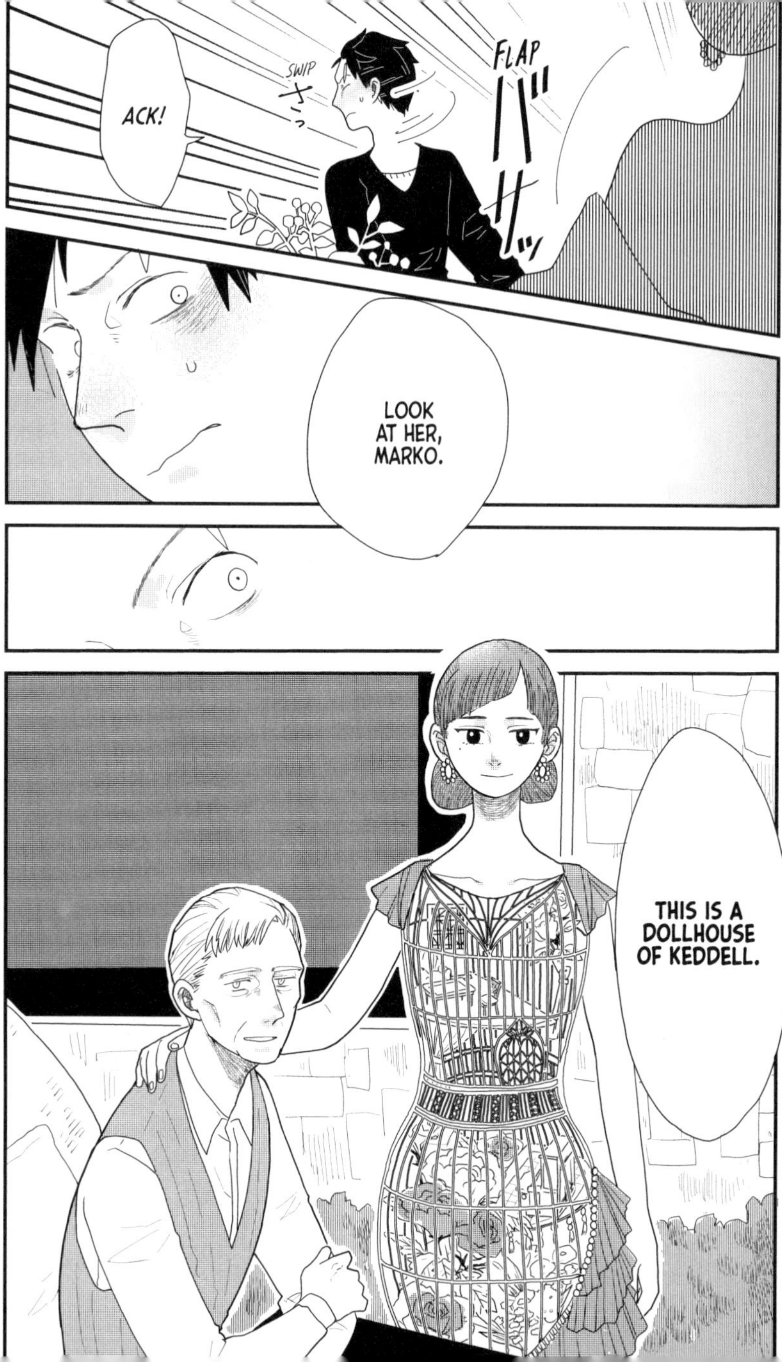
FLAP
SWIP
ACK!
LOOK AT HER, MARKO.
THIS IS A DOLLHOUSE OF KEDDELL.

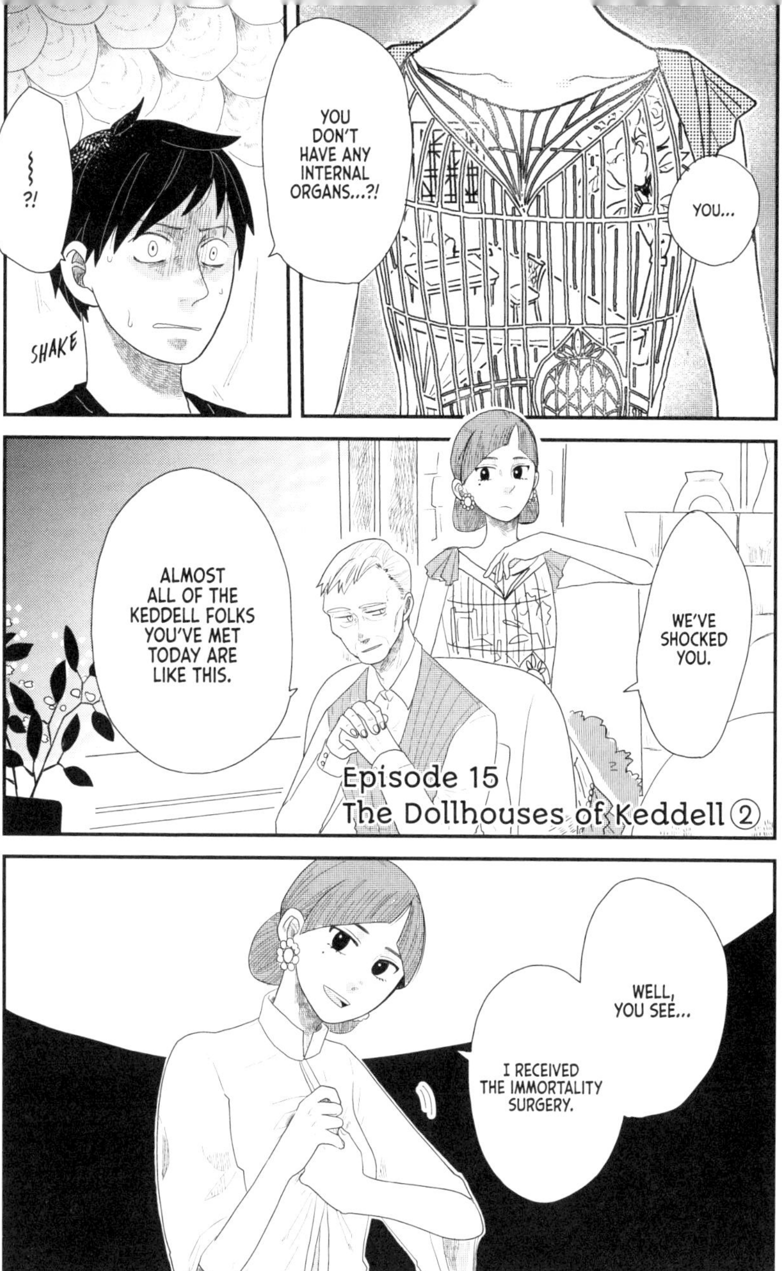
YOU...
YOU DON'T HAVE ANY INTERNAL ORGANS...?!
?!
SHAKE
WE'VE SHOCKED YOU.
ALMOST ALL OF THE KEDDELL FOLKS YOU'VE MET TODAY ARE LIKE THIS.
Episode 15
The Dollhouses of Keddell ②
WELL, YOU SEE...
I RECEIVED THE IMMORTALITY SURGERY.

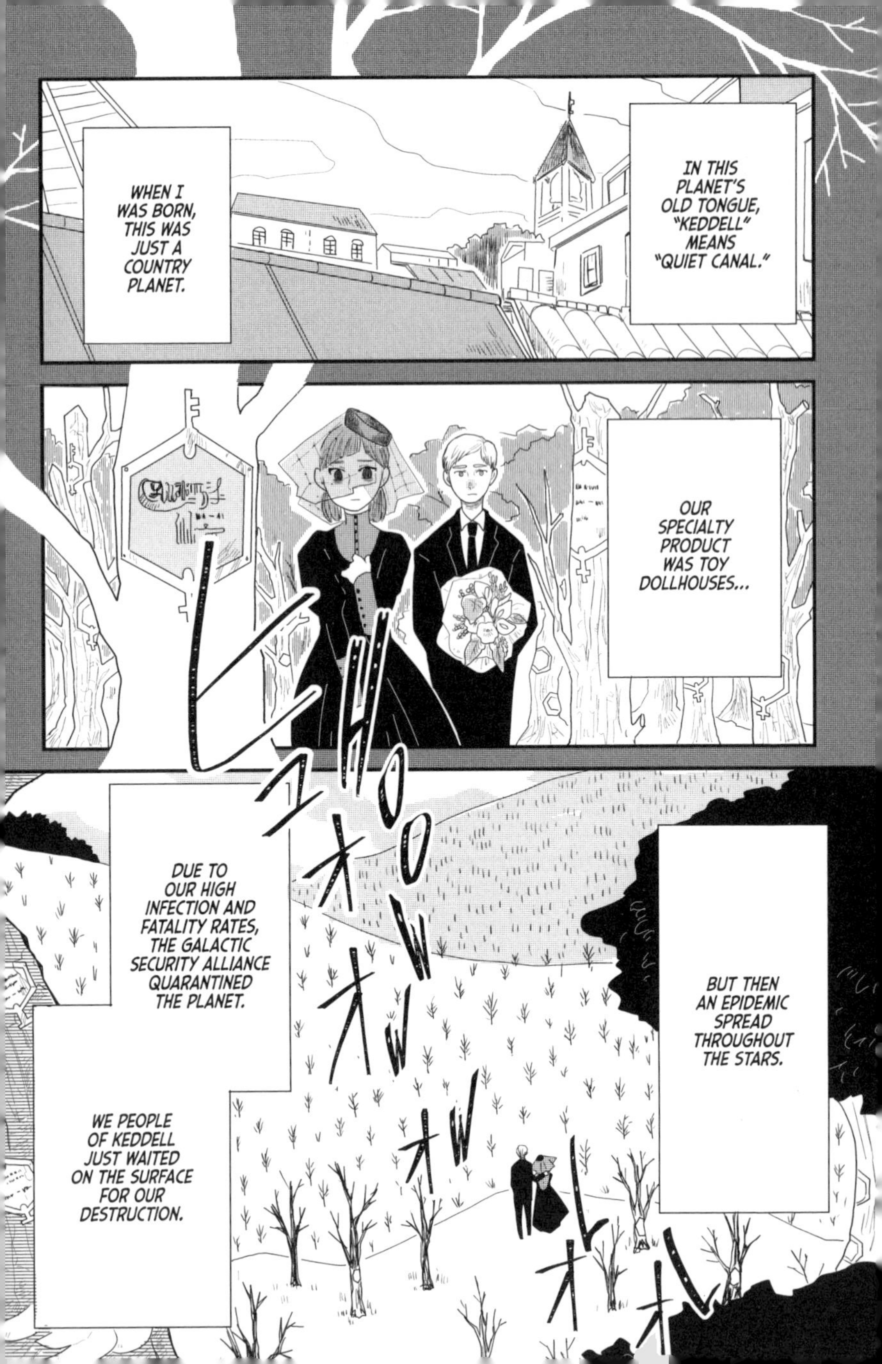
IN THIS PLANET'S OLD TONGUE, "KEDDELL" MEANS "QUIET CANAL."
WHEN I WAS BORN, THIS WAS JUST A COUNTRY PLANET.
OUR SPECIALTY PRODUCT WAS TOY DOLLHOUSES...
HOOOWWWW
BUT THEN AN EPIDEMIC SPREAD THROUGHOUT THE STARS.
DUE TO OUR HIGH INFECTION AND FATALITY RATES, THE GALACTIC SECURITY ALLIANCE QUARANTINED THE PLANET.
WE PEOPLE OF KEDDELL JUST WAITED ON THE SURFACE FOR OUR DESTRUCTION.

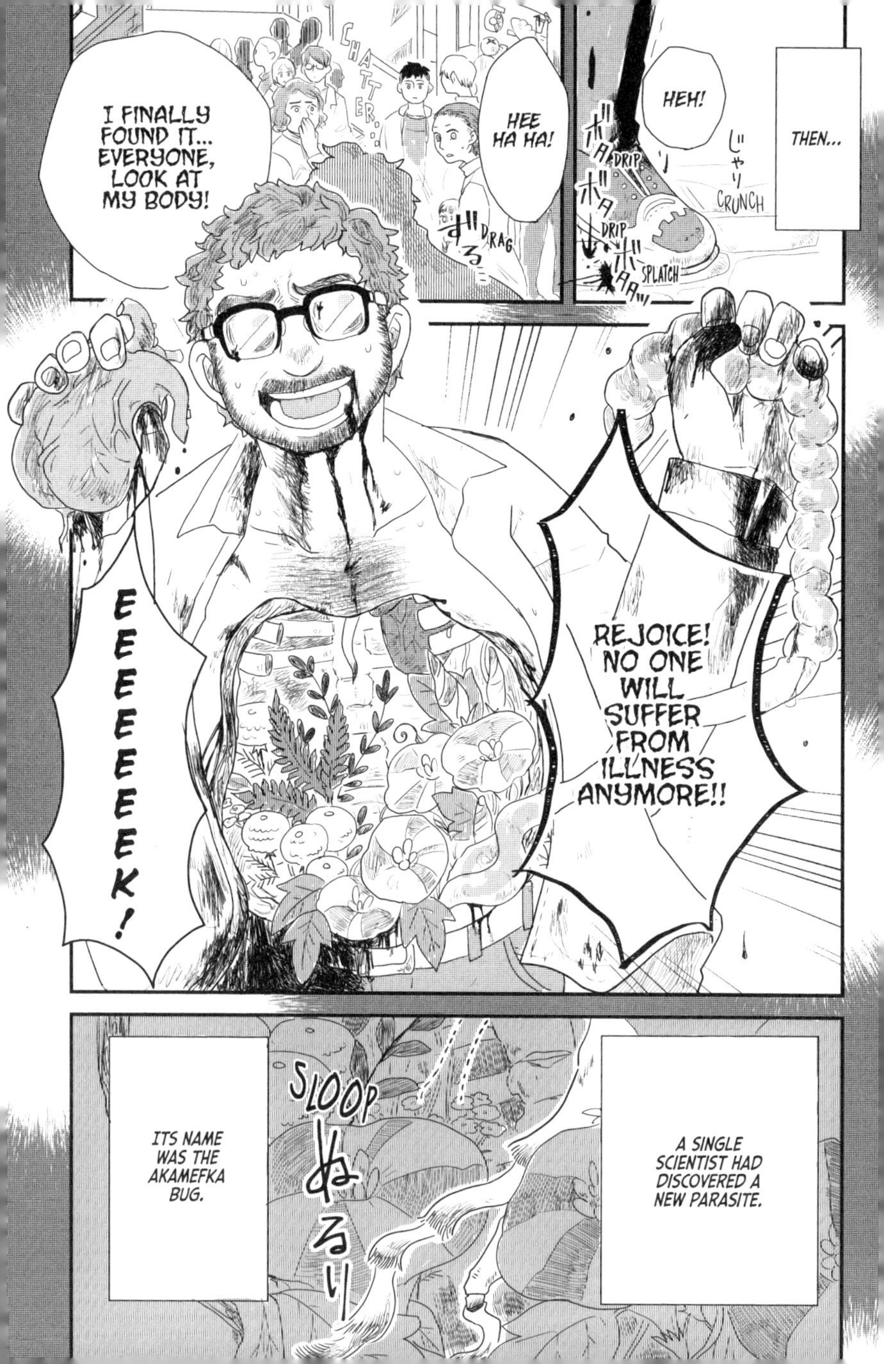
THEN...
HEH!
ボタ DRIP
ボタ DRIP
ボタタッ SPLATCH
じゃり CRUNCH
HEE HA HA!
I FINALLY FOUND IT... EVERYONE, LOOK AT MY BODY!
CHATTER
ずる DRAG
REJOICE! NO ONE WILL SUFFER FROM ILLNESS ANYMORE!!
EEEEEEEEEK!
A SINGLE SCIENTIST HAD DISCOVERED A NEW PARASITE.
SLOOP ぬるり
ITS NAME WAS THE AKAMEFKA BUG.

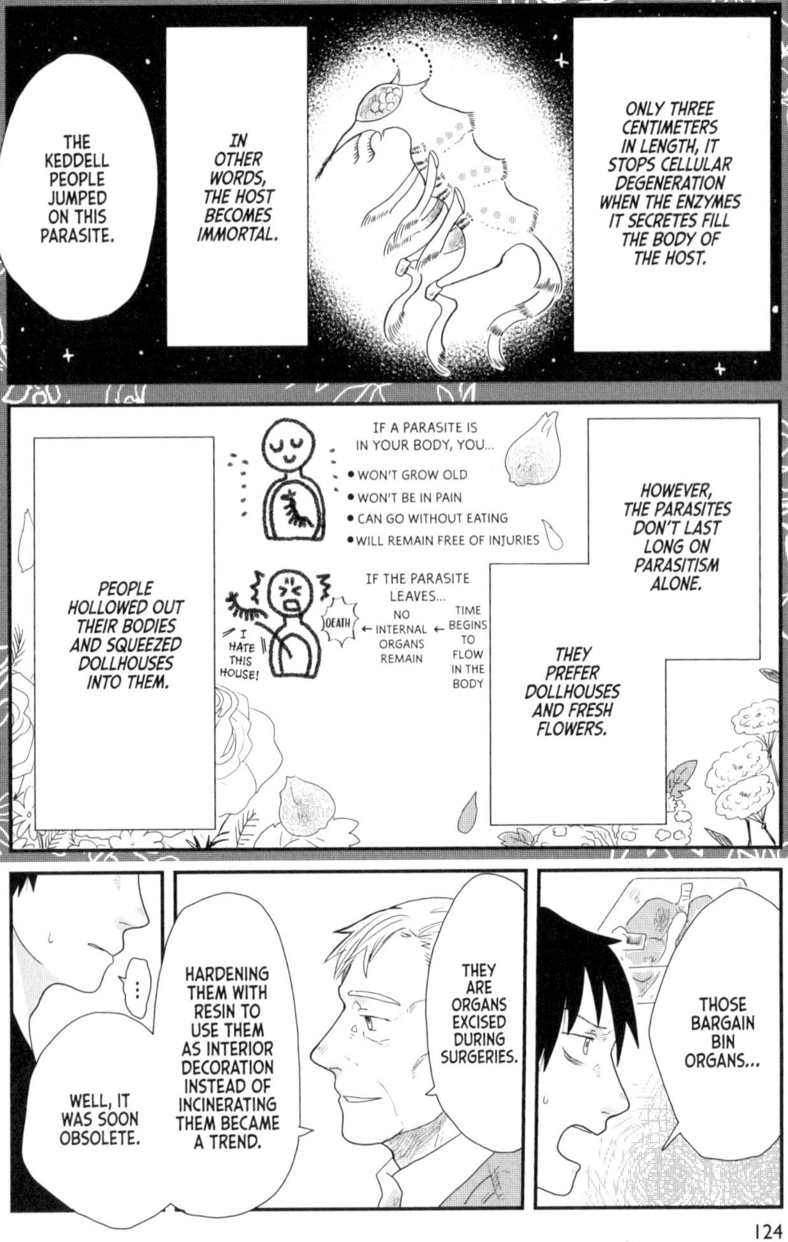
ONLY THREE CENTIMETERS IN LENGTH, IT STOPS CELLULAR DEGENERATION WHEN THE ENZYMES IT SECRETES FILL THE BODY OF THE HOST.
IN OTHER WORDS, THE HOST BECOMES IMMORTAL.
THE KEDDELL PEOPLE JUMPED ON THIS PARASITE.
HOWEVER, THE PARASITES DON'T LAST LONG ON PARASITISM ALONE.
THEY PREFER DOLLHOUSES AND FRESH FLOWERS.
IF A PARASITE IS IN YOUR BODY, YOU...
• WON'T GROW OLD
• WON'T BE IN PAIN
• CAN GO WITHOUT EATING
• WILL REMAIN FREE OF INJURIES
IF THE PARASITE LEAVES...
TIME BEGINS TO FLOW IN THE BODY
← NO INTERNAL ORGANS REMAIN
← DEATH
I HATE THIS HOUSE!
PEOPLE HOLLOWED OUT THEIR BODIES AND SQUEEZED DOLLHOUSES INTO THEM.
THOSE BARGAIN BIN ORGANS...
THEY ARE ORGANS EXCISED DURING SURGERIES.
HARDENING THEM WITH RESIN TO USE THEM AS INTERIOR DECORATION INSTEAD OF INCINERATING THEM BECAME A TREND.
WELL, IT WAS SOON OBSOLETE.
...

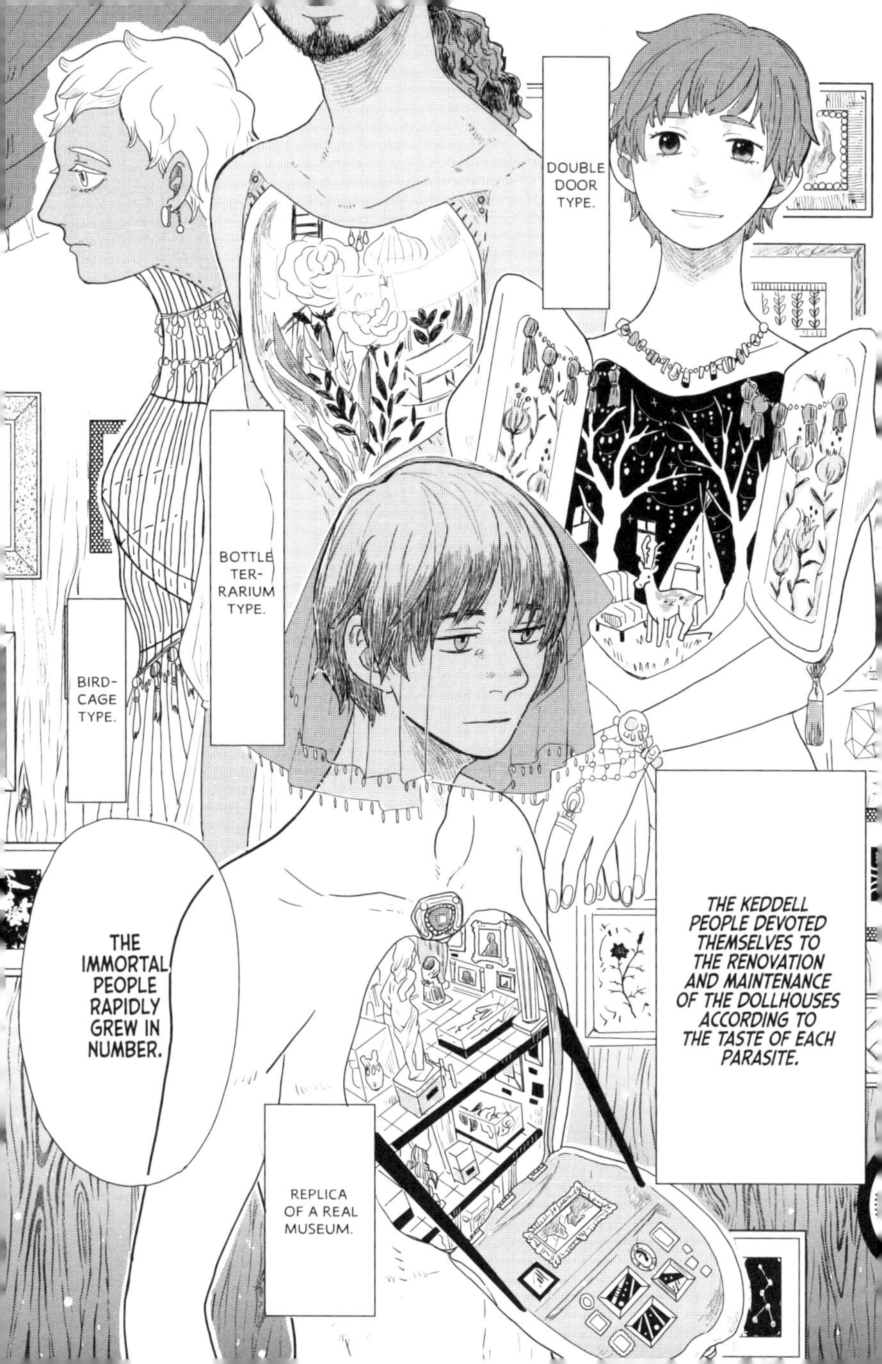
DOUBLE DOOR TYPE.
BOTTLE TERRARIUM TYPE.
BIRD-CAGE TYPE.
THE KEDDELL PEOPLE DEVOTED THEMSELVES TO THE RENOVATION AND MAINTENANCE OF THE DOLLHOUSES ACCORDING TO THE TASTE OF EACH PARASITE.
THE IMMORTAL PEOPLE RAPIDLY GREW IN NUMBER.
REPLICA OF A REAL MUSEUM.

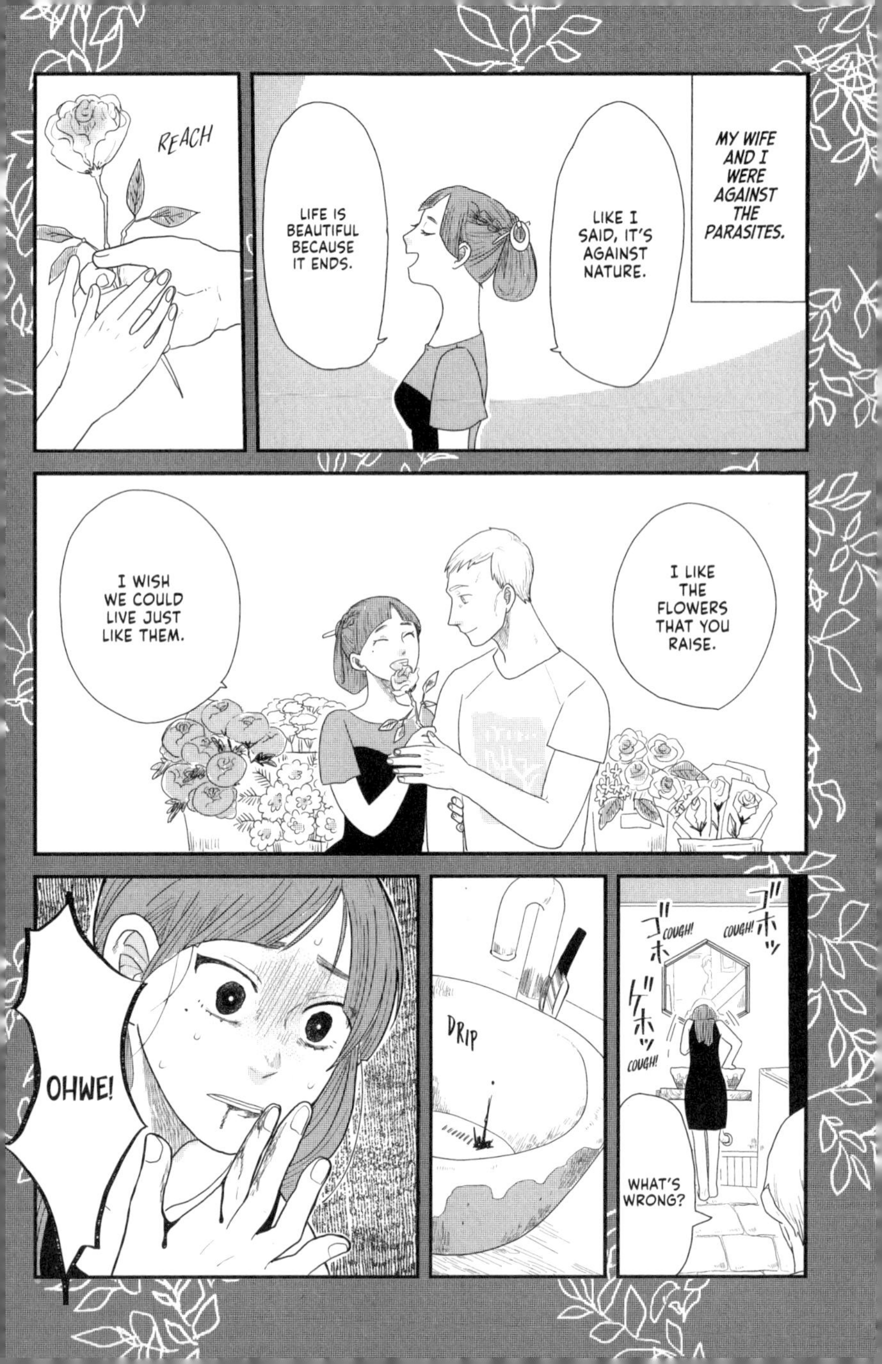
MY WIFE AND I WERE AGAINST THE PARASITES.
LIKE I SAID, IT'S AGAINST NATURE.
LIFE IS BEAUTIFUL BECAUSE IT ENDS.
REACH
I LIKE THE FLOWERS THAT YOU RAISE.
I WISH WE COULD LIVE JUST LIKE THEM.
ゴホッ
COUGH!
ゴホ
COUGH!
ゲホッ
COUGH!
WHAT'S WRONG?
DRIP
OHWE!

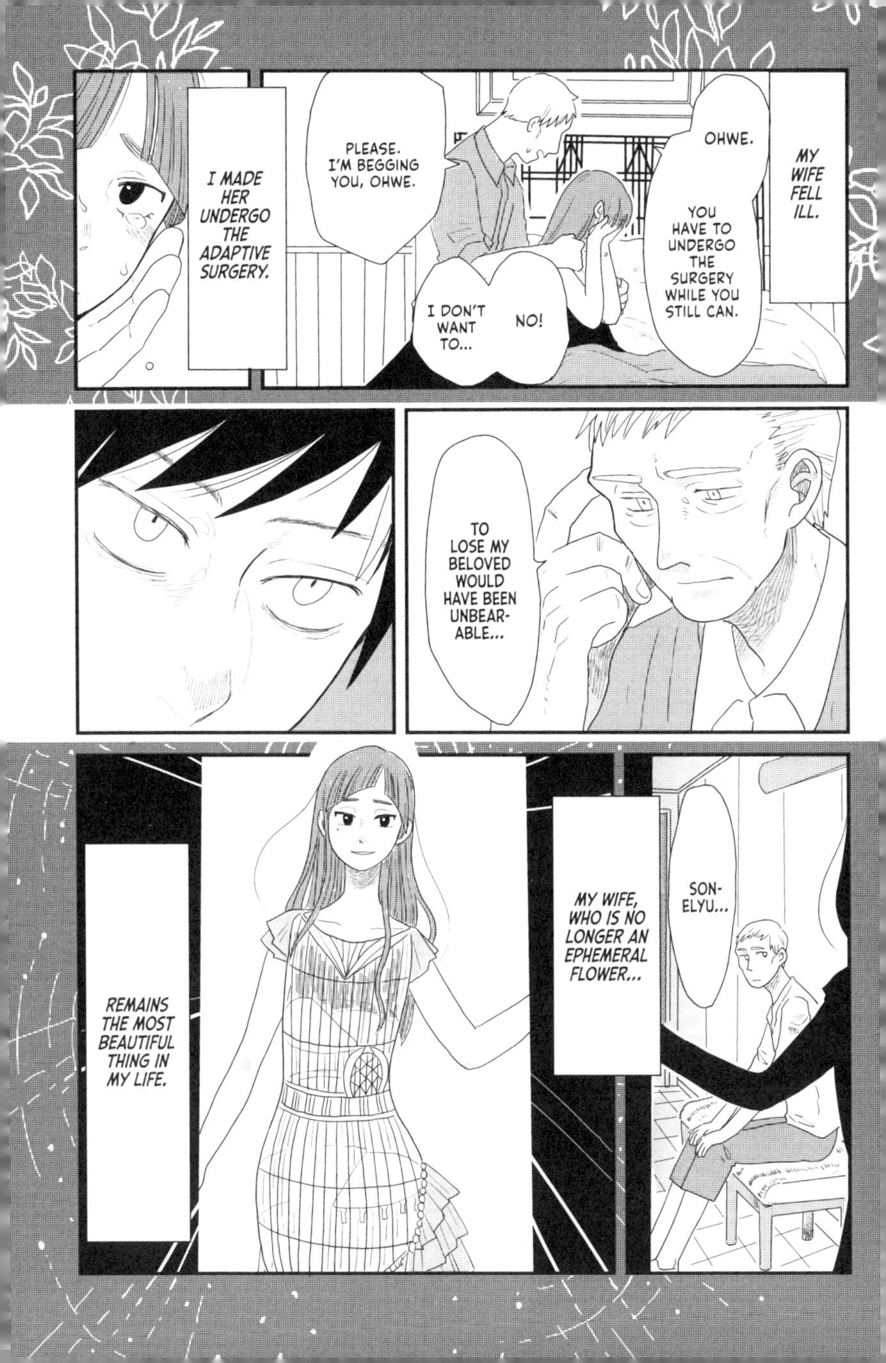
MY WIFE FELL ILL.
OHWE.
YOU HAVE TO UNDERGO THE SURGERY WHILE YOU STILL CAN.
NO!
I DON'T WANT TO...
PLEASE. I'M BEGGING YOU, OHWE.
I MADE HER UNDERGO THE ADAPTIVE SURGERY.
TO LOSE MY BELOVED WOULD HAVE BEEN UNBEAR-ABLE...
SON-ELYU...
MY WIFE, WHO IS NO LONGER AN EPHEMERAL FLOWER...
REMAINS THE MOST BEAUTIFUL THING IN MY LIFE.

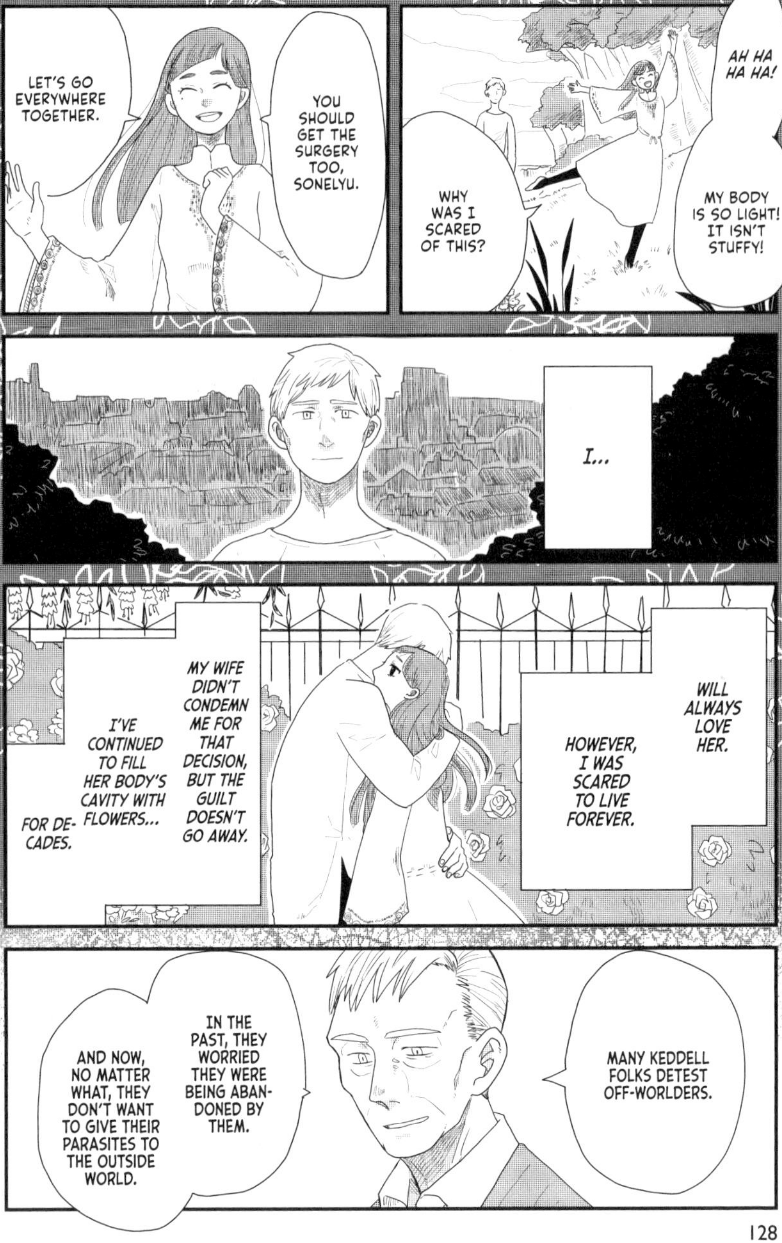
AH HA HA HA!
MY BODY IS SO LIGHT! IT ISN'T STUFFY!
WHY WAS I SCARED OF THIS?
YOU SHOULD GET THE SURGERY TOO, SONELYU.
LET'S GO EVERYWHERE TOGETHER.
I...
WILL ALWAYS LOVE HER.
HOWEVER, I WAS SCARED TO LIVE FOREVER.
MY WIFE DIDN'T CONDEMN ME FOR THAT DECISION, BUT THE GUILT DOESN'T GO AWAY.
I'VE CONTINUED TO FILL HER BODY'S CAVITY WITH FLOWERS...
FOR DE-CADES.
MANY KEDDELL FOLKS DETEST OFF-WORLDERS.
IN THE PAST, THEY WORRIED THEY WERE BEING ABAN-DONED BY THEM.
AND NOW, NO MATTER WHAT, THEY DON'T WANT TO GIVE THEIR PARASITES TO THE OUTSIDE WORLD.

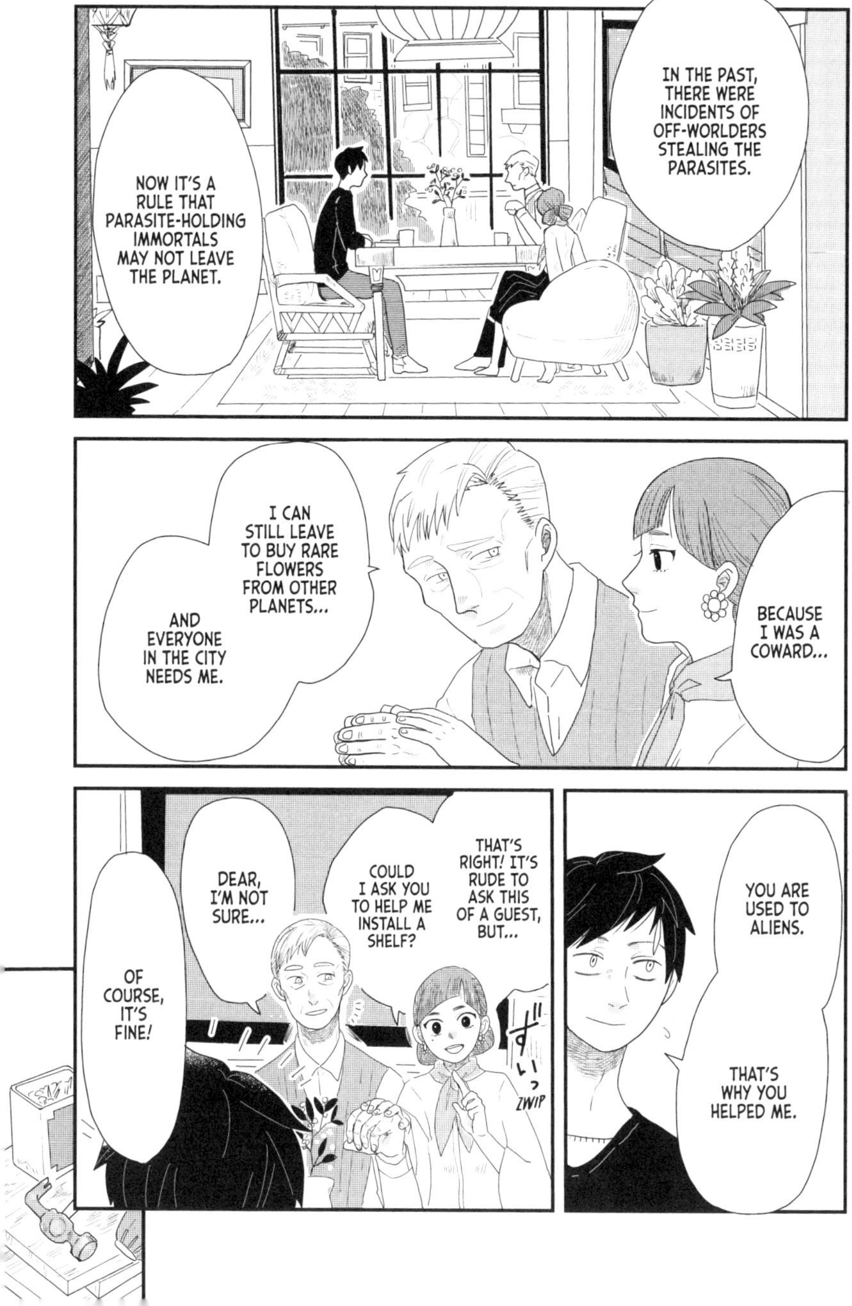
IN THE PAST, THERE WERE INCIDENTS OF OFF-WORLDERS STEALING THE PARASITES.
NOW IT'S A RULE THAT PARASITE-HOLDING IMMORTALS MAY NOT LEAVE THE PLANET.
BECAUSE I WAS A COWARD...
I CAN STILL LEAVE TO BUY RARE FLOWERS FROM OTHER PLANETS...
AND EVERYONE IN THE CITY NEEDS ME.
YOU ARE USED TO ALIENS.
THAT'S WHY YOU HELPED ME.
THAT'S RIGHT! IT'S RUDE TO ASK THIS OF A GUEST, BUT...
COULD I ASK YOU TO HELP ME INSTALL A SHELF?
ZWIP
DEAR, I'M NOT SURE...
OF COURSE, IT'S FINE!

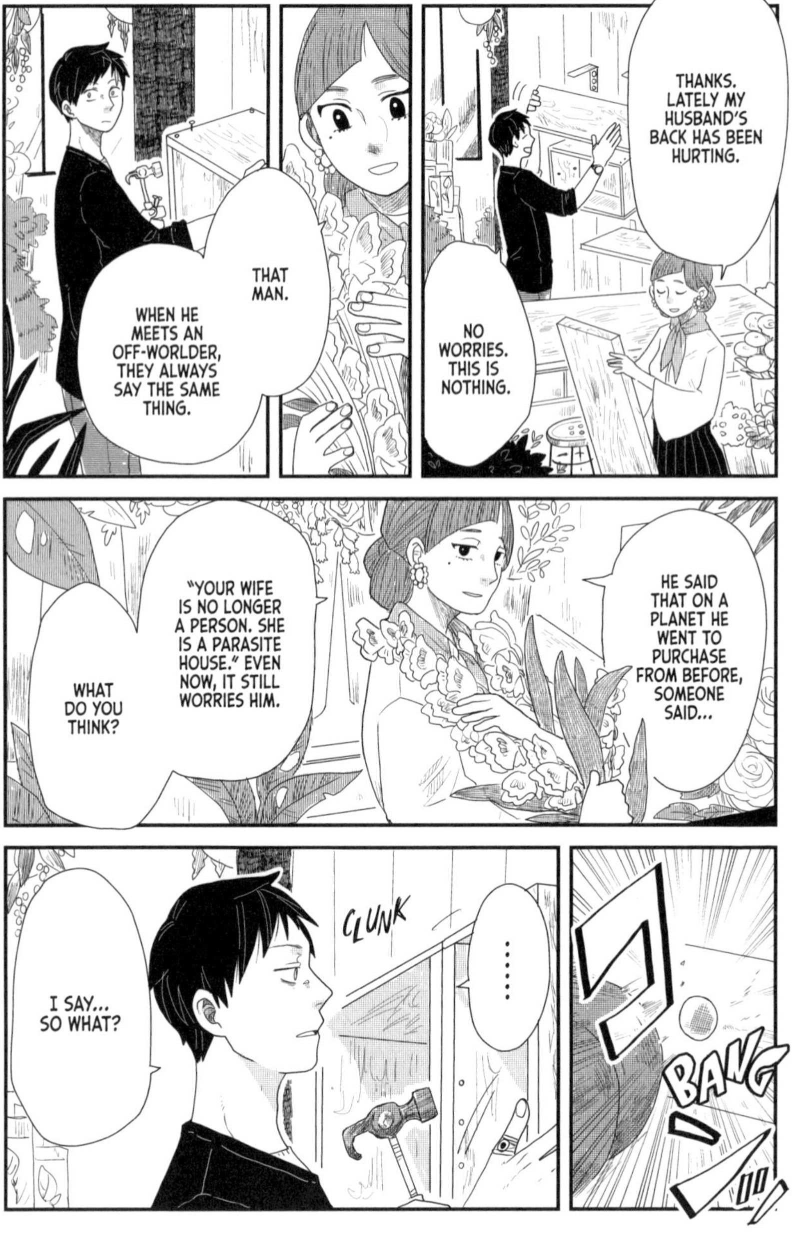
THANKS. LATELY MY HUSBAND'S BACK HAS BEEN HURTING.
NO WORRIES. THIS IS NOTHING.
THAT MAN.
WHEN HE MEETS AN OFF-WORLDER, THEY ALWAYS SAY THE SAME THING.
HE SAID THAT ON A PLANET HE WENT TO PURCHASE FROM BEFORE, SOMEONE SAID...
"YOUR WIFE IS NO LONGER A PERSON. SHE IS A PARASITE HOUSE." EVEN NOW, IT STILL WORRIES HIM.
WHAT DO YOU THINK?
BANG
......
CLUNK
I SAY... SO WHAT?

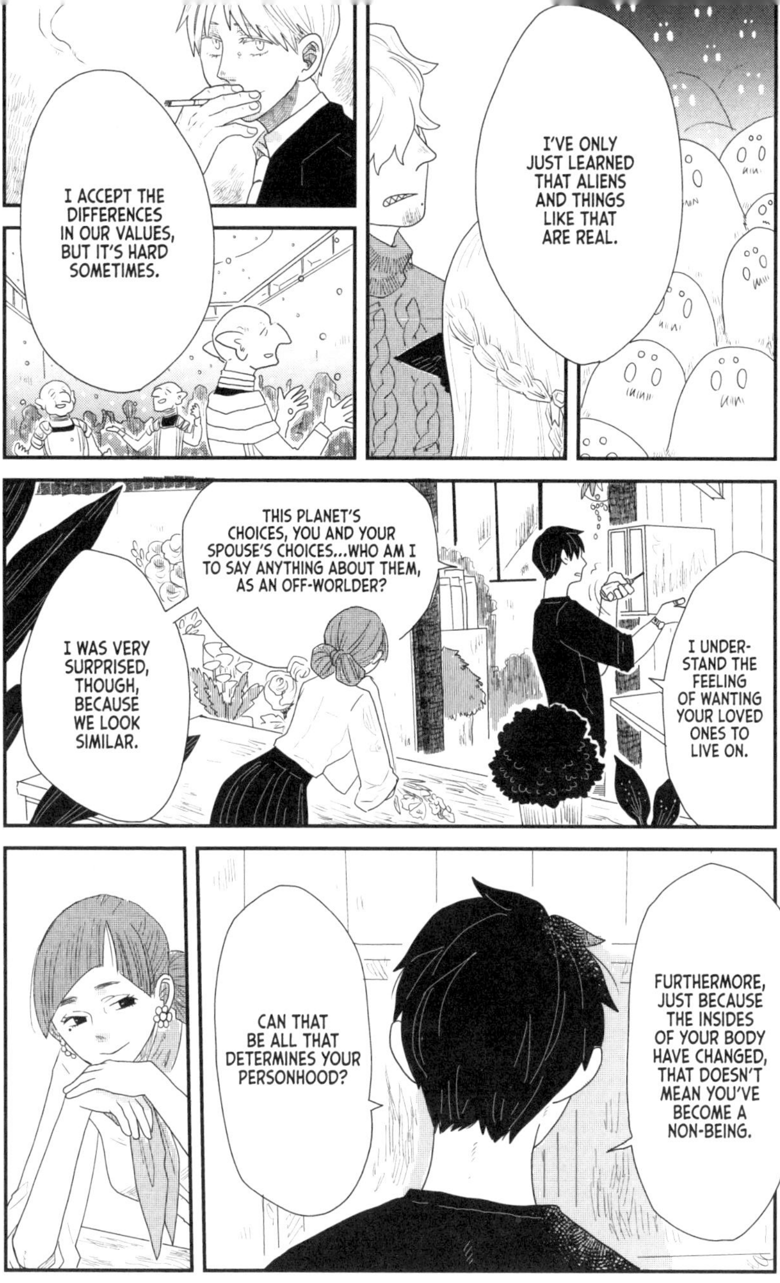
I'VE ONLY JUST LEARNED THAT ALIENS AND THINGS LIKE THAT ARE REAL.
I ACCEPT THE DIFFERENCES IN OUR VALUES, BUT IT'S HARD SOMETIMES.
I UNDER-STAND THE FEELING OF WANTING YOUR LOVED ONES TO LIVE ON.
THIS PLANET'S CHOICES, YOU AND YOUR SPOUSE'S CHOICES...WHO AM I TO SAY ANYTHING ABOUT THEM, AS AN OFF-WORLDER?
I WAS VERY SURPRISED, THOUGH, BECAUSE WE LOOK SIMILAR.
FURTHERMORE, JUST BECAUSE THE INSIDES OF YOUR BODY HAVE CHANGED, THAT DOESN'T MEAN YOU'VE BECOME A NON-BEING.
CAN THAT BE ALL THAT DETERMINES YOUR PERSONHOOD?

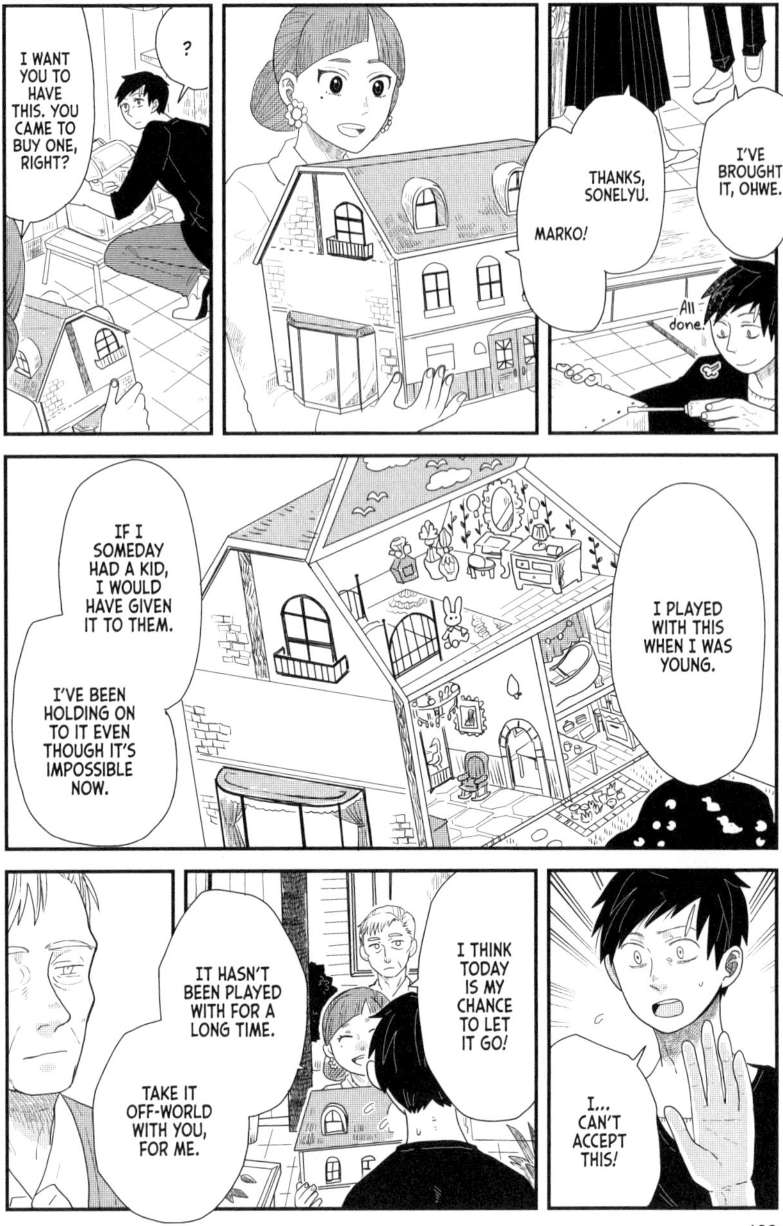
I'VE BROUGHT IT, OHWE.
THANKS, SONELYU.
MARKO!
All done.
?
I WANT YOU TO HAVE THIS. YOU CAME TO BUY ONE, RIGHT?
I PLAYED WITH THIS WHEN I WAS YOUNG.
IF I SOMEDAY HAD A KID, I WOULD HAVE GIVEN IT TO THEM.
I'VE BEEN HOLDING ON TO IT EVEN THOUGH IT'S IMPOSSIBLE NOW.
I... CAN'T ACCEPT THIS!
I THINK TODAY IS MY CHANCE TO LET IT GO!
IT HASN'T BEEN PLAYED WITH FOR A LONG TIME.
TAKE IT OFF-WORLD WITH YOU, FOR ME.

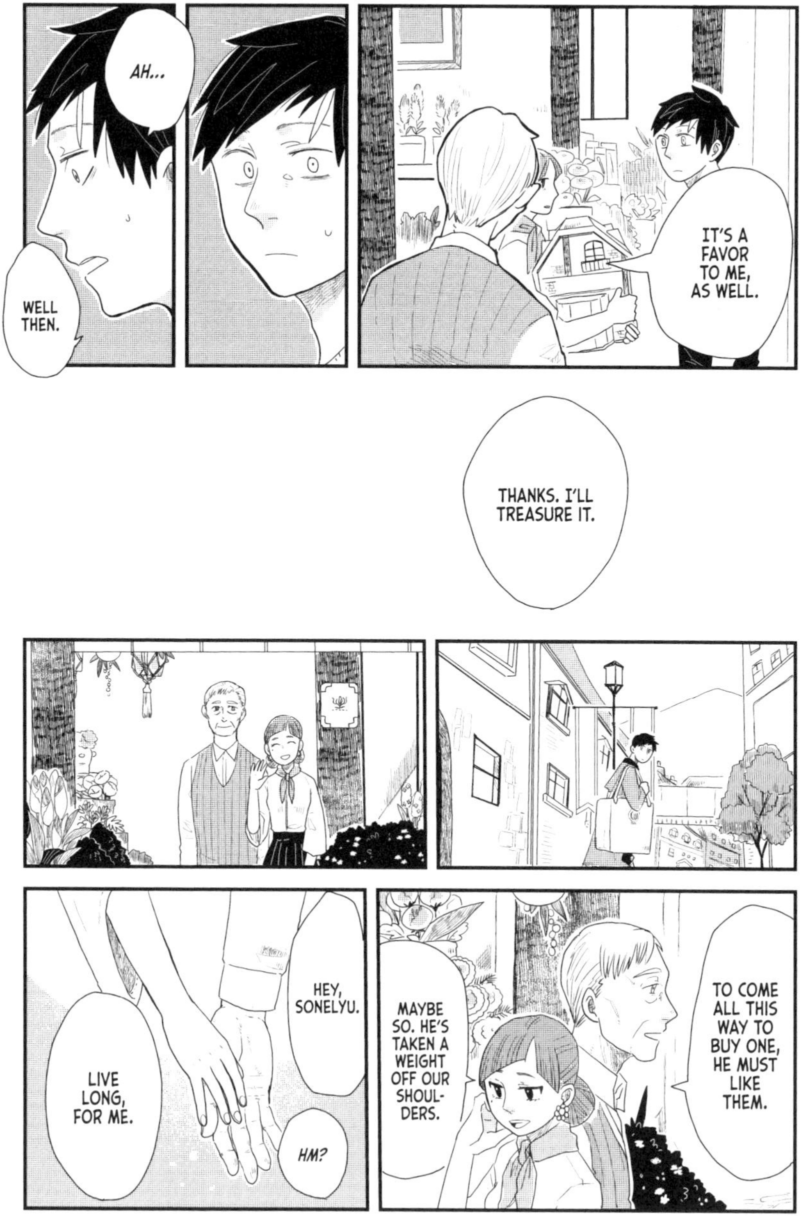
IT'S A FAVOR TO ME, AS WELL.
AH...
WELL THEN.
THANKS. I'LL TREASURE IT.
TO COME ALL THIS WAY TO BUY ONE, HE MUST LIKE THEM.
MAYBE SO. HE'S TAKEN A WEIGHT OFF OUR SHOULDERS.
HEY, SONELYU.
HM?
LIVE LONG, FOR ME.

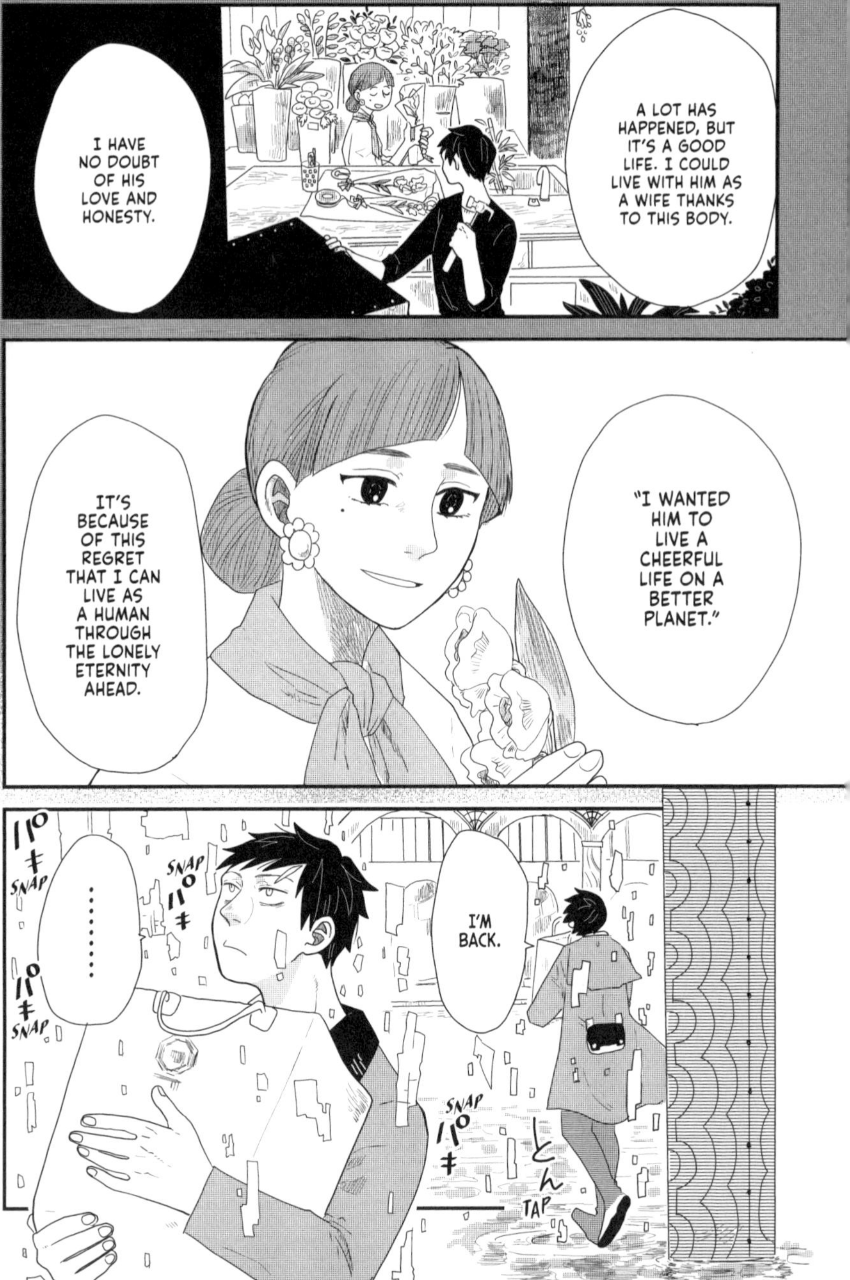
A LOT HAS HAPPENED, BUT IT'S A GOOD LIFE. I COULD LIVE WITH HIM AS A WIFE THANKS TO THIS BODY.
I HAVE NO DOUBT OF HIS LOVE AND HONESTY.
"I WANTED HIM TO LIVE A CHEERFUL LIFE ON A BETTER PLANET."
IT'S BECAUSE OF THIS REGRET THAT I CAN LIVE AS A HUMAN THROUGH THE LONELY ETERNITY AHEAD.
とん
TAP
パキ
SNAP
I'M BACK.
パキ
SNAP
パキ
SNAP
パキ
SNAP
....

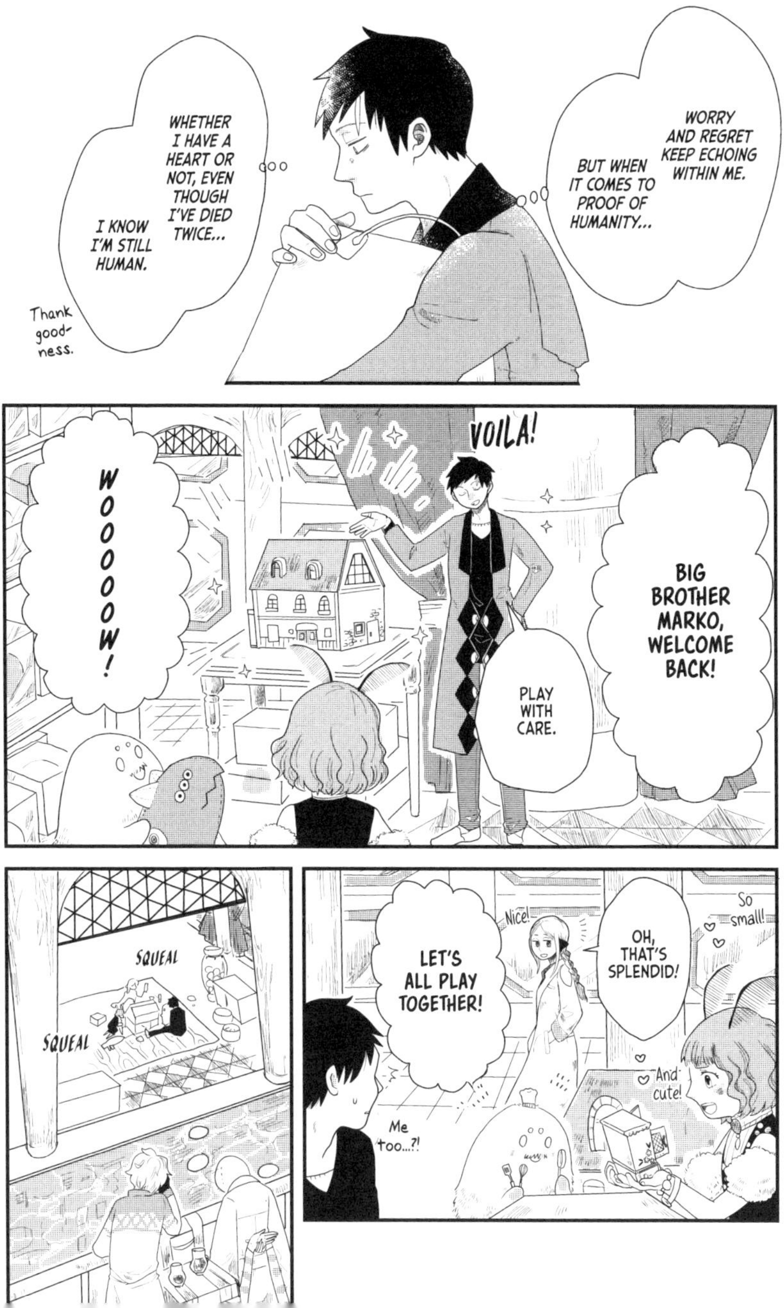
WORRY AND REGRET KEEP ECHOING WITHIN ME.
BUT WHEN IT COMES TO PROOF OF HUMANITY...
WHETHER I HAVE A HEART OR NOT, EVEN THOUGH I'VE DIED TWICE...
I KNOW I'M STILL HUMAN.
Thank good-ness.
VOILA!
BIG BROTHER MARKO, WELCOME BACK!
PLAY WITH CARE.
WOOOOOOW!
So small!
OH, THAT'S SPLENDID!
Nice!
LET'S ALL PLAY TOGETHER!
And cute!
Me too...?!
SQUEAL
SQUEAL

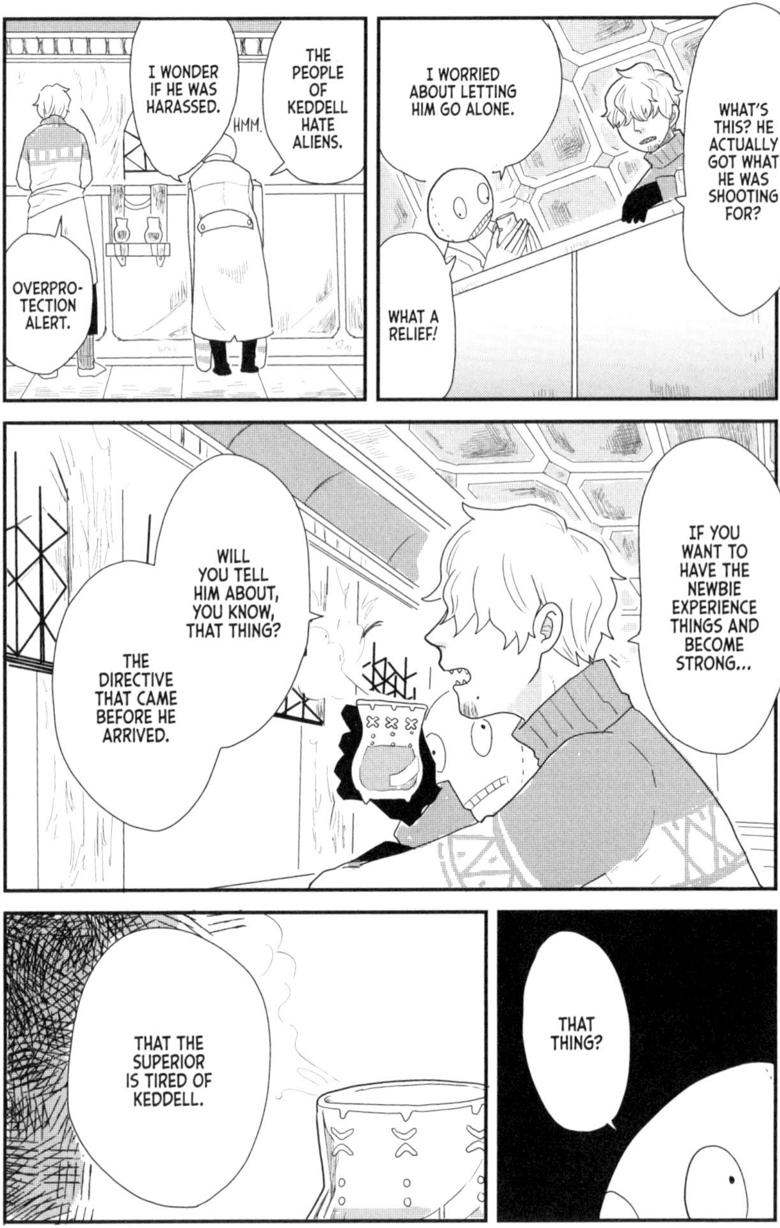
WHAT'S THIS? HE ACTUALLY GOT WHAT HE WAS SHOOTING FOR?
I WORRIED ABOUT LETTING HIM GO ALONE.
WHAT A RELIEF!
THE PEOPLE OF KEDDELL HATE ALIENS.
I WONDER IF HE WAS HARASSED.
HMM.
OVERPROTECTION ALERT.
IF YOU WANT TO HAVE THE NEWBIE EXPERIENCE THINGS AND BECOME STRONG...
WILL YOU TELL HIM ABOUT, YOU KNOW, THAT THING?
THE DIRECTIVE THAT CAME BEFORE HE ARRIVED.
THAT THING?
THAT THE SUPERIOR IS TIRED OF KEDDELL.

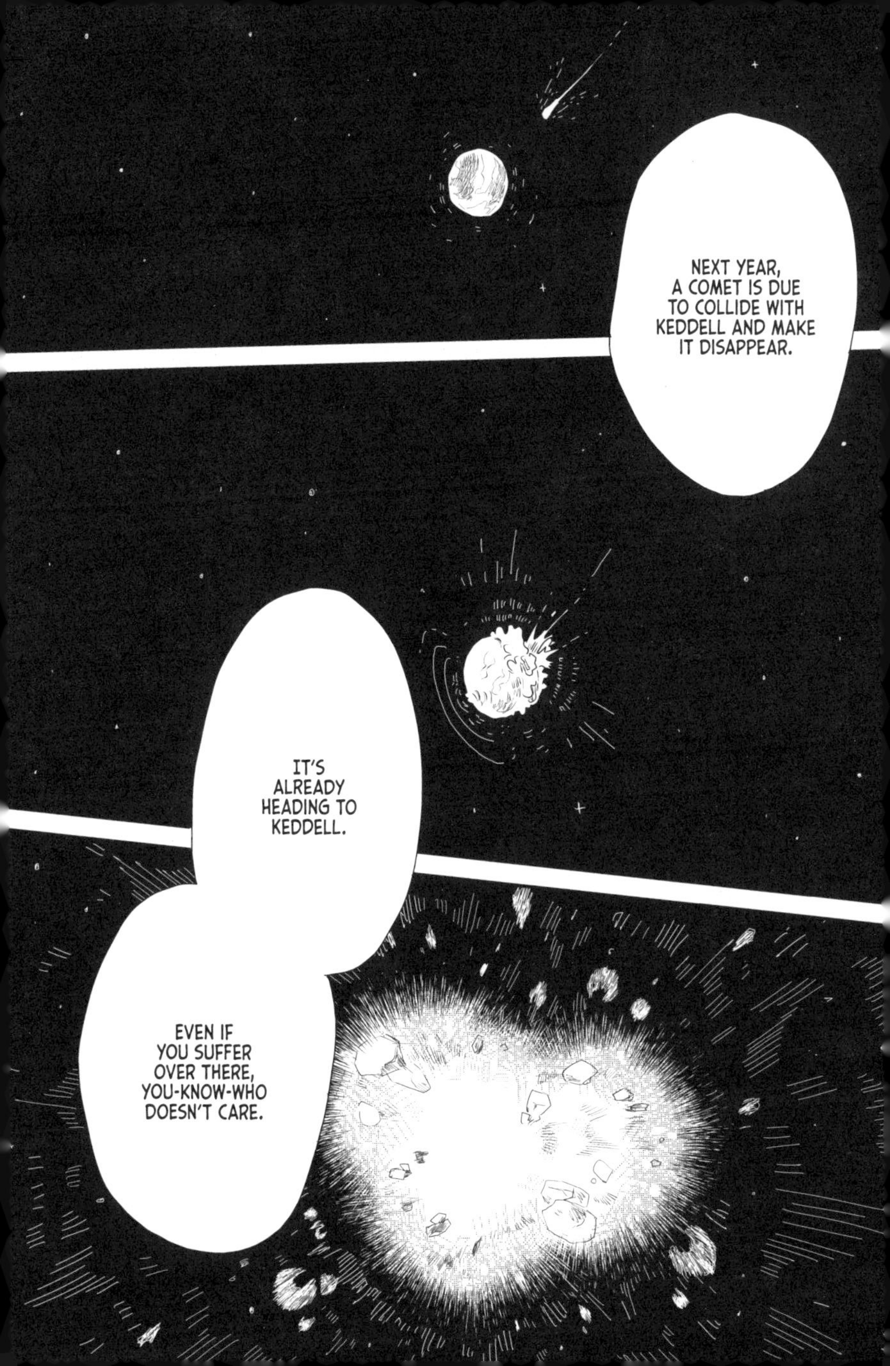
NEXT YEAR, A COMET IS DUE TO COLLIDE WITH KEDDELL AND MAKE IT DISAPPEAR.
IT'S ALREADY HEADING TO KEDDELL.
EVEN IF YOU SUFFER OVER THERE, YOU-KNOW-WHO DOESN'T CARE.

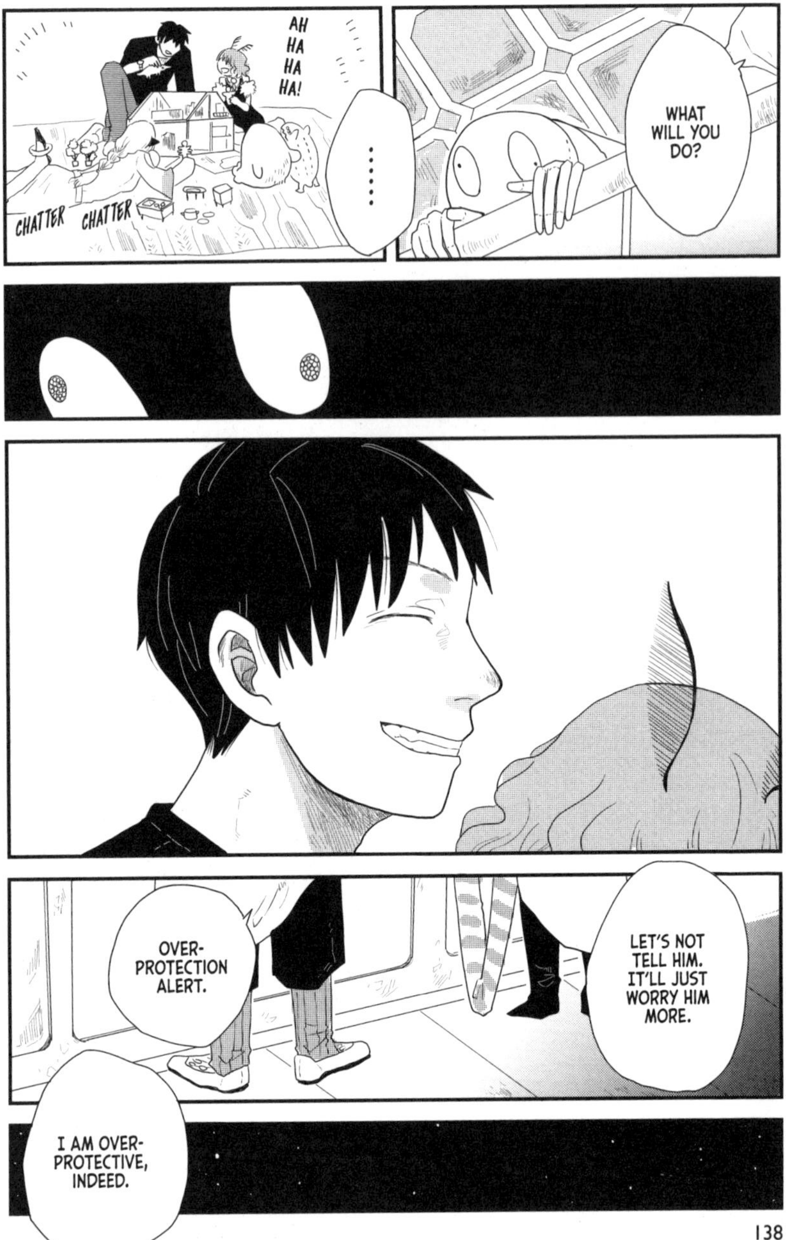
WHAT WILL YOU DO?
......
AH HA HA HA!
CHATTER CHATTER
LET'S NOT TELL HIM. IT'LL JUST WORRY HIM MORE.
OVER-PROTECTION ALERT.
I AM OVER-PROTECTIVE, INDEED.

Episode 16: The Yuno-za's Dinner Table

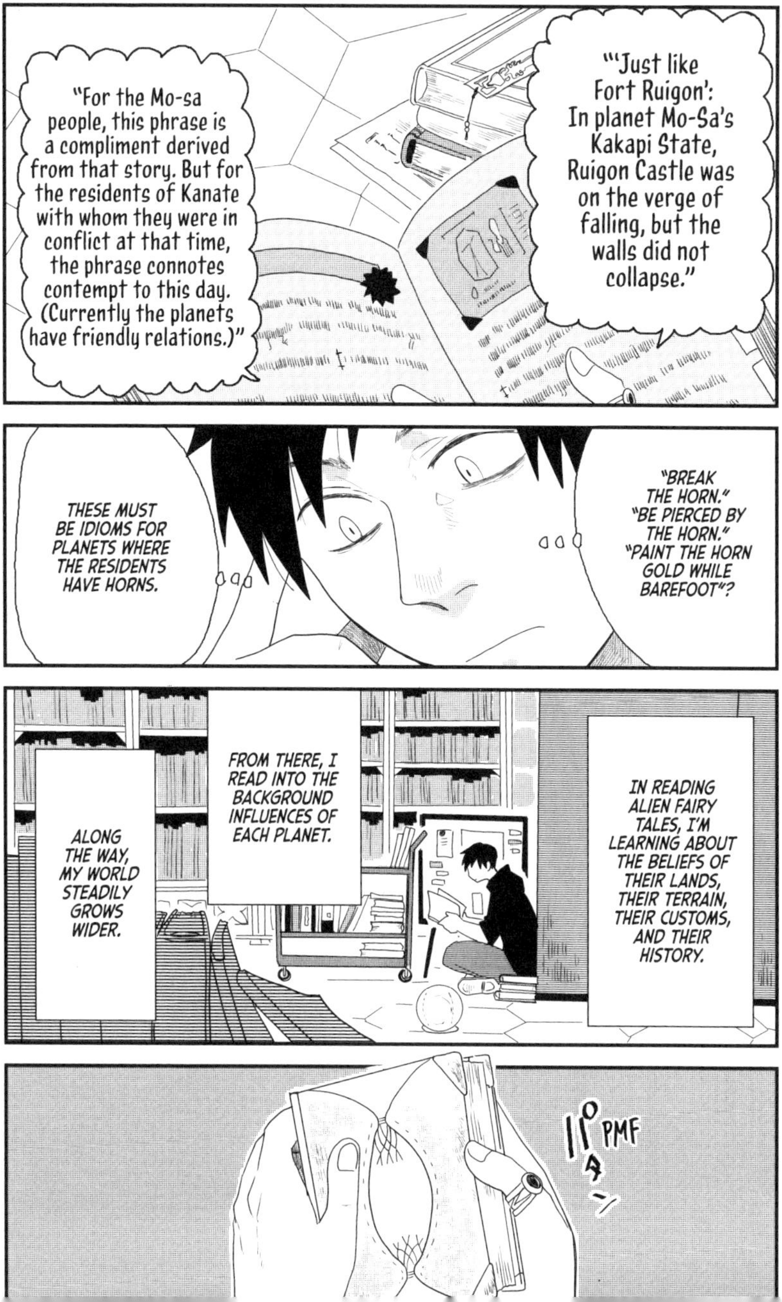
"'Just like Fort Ruigon': In planet Mo-Sa's Kakapi State, Ruigon Castle was on the verge of falling, but the walls did not collapse."
"For the Mo-sa people, this phrase is a compliment derived from that story. But for the residents of Kanate with whom they were in conflict at that time, the phrase connotes contempt to this day. (Currently the planets have friendly relations.)"
"BREAK THE HORN." "BE PIERCED BY THE HORN." "PAINT THE HORN GOLD WHILE BAREFOOT"?
THESE MUST BE IDIOMS FOR PLANETS WHERE THE RESIDENTS HAVE HORNS.
IN READING ALIEN FAIRY TALES, I'M LEARNING ABOUT THE BELIEFS OF THEIR LANDS, THEIR TERRAIN, THEIR CUSTOMS, AND THEIR HISTORY.
FROM THERE, I READ INTO THE BACKGROUND INFLUENCES OF EACH PLANET.
ALONG THE WAY, MY WORLD STEADILY GROWS WIDER.
PMF

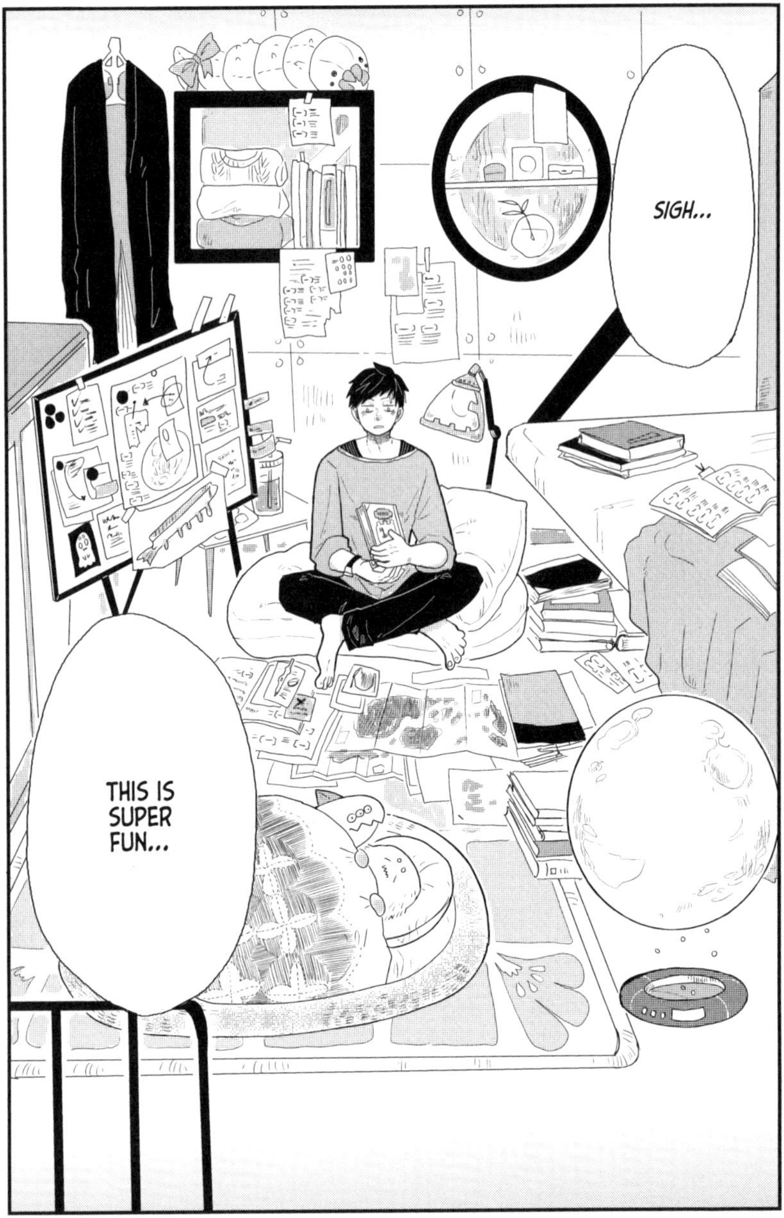
SIGH...
THIS IS SUPER FUN...

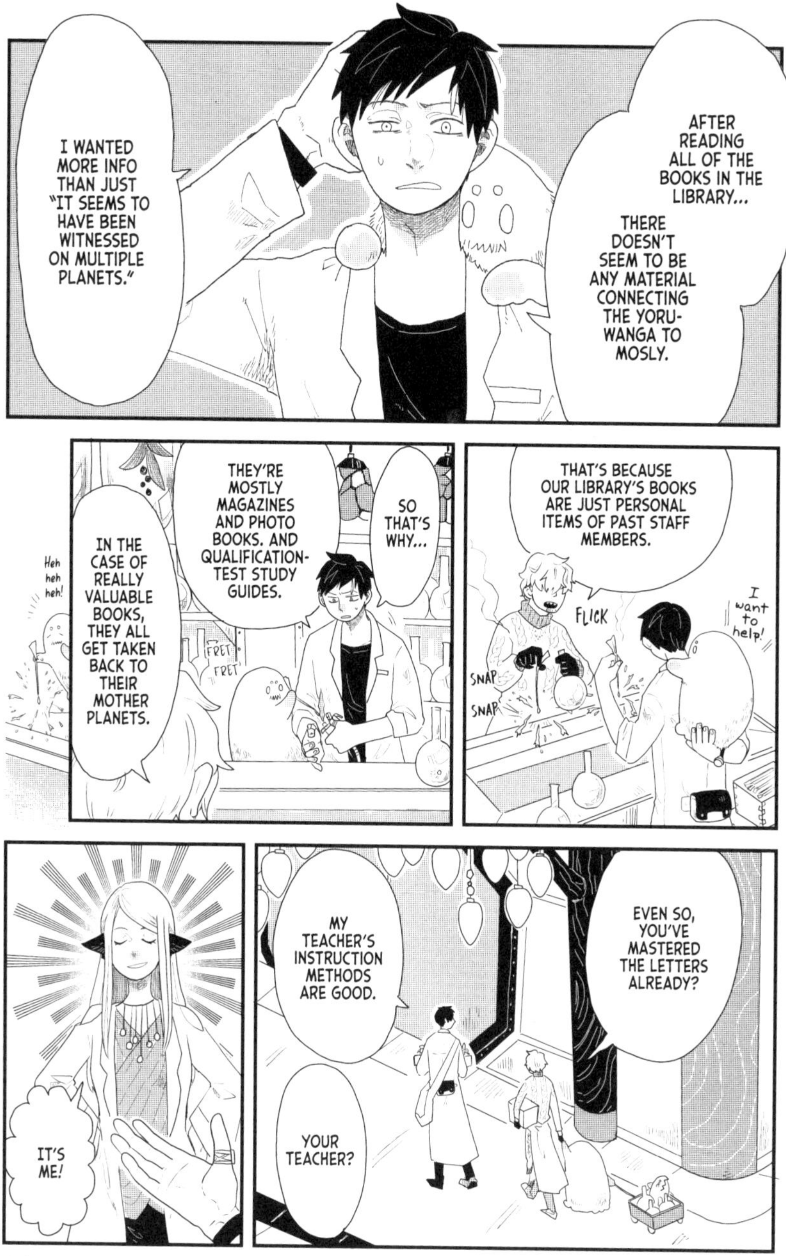
AFTER READING ALL OF THE BOOKS IN THE LIBRARY...
THERE DOESN'T SEEM TO BE ANY MATERIAL CONNECTING THE YORU-WANGA TO MOSLY.
I WANTED MORE INFO THAN JUST "IT SEEMS TO HAVE BEEN WITNESSED ON MULTIPLE PLANETS."
THAT'S BECAUSE OUR LIBRARY'S BOOKS ARE JUST PERSONAL ITEMS OF PAST STAFF MEMBERS.
FLICK
I want to help!
SNAP
SNAP
SO THAT'S WHY...
THEY'RE MOSTLY MAGAZINES AND PHOTO BOOKS. AND QUALIFICATION-TEST STUDY GUIDES.
IN THE CASE OF REALLY VALUABLE BOOKS, THEY ALL GET TAKEN BACK TO THEIR MOTHER PLANETS.
FRET
FRET
Heh heh heh!
EVEN SO, YOU'VE MASTERED THE LETTERS ALREADY?
MY TEACHER'S INSTRUCTION METHODS ARE GOOD.
YOUR TEACHER?
IT'S ME!

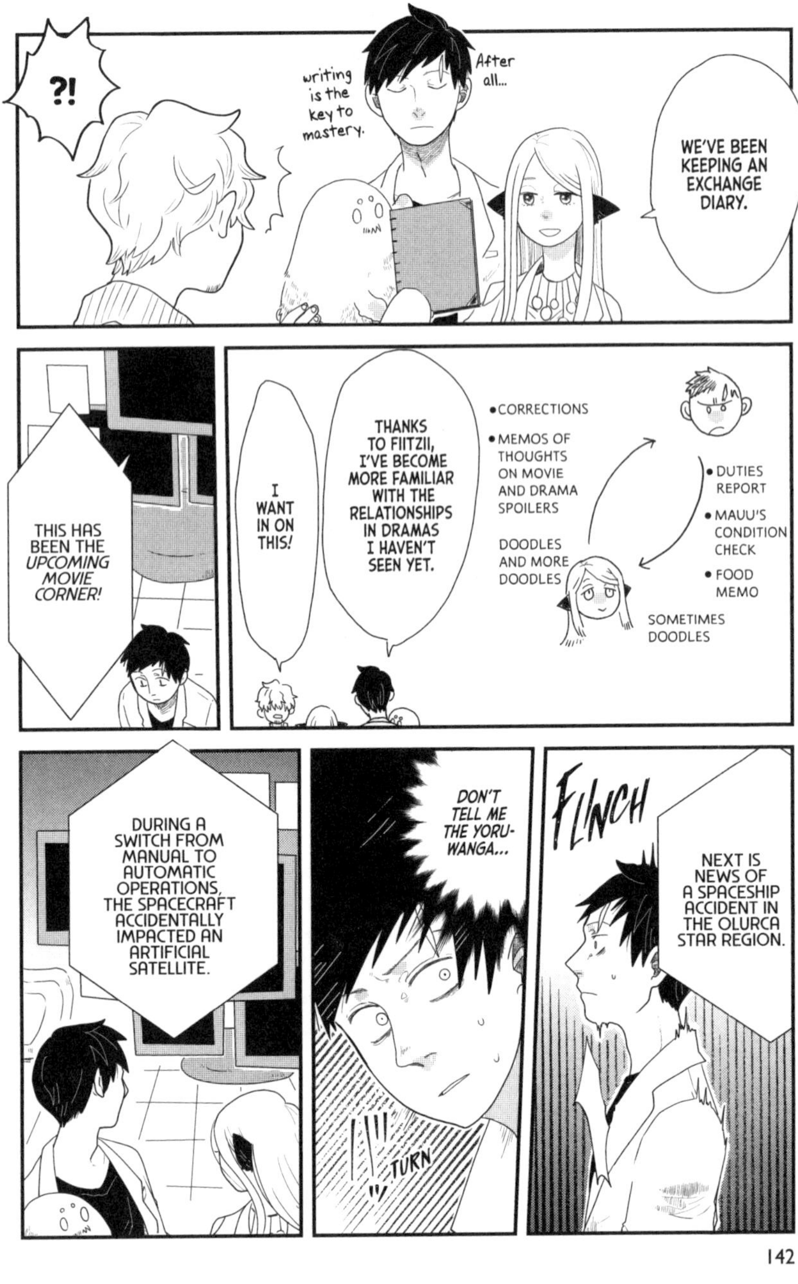
WE'VE BEEN KEEPING AN EXCHANGE DIARY.
After all...
writing is the key to mastery.
?!
THANKS TO FIITZII, I'VE BECOME MORE FAMILIAR WITH THE RELATIONSHIPS IN DRAMAS I HAVEN'T SEEN YET.
I WANT IN ON THIS!
• DUTIES REPORT
• MAUU'S CONDITION CHECK
• FOOD MEMO
SOMETIMES DOODLES
• CORRECTIONS
• MEMOS OF THOUGHTS ON MOVIE AND DRAMA SPOILERS
DOODLES AND MORE DOODLES
THIS HAS BEEN THE *UPCOMING MOVIE CORNER!*
FLINCH
NEXT IS NEWS OF A SPACESHIP ACCIDENT IN THE OLURCA STAR REGION.
DON'T TELL ME THE YORU-WANGA...
TURN
DURING A SWITCH FROM MANUAL TO AUTOMATIC OPERATIONS, THE SPACECRAFT ACCIDENTALLY IMPACTED AN ARTIFICIAL SATELLITE.

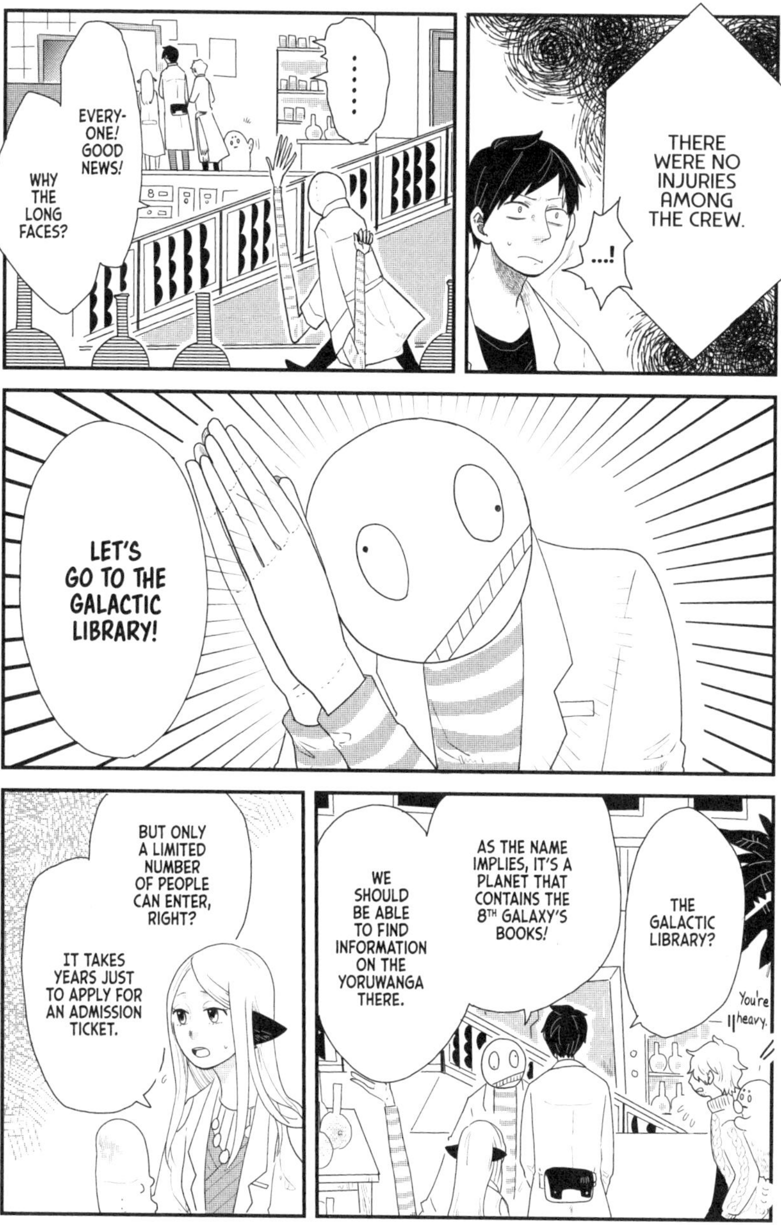
THERE WERE NO INJURIES AMONG THE CREW.
...!
......
EVERY-ONE! GOOD NEWS!
WHY THE LONG FACES?
LET'S GO TO THE GALACTIC LIBRARY!
THE GALACTIC LIBRARY?
You're heavy.
AS THE NAME IMPLIES, IT'S A PLANET THAT CONTAINS THE 8TH GALAXY'S BOOKS!
WE SHOULD BE ABLE TO FIND INFORMATION ON THE YORUWANGA THERE.
BUT ONLY A LIMITED NUMBER OF PEOPLE CAN ENTER, RIGHT?
IT TAKES YEARS JUST TO APPLY FOR AN ADMISSION TICKET.

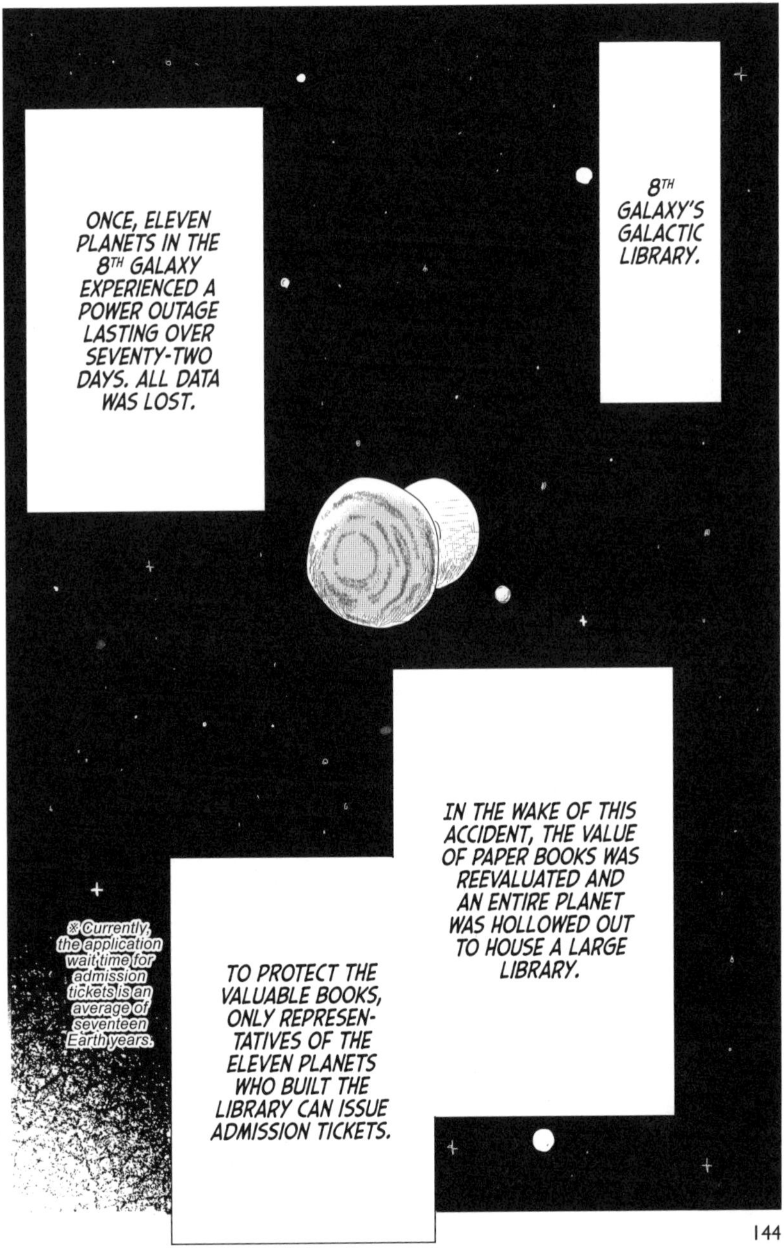
8TH GALAXY'S GALACTIC LIBRARY.
ONCE, ELEVEN PLANETS IN THE 8TH GALAXY EXPERIENCED A POWER OUTAGE LASTING OVER SEVENTY-TWO DAYS. ALL DATA WAS LOST.
IN THE WAKE OF THIS ACCIDENT, THE VALUE OF PAPER BOOKS WAS REEVALUATED AND AN ENTIRE PLANET WAS HOLLOWED OUT TO HOUSE A LARGE LIBRARY.
TO PROTECT THE VALUABLE BOOKS, ONLY REPRESEN-TATIVES OF THE ELEVEN PLANETS WHO BUILT THE LIBRARY CAN ISSUE ADMISSION TICKETS.
※ Currently, the application wait time for admission tickets is an average of seventeen Earth years.

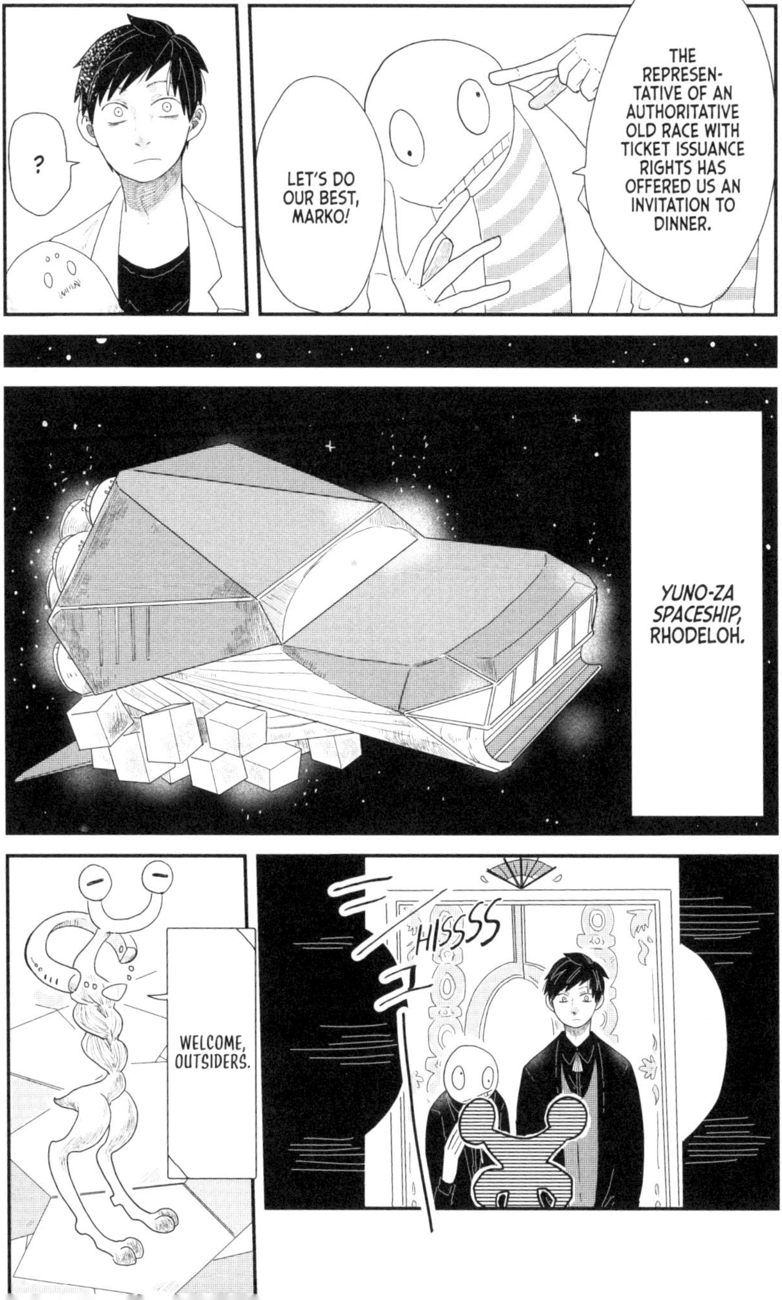
THE REPRESEN-TATIVE OF AN AUTHORITATIVE OLD RACE WITH TICKET ISSUANCE RIGHTS HAS OFFERED US AN INVITATION TO DINNER.
LET'S DO OUR BEST, MARKO!
?
YUNO-ZA SPACESHIP, RHODELOH.
HISSSS
WELCOME, OUTSIDERS.

ALIEN OF YUNO-ZA.

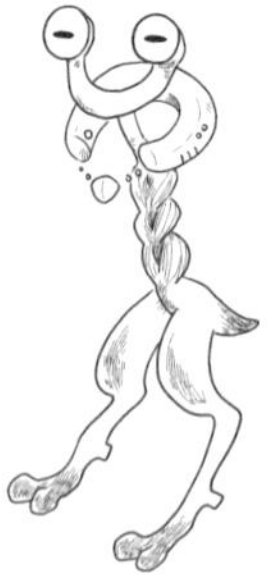

THE MOTHER PLANET OF THE ANCIENT YUNO-ZA RACE DISAPPEARED LONG AGO. SINCE THEN, THE YUNO-ZA HAVE MAINTAINED THEIR LIFESTYLE ON SPACESHIPS. THEIR SHIPS HAVE HAVE 3 TO 617 PASSENGERS, AND THEY PREFER AN ODD NUMBER OF CREW.

IN THE PROCESS OF ADAPTING TO SPACE LIFE, THE YUNO-ZA LOST THEIR DIGESTIVE SYSTEMS. THEY DON'T HAVE MOUTHS, BUT CONVERSATION IS POSSIBLE WITH VOCALIZERS WORN AROUND THEIR NECKS. RELATIVES COMMUNICATE TELEPATHICALLY.

THE YUNO-ZA PRODUCE MANY VIPS OF THE GALACTIC SECURITY ALLIANCE.

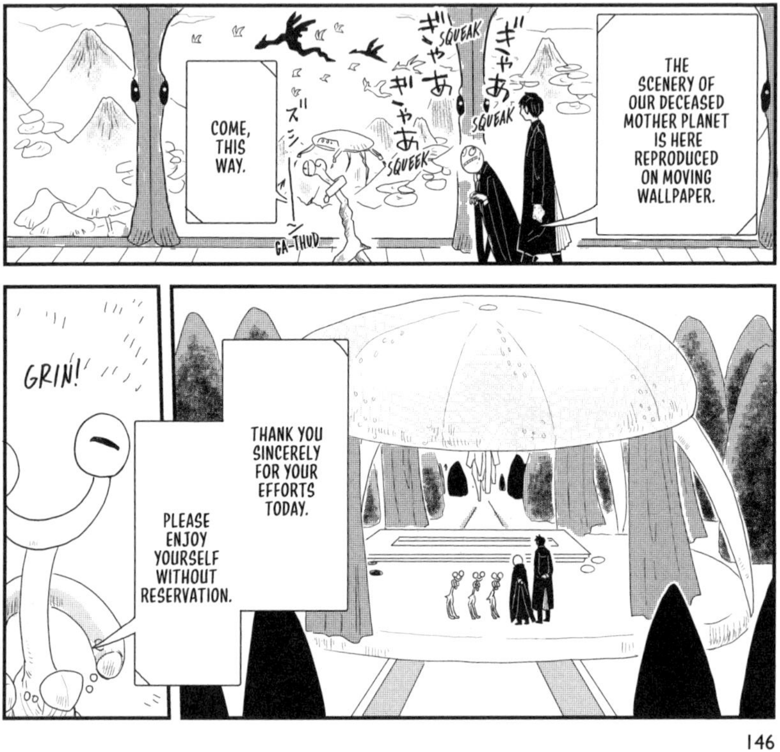
THE SCENERY OF OUR DECEASED MOTHER PLANET IS HERE REPRODUCED ON MOVING WALLPAPER.
ぎゃあ
SQUEAK
ぎゃあ
SQUEAK
ぎゃあ
SQUEEK
COME, THIS WAY.
ズシー
GA-THUD
THANK YOU SINCERELY FOR YOUR EFFORTS TODAY.
GRIN!
PLEASE ENJOY YOURSELF WITHOUT RESERVATION.

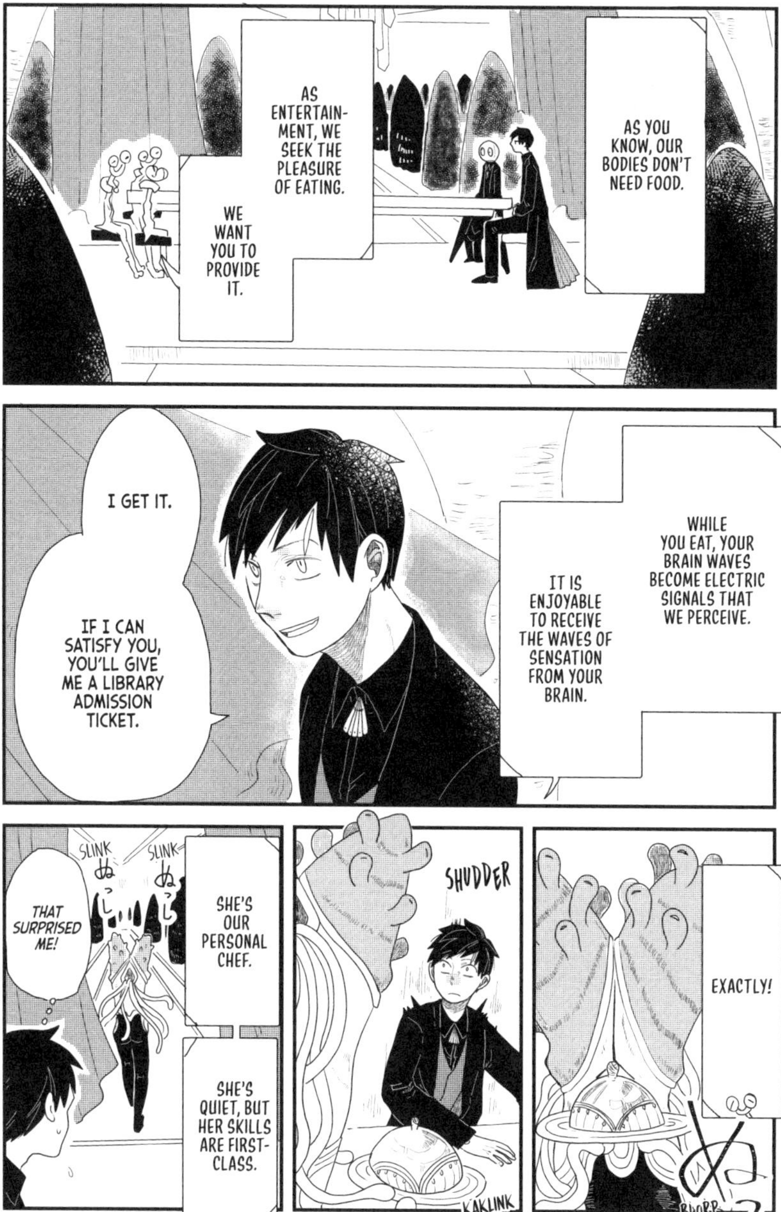

AS YOU KNOW, OUR BODIES DON'T NEED FOOD.
AS ENTERTAINMENT, WE SEEK THE PLEASURE OF EATING.
WE WANT YOU TO PROVIDE IT.
WHILE YOU EAT, YOUR BRAIN WAVES BECOME ELECTRIC SIGNALS THAT WE PERCEIVE.
IT IS ENJOYABLE TO RECEIVE THE WAVES OF SENSATION FROM YOUR BRAIN.
I GET IT.
IF I CAN SATISFY YOU, YOU'LL GIVE ME A LIBRARY ADMISSION TICKET.
EXACTLY!
BLORP
SHUDDER
KAKLINK
SHE'S OUR PERSONAL CHEF.
SLINK
SLINK
THAT SURPRISED ME!
SHE'S QUIET, BUT HER SKILLS ARE FIRST-CLASS.

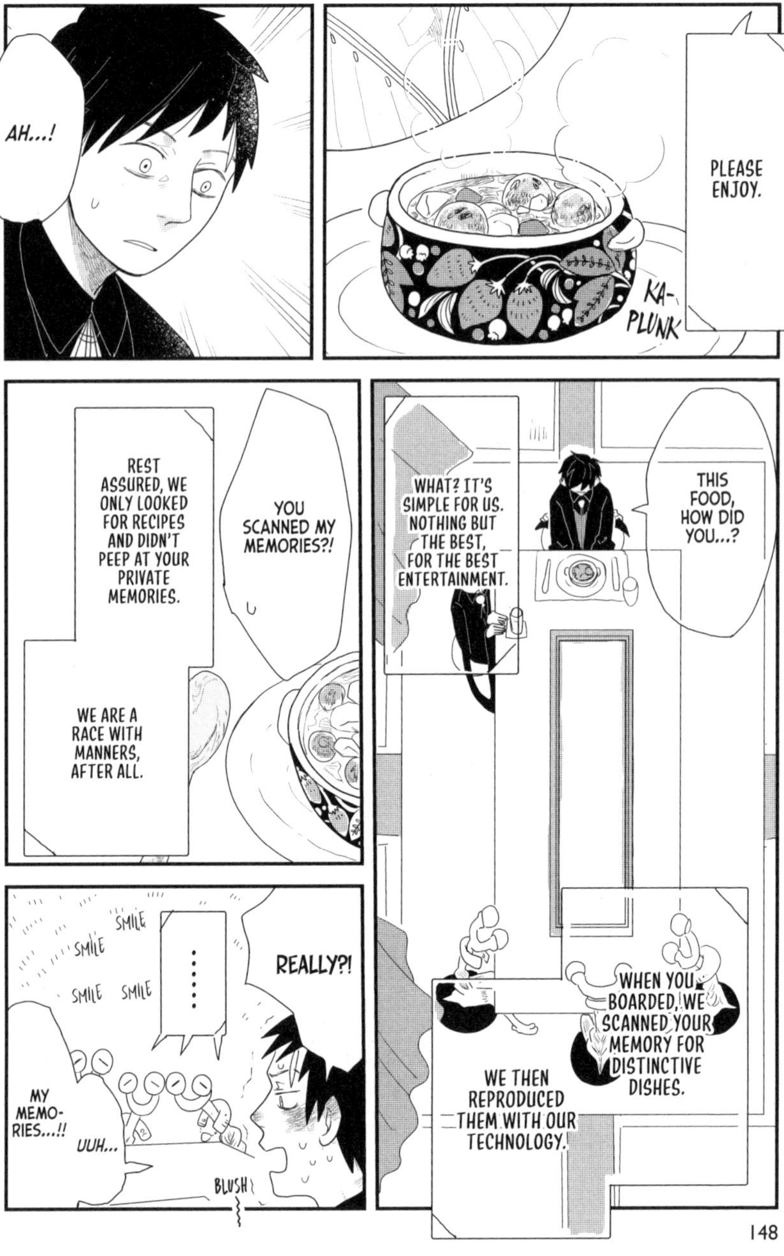
PLEASE ENJOY.
KA-PLUNK
AH...!
THIS FOOD, HOW DID YOU...?
WHAT? IT'S SIMPLE FOR US. NOTHING BUT THE BEST, FOR THE BEST ENTERTAINMENT.
WHEN YOU BOARDED, WE SCANNED YOUR MEMORY FOR DISTINCTIVE DISHES.
WE THEN REPRODUCED THEM WITH OUR TECHNOLOGY.
YOU SCANNED MY MEMORIES?!
REST ASSURED, WE ONLY LOOKED FOR RECIPES AND DIDN'T PEEP AT YOUR PRIVATE MEMORIES.
WE ARE A RACE WITH MANNERS, AFTER ALL.
REALLY?!
......
SMILE
SMILE
SMILE
SMILE
MY MEMO-RIES...!!
UUH...
BLUSH

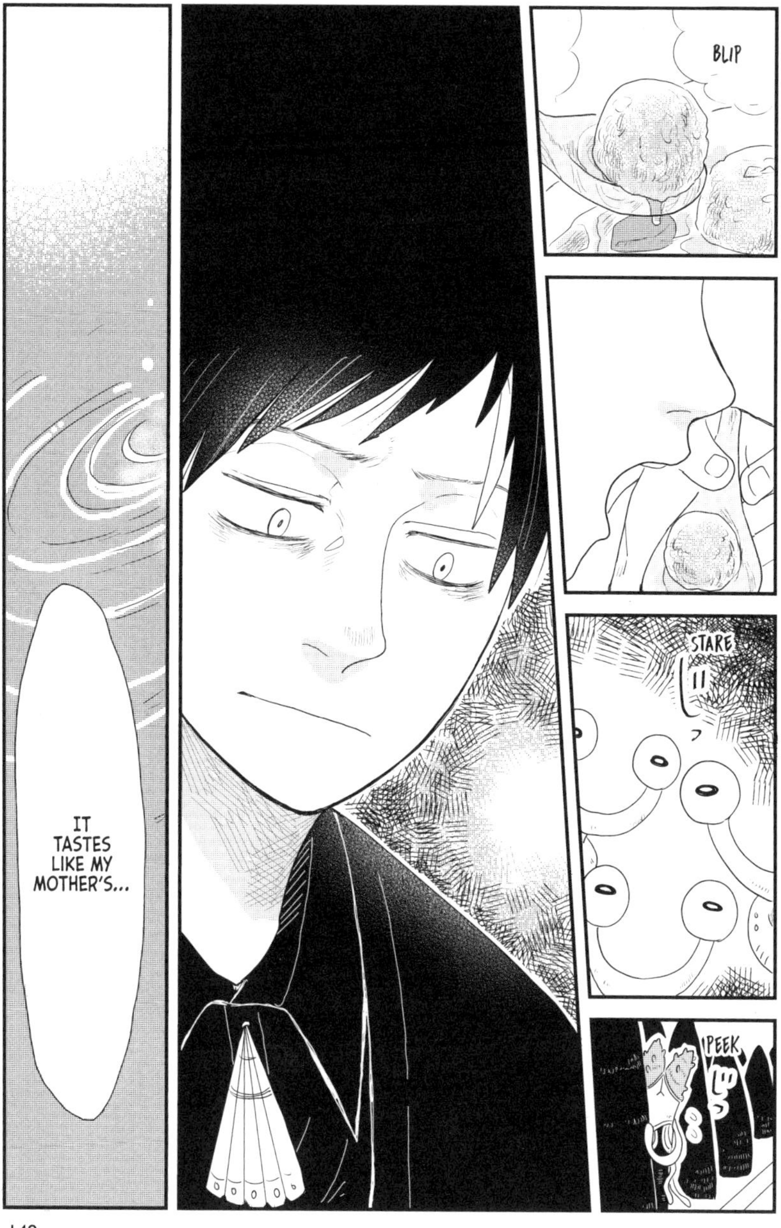
BLIP
STARE
PEEK
IT TASTES LIKE MY MOTHER'S...

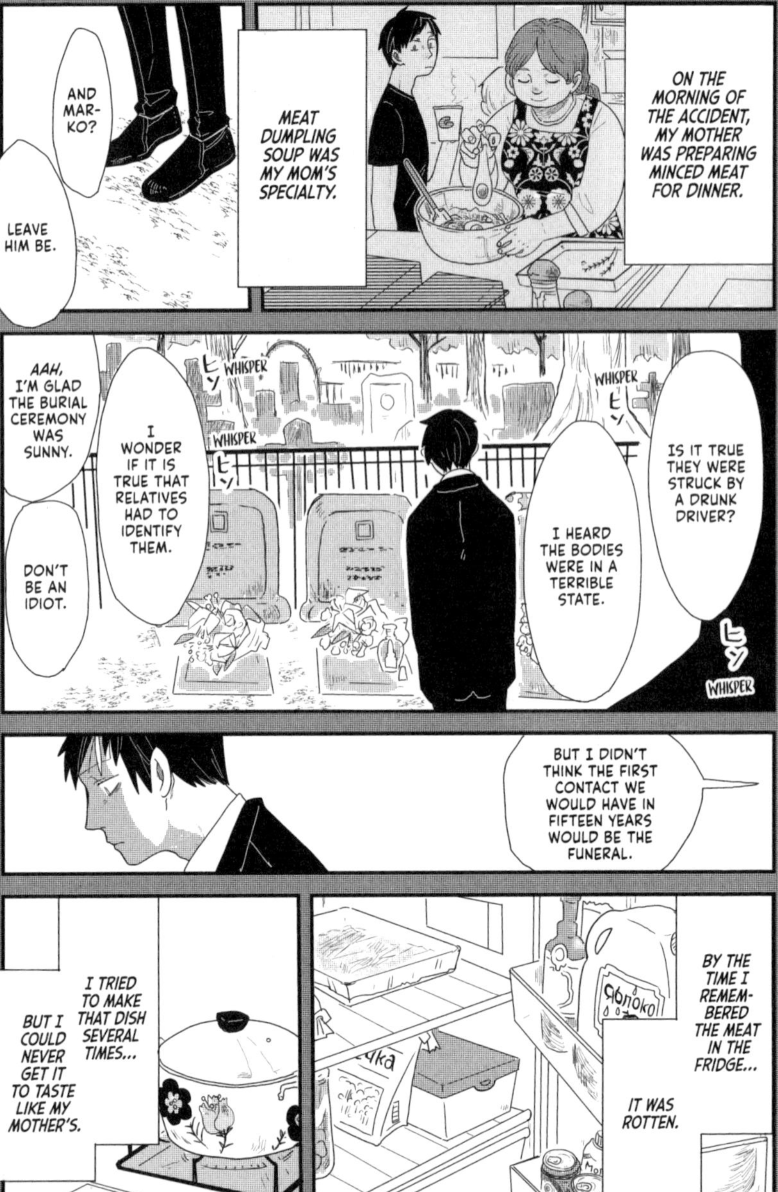
ON THE MORNING OF THE ACCIDENT, MY MOTHER WAS PREPARING MINCED MEAT FOR DINNER.
MEAT DUMPLING SOUP WAS MY MOM'S SPECIALTY.
AND MAR-KO?
LEAVE HIM BE.
ヒソ WHISPER
IS IT TRUE THEY WERE STRUCK BY A DRUNK DRIVER?
WHISPER ヒソ
I HEARD THE BODIES WERE IN A TERRIBLE STATE.
WHISPER ヒソ
WHISPER ヒソ
I WONDER IF IT IS TRUE THAT RELATIVES HAD TO IDENTIFY THEM.
AAH, I'M GLAD THE BURIAL CEREMONY WAS SUNNY.
DON'T BE AN IDIOT.
BUT I DIDN'T THINK THE FIRST CONTACT WE WOULD HAVE IN FIFTEEN YEARS WOULD BE THE FUNERAL.
BY THE TIME I REMEM-BERED THE MEAT IN THE FRIDGE...
IT WAS ROTTEN.
яблоко
I TRIED TO MAKE THAT DISH SEVERAL TIMES...
BUT I COULD NEVER GET IT TO TASTE LIKE MY MOTHER'S.

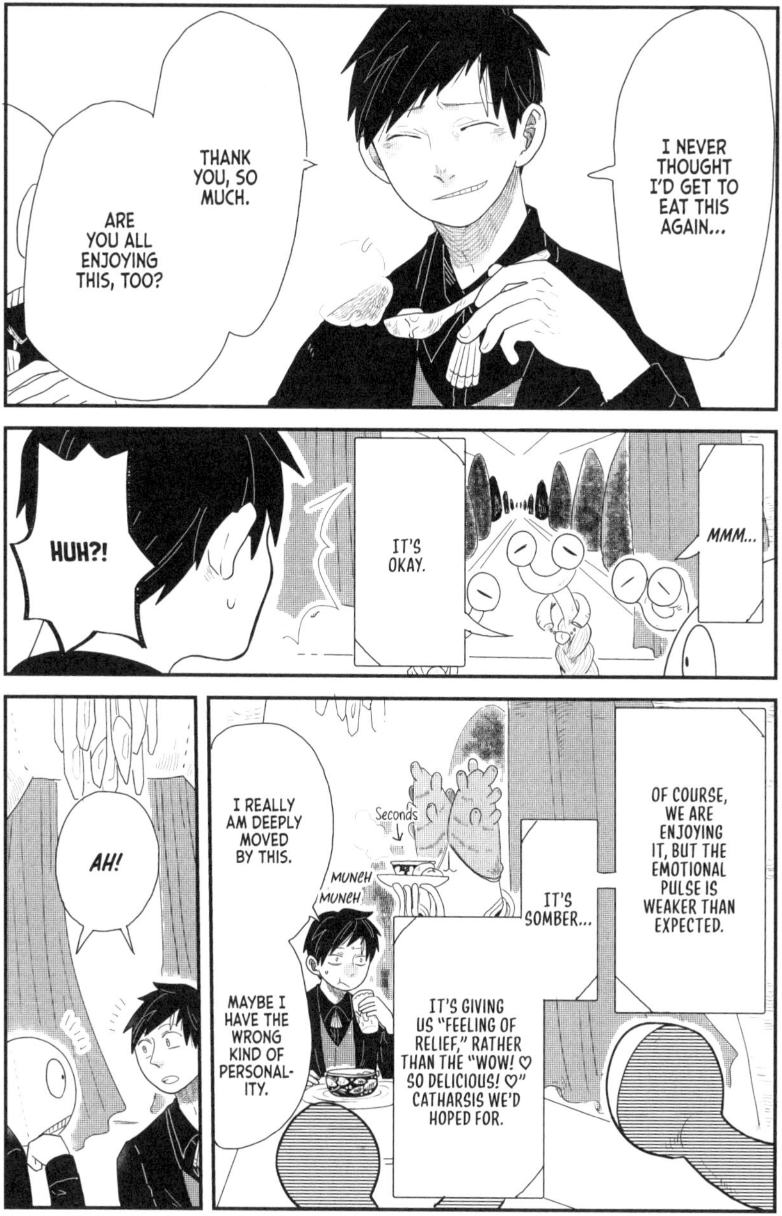
I NEVER THOUGHT I'D GET TO EAT THIS AGAIN...
THANK YOU, SO MUCH.
ARE YOU ALL ENJOYING THIS, TOO?
MMM...
IT'S OKAY.
HUH?!
OF COURSE, WE ARE ENJOYING IT, BUT THE EMOTIONAL PULSE IS WEAKER THAN EXPECTED.
IT'S SOMBER...
IT'S GIVING US "FEELING OF RELIEF," RATHER THAN THE "WOW! ♡ SO DELICIOUS! ♡" CATHARSIS WE'D HOPED FOR.
Seconds
MUNCH MUNCH
I REALLY AM DEEPLY MOVED BY THIS.
MAYBE I HAVE THE WRONG KIND OF PERSONALITY.
AH!

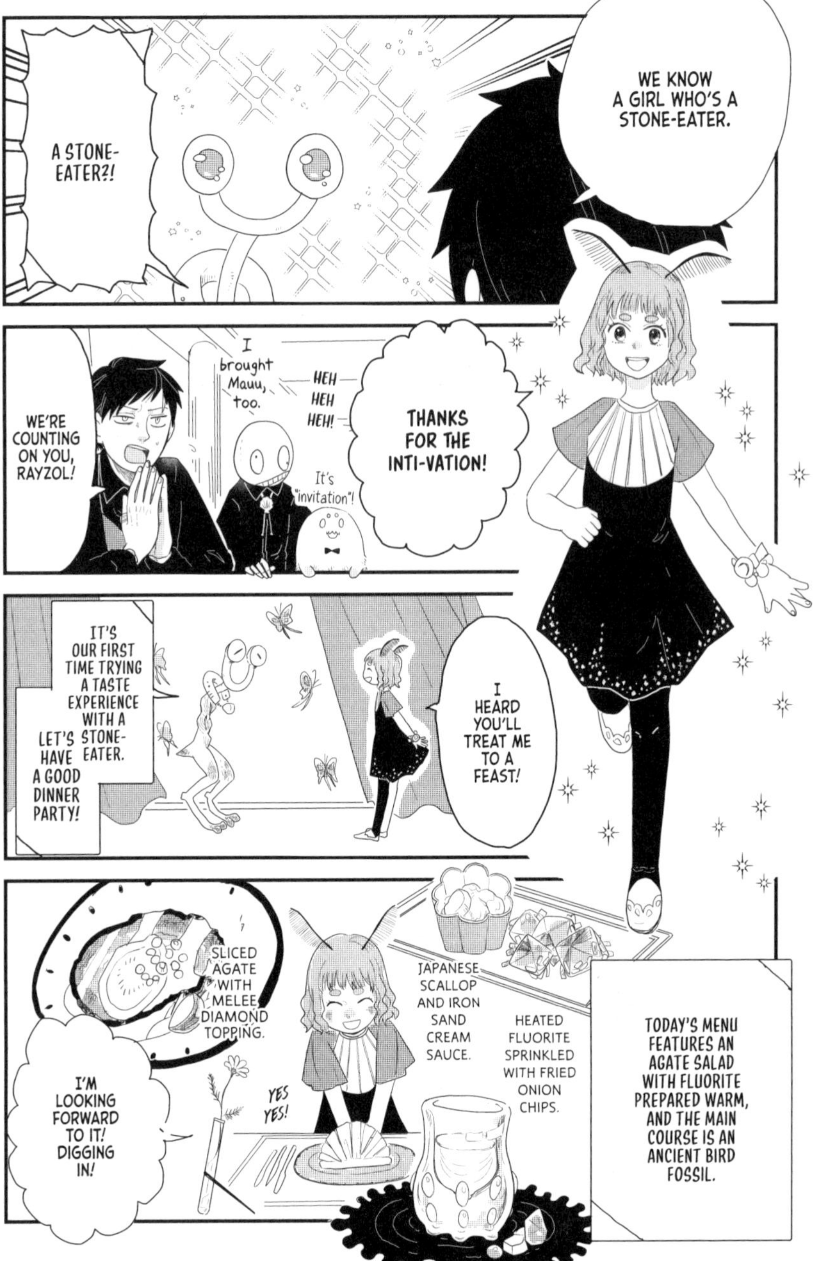
WE KNOW A GIRL WHO'S A STONE-EATER.
A STONE-EATER?!
THANKS FOR THE INTI-VATION!
HEH HEH HEH!
I brought Mauu, too.
It's "invitation"!
WE'RE COUNTING ON YOU, RAYZOL!
I HEARD YOU'LL TREAT ME TO A FEAST!
IT'S OUR FIRST TIME TRYING A TASTE EXPERIENCE WITH A STONE-EATER.
LET'S HAVE A GOOD DINNER PARTY!
TODAY'S MENU FEATURES AN AGATE SALAD WITH FLUORITE PREPARED WARM, AND THE MAIN COURSE IS AN ANCIENT BIRD FOSSIL.
HEATED FLUORITE SPRINKLED WITH FRIED ONION CHIPS.
JAPANESE SCALLOP AND IRON SAND CREAM SAUCE.
SLICED AGATE WITH MELEE DIAMOND TOPPING.
YES YES!
I'M LOOKING FORWARD TO IT! DIGGING IN!

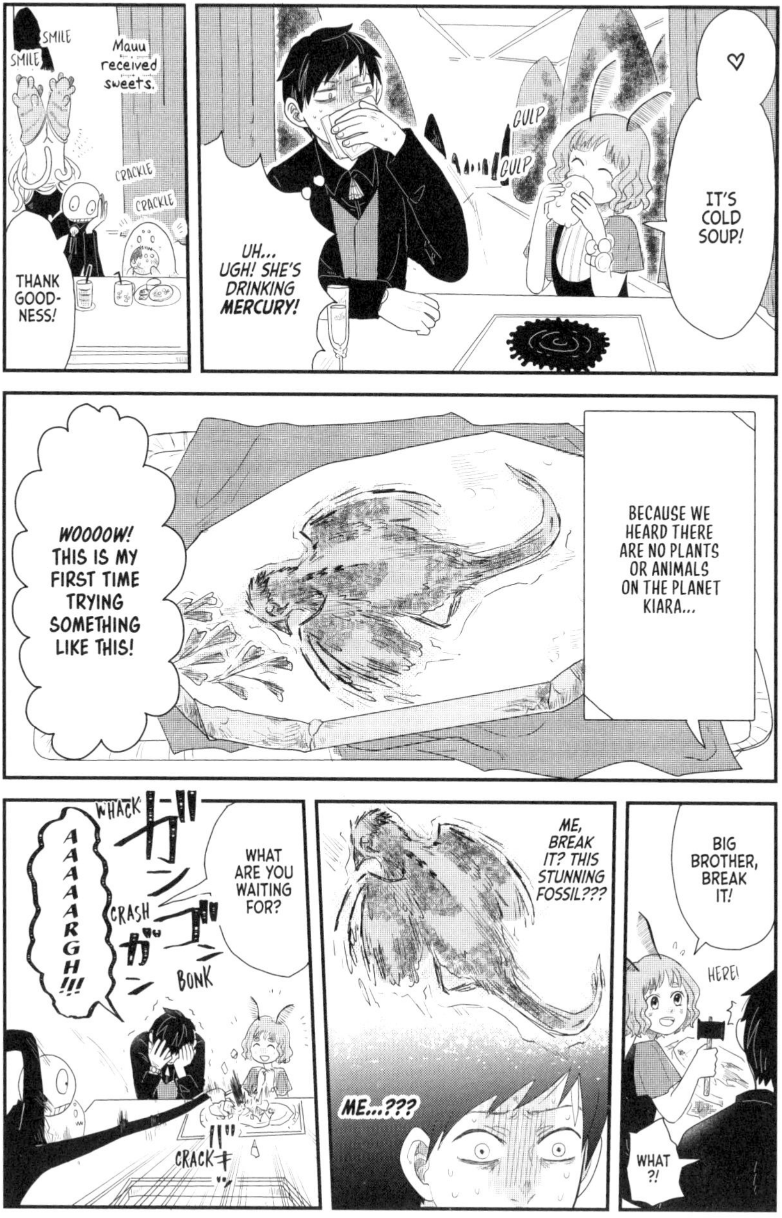
♡
IT'S COLD SOUP!
GULP
GULP
UH... UGH! SHE'S DRINKING MERCURY!
SMILE
SMILE
Mauu received sweets.
CRACKLE
CRACKLE
THANK GOODNESS!
BECAUSE WE HEARD THERE ARE NO PLANTS OR ANIMALS ON THE PLANET KIARA...
WOOOOW! THIS IS MY FIRST TIME TRYING SOMETHING LIKE THIS!
BIG BROTHER, BREAK IT!
HERE!
WHAT?!
ME, BREAK IT? THIS STUNNING FOSSIL???
ME...???
WHAT ARE YOU WAITING FOR?
WHACK
AAAAAAARGH!!!
CRASH
BONK
CRACK

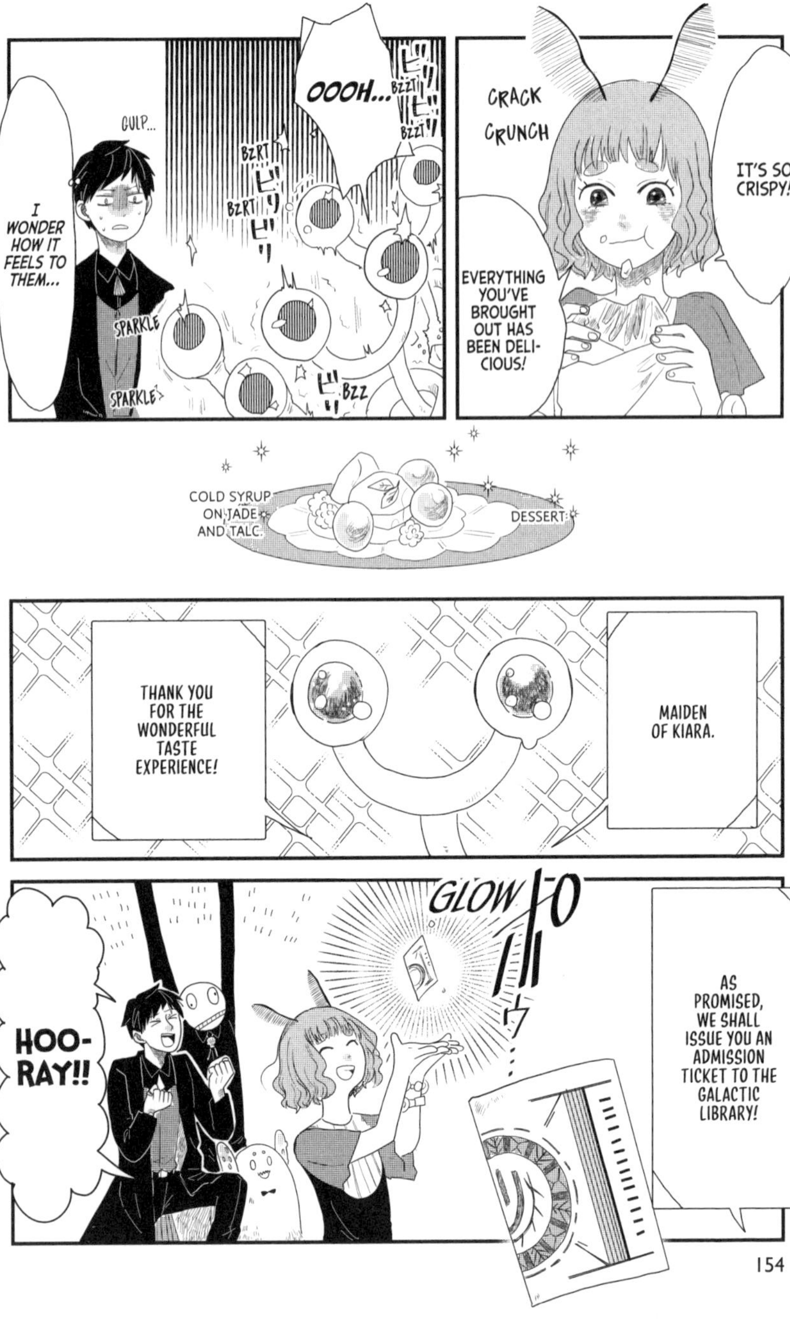
CRACK
CRUNCH
IT'S SO CRISPY!
EVERYTHING YOU'VE BROUGHT OUT HAS BEEN DELICIOUS!
OOOH...
BZZT
BZZT
BZRT
BZRT
BZZ
GULP...
I WONDER HOW IT FEELS TO THEM...
SPARKLE
SPARKLE
DESSERT:
COLD SYRUP ON JADE AND TALC
MAIDEN OF KIARA.
THANK YOU FOR THE WONDERFUL TASTE EXPERIENCE!
AS PROMISED, WE SHALL ISSUE YOU AN ADMISSION TICKET TO THE GALACTIC LIBRARY!
GLOW
HOO-RAY!!

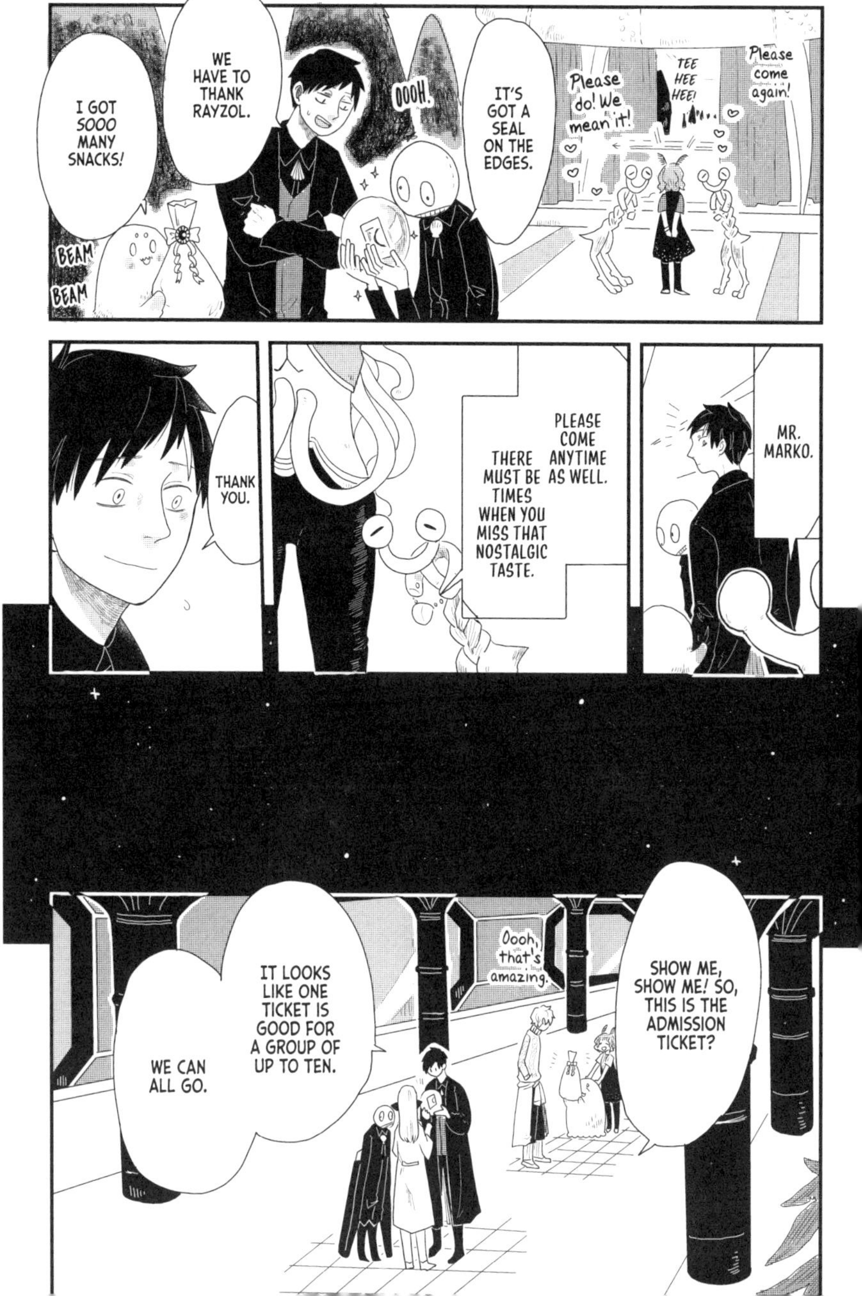

Please come again!
TEE HEE HEE!
Please do! We mean it!
IT'S GOT A SEAL ON THE EDGES.
OOOH.
WE HAVE TO THANK RAYZOL.
I GOT SOOO MANY SNACKS!
BEAM BEAM
MR. MARKO.
PLEASE COME ANYTIME AS WELL.
THERE MUST BE TIMES WHEN YOU MISS THAT NOSTALGIC TASTE.
THANK YOU.
SHOW ME, SHOW ME! SO, THIS IS THE ADMISSION TICKET?
Oooh, that's amazing.
IT LOOKS LIKE ONE TICKET IS GOOD FOR A GROUP OF UP TO TEN.
WE CAN ALL GO.

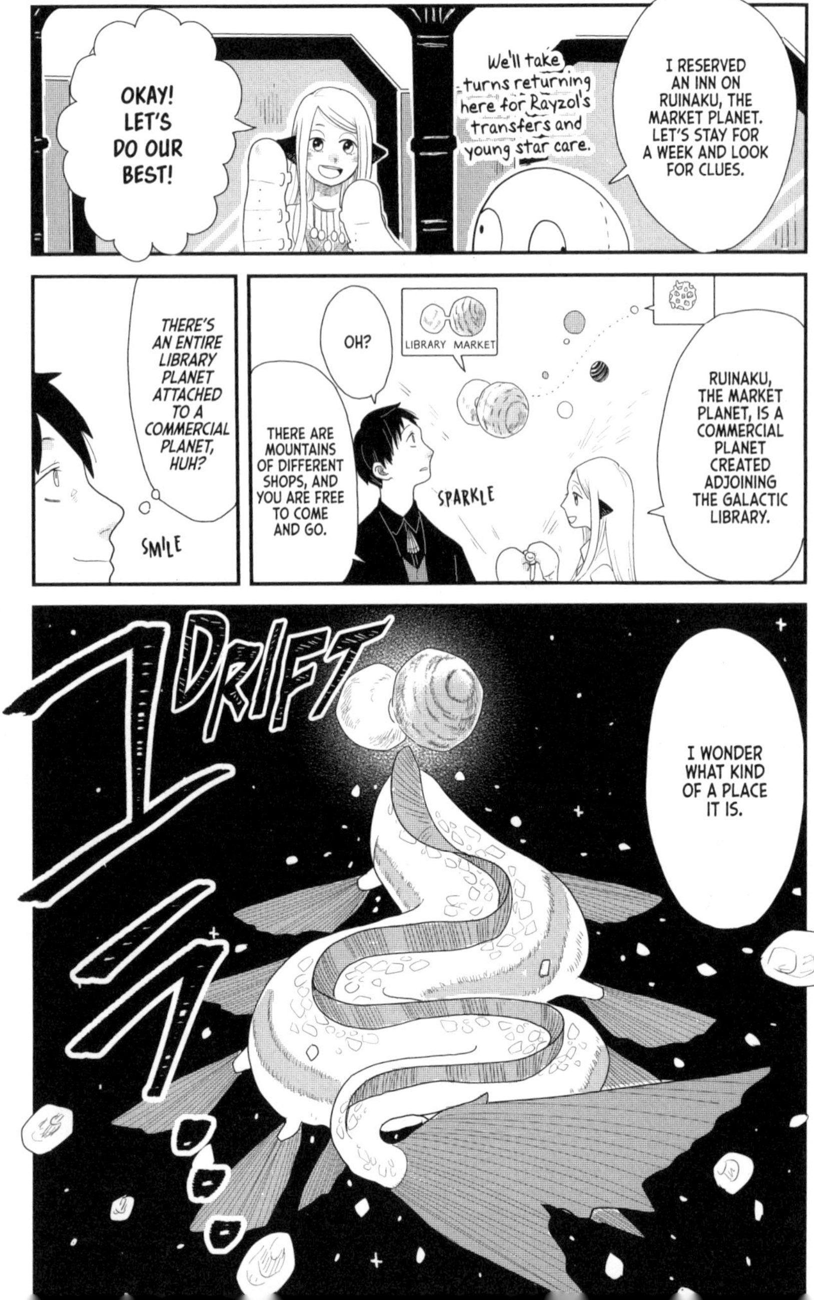
I RESERVED AN INN ON RUINAKU, THE MARKET PLANET. LET'S STAY FOR A WEEK AND LOOK FOR CLUES.
We'll take turns returning here for Rayzol's transfers and young star care.
OKAY! LET'S DO OUR BEST!
RUINAKU, THE MARKET PLANET, IS A COMMERCIAL PLANET CREATED ADJOINING THE GALACTIC LIBRARY.
LIBRARY MARKET
OH?
THERE ARE MOUNTAINS OF DIFFERENT SHOPS, AND YOU ARE FREE TO COME AND GO.
SPARKLE
THERE'S AN ENTIRE LIBRARY PLANET ATTACHED TO A COMMERCIAL PLANET, HUH?
SMILE
I WONDER WHAT KIND OF A PLACE IT IS.
DRIFT

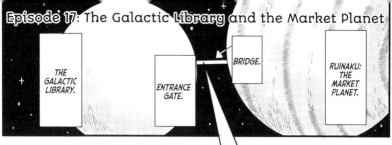

Episode 17: The Galactic Library and the Market Planet

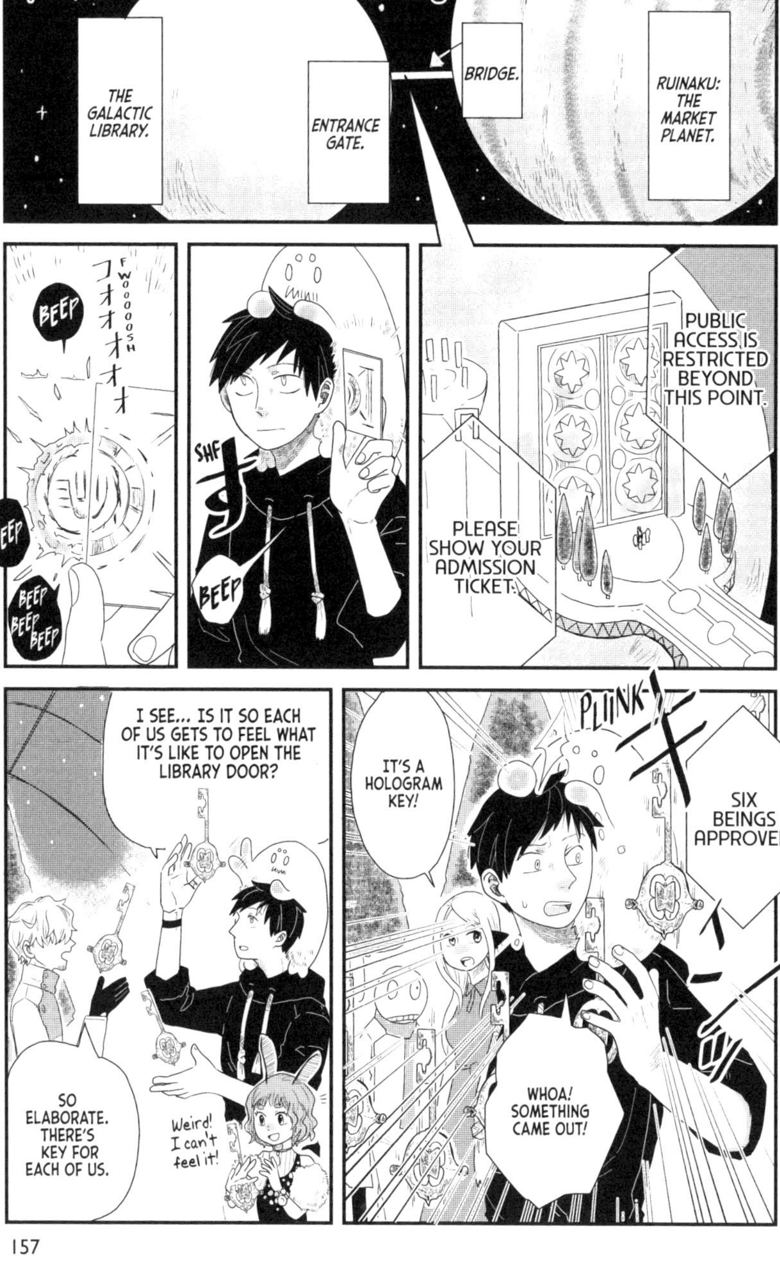

RUINAKU: THE MARKET PLANET.
BRIDGE.
ENTRANCE GATE.
THE GALACTIC LIBRARY.
PUBLIC ACCESS IS RESTRICTED BEYOND THIS POINT.
PLEASE SHOW YOUR ADMISSION TICKET.
SHF
BEEP
BEEP
FWOOOOOOSH
BEEP
BEEP BEEP BEEP
PLIINK
SIX BEINGS APPROVED.
IT'S A HOLOGRAM KEY!
WHOA! SOMETHING CAME OUT!
I SEE... IS IT SO EACH OF US GETS TO FEEL WHAT IT'S LIKE TO OPEN THE LIBRARY DOOR?
SO ELABORATE. THERE'S KEY FOR EACH OF US.
Weird! I can't feel it!

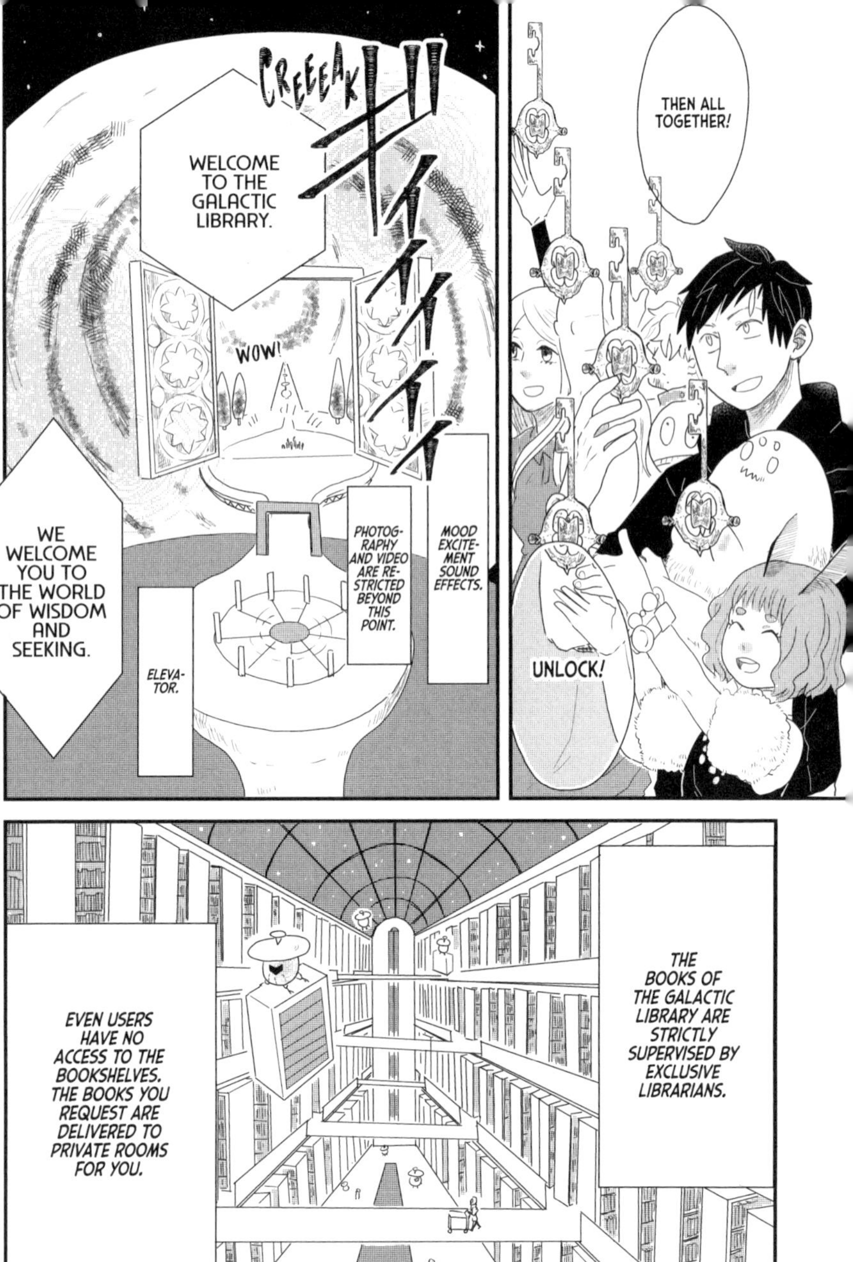
THEN ALL TOGETHER!
UNLOCK!
CREEEAK
WELCOME TO THE GALACTIC LIBRARY.
WOW!
MOOD EXCITEMENT SOUND EFFECTS.
PHOTOGRAPHY AND VIDEO ARE RESTRICTED BEYOND THIS POINT.
WE WELCOME YOU TO THE WORLD OF WISDOM AND SEEKING.
ELEVATOR.
THE BOOKS OF THE GALACTIC LIBRARY ARE STRICTLY SUPERVISED BY EXCLUSIVE LIBRARIANS.
EVEN USERS HAVE NO ACCESS TO THE BOOKSHELVES. THE BOOKS YOU REQUEST ARE DELIVERED TO PRIVATE ROOMS FOR YOU.

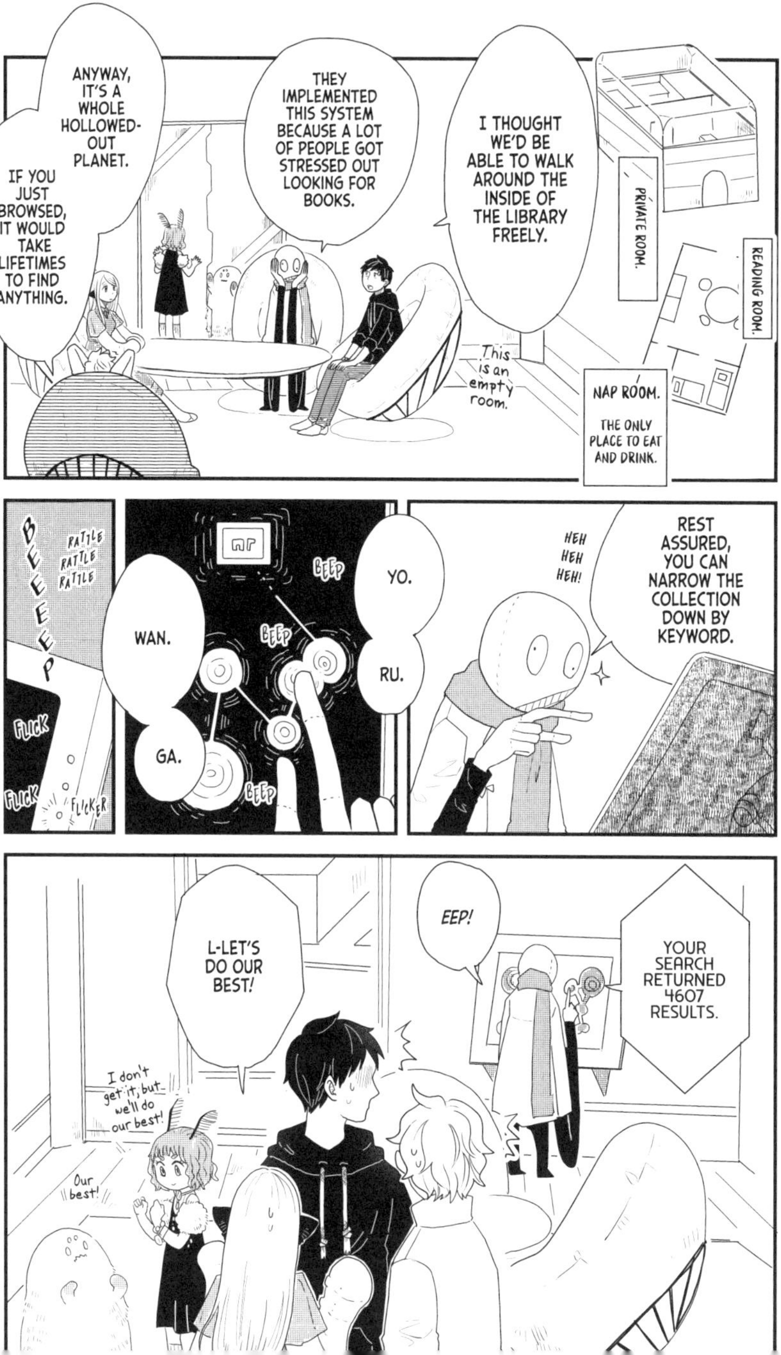
PRIVATE ROOM.
READING ROOM.
I THOUGHT WE'D BE ABLE TO WALK AROUND THE INSIDE OF THE LIBRARY FREELY.
THEY IMPLEMENTED THIS SYSTEM BECAUSE A LOT OF PEOPLE GOT STRESSED OUT LOOKING FOR BOOKS.
ANYWAY, IT'S A WHOLE HOLLOWED-OUT PLANET.
IF YOU JUST BROWSED, IT WOULD TAKE LIFETIMES TO FIND ANYTHING.
NAP ROOM.
THE ONLY PLACE TO EAT AND DRINK.
This is an empty room.
REST ASSURED, YOU CAN NARROW THE COLLECTION DOWN BY KEYWORD.
HEH HEH HEH!
YO.
RU.
BEEP
BEEP
WAN.
GA.
BEEP
BEEEEP
RATTLE RATTLE RATTLE
FLICK
FLICK
FLICKER
YOUR SEARCH RETURNED 4607 RESULTS.
EEP!
L-LET'S DO OUR BEST!
I don't get it, but we'll do our best!
Our best!

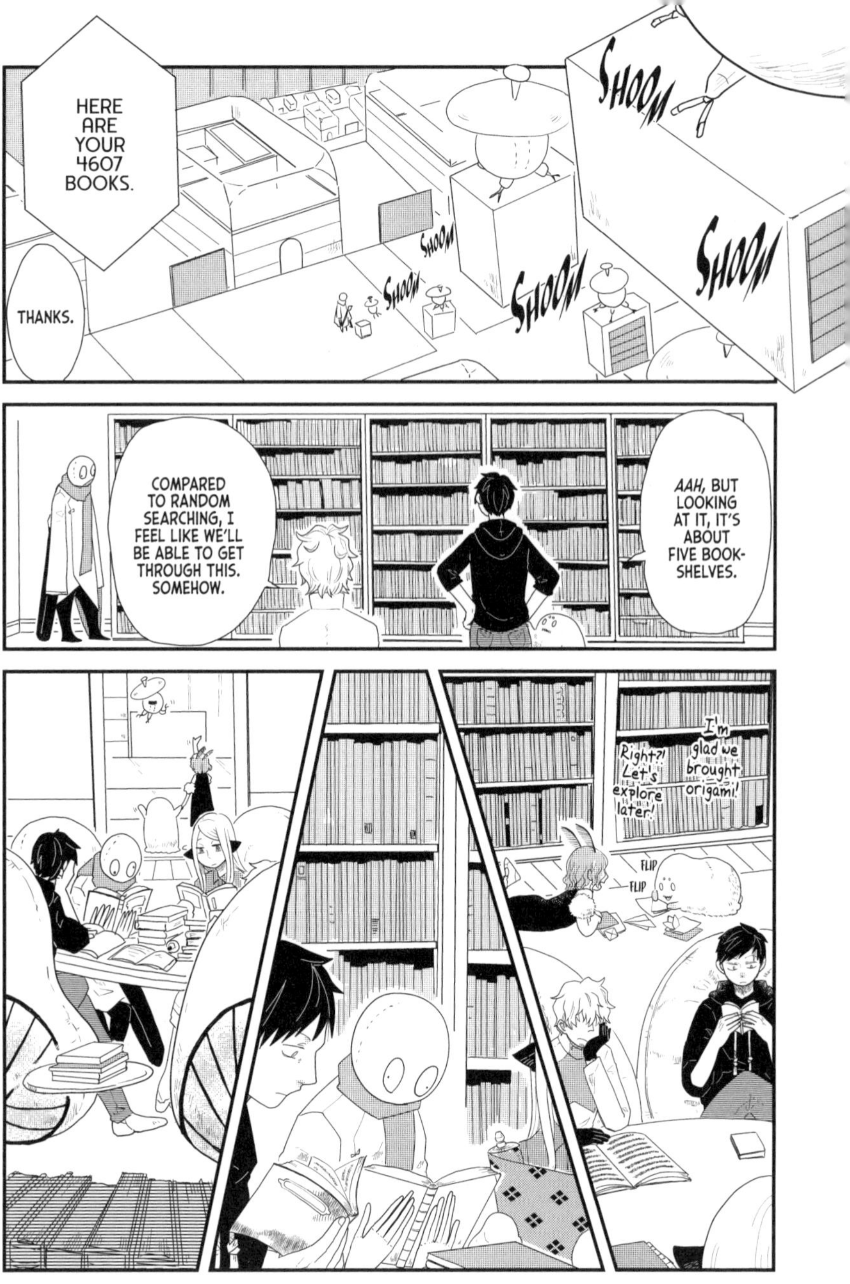
SHOOM
SHOOM
SHOOM
SHOOM
SHOOM
HERE ARE YOUR 4607 BOOKS.
THANKS.
AAH, BUT LOOKING AT IT, IT'S ABOUT FIVE BOOK-SHELVES.
COMPARED TO RANDOM SEARCHING, I FEEL LIKE WE'LL BE ABLE TO GET THROUGH THIS. SOMEHOW.
I'm glad we brought origami!
Right?! Let's explore later!
FLIP
FLIP

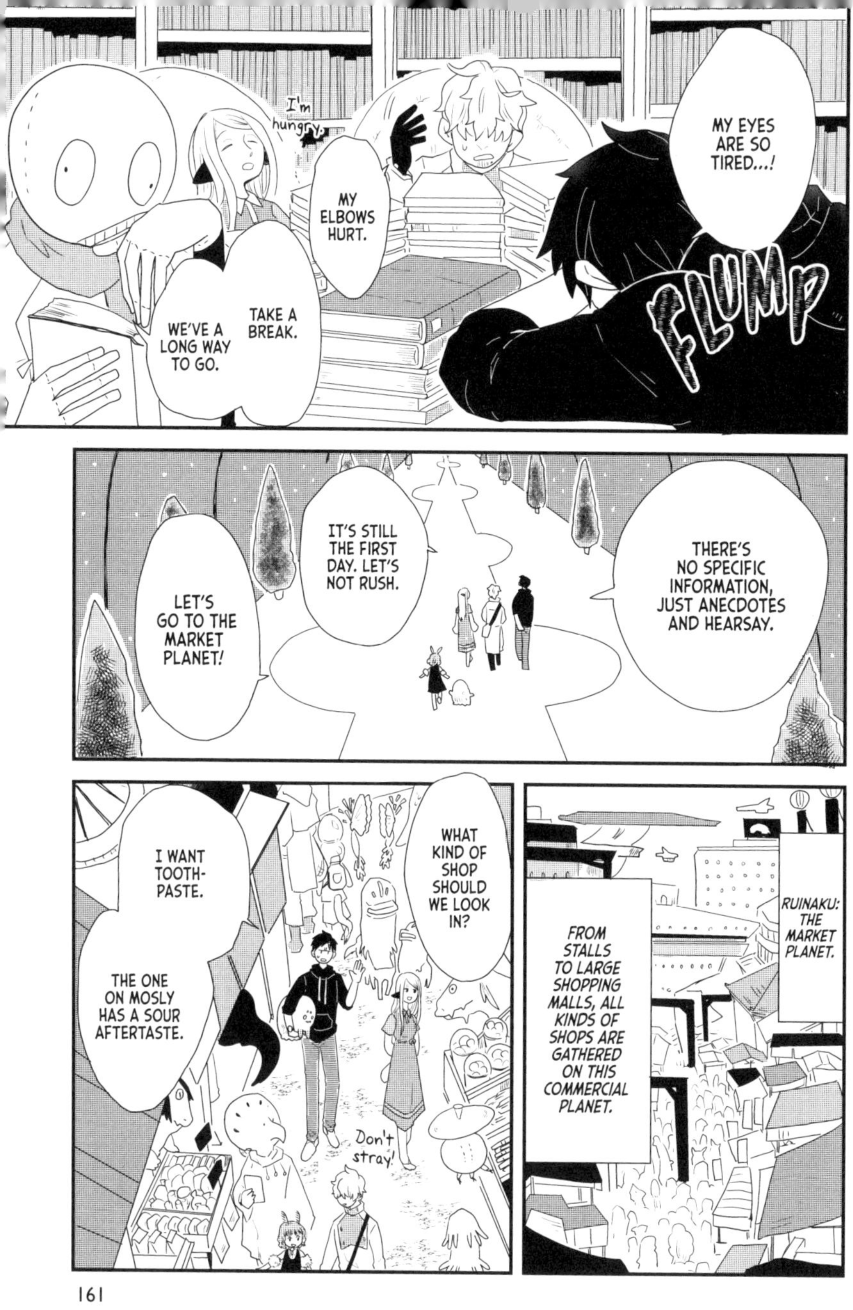
MY EYES ARE SO TIRED...!
FLUMP
I'm hungry.
MY ELBOWS HURT.
TAKE A BREAK.
WE'VE A LONG WAY TO GO.
THERE'S NO SPECIFIC INFORMATION, JUST ANECDOTES AND HEARSAY.
IT'S STILL THE FIRST DAY. LET'S NOT RUSH.
LET'S GO TO THE MARKET PLANET!
RUINAKU: THE MARKET PLANET.
FROM STALLS TO LARGE SHOPPING MALLS, ALL KINDS OF SHOPS ARE GATHERED ON THIS COMMERCIAL PLANET.
WHAT KIND OF SHOP SHOULD WE LOOK IN?
I WANT TOOTH-PASTE.
THE ONE ON MOSLY HAS A SOUR AFTERTASTE.
Don't stray!

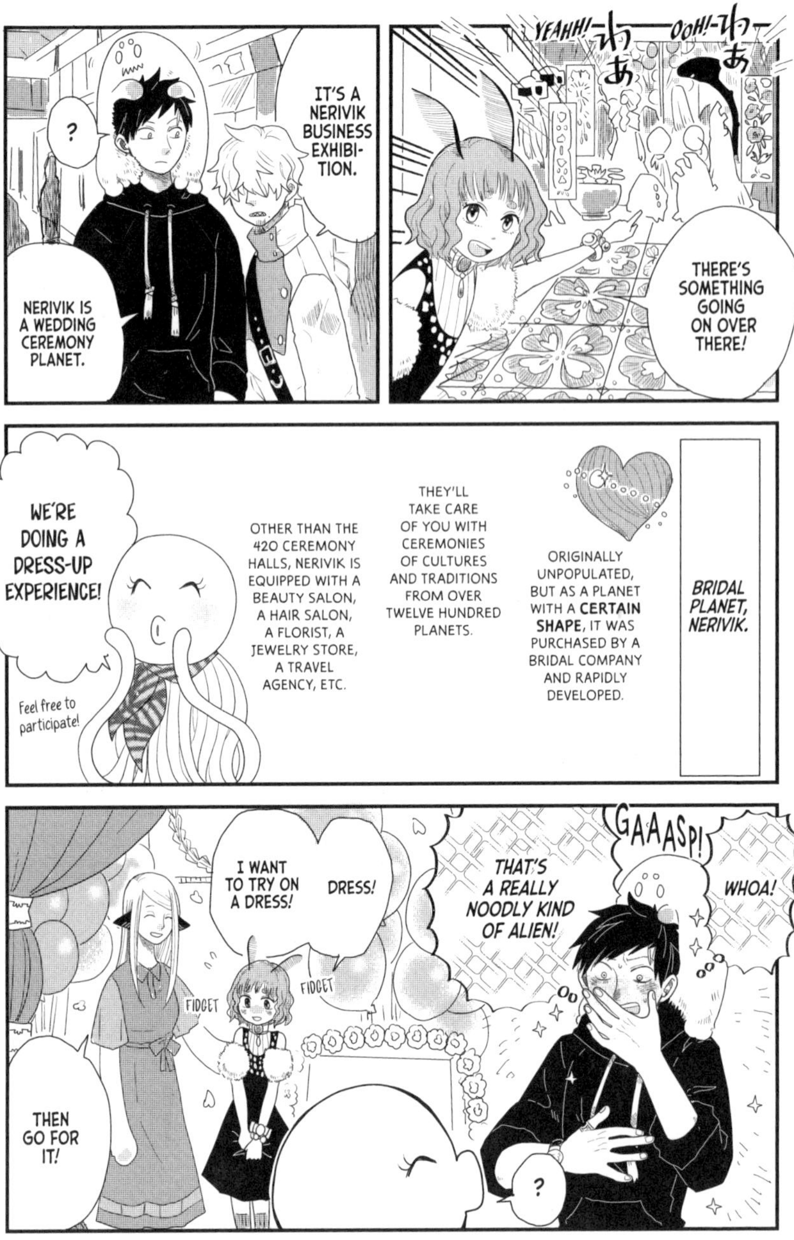

OOH!-わっ
あ
YEAHH!-わっ
あ
THERE'S SOMETHING GOING ON OVER THERE!
IT'S A NERIVIK BUSINESS EXHIBITION.
?
NERIVIK IS A WEDDING CEREMONY PLANET.
BRIDAL PLANET, NERIVIK.
ORIGINALLY UNPOPULATED, BUT AS A PLANET WITH A **CERTAIN SHAPE**, IT WAS PURCHASED BY A BRIDAL COMPANY AND RAPIDLY DEVELOPED.
THEY'LL TAKE CARE OF YOU WITH CEREMONIES OF CULTURES AND TRADITIONS FROM OVER TWELVE HUNDRED PLANETS.
OTHER THAN THE 420 CEREMONY HALLS, NERIVIK IS EQUIPPED WITH A BEAUTY SALON, A HAIR SALON, A FLORIST, A JEWELRY STORE, A TRAVEL AGENCY, ETC.
WE'RE DOING A DRESS-UP EXPERIENCE!
Feel free to participate!
GAAASP!
WHOA!
THAT'S A REALLY NOODLY KIND OF ALIEN!
DRESS!
I WANT TO TRY ON A DRESS!
FIDGET
FIDGET
?
THEN GO FOR IT!

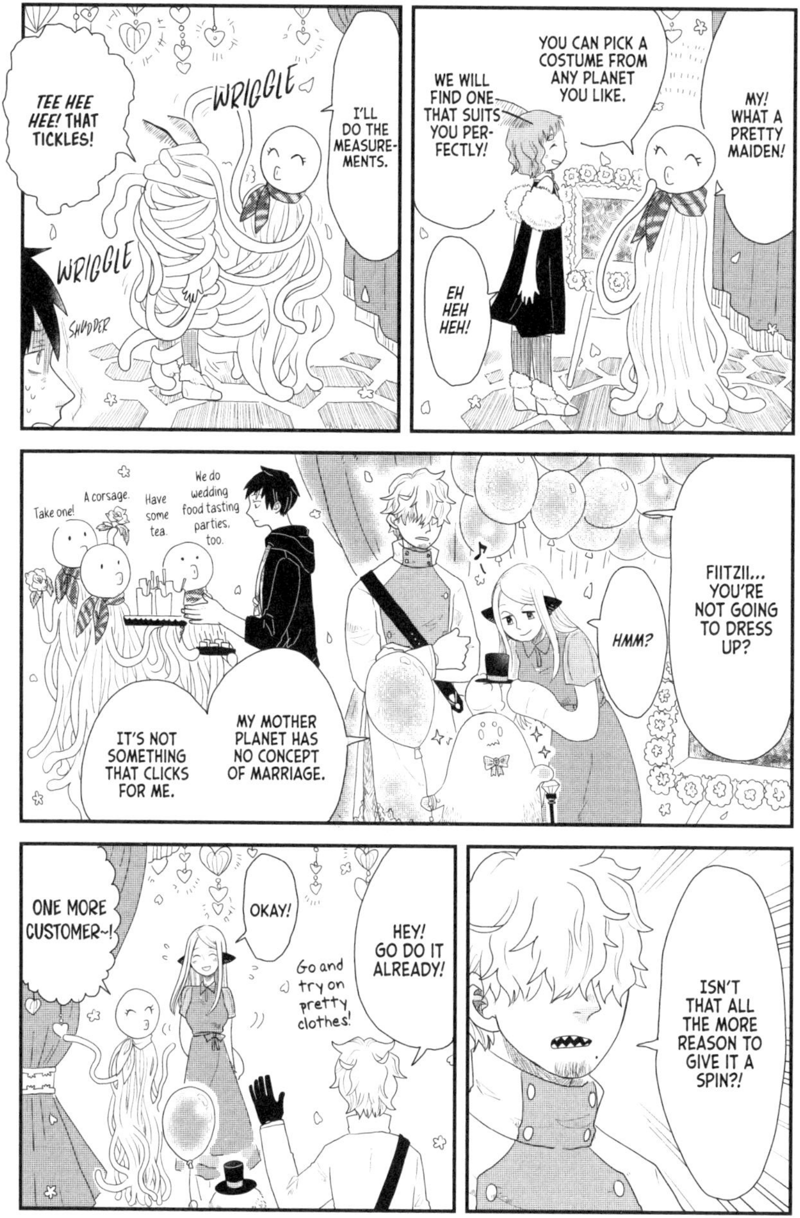
MY! WHAT A PRETTY MAIDEN!
YOU CAN PICK A COSTUME FROM ANY PLANET YOU LIKE.
WE WILL FIND ONE THAT SUITS YOU PERFECTLY!
EH HEH HEH!
I'LL DO THE MEASUREMENTS.
WRIGGLE
TEE HEE HEE! THAT TICKLES!
WRIGGLE
SHUDDER
FIITZII... YOU'RE NOT GOING TO DRESS UP?
HMM?
MY MOTHER PLANET HAS NO CONCEPT OF MARRIAGE.
IT'S NOT SOMETHING THAT CLICKS FOR ME.
We do wedding food tasting parties, too.
Have some tea.
A corsage.
Take one!
ISN'T THAT ALL THE MORE REASON TO GIVE IT A SPIN?!
HEY! GO DO IT ALREADY!
Go and try on pretty clothes!
OKAY!
ONE MORE CUSTOMER~!

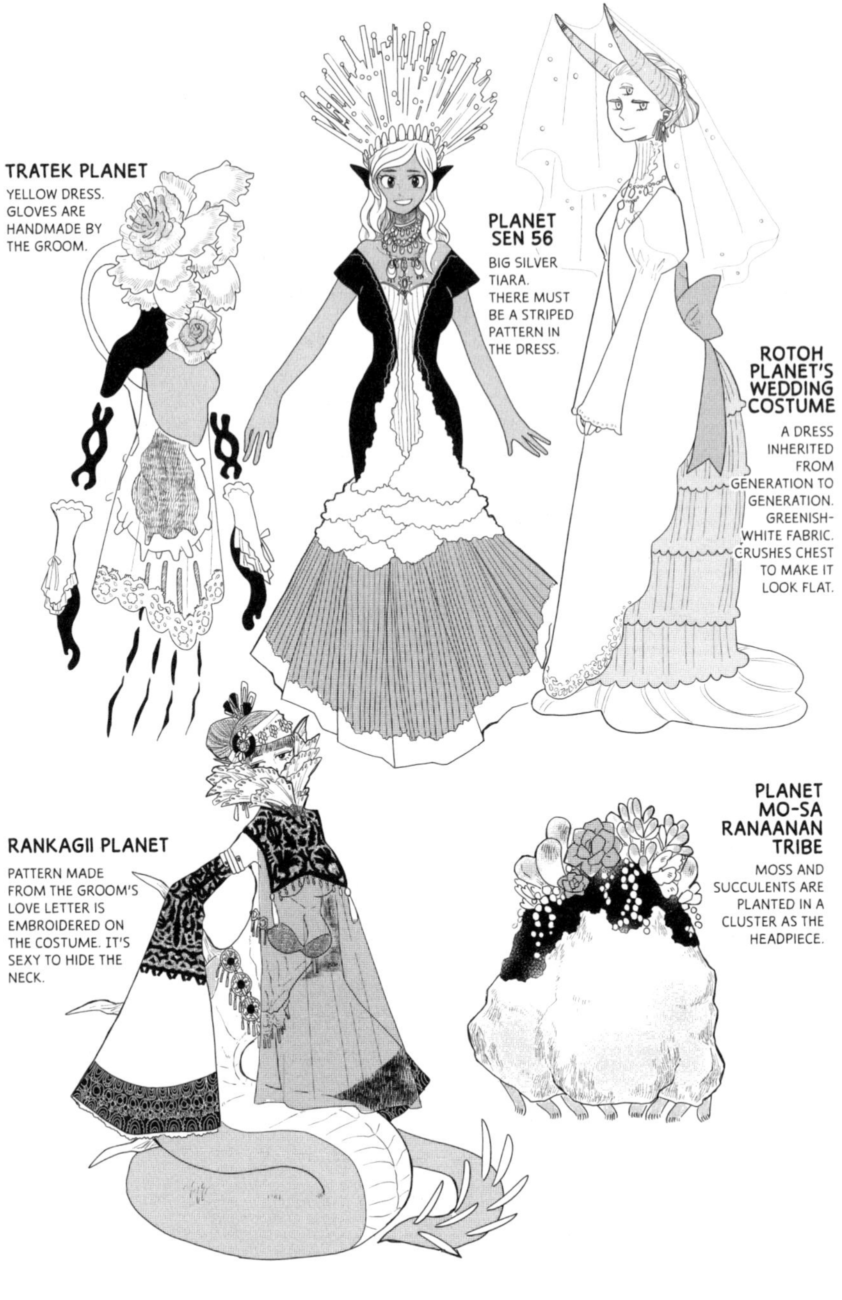
ROTOH PLANET'S WEDDING COSTUME
A DRESS INHERITED FROM GENERATION TO GENERATION. GREENISH-WHITE FABRIC. CRUSHES CHEST TO MAKE IT LOOK FLAT.
PLANET SEN 56
BIG SILVER TIARA. THERE MUST BE A STRIPED PATTERN IN THE DRESS.
TRATEK PLANET
YELLOW DRESS. GLOVES ARE HANDMADE BY THE GROOM.
PLANET MO-SA RANAANAN TRIBE
MOSS AND SUCCULENTS ARE PLANTED IN A CLUSTER AS THE HEADPIECE.
RANKAGII PLANET
PATTERN MADE FROM THE GROOM'S LOVE LETTER IS EMBROIDERED ON THE COSTUME. IT'S SEXY TO HIDE THE NECK.

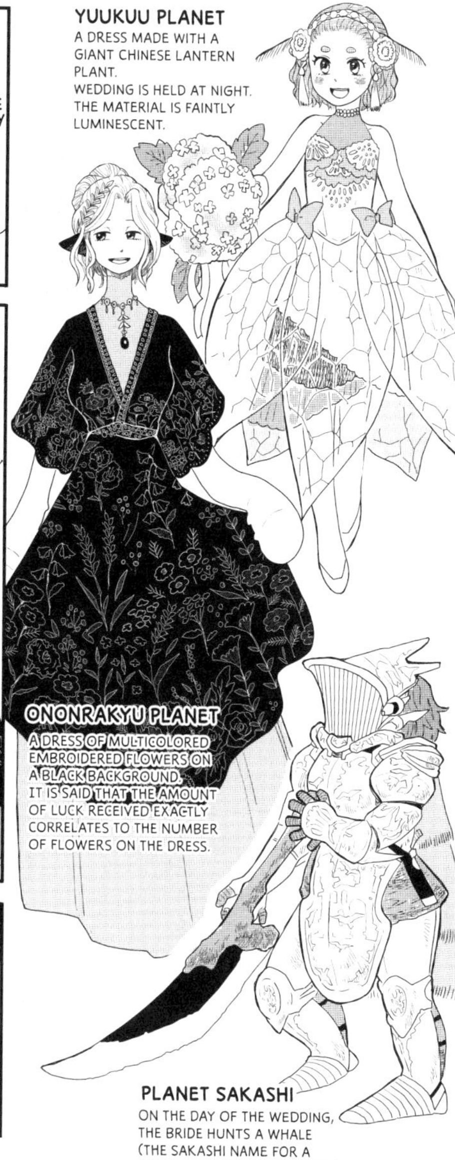
YUUKUU PLANET
A DRESS MADE WITH A GIANT CHINESE LANTERN PLANT.
WEDDING IS HELD AT NIGHT. THE MATERIAL IS FAINTLY LUMINESCENT.
ONONRAKYU PLANET
A DRESS OF MULTICOLORED EMBROIDERED FLOWERS ON A BLACK BACKGROUND.
IT IS SAID THAT THE AMOUNT OF LUCK RECEIVED EXACTLY CORRELATES TO THE NUMBER OF FLOWERS ON THE DRESS.
PLANET SAKASHI
ON THE DAY OF THE WEDDING, THE BRIDE HUNTS A WHALE (THE SAKASHI NAME FOR A LARGE TERRESTRIAL CREATURE), AND THE GROOM PREPARES THE OUTFIT.

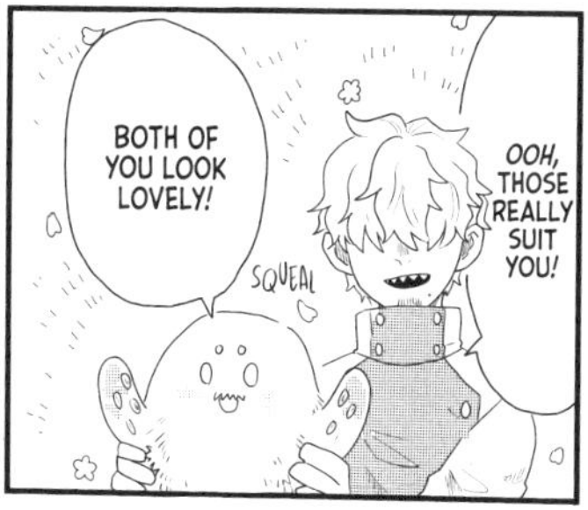
OOH, THOSE REALLY SUIT YOU!
BOTH OF YOU LOOK LOVELY!
SQUEAL

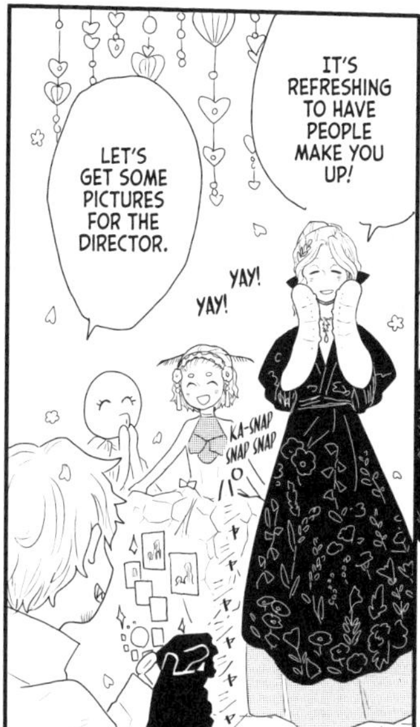
IT'S REFRESHING TO HAVE PEOPLE MAKE YOU UP!
LET'S GET SOME PICTURES FOR THE DIRECTOR.
YAY!
YAY!
KA-SNAP SNAP SNAP

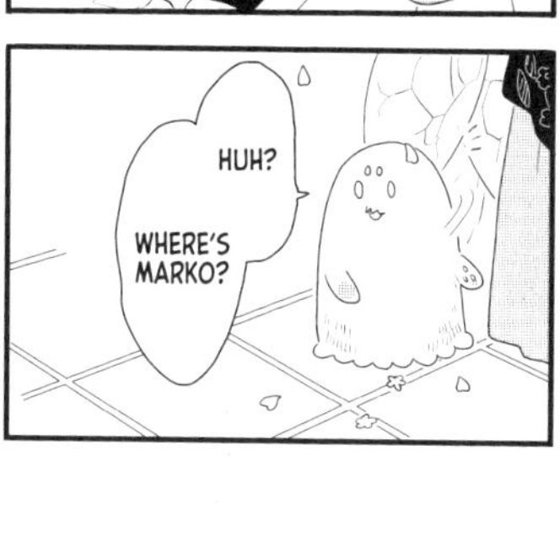
HUH?
WHERE'S MARKO?

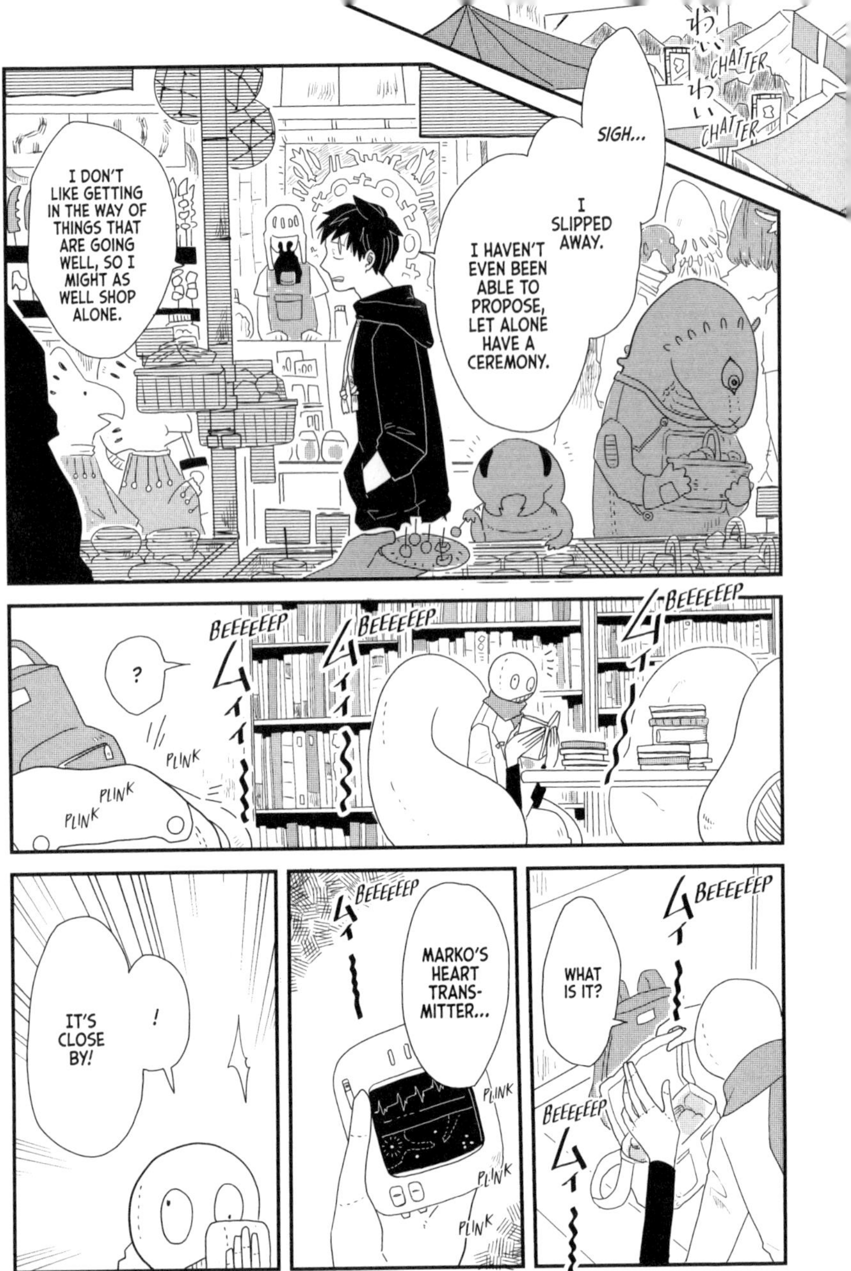
わい CHATTER
わい CHATTER
SIGH...
I SLIPPED AWAY.
I HAVEN'T EVEN BEEN ABLE TO PROPOSE, LET ALONE HAVE A CEREMONY.
I DON'T LIKE GETTING IN THE WAY OF THINGS THAT ARE GOING WELL, SO I MIGHT AS WELL SHOP ALONE.
BEEEEEEP
BEEEEEEP
BEEEEEEP
?
PLINK
PLINK
PLINK
BEEEEEEP
WHAT IS IT?
BEEEEEEP
BEEEEEEP
MARKO'S HEART TRANS-MITTER...
PLINK
PLINK
PLINK
!
IT'S CLOSE BY!

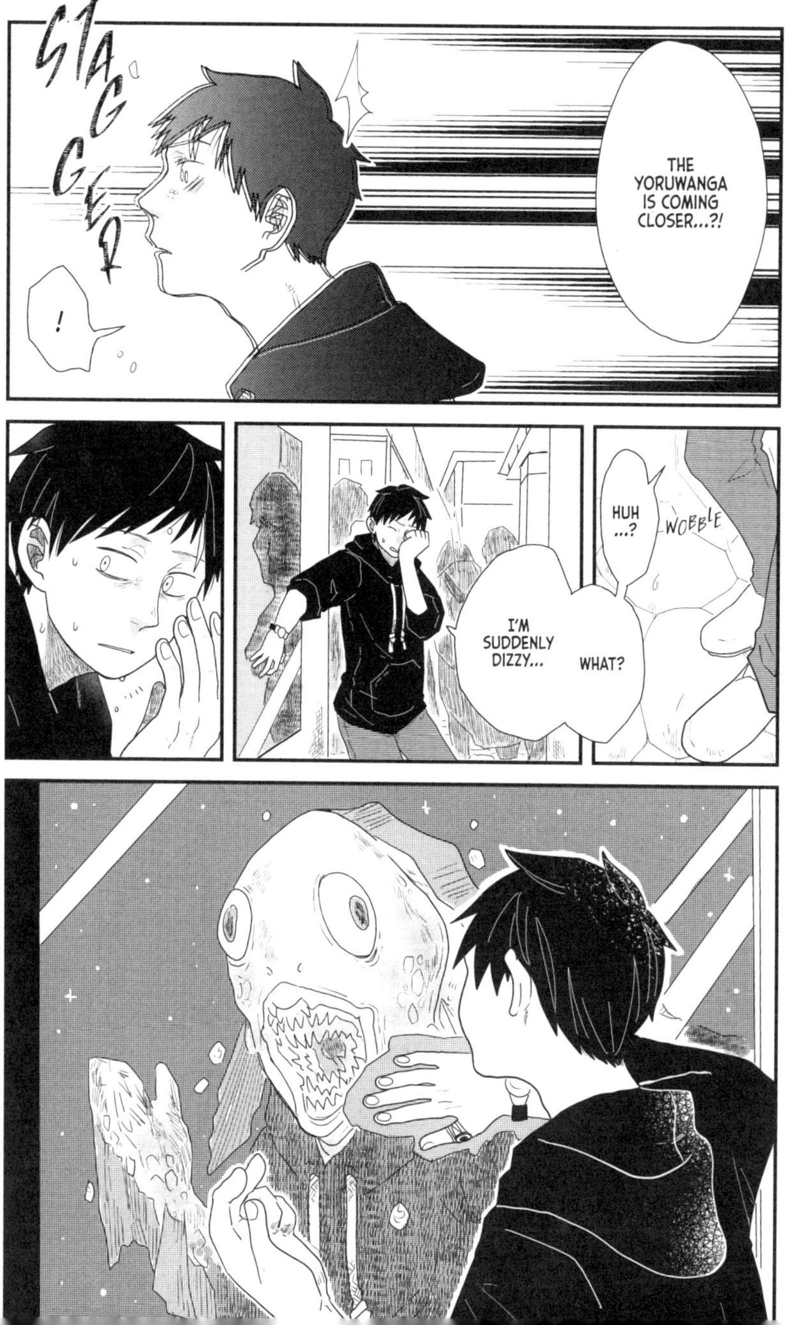
THE YORUWANGA IS COMING CLOSER...?!
STAGGER
!
HUH ...?
WOBBLE
WHAT?
I'M SUDDENLY DIZZY...

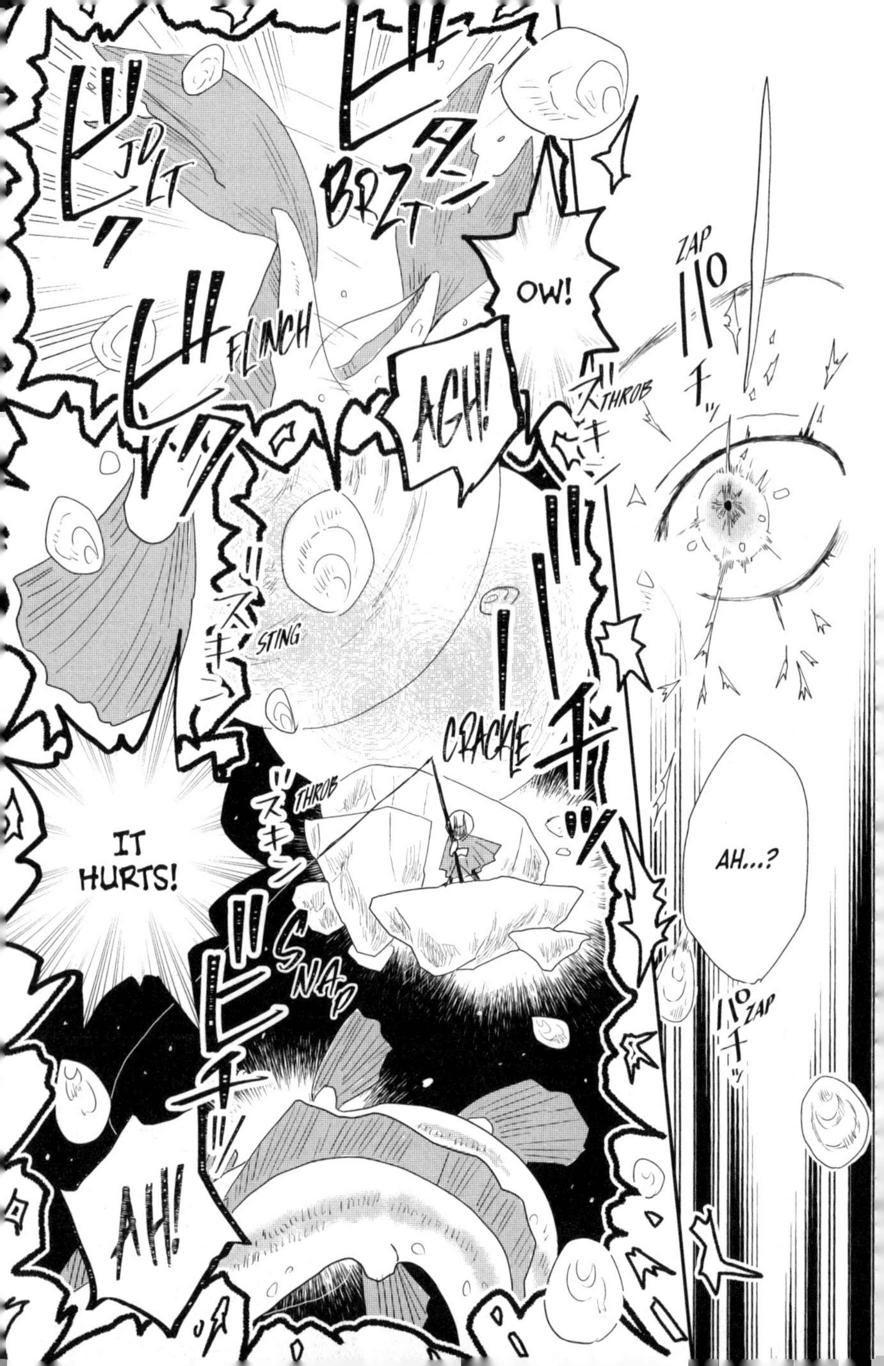
ZAP
AH...?
ZAP
BRZT
OW!
THROB
AGH!
JOLT
FLINCH
CRACKLE
STING
THROB
SNAP
IT HURTS!
AH!

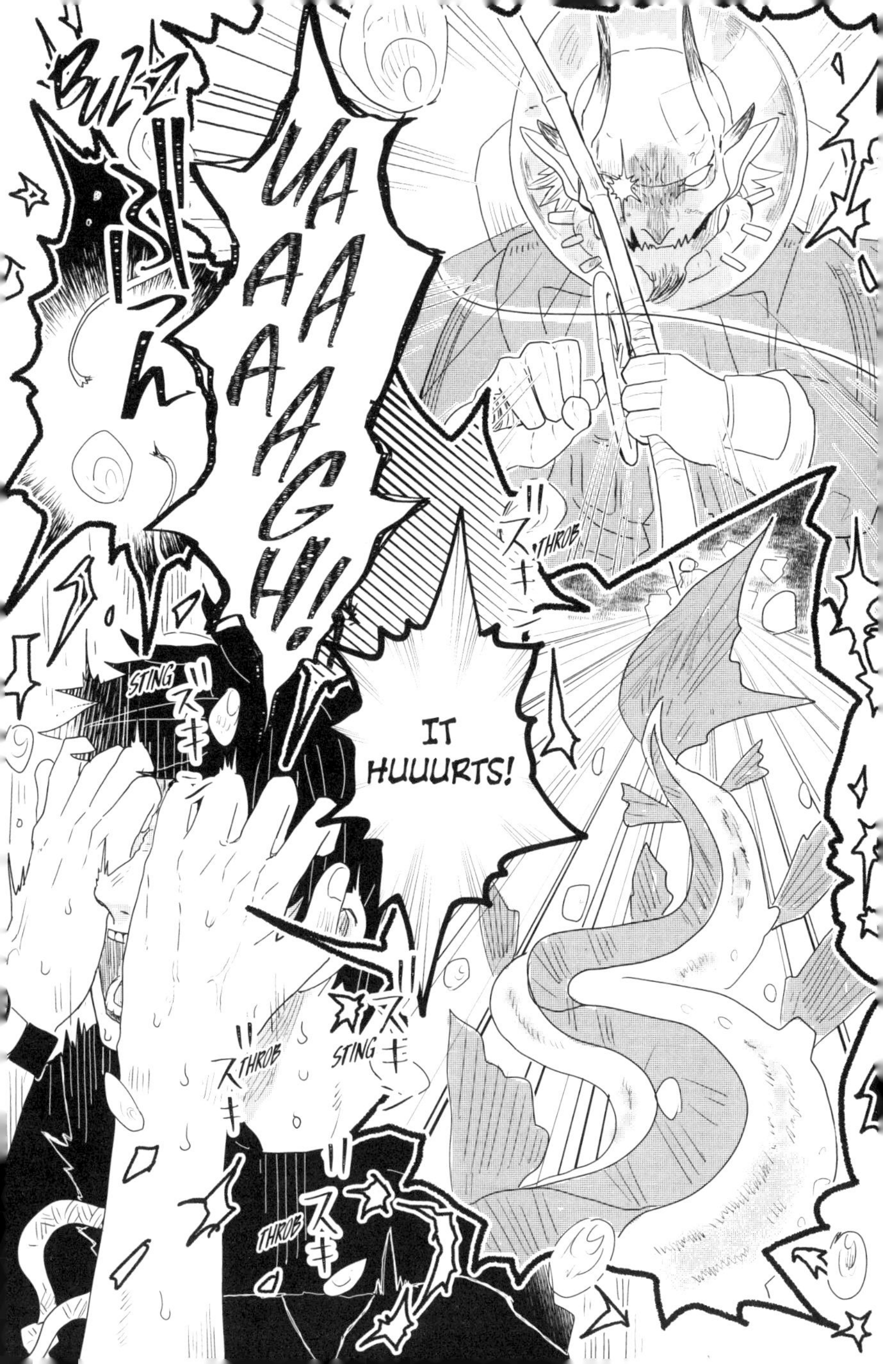
THROB
UAAAAAAGH!!
BUZZ
IT HUUURTS!
STING
STING
THROB
THROB

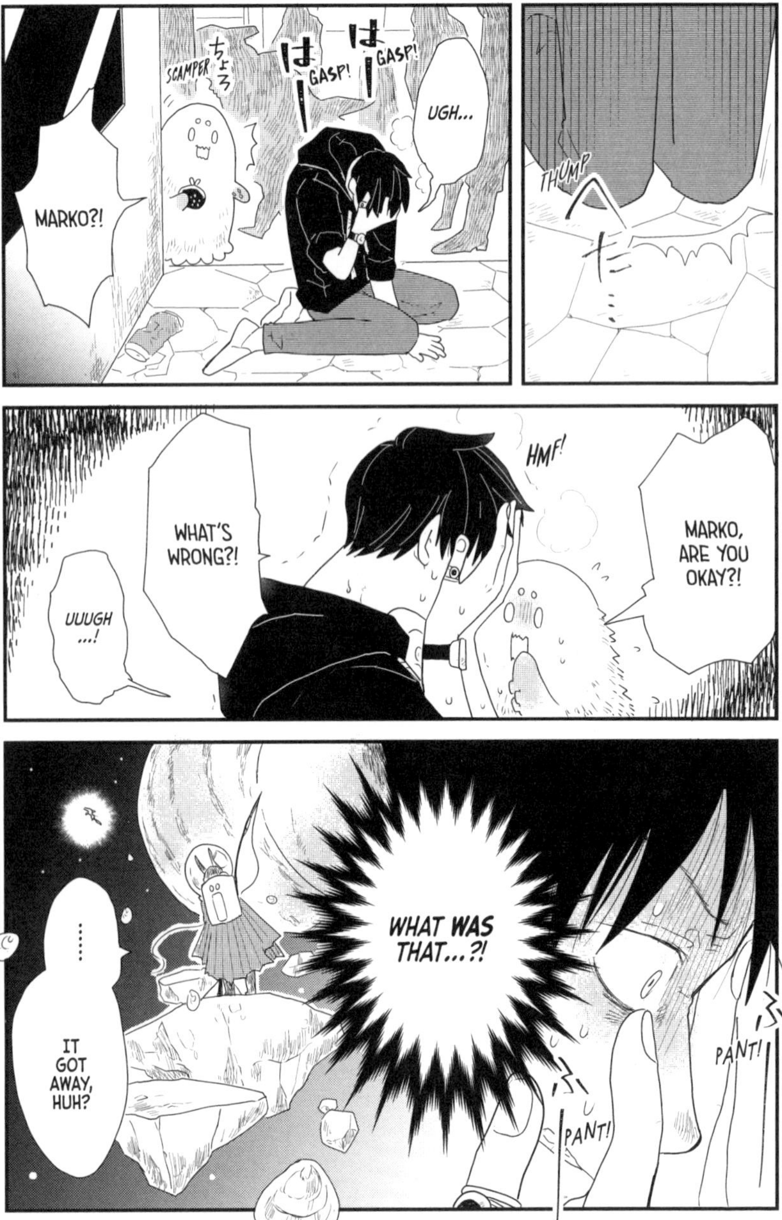
THUMP
UGH...
GASP!
は
GASP!
は
ちょろ
SCAMPER
MARKO?!
MARKO, ARE YOU OKAY?!
HMF!
WHAT'S WRONG?!
UUUGH ...!
ふ
PANT!
WHAT WAS THAT...?!
ふ
PANT!
......
IT GOT AWAY, HUH?

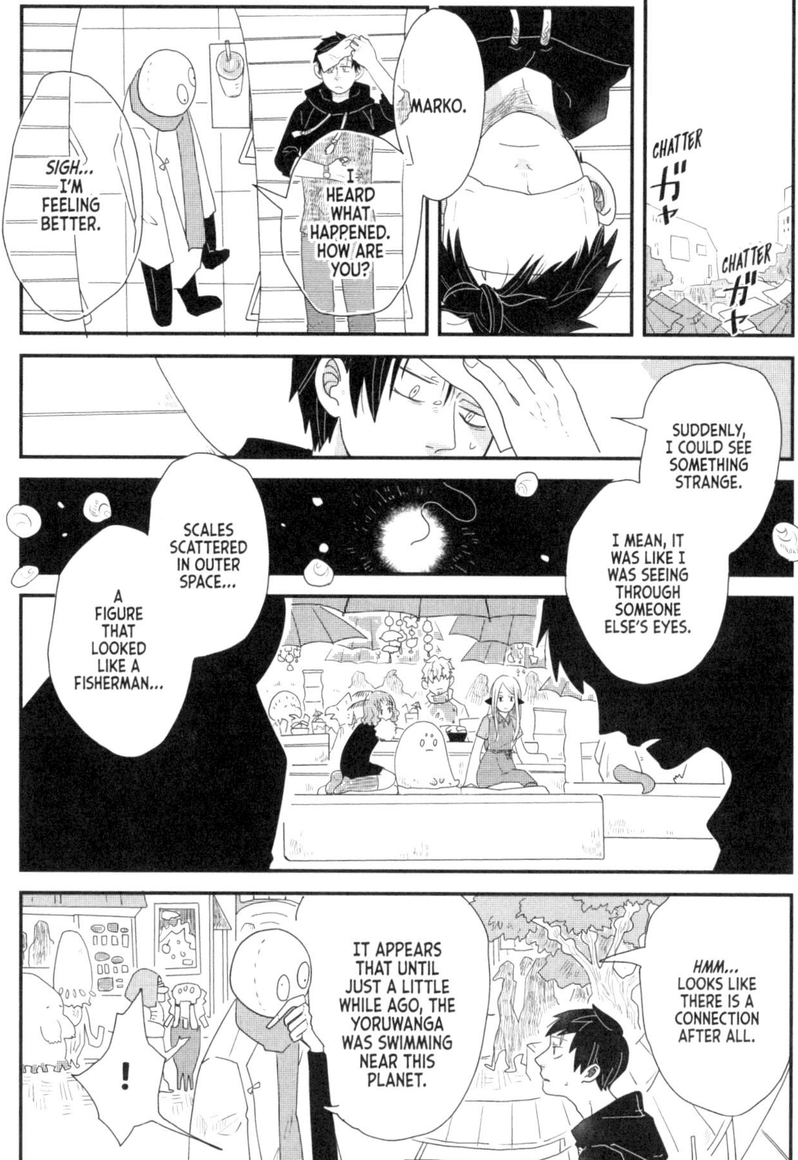
CHATTER
ガヤ
CHATTER
ガヤ
MARKO.
I HEARD WHAT HAPPENED. HOW ARE YOU?
SIGH... I'M FEELING BETTER.
SUDDENLY, I COULD SEE SOMETHING STRANGE.
I MEAN, IT WAS LIKE I WAS SEEING THROUGH SOMEONE ELSE'S EYES.
SCALES SCATTERED IN OUTER SPACE...
A FIGURE THAT LOOKED LIKE A FISHERMAN...
HMM... LOOKS LIKE THERE IS A CONNECTION AFTER ALL.
IT APPEARS THAT UNTIL JUST A LITTLE WHILE AGO, THE YORUWANGA WAS SWIMMING NEAR THIS PLANET.
!

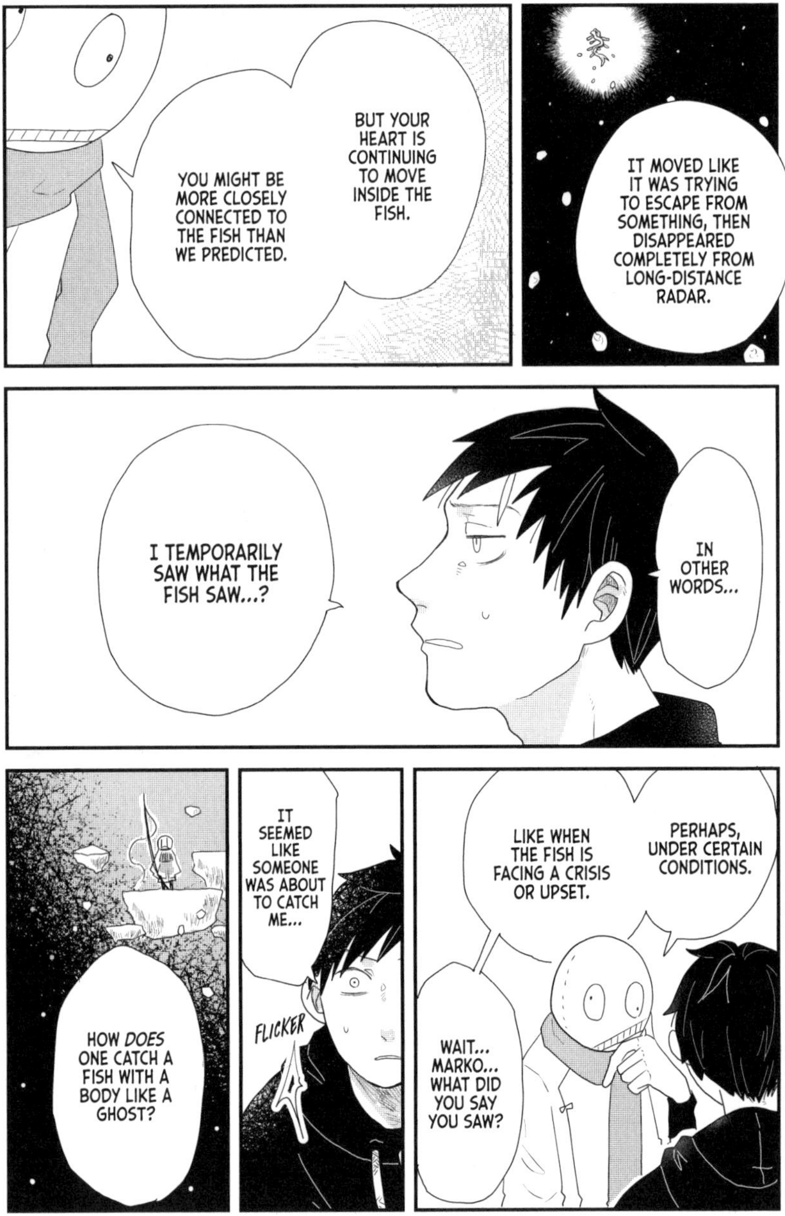
IT MOVED LIKE IT WAS TRYING TO ESCAPE FROM SOMETHING, THEN DISAPPEARED COMPLETELY FROM LONG-DISTANCE RADAR.
BUT YOUR HEART IS CONTINUING TO MOVE INSIDE THE FISH.
YOU MIGHT BE MORE CLOSELY CONNECTED TO THE FISH THAN WE PREDICTED.
IN OTHER WORDS...
I TEMPORARILY SAW WHAT THE FISH SAW...?
PERHAPS, UNDER CERTAIN CONDITIONS.
LIKE WHEN THE FISH IS FACING A CRISIS OR UPSET.
WAIT... MARKO... WHAT DID YOU SAY YOU SAW?
IT SEEMED LIKE SOMEONE WAS ABOUT TO CATCH ME...
FLICKER
HOW *DOES* ONE CATCH A FISH WITH A BODY LIKE A GHOST?

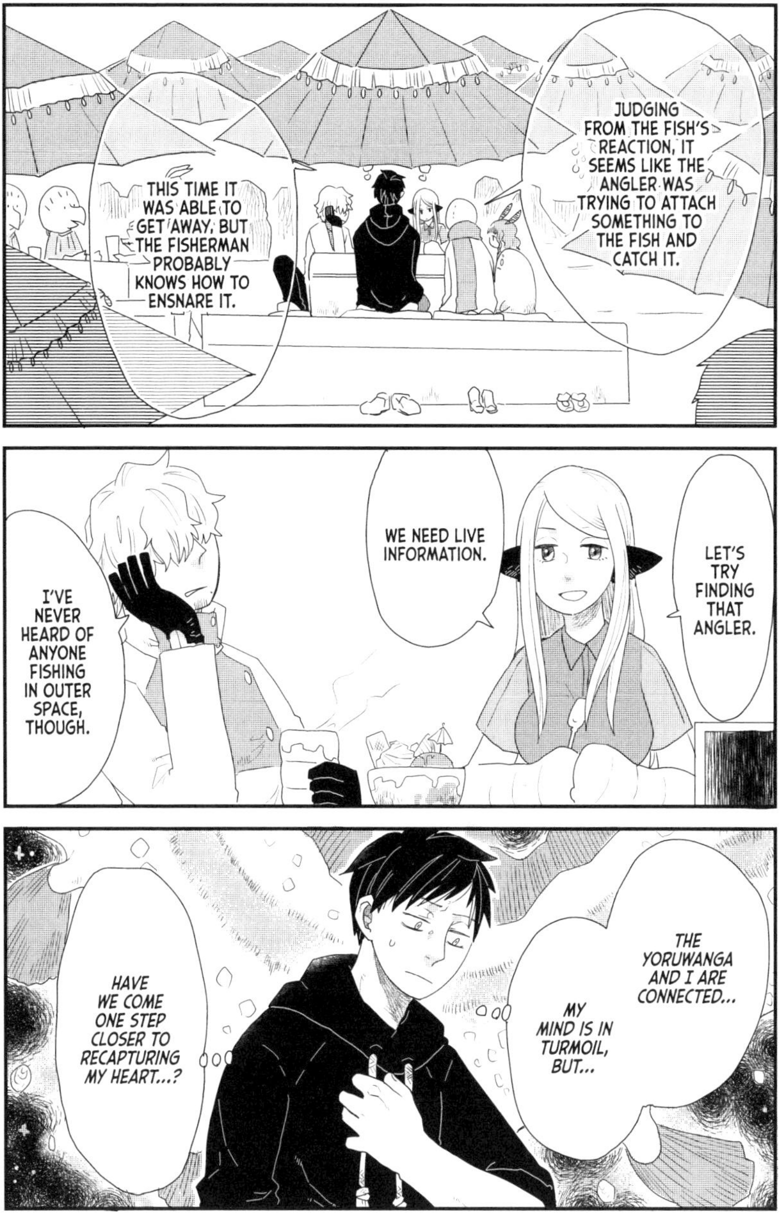
JUDGING FROM THE FISH'S REACTION, IT SEEMS LIKE THE ANGLER WAS TRYING TO ATTACH SOMETHING TO THE FISH AND CATCH IT.
THIS TIME IT WAS ABLE TO GET AWAY, BUT THE FISHERMAN PROBABLY KNOWS HOW TO ENSNARE IT.
LET'S TRY FINDING THAT ANGLER.
WE NEED LIVE INFORMATION.
I'VE NEVER HEARD OF ANYONE FISHING IN OUTER SPACE, THOUGH.
THE YORUWANGA AND I ARE CONNECTED...
MY MIND IS IN TURMOIL, BUT...
HAVE WE COME ONE STEP CLOSER TO RECAPTURING MY HEART...?

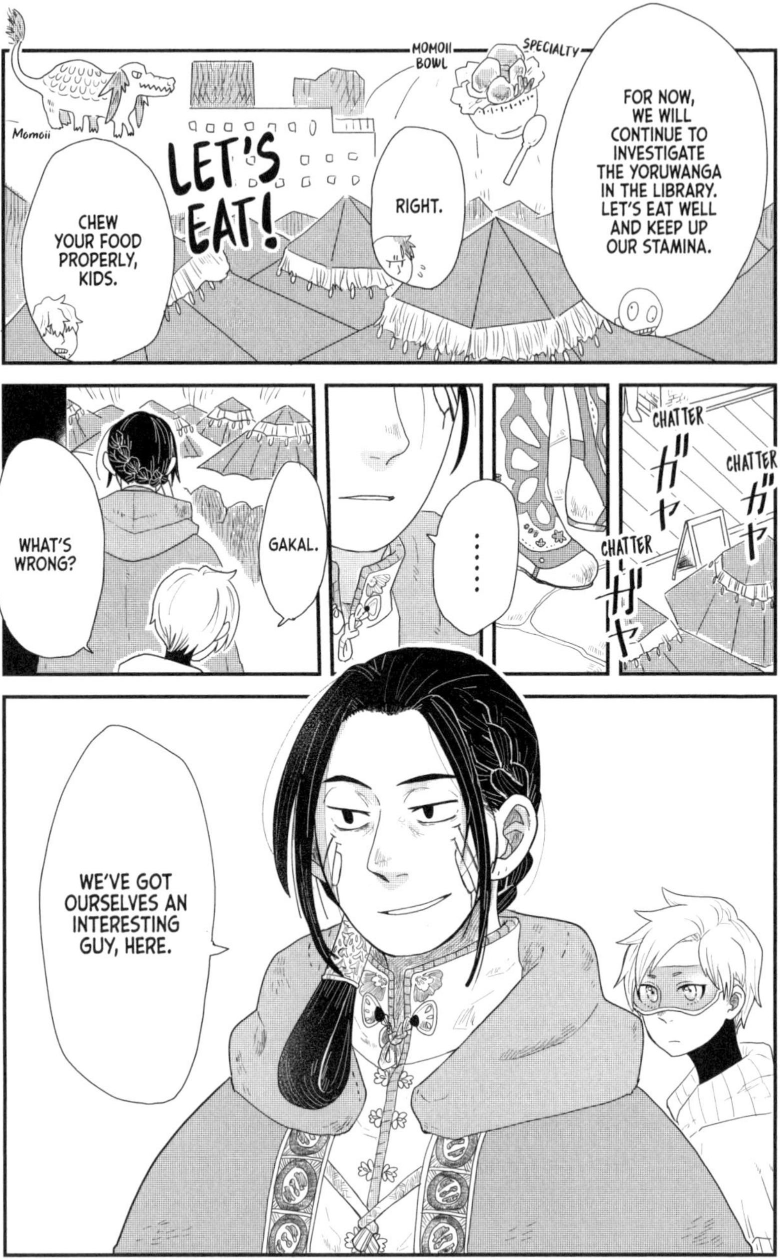
SPECIALTY
MOMOII BOWL
Momoii
FOR NOW, WE WILL CONTINUE TO INVESTIGATE THE YORUWANGA IN THE LIBRARY. LET'S EAT WELL AND KEEP UP OUR STAMINA.
RIGHT.
LET'S EAT!
CHEW YOUR FOOD PROPERLY, KIDS.
CHATTER ガヤ
CHATTER ガヤ
CHATTER ガヤ
……
GAKAL.
WHAT'S WRONG?
WE'VE GOT OURSELVES AN INTERESTING GUY, HERE.

To be continued...

- CHANGES TOOTHBRUSHES EVERY HALF-MONTH.

- DIFFERENT COLOR FOR PARTNER

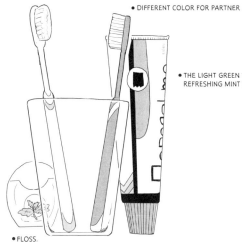

- THE LIGHT GREEN TOOTHPASTE IS A REFRESHING MINT FLAVOR.

- FLOSS.

- WANTS A TOOTHBRUSH STAND.

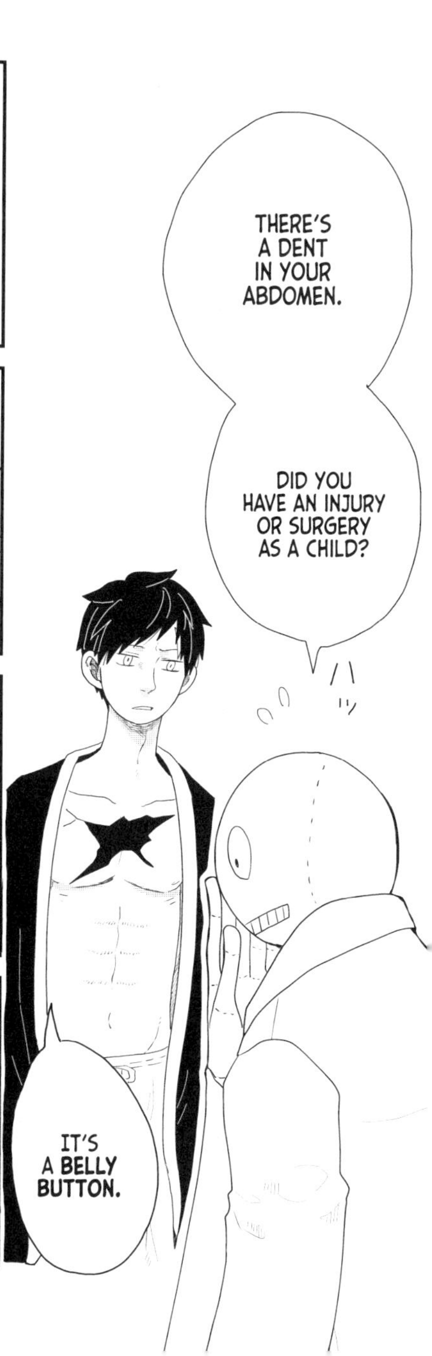
THERE'S A DENT IN YOUR ABDOMEN.
DID YOU HAVE AN INJURY OR SURGERY AS A CHILD?
IT'S A BELLY BUTTON.

Bottomless

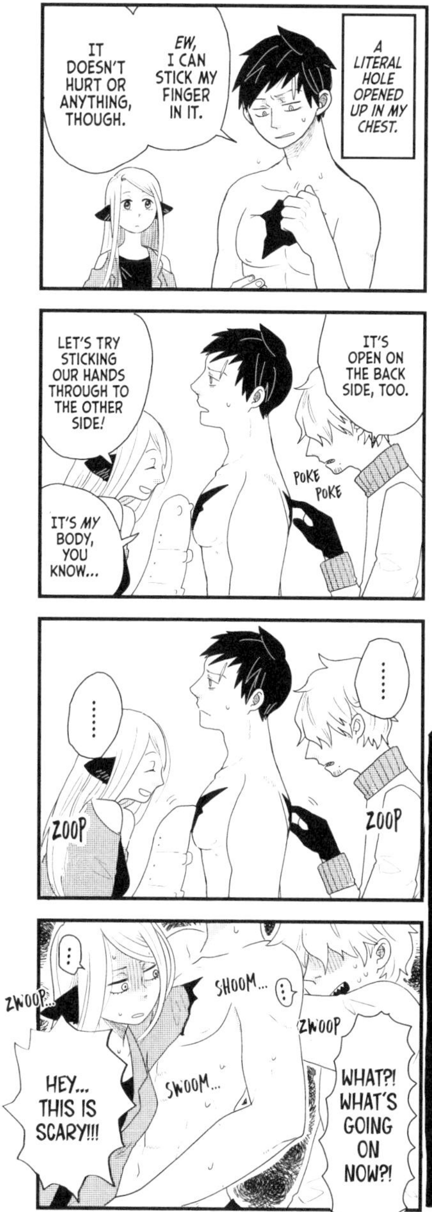
A LITERAL HOLE OPENED UP IN MY CHEST.
EW, I CAN STICK MY FINGER IN IT.
IT DOESN'T HURT OR ANYTHING, THOUGH.
IT'S OPEN ON THE BACK SIDE, TOO.
POKE POKE
LET'S TRY STICKING OUR HANDS THROUGH TO THE OTHER SIDE!
IT'S MY BODY, YOU KNOW...
......
ZOOP
......
ZOOP
WHAT?! WHAT'S GOING ON NOW?!
ZWOOP
SHOOM...
...
SWOOM...
...
ZWOOP...
HEY... THIS IS SCARY!!!

Hairdos

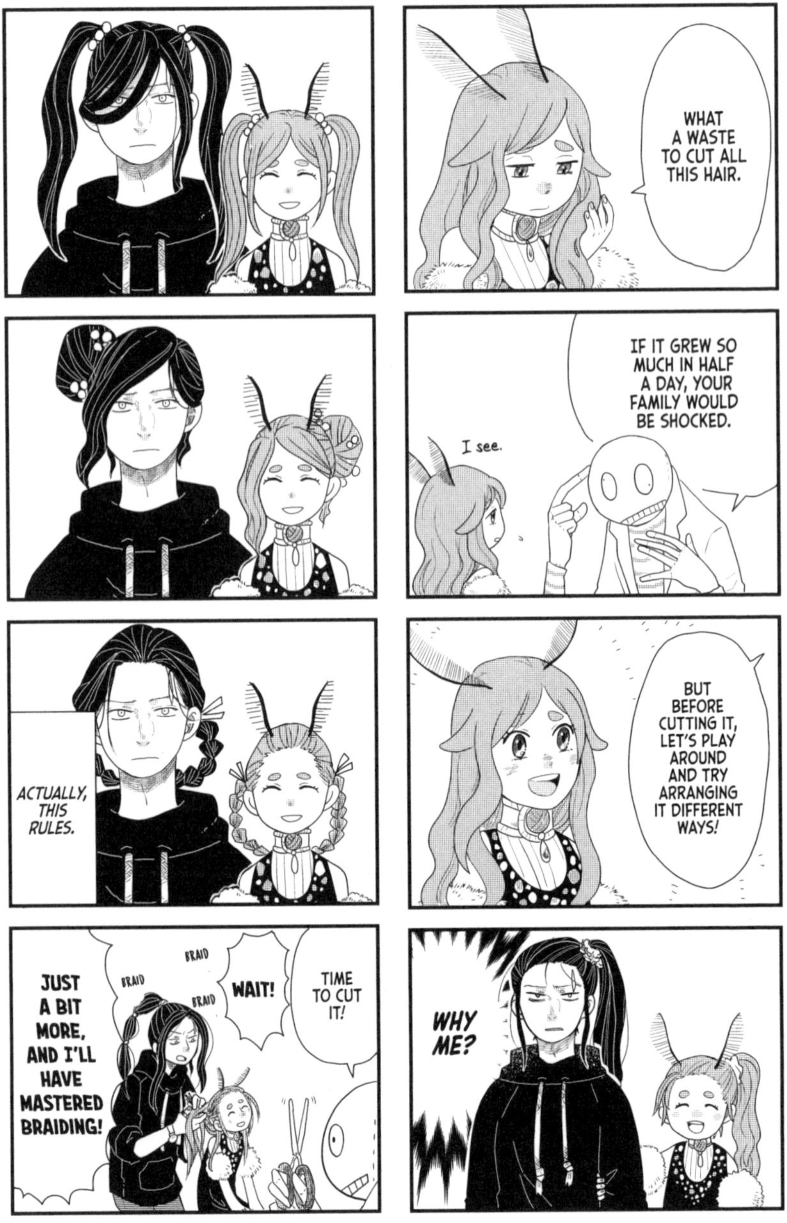

WHAT A WASTE TO CUT ALL THIS HAIR.
IF IT GREW SO MUCH IN HALF A DAY, YOUR FAMILY WOULD BE SHOCKED.
I see.
BUT BEFORE CUTTING IT, LET'S PLAY AROUND AND TRY ARRANGING IT DIFFERENT WAYS!
WHY ME?
ACTUALLY, THIS RULES.
TIME TO CUT IT!
WAIT!
BRAID
BRAID
BRAID
JUST A BIT MORE, AND I'LL HAVE MASTERED BRAIDING!

Crab Man

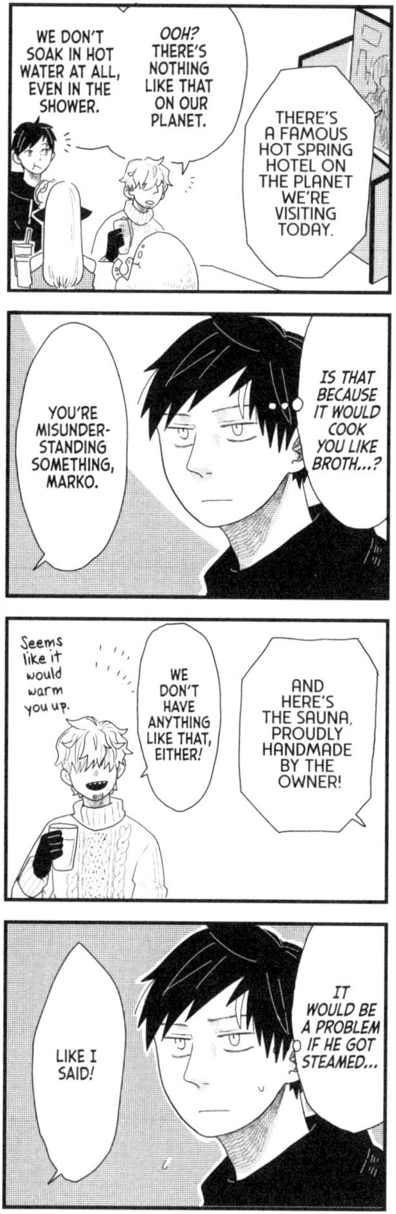
THERE'S A FAMOUS HOT SPRING HOTEL ON THE PLANET WE'RE VISITING TODAY.
OOH? THERE'S NOTHING LIKE THAT ON OUR PLANET.
WE DON'T SOAK IN HOT WATER AT ALL, EVEN IN THE SHOWER.
IS THAT BECAUSE IT WOULD COOK YOU LIKE BROTH...?
YOU'RE MISUNDERSTANDING SOMETHING, MARKO.
AND HERE'S THE SAUNA, PROUDLY HANDMADE BY THE OWNER!
WE DON'T HAVE ANYTHING LIKE THAT, EITHER!
Seems like it would warm you up.
IT WOULD BE A PROBLEM IF HE GOT STEAMED...
LIKE I SAID!

White Hair

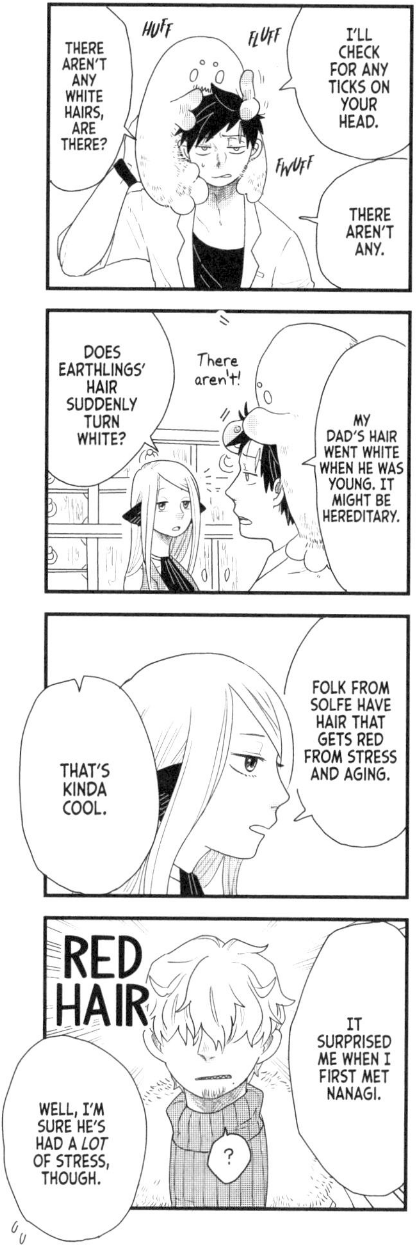
I'LL CHECK FOR ANY TICKS ON YOUR HEAD.
FLUFF
HUFF
THERE AREN'T ANY WHITE HAIRS, ARE THERE?
FWUFF
THERE AREN'T ANY.
There aren't!
DOES EARTHLINGS' HAIR SUDDENLY TURN WHITE?
MY DAD'S HAIR WENT WHITE WHEN HE WAS YOUNG. IT MIGHT BE HEREDITARY.
FOLK FROM SOLFE HAVE HAIR THAT GETS RED FROM STRESS AND AGING.
THAT'S KINDA COOL.
IT SURPRISED ME WHEN I FIRST MET NANAGI.
RED HAIR
?
WELL, I'M SURE HE'S HAD A *LOT* OF STRESS, THOUGH.

Mauu Becomes a Pâtissier

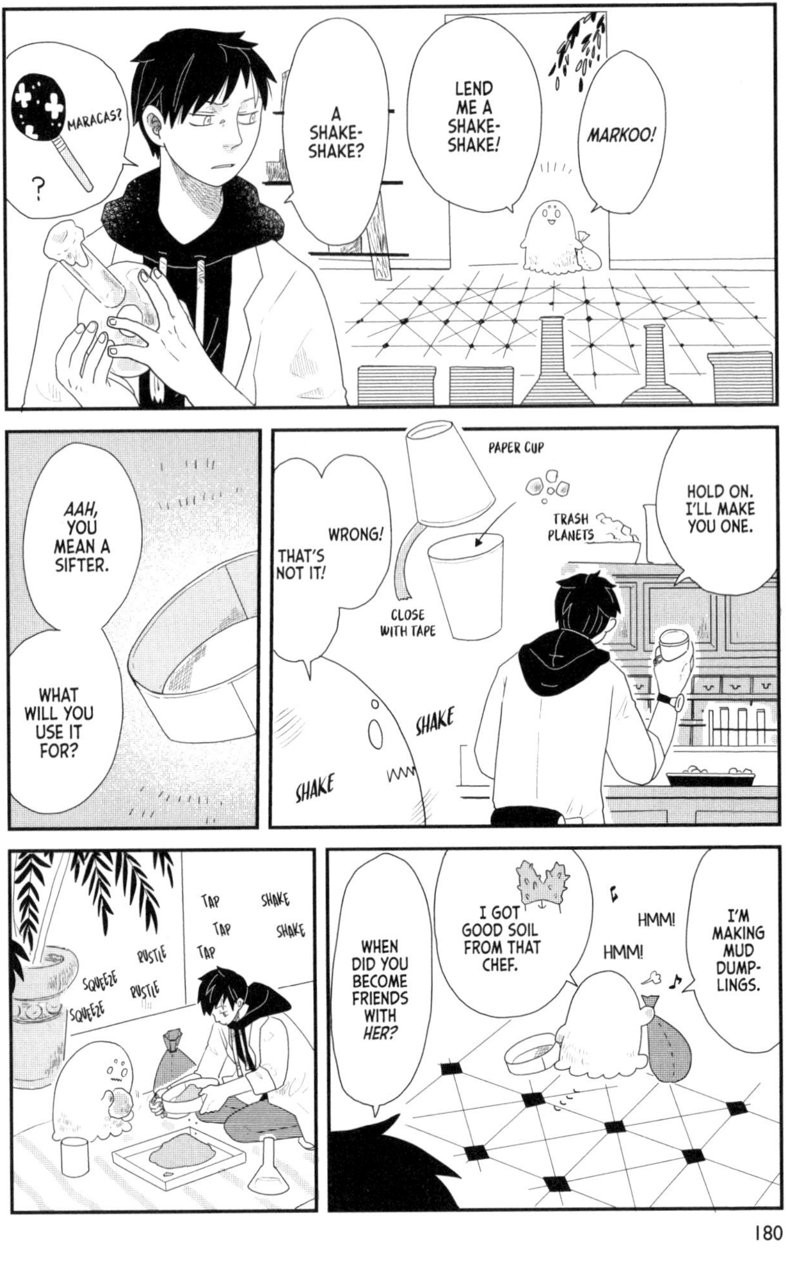
MARKOO!
LEND ME A SHAKE-SHAKE!
A SHAKE-SHAKE?
MARACAS?
?
HOLD ON. I'LL MAKE YOU ONE.
PAPER CUP
TRASH PLANETS
CLOSE WITH TAPE
WRONG!
THAT'S NOT IT!
SHAKE
SHAKE
AAH, YOU MEAN A SIFTER.
WHAT WILL YOU USE IT FOR?
I'M MAKING MUD DUMP-LINGS.
HMM!
HMM!
I GOT GOOD SOIL FROM THAT CHEF.
WHEN DID YOU BECOME FRIENDS WITH HER?
SHAKE
SHAKE
TAP
TAP
TAP
RUSTLE
RUSTLE
SQUEEZE
SQUEEZE

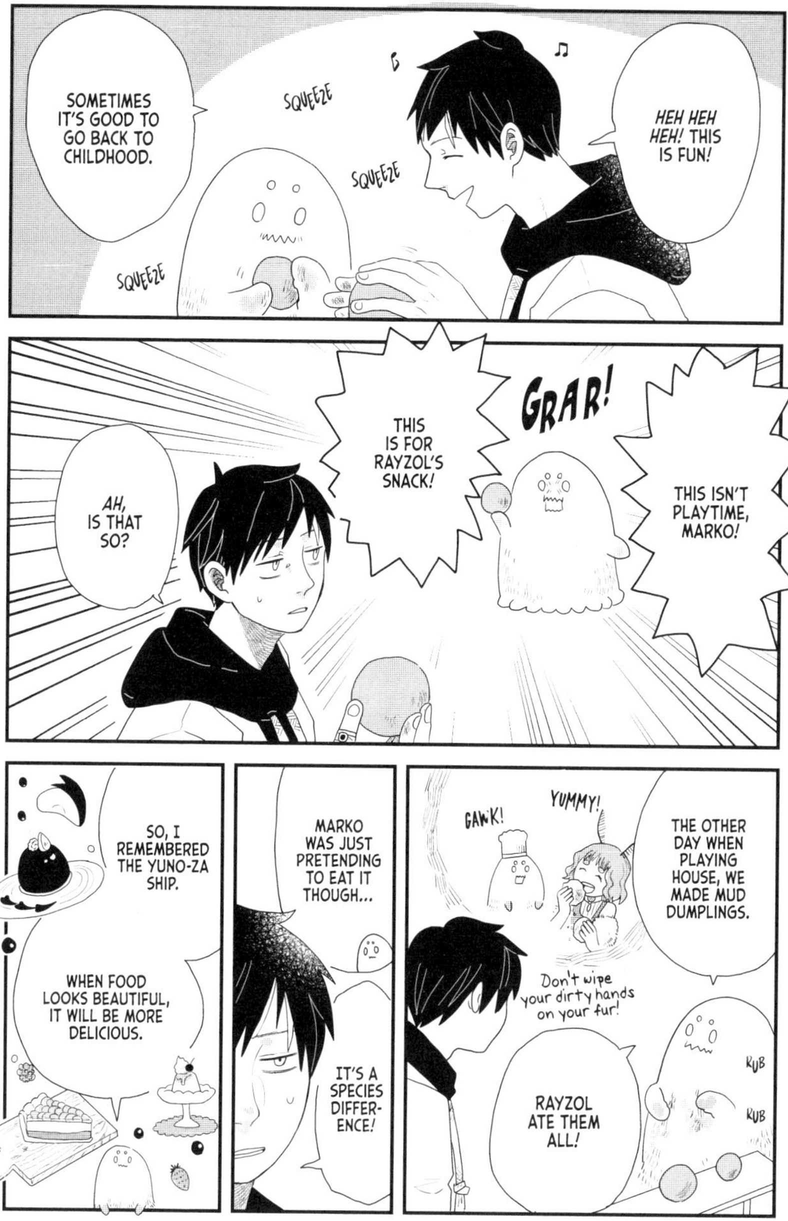
HEH HEH HEH! THIS IS FUN!
SQUEEZE
SQUEEZE
SQUEEZE
SOMETIMES IT'S GOOD TO GO BACK TO CHILDHOOD.
THIS ISN'T PLAYTIME, MARKO!
GRAR!
THIS IS FOR RAYZOL'S SNACK!
AH, IS THAT SO?
THE OTHER DAY WHEN PLAYING HOUSE, WE MADE MUD DUMPLINGS.
YUMMY!
GAWK!
Don't wipe your dirty hands on your fur!
RUB
RUB
RAYZOL ATE THEM ALL!
MARKO WAS JUST PRETENDING TO EAT IT THOUGH...
IT'S A SPECIES DIFFERENCE!
SO, I REMEMBERED THE YUNO-ZA SHIP.
WHEN FOOD LOOKS BEAUTIFUL, IT WILL BE MORE DELICIOUS.

Dumplings Drying

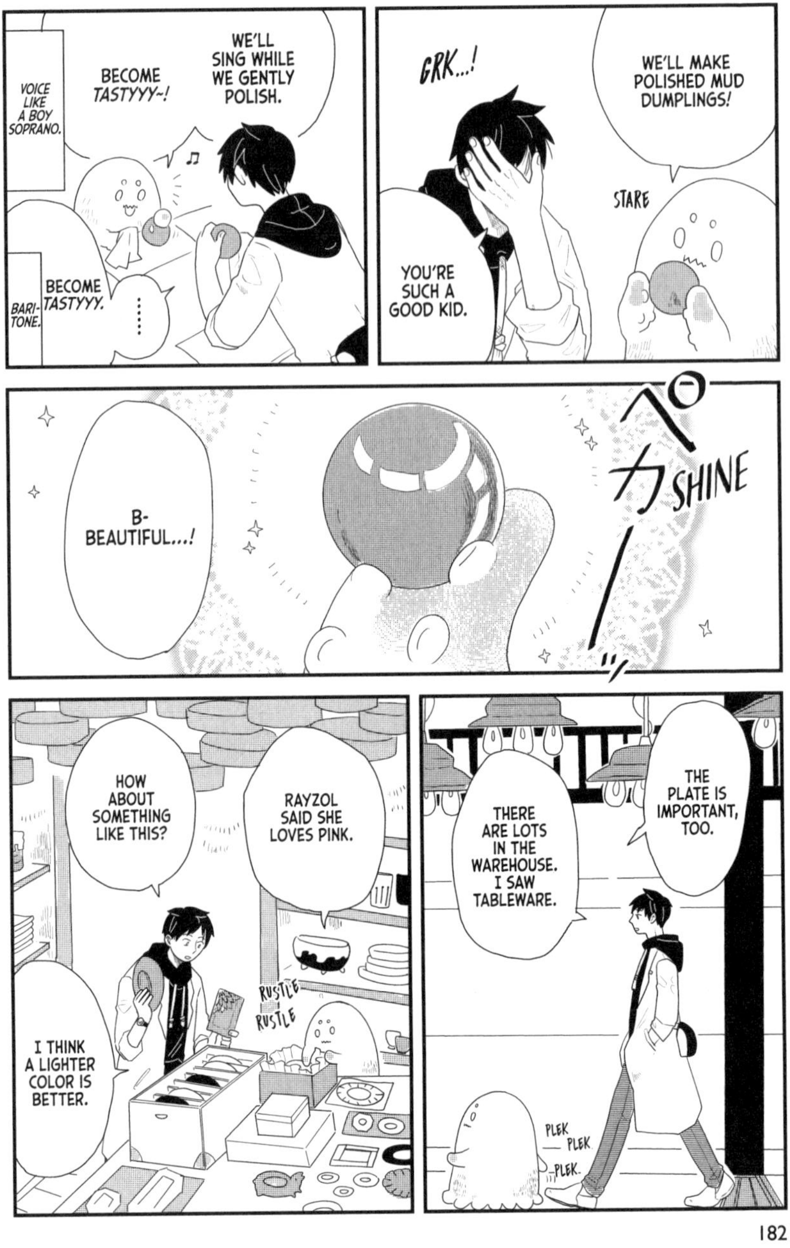
WE'LL MAKE POLISHED MUD DUMPLINGS!
GRK...!
STARE
YOU'RE SUCH A GOOD KID.
WE'LL SING WHILE WE GENTLY POLISH.
BECOME TASTYYY~!
VOICE LIKE A BOY SOPRANO.
BECOME TASTYYY.
BARI-TONE.
......
SHINE
B-BEAUTIFUL...!
THE PLATE IS IMPORTANT, TOO.
THERE ARE LOTS IN THE WAREHOUSE. I SAW TABLEWARE.
PLEK PLEK PLEK
RAYZOL SAID SHE LOVES PINK.
HOW ABOUT SOMETHING LIKE THIS?
RUSTLE RUSTLE
I THINK A LIGHTER COLOR IS BETTER.

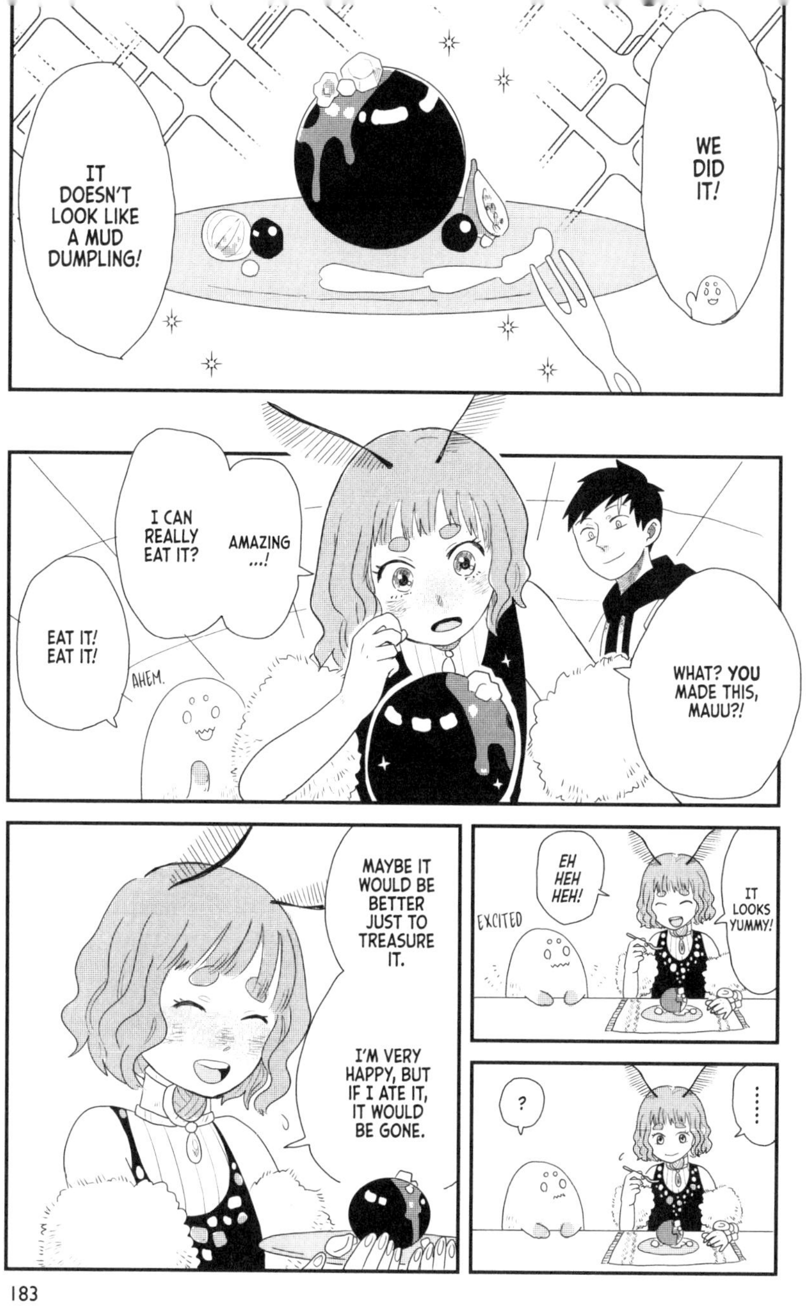
WE DID IT!
IT DOESN'T LOOK LIKE A MUD DUMPLING!
WHAT? YOU MADE THIS, MAUU?!
AMAZING ...!
I CAN REALLY EAT IT?
EAT IT! EAT IT!
AHEM.
IT LOOKS YUMMY!
EH HEH HEH!
EXCITED
......
?
MAYBE IT WOULD BE BETTER JUST TO TREASURE IT.
I'M VERY HAPPY, BUT IF I ATE IT, IT WOULD BE GONE.

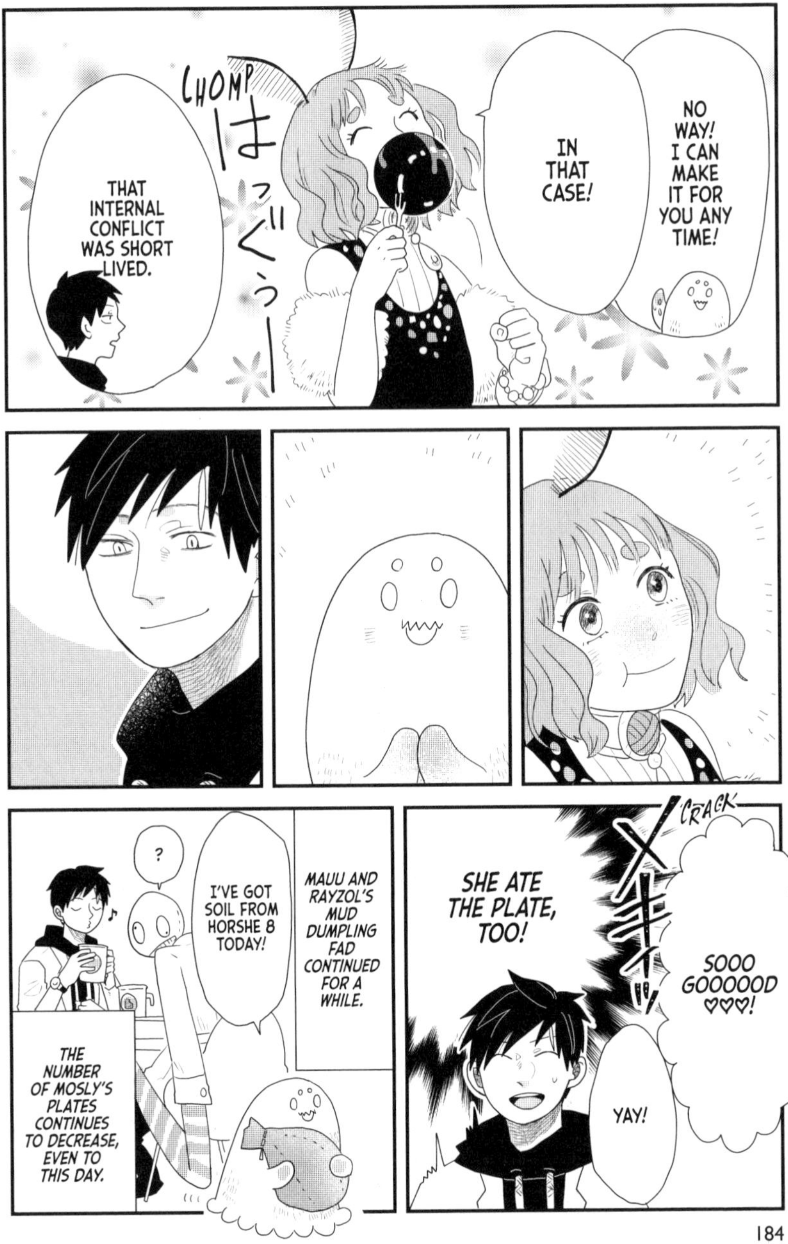
NO WAY! I CAN MAKE IT FOR YOU ANY TIME!
IN THAT CASE!
CHOMP
はっぐぅー
THAT INTERNAL CONFLICT WAS SHORT LIVED.
CRACK
メキッ
SOOO GOOOOOD ♡♡♡!
SHE ATE THE PLATE, TOO!
YAY!
MAUU AND RAYZOL'S MUD DUMPLING FAD CONTINUED FOR A WHILE.
I'VE GOT SOIL FROM HORSHE 8 TODAY!
?
THE NUMBER OF MOSLY'S PLATES CONTINUES TO DECREASE, EVEN TO THIS DAY.

Marko and the Movie Planet

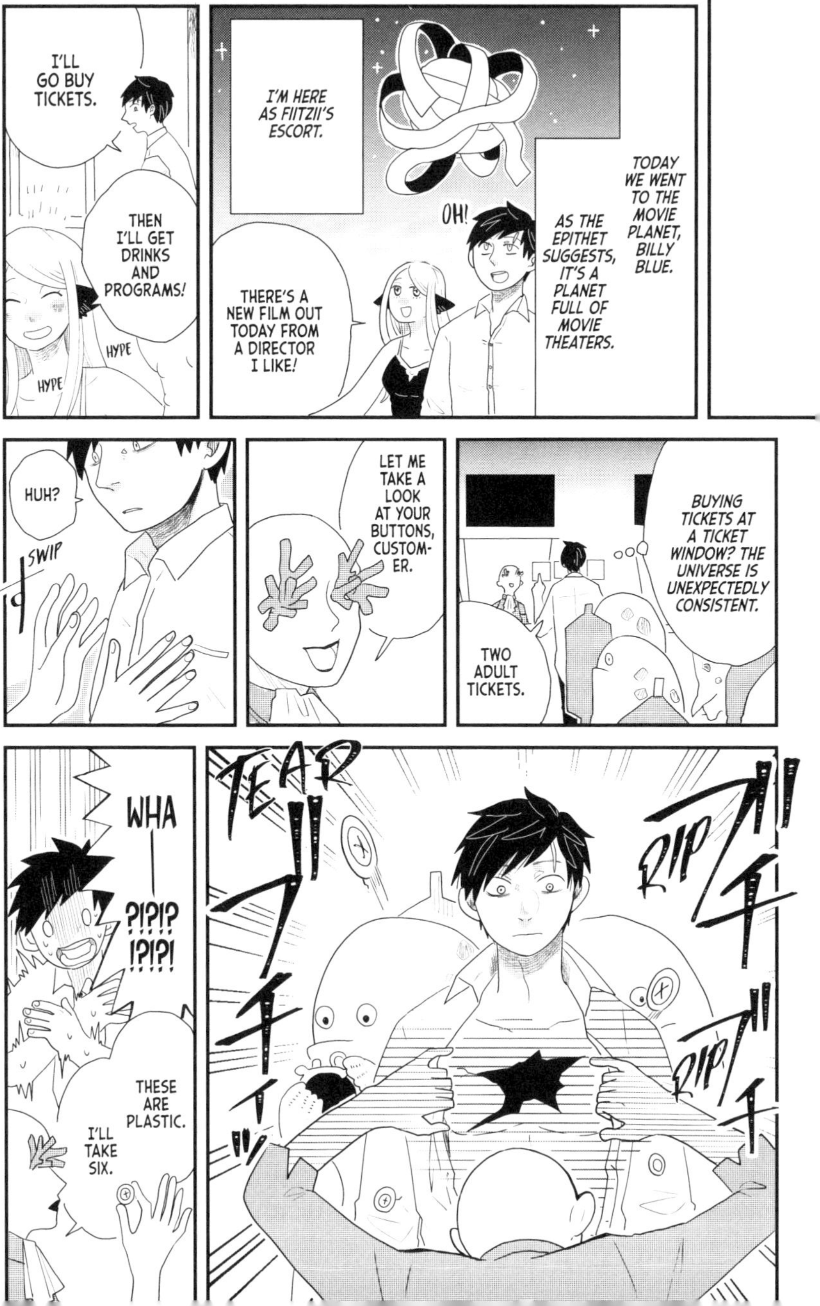
TODAY WE WENT TO THE MOVIE PLANET, BILLY BLUE.
AS THE EPITHET SUGGESTS, IT'S A PLANET FULL OF MOVIE THEATERS.
I'M HERE AS FIITZII'S ESCORT.
OH!
THERE'S A NEW FILM OUT TODAY FROM A DIRECTOR I LIKE!
I'LL GO BUY TICKETS.
THEN I'LL GET DRINKS AND PROGRAMS!
HYPE
HYPE
BUYING TICKETS AT A TICKET WINDOW? THE UNIVERSE IS UNEXPECTEDLY CONSISTENT.
TWO ADULT TICKETS.
LET ME TAKE A LOOK AT YOUR BUTTONS, CUSTOMER.
HUH?
SWIP
RIP
RIP
TEAR
WHA—?!?!?!?!?!
THESE ARE PLASTIC.
I'LL TAKE SIX.

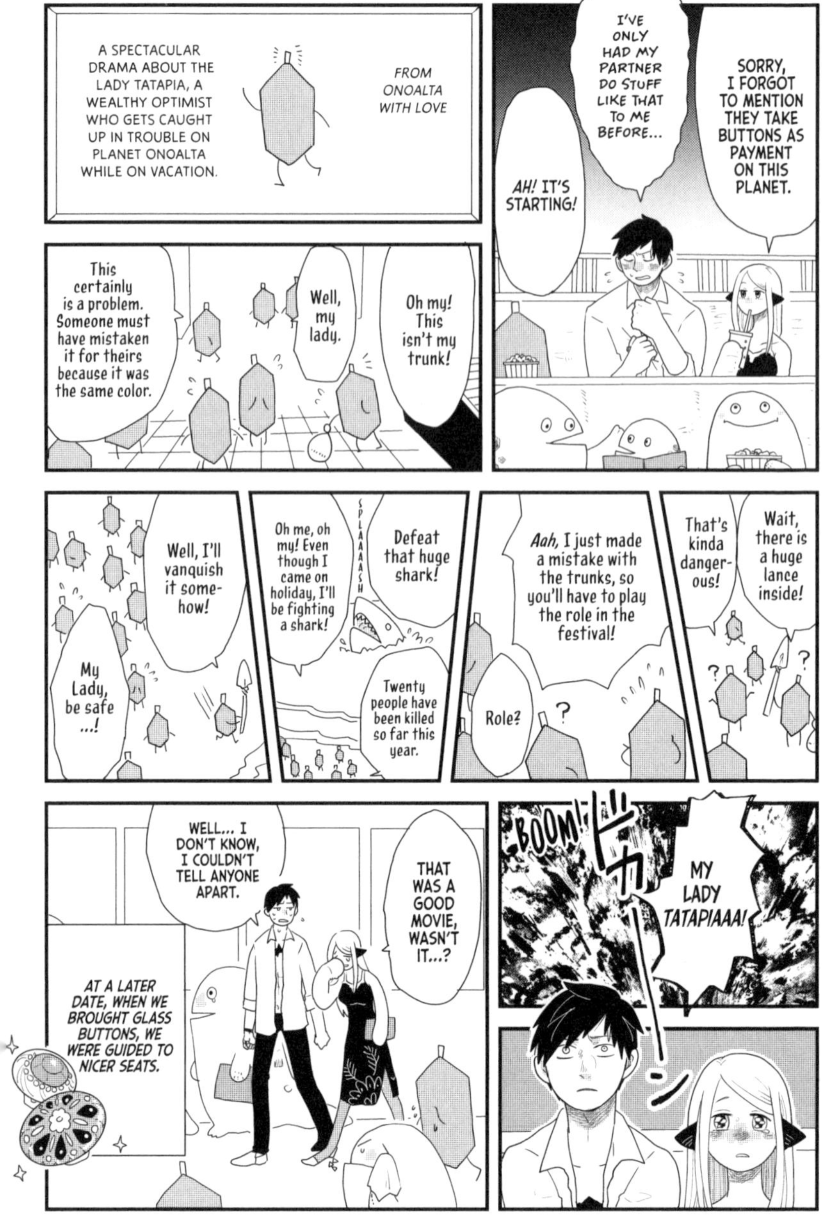
SORRY, I FORGOT TO MENTION THEY TAKE BUTTONS AS PAYMENT ON THIS PLANET.
I'VE ONLY HAD MY PARTNER DO STUFF LIKE THAT TO ME BEFORE...
AH! IT'S STARTING!
FROM ONOALTA WITH LOVE
A SPECTACULAR DRAMA ABOUT THE LADY TATAPIA, A WEALTHY OPTIMIST WHO GETS CAUGHT UP IN TROUBLE ON PLANET ONOALTA WHILE ON VACATION.
Oh my! This isn't my trunk!
Well, my lady.
This certainly is a problem. Someone must have mistaken it for theirs because it was the same color.
Wait, there is a huge lance inside!
That's kinda danger-ous!
Aah, I just made a mistake with the trunks, so you'll have to play the role in the festival!
Role?
Defeat that huge shark!
SPLAAAAASH
Oh me, oh my! Even though I came on holiday, I'll be fighting a shark!
Twenty people have been killed so far this year.
Well, I'll vanquish it some-how!
My Lady, be safe ...!
MY LADY TATAPIAAA!
BOOM!
ドカーン
THAT WAS A GOOD MOVIE, WASN'T IT...?
WELL... I DON'T KNOW, I COULDN'T TELL ANYONE APART.
AT A LATER DATE, WHEN WE BROUGHT GLASS BUTTONS, WE WERE GUIDED TO NICER SEATS.

Correspondence
from the End of the Universe

Setting Information Staff Room Furnishings

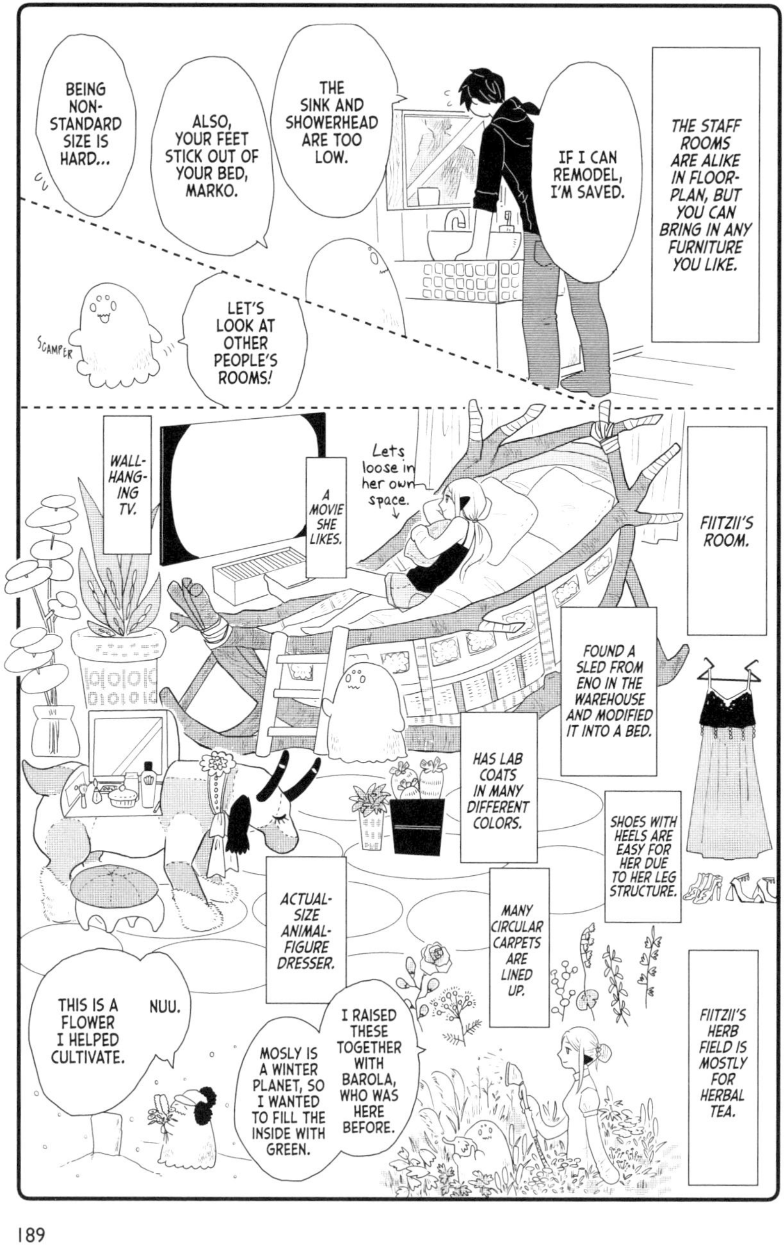

THE STAFF ROOMS ARE ALIKE IN FLOOR-PLAN, BUT YOU CAN BRING IN ANY FURNITURE YOU LIKE.
IF I CAN REMODEL, I'M SAVED.
THE SINK AND SHOWERHEAD ARE TOO LOW.
ALSO, YOUR FEET STICK OUT OF YOUR BED, MARKO.
BEING NON-STANDARD SIZE IS HARD...
LET'S LOOK AT OTHER PEOPLE'S ROOMS!
SCAMPER
FIITZII'S ROOM.
Lets loose in her own space.
A MOVIE SHE LIKES.
WALL-HANGING TV.
FOUND A SLED FROM ENO IN THE WAREHOUSE AND MODIFIED IT INTO A BED.
SHOES WITH HEELS ARE EASY FOR HER DUE TO HER LEG STRUCTURE.
HAS LAB COATS IN MANY DIFFERENT COLORS.
MANY CIRCULAR CARPETS ARE LINED UP.
ACTUAL-SIZE ANIMAL-FIGURE DRESSER.
FIITZII'S HERB FIELD IS MOSTLY FOR HERBAL TEA.
I RAISED THESE TOGETHER WITH BAROLA, WHO WAS HERE BEFORE.
MOSLY IS A WINTER PLANET, SO I WANTED TO FILL THE INSIDE WITH GREEN.
NUU.
THIS IS A FLOWER I HELPED CULTIVATE.

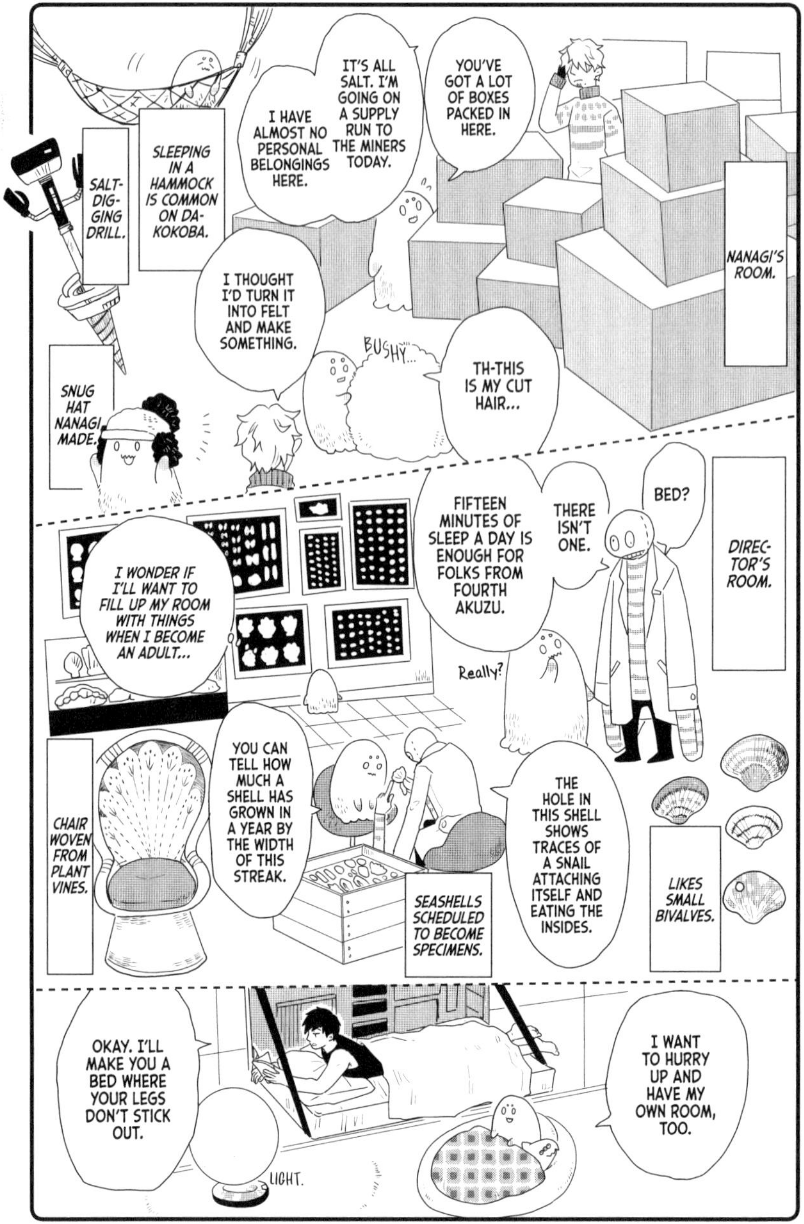
NANAGI'S ROOM.
YOU'VE GOT A LOT OF BOXES PACKED IN HERE.
IT'S ALL SALT. I'M GOING ON A SUPPLY RUN TO THE MINERS TODAY.
I HAVE ALMOST NO PERSONAL BELONGINGS HERE.
SLEEPING IN A HAMMOCK IS COMMON ON DA-KOKOBA.
SALT-DIG-GING DRILL.
TH-THIS IS MY CUT HAIR...
BUSHY...
I THOUGHT I'D TURN IT INTO FELT AND MAKE SOMETHING.
SNUG HAT NANAGI MADE.
DIREC-TOR'S ROOM.
BED?
THERE ISN'T ONE.
FIFTEEN MINUTES OF SLEEP A DAY IS ENOUGH FOR FOLKS FROM FOURTH AKUZU.
Really?
I WONDER IF I'LL WANT TO FILL UP MY ROOM WITH THINGS WHEN I BECOME AN ADULT...
LIKES SMALL BIVALVES.
THE HOLE IN THIS SHELL SHOWS TRACES OF A SNAIL ATTACHING ITSELF AND EATING THE INSIDES.
SEASHELLS SCHEDULED TO BECOME SPECIMENS.
YOU CAN TELL HOW MUCH A SHELL HAS GROWN IN A YEAR BY THE WIDTH OF THIS STREAK.
CHAIR WOVEN FROM PLANT VINES.
I WANT TO HURRY UP AND HAVE MY OWN ROOM, TOO.
OKAY. I'LL MAKE YOU A BED WHERE YOUR LEGS DON'T STICK OUT.
LIGHT.

Solfe View of Marriage

- WHILE THIS SECTION IS CALLED "SOLFE VIEW OF MARRIAGE," THESE ALIENS LACK A MARRIAGE-ANALOGOUS ARRANGEMENT.
- SOLFE WAS CREATED IN ORDER TO DISPATCH HEALTHCARE PROFESSIONALS TO THE 8TH GALAXY.
- SOME OF THEIR PEOPLE CHOOSE DIFFERENT OCCUPATIONS, BUT LEARNING ABOUT HEALTHCARE IS A STEP OF THEIR COMPULSORY EDUCATION.
- COMPULSORY EDUCATION LASTS FIFTEEN YEARS FROM AGES THREE TO EIGHTEEN.
- THE GOVERNMENT AGENCIES MANAGE FERTILITY, AND ALL SOLFE FOLK ARE GESTATED IN ARTIFICIAL WOMBS.

  WHEN ONE IS AN ADULT (TWENTY-TWO YEARS OLD), IT IS MANDATORY TO PROVIDE GENETIC INFORMATION TO THE GOVERNMENT, WHICH IS USED TO GENERATE FETUSES.
  SOLFE FOLK KNOW NOTHING ABOUT THEIR GENETIC PARENTS.

CHILD.
FIRST GUARDIANS.
SECOND GUARDIANS.
ALIENS OBTAINING PERMANENT RESIDENCE.

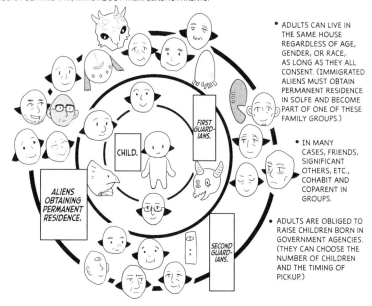

- ADULTS CAN LIVE IN THE SAME HOUSE REGARDLESS OF AGE, GENDER, OR RACE, AS LONG AS THEY ALL CONSENT. (IMMIGRATED ALIENS MUST OBTAIN PERMANENT RESIDENCE IN SOLFE AND BECOME PART OF ONE OF THESE FAMILY GROUPS.)
- IN MANY CASES, FRIENDS, SIGNIFICANT OTHERS, ETC., COHABIT AND COPARENT IN GROUPS.
- ADULTS ARE OBLIGED TO RAISE CHILDREN BORN IN GOVERNMENT AGENCIES. (THEY CAN CHOOSE THE NUMBER OF CHILDREN AND THE TIMING OF PICKUP.)

- THE ADULTS WHO LIVE IN THE SAME HOUSEHOLD AS THE KIDS THEY HAVE CHARGE OF ARE CALLED FIRST GUARDIANS. (ON EARTH, THESE ARE ROLE-EQUIVALENT TO FATHERS AND MOTHERS.) THE FIRST GUARDIANS OF THE FIRST GUARDIANS ARE SECOND GUARDIANS, AND AT LEAST FIVE MAIN CAREGIVERS ARE REQUIRED AT ALL TIMES. FOR EXAMPLE, IN A HOME WITH ONE CHILD AND FIVE FIRST GUARDIANS, WHEN TWO OF THEM ARE ABSENT AND DISPATCHED TO OTHER STARS, TWO OF THE SECOND GUARDIANS ARE DELEGATED AS CONSTANT CHILDCARE PROVIDERS.
- CONSTANT CHILDCARE PROVIDERS RECEIVE VARIOUS MEANS OF COMPENSATION FROM THE GOVERNMENT.
- IN THE CASE THAT THE CHILD WHO IS BEING TAKEN CARE OF FEELS THAT A HOUSE IS NOT FOR THEM, THE CHILD CAN CHOOSE FROM THE FOLLOWING AT WILL:
  1) GET EDUCATED WHILE LIVING AT A GOVERNMENT REARING FACILITY.
  2) TRY LIVING IN A DIFFERENT HOME.
  3) REPEAT BOTH OF THE ABOVE ALTERNATELY.
- FIITZII WAS FROM A HOME OF SEVEN FIRST GUARDIANS, RAISED WITH THREE CHILDREN OF THE SAME AGE.

Toys for Mauu

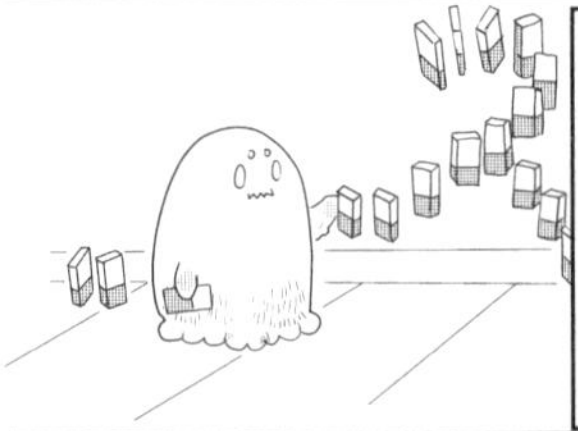

Aerial Dominoes

- DOMINOES THAT CAN BE LINED UP IN THE AIR.
- ALTHOUGH THEY CAN BE MADE FROM VARIOUS MATERIALS, WOOD AND SUPER HARD GLASS FUSED TOGETHER ARE COMMON.
- A BRAND THAT LIGHTS UP ON IMPACT IS POPULAR ACROSS A WIDE RANGE OF GENERATIONS.

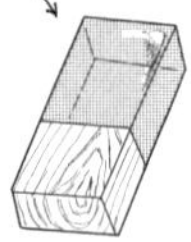
THIS PART LIGHTS UP.

Scale Plant

- A CULTIVATION AND OBSERVATION KIT FOR A PLANT THAT MAKES THE SOUND OF A SPECIFIC MUSICAL INSTRUMENT WHEN YOU TOUCH THE LEAVES.
- AFTER GERMINATION, THE RANGE OF SOUNDS INCREASE AS THE NUMBER OF LEAVES INCREASE.
- THERE ARE SOME MUSICIANS WHO CONDUCT PERFORMANCES BY DROPPING WATER ON THE LEAVES IN SPECIFIC ORDER.
- WHEN THE PLANT WITHERS, THE SOUND GOES STEADILY WILD.
- IT'S FUN TO HEAR THE SOUND OF MUSICAL INSTRUMENTS EVERY TIME THERE IS A QUARREL, AND IT'S ALSO GOOD FOR OVERCOMING CHILDREN'S DISLIKE OF VEGETABLES.

(IN THE NAME OF ETIQUETTE, SOME PLANETS PROHIBIT ITS USE IN SCHOOL LUNCHES.)

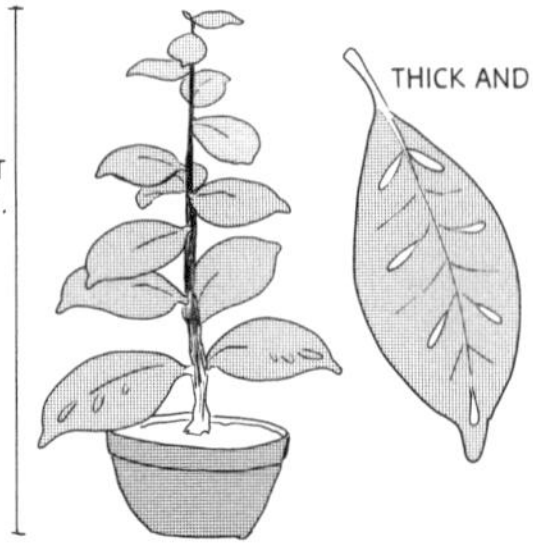
ABOUT 40 CM.
THICK AND PLIANT.

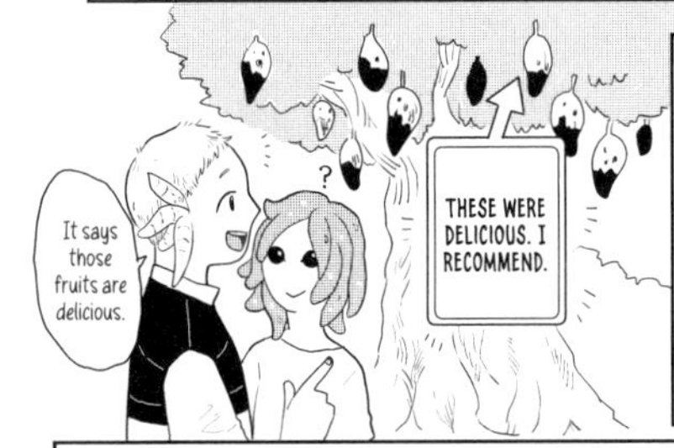
THESE WERE DELICIOUS. I RECOMMEND.
?
It says those fruits are delicious.

Torokkakarokka

- A COINED WORD COMBINING THE WORDS SECRET, MAP, FRIEND, AND ADVENTURE.
- CONTACT LENS-TYPE TOYS. (THE NUMBER OF LENSES SOLD IS DIFFERENT ACCORDING TO THE PLANET THEY ARE SOLD ON.)
- DISPLAYS PICTURES AND MESSAGES AND SUCH THAT CAN ONLY BE SEEN BY REGISTERED FRIENDS. (TO WRITE REQUIRES SPECIAL INK SOLD SEPARATELY.)
- USED AS AN AID IN PLAYING GAMES OF MAKE-BELIEVE EXPLORATION.

Magic Carpet Transformer

- BORN IN THE PROCESS OF DEVELOPING A WHEELCHAIR WITHOUT WHEELS.
- A MACHINE FOR MAKING THINGS FLOAT IN THE AIR. ATTACHES BELOW CHAIRS, CARPETS, BOARDS, THICK PAPER, AND SUCH.
- MAXIMUM LOAD IS 20 KILOS PER MACHINE.
- THE MAXIMUM SPEED IS ABOUT THE TROTTING PACE OF AN ADULT MALE EARTHLING.

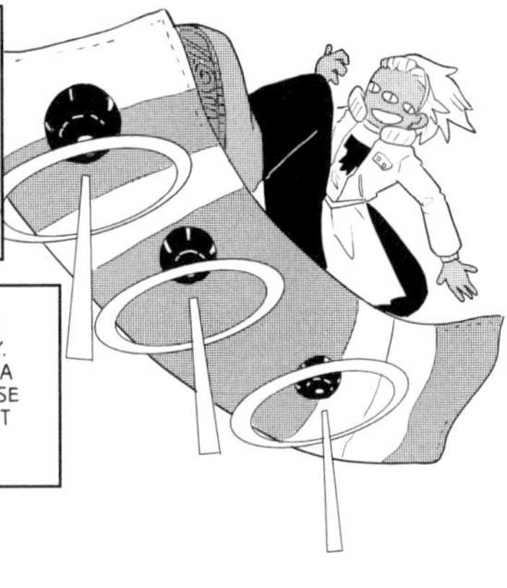

FORTY-SEVEN DOCTOR SETS ARE ON SALE TO MATCH THE VARIOUS RACES IN THE 8TH GALAXY. AMONG THE SETS MARKO FOUND, THERE WAS A RETRO-STYLE SOLFE DOCTOR PLAY SET. BECAUSE MARKO DIDN'T KNOW HOW TO USE IT, IT DIDN'T SEEM LIKE A TOY TO HIM.

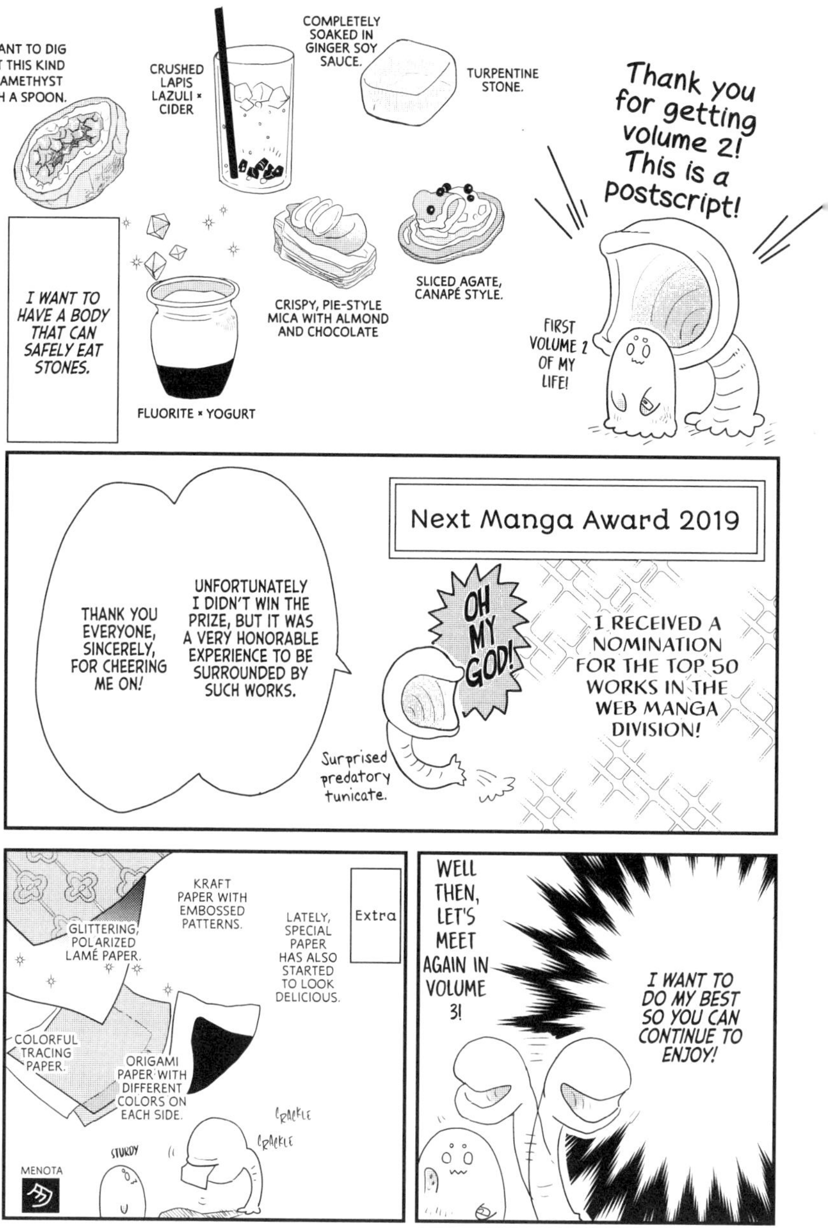

Thank you for getting volume 2! This is a postscript!
FIRST VOLUME 2 OF MY LIFE!
TURPENTINE STONE.
COMPLETELY SOAKED IN GINGER SOY SAUCE.
CRUSHED LAPIS LAZULI × CIDER
I WANT TO DIG OUT THIS KIND OF AMETHYST WITH A SPOON.
SLICED AGATE, CANAPÉ STYLE.
CRISPY, PIE-STYLE MICA WITH ALMOND AND CHOCOLATE
FLUORITE × YOGURT
I WANT TO HAVE A BODY THAT CAN SAFELY EAT STONES.
Next Manga Award 2019
I RECEIVED A NOMINATION FOR THE TOP 50 WORKS IN THE WEB MANGA DIVISION!
OH MY GOD!
Surprised predatory tunicate.
UNFORTUNATELY I DIDN'T WIN THE PRIZE, BUT IT WAS A VERY HONORABLE EXPERIENCE TO BE SURROUNDED BY SUCH WORKS.
THANK YOU EVERYONE, SINCERELY, FOR CHEERING ME ON!
I WANT TO DO MY BEST SO YOU CAN CONTINUE TO ENJOY!
WELL THEN, LET'S MEET AGAIN IN VOLUME 3!
Extra
LATELY, SPECIAL PAPER HAS ALSO STARTED TO LOOK DELICIOUS.
KRAFT PAPER WITH EMBOSSED PATTERNS.
GLITTERING, POLARIZED LAMÉ PAPER.
COLORFUL TRACING PAPER.
ORIGAMI PAPER WITH DIFFERENT COLORS ON EACH SIDE.
CRACKLE
CRACKLE
STURDY
MENOTA

DR. KUNEKAYAF AND HIS FIVE CHILDREN

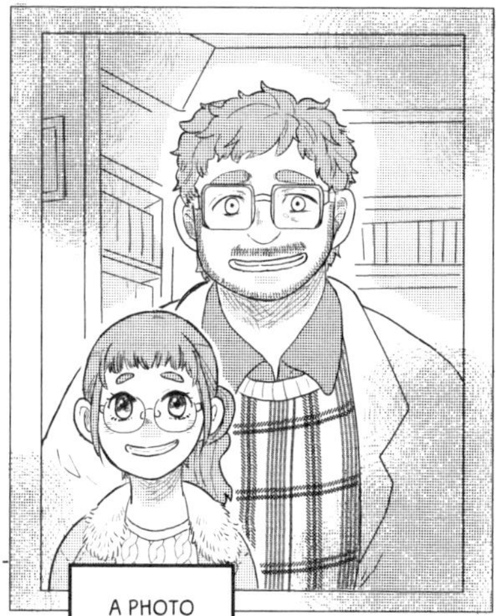

A PHOTO WITH A LABEL THAT READS, "YOUR SMILES LOOK EXACTLY ALIKE!" THE DOCTOR AND HIS ELDEST DAUGHTER, EVENY (AGE SIX).

DR. KUNEKAYAF DISCOVERED THE AKAMEFKA BUGS ON KEDDELL. AS A PARASITOLOGIST, HE WAS A BRAVE SCIENTIST FLYING AROUND THE GALAXY. HE WAS BLESSED WITH A WIFE AND FOUR CHILDREN AND KNOWN TO HAVE A MEEK PERSONALITY.

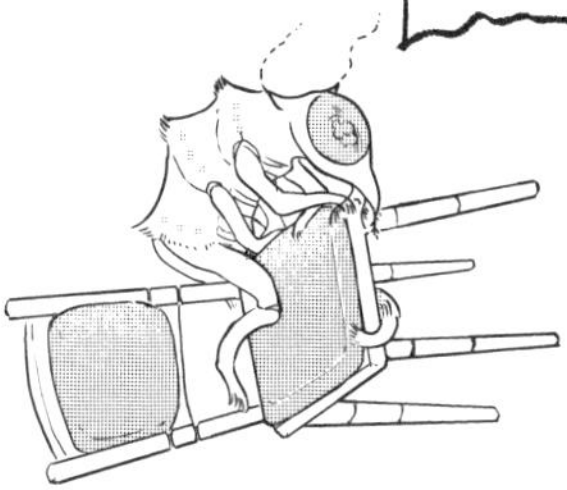

DR. KUNEKAYAF'S WIFE DIED AFTER GIVING BIRTH TO WHAT WOULD BECOME THEIR FIFTH CHILD, THEIR THIRD SON.

AND DUE TO A NEW EPIDEMIC THAT BROKE OUT ON KEDDELL, THE DOCTOR LOST HIS SON SOON AFTER.

DR. KUNEKAYAF AND HIS CHILDREN DESCENDED INTO GRIEF, AND WITH NO KNOWLEDGE OF HOW TO STOP THE DISEASE, IT SPREAD THROUGH THE PLANET.

THE GALACTIC SECURITY ALLIANCE RUSHED TO DEVELOP A VACCINE, BUT EVERY TIME THE VACCINE WAS COMPLETED, THE VIRUS WOULD MUTATE AND THE INFECTION AND FATALITY RATES WOULD RISE. TO PREVENT A PANDEMIC FROM SPREADING INTO THE GALAXY WITH EVACUEES, THE ALLIANCE ENFORCED A QUARANTINE OF KEDDELL.

(AS AN ASIDE, ONE OF THE MEMBERS WHO SIGNED THE KEDDELL QUARANTINE ORDER HAD ROOTS ON KEDDELL. IN LATER YEARS, HE LEFT A LETTER SAYING HE REGRETTED THE ORDER BEFORE GOING MISSING.)

AFTER THE BLOCKADE, DR. KUNEKAYAF'S ELDEST DAUGHTER DIED OF THE EPIDEMIC AT SIX YEARS OLD. KUNEKAYAF ILLEGALLY COMMUNICATED WITH ALIEN FRIENDS ASKING FOR HELP IN ESCAPING THE PLANET. TWENTY-SIX ALIEN COLLABORATORS WHO TRIED TO HELP KUNEKAYAF WERE ARRESTED. SIMILAR INCIDENTS OCCURRED FREQUENTLY IN KEDDELL AROUND THIS TIME.

DR. KUNEKAYAF WAS IN A PIT OF DESPAIR UNTIL HE MET SOMEONE.

THE MAN IN QUESTION WAS A FAN OF KUNEKAYAF'S BOOK AND CAME FROM A PLANET FAR AWAY, CALLING HIMSELF A FORTUNE-TELLER. HE SAID, "YOU WILL BE THE ONE TO SAVE KEDDELL FROM ITS DESTRUCTION," AND TOLD KUNEKAYAF TO SEARCH FOR AKAMEFKA. AKAMEFKA, IN KEDDELL'S OLD TONGUE, MEANS "THE PLACE WHERE THERE ARE SMALL SHOES." WHEN KUNEKAYAF LOOKED IN ONE OF HIS CHILDREN'S ROOMS, HE DISCOVERED MANY PARASITES WRIGGLING IN THE UNOPENED DOLLHOUSE HE HAD BOUGHT FOR HIS THIRD SON. EVER SINCE, THIS PARASITE HAS BEEN FOUND THROUGHOUT KEDDELL. THE FORTUNE-TELLER NEVER APPEARED BEFORE KUNEKAYAF AGAIN, AND AS HE WAS VERY DRUNK AT THE TIME, IT IS STILL NOT KNOWN IF THE FORTUNE-TELLER EXISTED OR NOT. ANYWAY, UNDER DIFFICULT-TO-EXPLAIN INSPIRATION, DR. KUNEKAYAF STUDIED PARASITES WHILE KNOWING THE EFFECTS OF THE ENZYMES THEY PRODUCED, IN ORDER TO ESCAPE FROM THE INTERPLANETARY PANDEMIC.

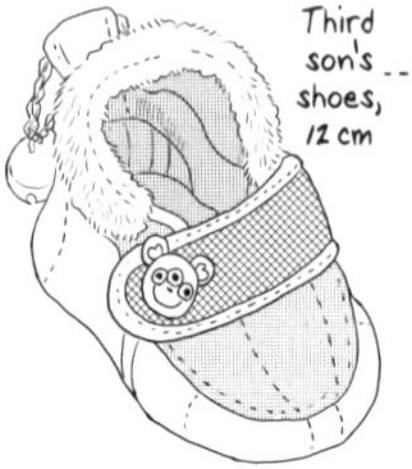
Third son's shoes, 12 cm

THIS SAVED MANY KEDDELLITES BY RENDERING THEM UNABLE TO DIE, WHICH LIFTED THE PLANET TO ITS CURRENT STATE OF PROSPERITY.

MAKING PEOPLE'S BODIES INTO DOLLHOUSES VIA SURGERY WAS CRITICIZED BY COUNTLESS GROUPS. ALSO, BECAUSE ONLY THOSE IN THEIR LATE TEENS TO THIRTIES COULD WITHSTAND THE SURGERY, CHILDREN AND THE ELDERLY WERE WIPED OUT.

FIVE YEARS AFTER DR. KUNEKAYAF DISCOVERED THE AKAMEFKA PARASITES, AN ALL-PURPOSE VACCINE WAS COMPLETED, AND THE OPEN PLANETS OF THE 8TH GALAXY MADE THE VACCINE MANDATORY FOR ALL CHILDREN.

IN KEDDELL, HOWEVER, WHERE XENOPHOBIA HAD BECOME COMMON, THE VACCINE WAS NOT POPULAR.

DR. KUNEKAYAF'S ELDEST SON WAS ATTACKED ON THE STREET BY THOSE WHO OPPOSED THE PROCEDURE IMMEDIATELY AFTER HIS OWN SURGERY. THE PARASITE WAS FORCIBLY EXTRACTED FROM HIS BODY, AND HE DIED.

KUNEKAYAF'S SECOND SON ASSISTED WITH HIS FATHER'S RESEARCH AFTER HIS SURGERY. THE SECOND DAUGHTER REFUSED SURGERY AND EMIGRATED TO AN ALIEN PLANET. DR. KUNEKAYAF'S LIFE HAS BEEN IMMORTALIZED ON FILM MANY TIMES BY ALIEN DIRECTORS, BUT MANY OF THEM PORTRAY THE DOCTOR AS A MAD SCIENTIST. ALSO, MANY GAMES AND NOVELS AND SUCH HAVE HAD CHARACTERS SEEMINGLY MODELED IN APPEARANCE ON KUNEKAYAF, BUT AGAIN, THE IMAGE THEY DEPICT IS THAT OF A MAD SCIENTIST. ALTHOUGH DR. KUNEKAYAF IS ALIVE, HIS CURRENT RESIDENCE IS NOT PUBLIC KNOWLEDGE.

THE NAME OF THE FORTUNE-TELLER THE DOCTOR MET WAS RANKAMARCH. HE APPEARS IN FOLK TALES OF PLANETS FAR AWAY FROM KEDDELL AND SHARES A NAME WITH A DEVIL THAT DESTROYS PEOPLE.

Correspondence
from the End of the **Universe**

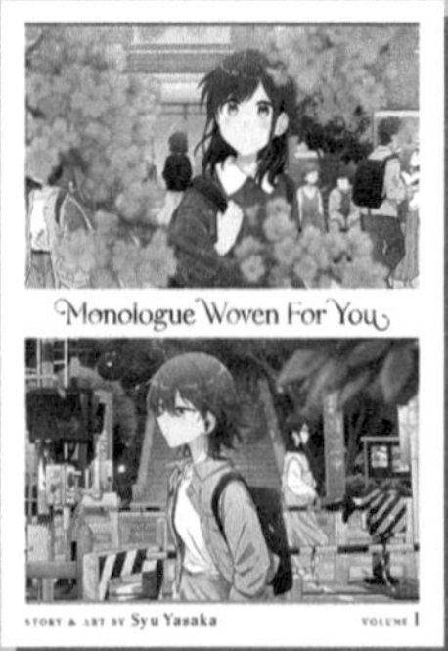
Monologue Woven For You
STORY & ART BY Syu Yasaka
VOLUME 1
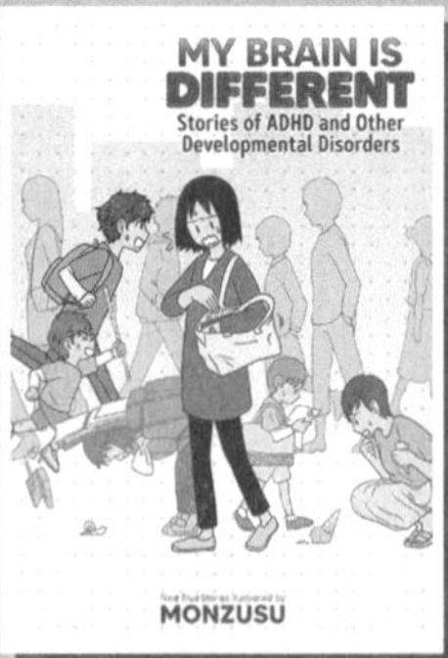
MY BRAIN IS
DIFFERENT
Stories of ADHD and Other Developmental Disorders
MONZUSU
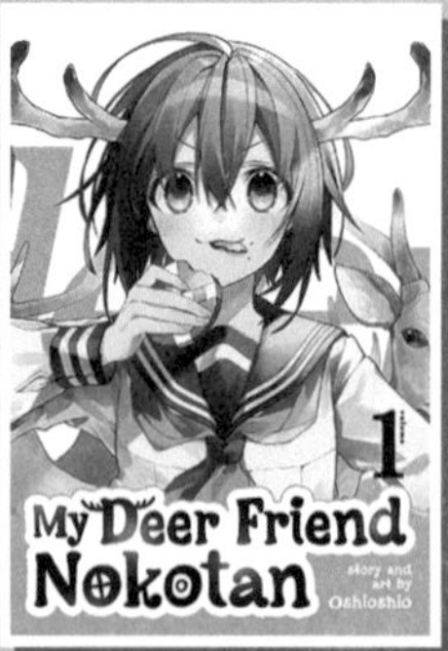
1
My Deer Friend
Nokotan
story and art by
Oshioshio
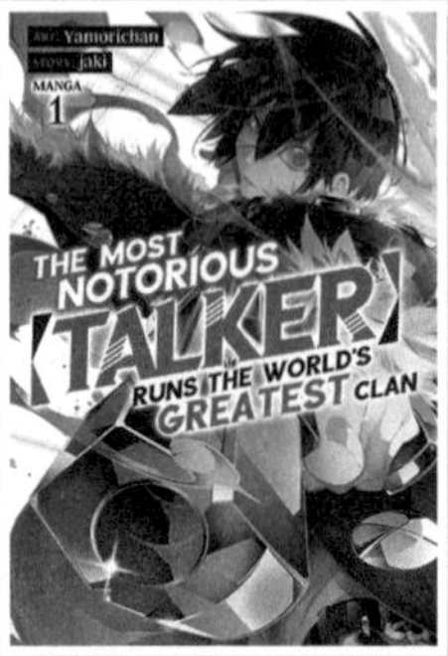
Yamorichan
jaki
MANGA
1
THE MOST
NOTORIOUS
TALKER
RUNS THE WORLD'S
GREATEST CLAN
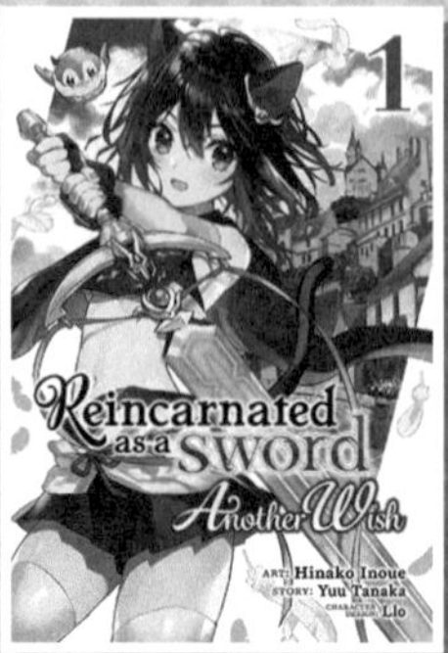
1
Reincarnated as a Sword
Another Wish
ART: Hinako Inoue
STORY: Yuu Tanaka
Llo
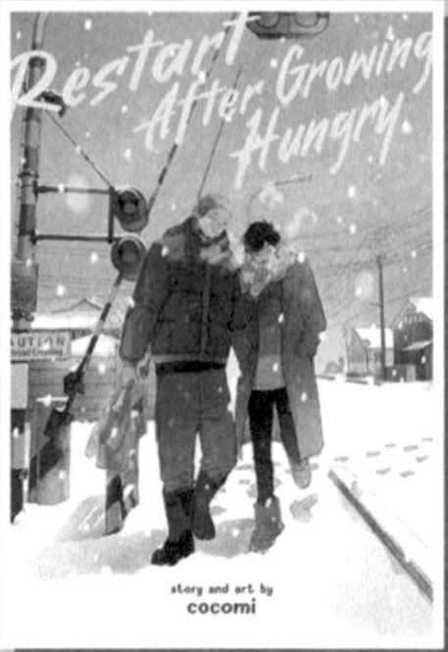
Restart After Growing Hungry
story and art by
cocomi
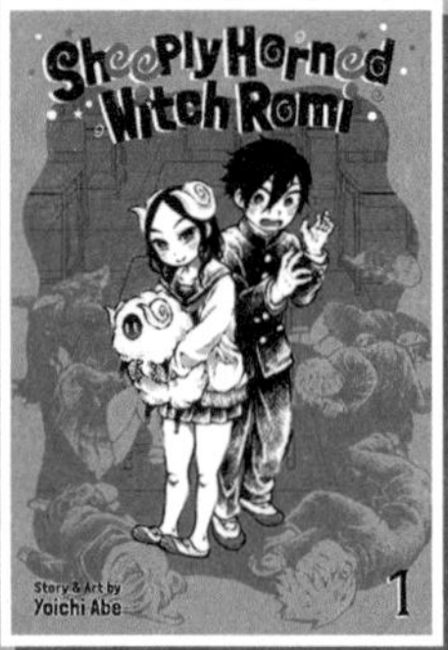
Sheeply Horned
Witch Romi
Story & Art by
Yoichi Abe
1
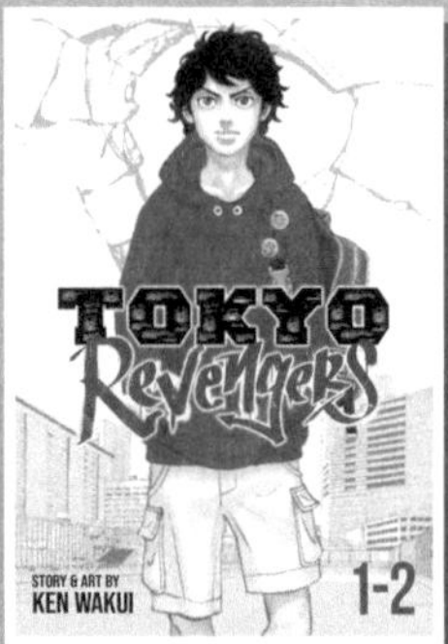
TOKYO
Revengers
STORY & ART BY
KEN WAKUI
1-2
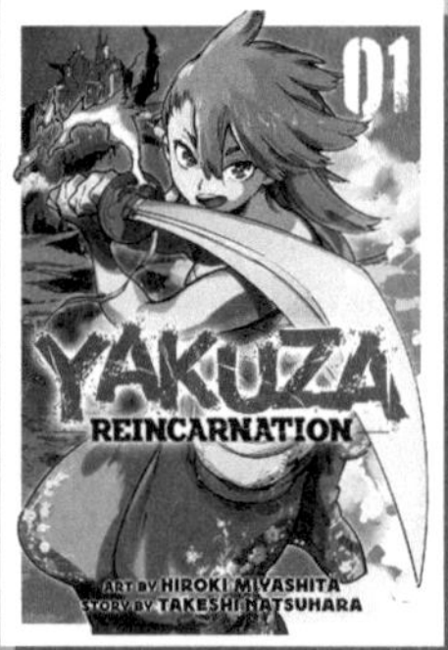
01
YAKUZA
REINCARNATION
ART BY HIROKI MIYASHITA
STORY BY TAKESHI NATSUHARA

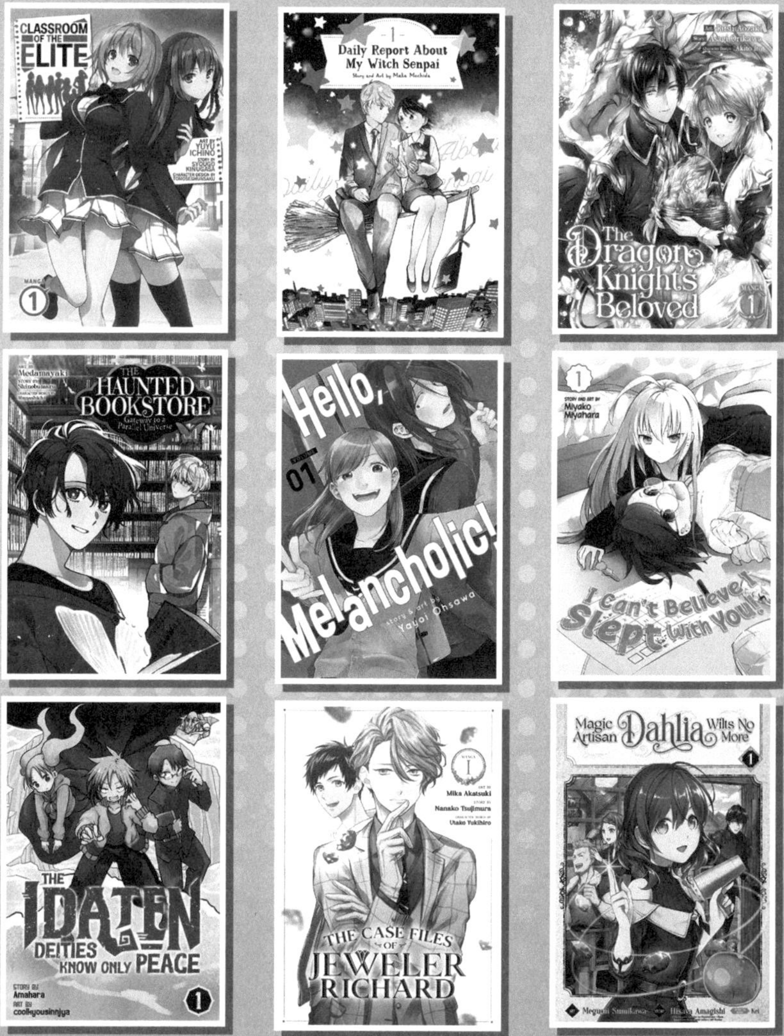
CLASSROOM OF THE ELITE
ART BY YUYU ICHINO
STORY BY SYOUGO KINUGASA
MANGA 1
Daily Report About My Witch Senpai
Story and Art by Maka Mochida
The Dragon Knight's Beloved
MANGA 1
THE HAUNTED BOOKSTORE
Gateway to a Parallel Universe
Hello, Melancholic!
01
story & art by Yayoi Ohsawa
1
STORY AND ART BY Miyako Miyahara
I Can't Believe I Slept With You!
THE IDATEN DEITIES KNOW ONLY PEACE
STORY BY Amahara
ART BY coolkyousinnjya
1
MANGA I
ART BY Mika Akatsuki
STORY BY Nanako Tsujimura
CHARACTER DESIGN BY Utako Yukihiro
THE CASE FILES OF JEWELER RICHARD
Magic Artisan Dahlia Wilts No More
1

SEVEN SEAS ENTERTAINMENT PRESENTS

Correspondence

from the End of the Universe

story and art by MENOTA   VOLUME 2

TRANSLATION
Kathryn Henzler

LETTERING
Nicole Roderick

COVER DESIGN
Shi Briggs

PROOFREADER
Krista Grandy

SENIOR COPY EDITOR
Dawn Davis

EDITOR
Jay Edidin

PRODUCTION DESIGNER
Christina McKenzie

PRODUCTION MANAGER
Lissa Pattillo

PREPRESS TECHNICIAN
Melanie Ujimori

PRINT MANAGER
Rhiannon Rasmussen-Silverstein

EDITOR-IN-CHIEF
Julie Davis

ASSOCIATE PUBLISHER
Adam Arnold

PUBLISHER
Jason DeAngelis

HATENO SHOU TSUSHIN Vol. 2
© MENOTA 2019
Originally published in Japan in 2019 by SHUFU TO SEIKATSU SHA CO.,LTD., Tokyo.
English translation rights arranged with SHUFU TO SEIKATSU SHA CO.,LTD.,Tokyo,
through TOHAN CORPORATION, Tokyo.

Seven Seas press and purchase enquiries can be sent to Marketing Manager Lianne
Sentar at press@gomanga.com. Information regarding the distribution and purchase of
digital editions is available from Digital Manager CK Russell at digital@gomanga.com.

Seven Seas and the Seven Seas logo are trademarks of
Seven Seas Entertainment. All rights reserved.

ISBN: 978-1-64827-897-6
Printed in USA
First Printing: October 2022   Withdrawn
10 9 8 7 6 5 4 3 2 1

READING DIRECTIONS

This book reads from *right to left*,
Japanese style. If this is your first time
reading manga, you start reading from
the top right panel on each page and
take it from there. If you get lost, just
follow the numbered diagram here.
It may seem backwards at first,
but you'll get the hang of it! Have fun!!

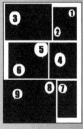

Follow us online: www.SevenSeasEntertainment.com